THE WEASEL

A DOUBLE LIFE IN THE MOB

ADRIAN HUMPHREYS

HarperCollins*Publishers*Ltd

Published by HarperCollins Publishers Ltd

Originally published by John Wiley & Sons Canada, Ltd.: 2012

First published by HarperCollins Publishers Ltd in an EPub edition: 2013
This HarperCollins Publishers Ltd trade paperback edition: 2014

HarperCollins books may be purchased for educational, business, or sales
promotional use through our Special Markets Department.

HarperCollins Publishers Ltd
2 Bloor Street East, 20th Floor
Toronto, Ontario, Canada
M4W 1A8

www.harpercollins.ca

Library and Archives Canada Cataloguing in Publication
information is available upon request

ISBN 978-1-44342-804-0

Printed and bound in the United States of America
RRD 9 8 7 6 5 4 3 2 1

To Eliana,
My gold standard.

CONTENTS

PROLOGUE

DETROIT-WINDSOR BORDER, 1986

"This is Marvin 'The Weasel' Elkind, he's a well-connected guy."

It was the introduction Marvin wanted: a crook vouching for him as a fellow crook to a third crook a little further up the underworld food chain. From where he had parked his car in downtown Windsor, The Weasel could see the gleaming dark towers of Detroit's Renaissance Center and, if he squinted to the west, the cabled arches of the Ambassador Bridge that spans the river, linking Detroit on the American side to Windsor in Canada. It is the continent's most heavily travelled border point and Marvin knew the seamless link between automotive giants in both cities had long ago been appropriated by gangsters, making the 32-mile length of the river the carotid artery of contraband.

Marvin chomped on the end of a fat Tuero cigar, grown and rolled in Canada using tobacco seeds from Havana, letting him think he was smoking a Cuban without coughing up so many pesos. The cigars became a smoky signature of his presence that constantly floated back and forth from his thin lips to his corpulent, ring-heavy fingers. Marvin was meeting the owners of a chain of strip clubs who also sold drugs. They wanted to expand and that's where Marvin said he could help.

"My Detroit friends want to get into business in Ontario," Marvin told them, giving the businessmen a hard stare to emphasize the dark nature of his proposal. "They're looking for partners who can handle it."

The strip club owners had already checked Marvin out, in the haphazard, oral-history sort of way gangsters do, especially in the days before one could Google a name to see if he had been in the newspapers, testifying at a trial, maybe, or otherwise revealed as a snitch. In this cutthroat world, a personal recommendation was the only sure way of getting behind closed doors, which is where Marvin needed to be. Before the meeting, the businessmen had called friends in both countries asking about The Weasel. They spoke to a major boxing promoter in Detroit who knew all the bandits from ringside; he told them Marvin hung around with serious Mafia guys all the time. The club owners also talked with career criminals in Toronto who had known Marvin for decades as a street enforcer, loan collector and mob driver. The owners had themselves seen Marvin hanging around one of their clubs with Ernie Kanakis, a big-time gambler rumoured to have killed three Detroit mobsters coming at him with ice picks.

Marvin was given the nod on all fronts as a known hood and connected guy, and the backroom doors were flung open. They always were.

Marvin brought three Detroit friends to his next meeting. The club owners cleared out their VIP room for them. Shockingly young women gyrated amid a river of booze and food as the talk turned to drugs. The deal was looking good for everyone and as Marvin reluctantly got up to leave, one of his American friends, a firmly built Italian man with a thick moustache, gave the Canadian businessmen his phone number in Detroit.

* * *

The mustachioed American looked out across the border from the 26th floor of a skyscraper on Detroit's Michigan Avenue and could just about see—a mile away—the tawdry strip club where he had been with The Weasel. In the daytime, with the bright neon lights dimmed, it looked nowhere near as impressive.

If anyone dialled the number he had given out, the phone that would ring was a few feet away, across his office and locked in the bottom drawer of his desk. Special Agent Rich Mazzari was the only person with a key to that drawer. The phone was a special hotline he used only in undercover operations, secured inside the Detroit field office of the Federal Bureau of Investigation. Mazzari didn't want anyone else answering it, jeopardizing his investigations or putting the lives of his agents or prized informants at risk. Informants like The Weasel.

The truth was, despite the furtive checking on Marvin's background by the strip club owners, despite Marvin's fearsome streetwise stare and calm demeanour, Marvin was part of this emerging drug conspiracy not as a criminal, although he sometimes was one, and not as a mobster, although he had been that, and not as a thuggish enforcer, although he did that kind of work as well, but as a paid police informant. A career fink. In fact, because of his unique life and special abilities, one of the best. He achieved secret success solving a staggering number of crimes in several countries by infiltrating criminal gangs and conspiracies, bringing down drug traffickers and con men, foreign agents and spies, Mafia bosses and pornography kingpins, corrupt union fat cats and crooked businessmen. He helped to thwart Third World coups, multimillion-dollar frauds, union corruption, political blackmail and murders. He worked for the FBI, U.S. Customs and Border Protection, the

Internal Revenue Service, Scotland Yard, Mexican federal police, Royal Canadian Mounted Police, Ontario Provincial Police, city forces and more. He had infiltrated crime gangs in Canada, the United States, Mexico, Ecuador, the Netherlands and the Middle East.

In a beautiful hide-in-plain-sight accident, Marvin was known on the street as "The Weasel," but no one could have suspected how masterful a weasel he really was.

Marvin's job—his "government work," as he calls it—was to introduce into this drug conspiracy four people who would not pass such a background check by the crooks: three agents with the FBI and a detective with the OPP. The only way these four were getting past the closed backroom doors was if someone like The Weasel brought them in with him.

This was what Marvin got paid for. This was what he was good at.

This was what he loved.

* * *

While Mazzari waited in his Detroit office, Marvin was heading back into the club for another meeting, this time bringing another undercover cop with him.

OPP Detective-Constable Al Robinson was Marvin's police handler. He was known by all of his friends as Robbie, but to the criminals Marvin introduced him to he was Colonel Al Gibson, a former air force officer who had left the military under a cloud of disgrace. The military co-operated in the subterfuge and created false records for a discharged Colonel Gibson in case someone with deep contacts checked on him. Robbie had two wallets, one with his real ID and a second for Col. Gibson. He even had a tattoo on his right forearm, an image of a heart hugged by a flowing ribbon inscribed with the word "Mother." Cheaply inked when he was a teenager in homage to his dead mom, it had blurred with age. In the 1980s, the tattooed arm alone deflected suspicion he might be a cop. None the wiser, the crooks all called him "The Colonel."

As they headed into the strip club together, passing several well-muscled and unsmiling bouncers who eyed them as they entered, The Weasel and The Colonel were walking into another wild adventure.

"They're expecting us," Marvin said to the bartender, raising his grating voice above the thumping music that, along with amphetamines and cigarettes, kept the dancers moving. "Tell them The Weasel and The Colonel are here."

"I'll pass it on," the barman said.

Inside the back office, one of the club operators wanted to talk to his new Detroit partners before heading out to see Marvin. He searched through the papers in his wallet for the phone number.

Across the river, Mazzari looked at his watch. He knew Marvin and Robbie were going back into the club and he might get a phone call from the club owners. He unlocked the drawer containing his hidden hotline. Then nature called. Unsure of how long he might have to wait, Mazzari dashed to the bathroom so he would be ready for round-the-clock action once things got started.

Just after the agent ran out of his office, the phone started ringing.

And just as it rang, a fellow agent walking past heard the mysterious sound and traced it to the jangling phone in the open drawer.

The perplexed young agent liked to be helpful. So he answered it.

"Hello, FBI Detroit."

At the other end of the phone, there was a stunned, confused silence. Meanwhile, not knowing of the slip-up, Marvin and Robbie stood waiting expectantly at the bar.

PART ONE

PART ONE

CHAPTER 1

TORONTO, 1934

A surprise surge of warmth after a frigid weekend put the city in a good mood on March 13, 1934, and if Beatrice Elkind read the local newspapers that day before entering Toronto General Hospital with labour pains she would have seen a screaming headline—"Accounts Juggled"—about secret payments by city officials; overseas news highlighting fears of war against "Nazi encroachment"; and, to the south in Mason City, Iowa, a story about John Dillinger and Baby Face Nelson hitting the First National Bank, an event that ushered in a new golden age of the American gangster. Beyond the headlines of that day are themes that would have a deep impact on Beatrice and her family—corruption, anti-Semitism and gangster tales—but the only thing on her mind was the struggle inside the delivery room.

Her baby was breeched in her womb, upside down with his chubby legs bent up near his tiny ears. Slippery and stubborn, he had to be dragged out with metal forceps.

Marvin Elkind was a handful before he had even taken his first gasp of air.

Looking at him all tiny, bruised and helpless, no one could have predicted the bizarre life he would go on to live.

* * *

"I was born on March 13. I wonder if that was a Friday—Friday the 13th—with all the luck I've had in my life," says Marvin, now 77.

He chuckles, and his heavy jowls quiver, giving him the look of an English bulldog. Standing five feet six and weighing close to 300 pounds, he is decidedly round, as is his face, with cheeks that ball tight under his eyes into red apples that, in full smile, give him the appearance of a cartoon character.

As he laughs, his hairy chest heaves. From beneath his shirt, which is unbuttoned more than it should be, light glints off the gold chains he likes to drape around his neck. Like most things involving The Weasel, there's a juicy story behind each of them. His enormous sausage fingers are also circled in gold, his pinkies squeezed into chunky rings. Each wrist, too; a heavy gold bracelet around his right and a gold Oscar de la Renta watch around his left. When clenched, his fists are shockingly large, a sign of the boxer he once was, a southpaw with a mixed record in the ring—just as in life.

Despite his age, he maintains a good head of hair, more salt than pepper now, and his once curly locks fall straight and are kept short. A broken front tooth hints at a difficult past.

His eyes, though, are what captivate.

Slate grey, they are a wonder of expression. When laughing, as he does often, his eyes are moist and bright, but when serious or stern, which he has frequent cause to be, they narrow considerably, one slightly more than the other. With eyelids that retract deep under his brow, he conjures the cold look of a shark. His chuckle fades.

"My daughter said I am the luckiest guy in town and I said, 'What are you talking about? How do you figure that

I'm lucky? Look at my life.' She said, 'They never got you. All the guys you did jobs on, all you been through, none of them got you. You made it through. You're the luckiest guy in town.' She might be right in a way," he says. Then, after a long pause: "I don't feel lucky."

***

Marvin was not born on Friday the 13th—it was a Tuesday— but neither was he born into fortunate circumstances, although, at the start, it was hardly an exceptional story for blue-collar immigrants in Toronto, which was then Canada's second-largest city, after Montreal.

Marvin's mother, Beatrice Feldstein, was born in 1911 in Romania and emigrated with her family to Canada. It was a hard journey. Her eldest brother died during the voyage and was hastily buried when the ship pulled into port. The Feldsteins settled in Cabbagetown, a tough neighbourhood near the centre of Toronto, where disputes among residents were settled without the police whenever possible. A high-school graduate, Beatrice was unusually well educated for a poor immigrant Jewish girl at the time. Her handwriting was deemed to be so exquisite that it was showcased at the Canadian National Exhibition. Her abilities earned her a job in the shipping office of Society Shirt. It was there that she met a strapping young janitor who swept her off her feet.

Aaron Elkind, born in 1904, had come to Canada from Russia in 1927 with his younger brother Morris. They joined their older brothers, Sam and Harry, who had arrived earlier when their father, Menachem, was working as a Hebrew teacher in nearby Hamilton, Ontario. Aaron and Beatrice were married in 1931. Three years later, Marvin was born.

But, as cheers of *mazel tov* rang out, there was little joy in the home. Marvin's timing was terrible.

"My father was a bad guy," Marvin says. "He hung around with bad guys and was always getting into some trouble. My mother didn't know that at the time she married him. When she found out the kind of person he was, it was too late—she was pregnant with me. In those days, abortion was completely unheard of in the Jewish faith and so was divorce if you had a child. She said that if she hadn't had me, she would have left him. So my mother and maternal grandmother always blamed me for the fact that she was with him for so long. The person who always gave her support was Morris, my father's brother."

Morris Elkind also worked at Society Shirt but was cut from different cloth than Aaron. While Morris always wore a yarmulke, the skullcap of Orthodox Judaism, Aaron shunned the trappings of his faith. As Aaron swept the floors, Morris secured a better job as a cutter, forging a reputation as one of the best. And whenever Aaron had a fight with Beatrice, Morris was there to support her. Aaron was the black sheep, Morris the white knight.

* * *

Aaron kept a close eye on the comings and goings at what would later become the Toronto-Dominion Bank on the corner of Dundas Street West and Ossington Avenue. With three friends, he was planning to rob it. It was 1937, and Marvin was three years old.

Their plan was to go for the bank vault at night, to avoid the complications of tellers and customers, guns and getaway cars. But the heist didn't go cleanly. Somebody had ratted and police were waiting.

"The guys had no weapons, but one of them reached for a cigarette and the cops thought he was going for a gun, so they shot him and killed him. My father got away. But we never saw him again. According to my grandmother—my maternal grandmother, who didn't like my father—they suspected he had a beef with police and made a deal to turn the other guys in, and in return he would be allowed to leave the country. He hightailed it back to Russia."

In Russia, Aaron didn't abandon his sneaky ways.

"It was never proven that this was the case and I hope, I hope, I hope that it isn't true, but my grandmother told me this; my grandmother told me that she found out later that my father got executed in 1946 because the Russians found out he had been selling secrets to the Germans during the war. My grandmother was happy to believe it. She always said that the one good thing he did for us was to leave. I'll tell you how much my grandmother liked him: she told me that when she heard about the robbery and that one guy got killed in it, she was very disappointed to find out it wasn't my father.

"My grandmother was only too happy to believe it, she delighted in it, because it gave her an excuse for me, that his genes were my problem, the reason for my behaviour."

It is an intriguing revelation: The Weasel might be the son of a weasel.

"Don't think that hasn't come up through my mind many, many times."

* * *

Six months after Aaron fled the bank job, when their rabbi confirmed his betrayal of the family and his move back to

Russia, Beatrice married another Elkind, this time Morris, the steady brother.

The new version of the Elkind family moved into a two-storey brown-brick house at the corner of Roxton Road and Harrison Street. Across the road was Fred Hamilton Park, where Marvin played baseball and an outdoor ice rink was flooded each winter for hockey.

Here Beatrice found the stability she craved. About 10 months after she and Morris were married, she gave birth to another son, Stanley. Some seven years later, a daughter, Marilyn, was born.

The family dynamics were hard on young Marvin. Morris was deeply ashamed of his disgraced brother and seemed to see the very image of Aaron in Marvin's face, a daily reminder of his family's shame. Morris, for all his piety, did not extend the love of a father to Marvin.

"My stepfather was a very nice guy to everyone but me. Morris and I didn't get along until the last day of his life," Marvin says.

There was a streak of Aaron in Marvin. He was rebellious and drawn to the excitement outside Morris's insular world of faith, family and work. Marvin loved physical sports and neighbourhood talk of street toughs.

In kindergarten, Marvin's teacher told him that if his father was not his real dad that meant he was adopted.

"I found out at school you adopted me," Marvin told Morris that evening.

"No, I didn't," was the curt reply. "I'm not your father. Don't call me dad." Not knowing what to do or say, he went to his mother.

"Should I call him 'Uncle Morris,' then?" he asked her.

"No, that doesn't sound right."

"But he told me I can't call him dad."

"Then call him pops." And Marvin did, but the distinction between "dad" and "pops" weighed on him, robbing him of the sense of belonging and comfort that he longed for.

Morris could not forget that Marvin was his father's son. Whenever the boy got into trouble, which was often in the years ahead, Morris would say: "I expected it. He's Aaron's son. The apple doesn't fall far from the tree."

Morris really believed it.

* * *

While building his new family, Morris Elkind unleashed his entrepreneurial side. His brother Sam had a successful menswear shop, named Elkind's, and was ready to expand. Morris left Society Shirt and with Sam established a second Elkind's outlet on Dundas Street West. Years later, the stores would grow to become a popular chain of menswear stores called Elk's, but at the start, each day was a struggle for Morris and Beatrice. The long hours drained them. To help, Beatrice's sister and her husband moved into their home.

"My parents had a business and it kept them busy," Marvin recalls. "I didn't actually see them that much outside of Sundays. They left early in the morning to attend to the business and came home late. And on Sundays I would be getting hell from them for all of the things my uncle was saying that I did during the week. We were mostly looked after by my uncle. He couldn't stand me and I couldn't stand him; and he loved my brother and my brother loved him. Which made me all the madder.

"I didn't like to come home. I didn't like to be home at all. I'd go to a friend's house after school and my parents wouldn't know where I was. I'd stay and sleep there. There was also an alley nearby with old cars in it and sometimes I'd sleep in one of those.

"Not my father, not my mother, not my aunt, not my uncle ever hit me. What they did when they were upset with me was call the school about it and the next day the school would strap me for it."

Just as Morris and Beatrice were struggling with family strife, they faced a crisis at work as well.

"Their shop was in a strip of buildings owned by Dr. Clendenan. He was their landlord. There's a street named after him, Clendenan Avenue. This was in a neighbourhood called the Junction, and Dr. Clendenan was the wealthiest man in the Junction. He was very wealthy and very WASP. My stepfather was an Orthodox Jew—he always wore a skullcap. They were very, very different men but they were very, very fond of each other."

Whenever Morris was short of money, he would borrow a few hundred dollars from Clendenan, and he made a point of paying it back the day before it was due. "Always the day before, never on the day it was due, never after," Marvin says. Dr. Clendenan liked that. But the neighbourhood was in flux. Development pressure was building and rents increased.

Young Marvin would lie awake at night, listening to his parents talk in their bedroom next to his. The couple always spoke to each other in Yiddish. Through the thin walls of their Roxton Road home, Marvin listened as his mother fretted.

"Don't worry," Morris said. "Dr. Clendenan would never throw us out." Morris was right. Instead, Clendenan loaned Morris the money to buy the business outright from his brother and, in recognition of the men's special bond, instead of a month-to-month lease like the other tenants, Morris was given a 49-year lease.

"After Clendenan's death, his sons wanted to sell the whole block to a developer, so they got all of the tenants out but my father. He had the long-term lease. They had to buy him out. It was a lot of money. That changed his life. It made him a rich man. He bought a large home on Strathearn Road near Cedarvale Park, invested the rest and lived a semi-retired life."

While Clendenan's influence was an economic blessing, one piece of advice he gave Morris would have tragic consequences for Marvin. In fact, in any search back through time for the answers to how Marvin Elkind became The Weasel, what happened next must surely rank high.

CHAPTER 2

TORONTO, 1941

It was weighty stuff for students as young as seven, but a school trip to a local theatre was still better than the usual routine at Dewson Street Junior Public School, even if it was to see William Shakespeare's *The Merchant of Venice*.

The archaic language proved a muddle for many, but the colourful presentation of the character Shylock, a greedy and spiteful Jewish moneylender, caught their attention. The students watched as the nasty Shylock, contemptuously called "Jew," demanded his "pound of flesh" from his rival, the good-hearted Christian merchant Antonio, when he was unable to repay a debt. The students saw a parallel between the play and their class. Both had a Jew in it. By the end of the trip, many of the kids had taken to calling Marvin "Jew," in the same way it was spat at Shylock. By the time he got home from school, he had been in five fights.

"I had a big, round, fat kisser," Marvin says, describing his emerging physical form. His face, at that age, was cherubic; round and smooth, with a curl in a long forelock that sent his light brown hair swooping up and down over his right eye. He looked younger and smaller than his classmates, and more innocent. He looked the sort that would get picked on no matter what his ethnic background. And his religion, certainly in those days, made it worse. "My family were Orthodox Jews and I went to school in a non-Jewish area, maybe ninety per cent Italian. Anti-Semitism was very popular. I was getting beat up outside the schoolyard on a regular basis."

One afternoon, a man who lived near the school wandered over to Marvin after catching the tail end of another bruising. The neighbour, Tony Canzanno, a former boxer who went on to be coach of the University of Toronto boxing team, had seen it too many times.

"You know, I'm not a big guy," he said to Marvin.

"I can see that," Marvin said, showing his troublesome lip.

"When I was your age, I was small, too. The guys picked on me, so I learned to fight. Once they saw I knew how to fight, they didn't bother me. The big thing is, don't be scared to punch guys. Once you do, they will be scared to punch you first."

It was an epiphany for Marvin. It was so clear. It made such good sense.

"I followed that advice. It worked like magic. I was a very good street fighter, eventually. I learned how to street-fight out of necessity."

His family didn't approve of Marvin's fighting, but some of his relatives weren't above taking advantage of it.

"It was very convenient for Jewish kids to learn either how to fight or how to run fast. I had a cousin who could do neither. Because my father was a partner with his father in the store, I had to fight for him, too. This is when I was seven or eight. After school, I used to have to go to his school and he would wait for me to go home with him and I would get into the fights for him. It used to be a bit of a joke because he was twice my size."

The fighting wasn't good for Marvin's school record.

"I was also a lefty. I wrote with my left hand and ate with my left hand. Now this was a different time, a different age.

They wanted me to switch from my left hand to my right. From the day I started school to the day I quit, anytime I wrote with my left hand they strapped me. They strapped me all the time to get me to write with my right hand. It didn't work. I kept writing with the left." He does still.

* * *

Some days Marvin would be strapped when he got to school for something that had happened at home, strapped later in the day when he held his pencil with his left hand and strapped in the afternoon for being in a fight at lunch. Marvin started skipping school altogether. Notes were sent home and Marvin was increasingly labelled "incorrigible." His behaviour came to the attention of the school board.

At a time when the board had tremendous influence over family life, Marvin, who was just turning nine, joined his mother and stepfather in a meeting with Dr. C.C. Goldring, director of education for the Toronto board, who recommended that Marvin be moved out of the family home and placed in the custody of the Children's Aid Society, where he might find sterner discipline in a foster home. Before making a decision, as with all important matters, Morris asked Clendenan, his revered friend and landlord, for advice. It turned out that Clendenan and Goldring were friends. His advice was simple: "Take Dr. Goldring's advice."

From his bedroom that night, Marvin again heard his parents talking in their room next door.

"My mother was crying and saying 'No, no,' but my father, he said, in Yiddish, he said: 'Dr. Clendenan said so.' That put it in stone. If Dr. Clendenan said it, then it would be done. I knew that was that. I knew what would happen."

* * *

The week of Marvin's ninth birthday, on Friday, March 19, 1943, he was taken to family court by his mother and grandmother. His mother promised that, no matter what happened, he would be coming back home with her that day. They were reassuring words. Marvin had earlier canvassed neighbourhood toughs for advice. One lad, Les Irwin, three years older than Marvin, told him how to handle himself: when the judge speaks to you, keep your head down, look at your shoes and, if you can, cry, and then say, "I'm sorry. If you let me stay, I promise to be a good boy." For Marvin, who held the streetwise boy in the same esteem as Morris did Dr. Clendenan, his words were gospel.

"I was practising saying that ahead of time. I practised hanging my head and saying that line. I practised it and practised it and practised it. But I never got to use it."

As he waited outside the court with his mother and grandmother, a clerk came to greet them.

"The judge has signed the papers. Everything's in order," she said.

"We haven't spoken to the judge yet. Don't we have to see the judge? Doesn't he have to talk to Marvin?" his mother asked.

"No, he's signed the papers. It's not necessary. He's reviewed the case and agrees the boy should become a ward of Children's Aid."

"So what does that mean? When does he go?"

"He goes now. They're coming to get him."

"But he needs his clothes and his toys. He's not ready to go. I need to take him home to get his things and get him ready."

"No, he goes now. That'll all be taken care of."

The Children's Aid workers, a man and a woman, explained the rules to the stunned family. His mother could not go to Marvin's foster home. Neither could Marvin visit his family's home. The only time they could visit was at school. They also learned a Jewish home wasn't available and he was being placed in an Italian home. At least, they were told, it was not far away. Then his mother and grandmother were asked to leave.

Beatrice leaned down to Marvin, hugged him and spoke to him in Yiddish: "It will not be forever."

Marvin was too shocked to be scared.

"When they told me I wasn't going back home, I was in shock. Shock. It was like I was in a dream. A couple from Children's Aid came to get me. The lady sat in the back of the car with me and I remember she held my hand as we drove over to the foster home. The social workers explained how things work. They told me I wasn't the only foster kid, that there were others in the house where I was going. She said the woman there is not my mother but I have to obey her like she was and that she gets paid by them to take kids in."

CHAPTER 3

TORONTO, 1941

The Children's Aid Society workers stopped the car outside 250 Shaw Street, across from the western edge of Trinity Bellwoods Park, and Marvin looked up at the three-storey red-brick house and wondered if this was where he could feel he belonged.

If the social workers were truly looking to put Marvin in a place where his trouble-making tendencies would be curbed, they had stopped at the wrong address. From the outside, it was a fine-looking home in a working-class neighbourhood, but inside it was bedlam. Marvin and the social workers were greeted on the porch by Lena Pasquale, his new foster mother.

"Mrs. Pasquale, this is Marvin. Marvin, this is your new home," the female social worker said.

"Go to your room, we'll call you down for lunch," was Mrs. Pasquale's welcome.

Inside the Pasquale home, it was all discord and noise. Mrs. Pasquale had five children of her own, all in their teens, and took in three foster children for the money social services paid. Marvin soon learned the foster money supplemented Mrs. Pasquale's bootlegging business, in which she was a partner with the mother of future Toronto Mafia boss Paul Volpe. Liquor was sold from the house for close to double the price of the legal stores. The women's best customers were those on the so-called "Indian List," a sad collection of problem drunks who were prohibited from buying booze at the licensed outlets. Business was best on Sundays when no legal liquor was sold in the city. Marvin was soon delivering bottles of whisky to neighbourhood customers as part of his household chores. Living separately downstairs, in an unfinished basement, was Tony, the Pasquale father. He steered clear of the kids. And his wife. About a year after Marvin arrived, Tony was killed in a knife fight. His children ransacked his possessions and found the only thing worth keeping was a pair of slippers still in their box that his eldest son, Roy, had stolen and given him.

Roy, who was 19 at the time, was the worst role model a guy like Marvin could have. Six months before, Roy and a friend had barged into a house, pulled a handgun and ordered the two women inside to hand over all their money. Between them, the terrified women could muster only $29. Roy was arrested the next day.

But for young Marvin, Roy's presence was one of the highlights of his new life. "It was startling to me, all of these people running around the house. I was unsettled. But I find out that my oldest foster brother is Roy Pasquale, who had a real tough reputation. I felt good about that; I'd be living with a guy like that, a real tough guy who was known around town."

The strange, unhealthy attraction to Roy would last for four decades but, important for Marvin, he learned at an early age the value of being friends with the toughest guy around. The schoolyard scraps were almost a thing of the past. "Most guys didn't want to fight me. They were scared that if they beat me up, Roy would come and get them."

* * *

When Marvin and the other kids were called down for lunch, his first meal in his new home, Marvin noticed something about Mrs. Pasquale that was not there when she had greeted the social workers. Tucked into the pocket of her apron was a leather strap. One of the other foster kids told him that's what you get if she gets mad at you.

"She was a very tough old broad," Marvin says. "Roy was a tough guy but she used to take that strap and give him a whack right across the kisser. Even he didn't argue with her. No one ever objected. She was in complete control.

"When we came downstairs from our room in the attic and sat down for lunch, they had a big table we all ate at. I start eating and the Old Lady immediately gets up, walks over to me and, without any warning, grabs me by the hair and yanks me right up out of the seat and away from the table and bellows: 'You won't eat in this house with your left hand.' I stopped eating with my left immediately. Right there, in two seconds. They strapped the shit out of me at school every day over my writing and it didn't change a thing, but in two seconds with her over my eating, it changed right there. I started eating with my right hand." He does still.

* * *

Although he was nine, Marvin looked more like five because of his short, pudgy frame and round baby face with pinchable cheeks. He was the youngest child in the house. The other foster boys—Peter and Gerald—were both tall, strapping lads, which accentuated the age difference even more. His foster mother liked having a bambino in the house again. Marvin noted what marked the foster kids from her biological children: her children called her "Mama Pasquale" while the foster kids called her "Mrs. Pasquale."

On that first evening, Mrs. Pasquale laid out the plan for Marvin. Tomorrow, she would take him to get all the clothes he needed, and on Monday, her daughter Norma would take him to register at his new school down the road. His survival instincts suddenly kicked in.

"When I go to the new school," Marvin asked, "can I be registered under the name of Pasquale, so I will be like your real child?"

Mrs. Pasquale's eyes lit up. She smiled broadly.

"Yes. Yes, you can," she said. "But Marvin Pasquale doesn't sound right. From now on we'll call you Mario. Mario Pasquale. Is that OK?"

His answer was a stroke of manipulative genius. "Thank you, Mama Pasquale."

He pulled the same trickery on Roy. When the kids would sit around talking about who could take whom in a fight, and how strong one neighbourhood kid was and how tough another was, Marvin would keep interjecting: "He's not as tough as you, Roy." It worked as well on Roy as it did on Roy's mother.

"That was survival," Marvin recalls. "It was the same survival instinct that kept me going all those years as a fink. Don't think I'm kidding. That's not something you can learn. It's got to come to you naturally. All you can do is learn how to do it better, but it's got to be already in you."

That night, Peter and Gerald made room for Marvin in their attic bedroom, which was easy since he had brought nothing with him, not even pyjamas. At bedtime, he said he would sleep in his underwear, but Mama Pasquale would not hear of it. Whatever her flaws, she was a stickler for hygiene. She gave him one of Roy's shirts to wear. With Marvin in it, the shirttail draped to the floor. He climbed into bed and thought his first weary day at his new home was over. About an hour later, however, he heard Norma at the door to the attic whispering.

"Psst, Mario," she said. "Mario."

Not yet accustomed to his new name, Marvin didn't know whom she was talking to and ignored her. She got louder and more insistent until she was no longer whispering.

"Mario. Mario! Don't you know your own name?"

It finally clicked.

"Oh, that's right, I'm Mario now, sorry."

"My mother wants to see you," Norma said and led him downstairs to Mama Pasquale's bedroom, where the woman sat on the edge of her bed. Norma ushered Marvin in and quickly left.

"Mario, you've been a very bad boy today," the woman said quietly. As Marvin tried to figure out what he had done wrong, Mama Pasquale unbuttoned his oversized nightshirt, leaving him standing beside her, naked.

"You've been a very bad boy," she repeated, turning him around and spanking his bum with her hand until it was red and burning. Then she pulled him up and into her bed, turned him onto his stomach and lay down beside him. Gently she started to rub his reddened, bare bottom, whispering, "What a good boy you are. What a good boy." This went on long into the night. She woke Marvin up early and told him to go back to the attic bedroom.

The next morning, everything was as it had been the day before. Neither Norma nor Mama Pasquale—and certainly not Marvin—gave any hint of what had taken place that night. Breakfast came and went, with Marvin sitting quietly, carefully holding his cereal spoon in his right hand.

"I didn't know what to make of this," Marvin says now, showing his embarrassment by looking away when he speaks. "I figured that what I did wrong that day was to eat with my left hand and if I behaved myself, this weird shit wouldn't happen again. So the next day I watched myself so closely so I wouldn't do anything wrong. I was polite and quiet. I ate with my right hand. I didn't talk back. I was an angel. I was an absolute angel."

That day, a Saturday, Marvin, Norma and Mama Pasquale headed downtown to Eaton's, the landmark department store on Yonge Street, Toronto's main shopping drag. Mama Pasquale took with her a folded slip of paper from Children's Aid listing all of the things Marvin was entitled to: one sweater, five pairs of underwear, three pairs of socks, two pairs of pants and so on. Eaton's had an arrangement with Children's Aid to provide the items to the foster mother and the bill was sent to the government.

"Eaton's wasn't just a store. Back then it was an institution. You could return anything to Eaton's if it had an Eaton's label on it. There were two Eaton's stores here—one on Yonge Street and one on College Street. We would go to one of the Eaton's and buy our list of stuff. Then, when we got home, the Old Lady wouldn't let us take the windbreakers and sweaters and shoes and so forth out of the box. What would happen is the Old Lady would give us old stuff from her kids to wear; then, if she bought them at the Yonge store she would return them to the College store and pocket the money. It was all part of her scam, why she took kids in.

"One time much later, we were in Eaton's and one of the other foster kids was trying on pants and I was there to get a jacket and the store clerk asked me if I wanted to try it on and, without thinking, I said, 'Doesn't matter, I won't get to keep it anyways.' The Old Lady gave me such a whack I nearly fell over the other side of the counter."

That second night in the foster home, after a day of acting like an angel, Marvin got ready for bed, pulling on the new Eaton's pyjamas he had received that day. He climbed into bed. Then he heard it again.

"Psst, Mario," Norma whispered.

Once again he was led to Mama Pasquale's bedroom where she removed his pyjamas, told him he had been a naughty boy, spanked him until he was red and pulled him naked into bed with her, rubbing his buttocks.

"First night she did it, on the Friday, I didn't catch on. I got upset. I tried to figure out what I did wrong. The next night, on Saturday, after being very, very careful not to do anything wrong, it was the exact same ball game. That's when I knew the score. It was the same thing on Sunday night. And the next and the next. She did that the whole two years I was there; every fucking night. I went through all of my childhood illnesses while in that home—mumps, measles, chicken pox, scarlet fever—it didn't make any difference. Not one single night did the system change. Not once did I not get called down to her room. She didn't miss a night. She wouldn't let me go one night. I used to just close my eyes and pretend it wasn't happening."

* * *

On Monday, Norma took Marvin by the hand for the short walk down Shaw Street to register him at his new school, Givens Junior Public. About halfway there, when they were out of sight of the Pasquale home, Roy appeared behind them, pulled Marvin's hand out of Norma's grip and jerked him back toward him as Norma continued to walk ahead.

"I know what's going on with you and my mother," Roy said, bending down and pushing his face close to Marvin's, his voice low and menacing. He wrapped his powerful right hand around the back of the boy's neck and squeezed hard.

"If you tell anyone, no one will believe you, first of all, and second, I'll knock the hell out of you every day. But if you keep your mouth shut you'll be her favourite and I'll leave you alone as well." Roy paused, then asked, "Now, what's happening between you and my mother?"

"Nothing," said Marvin. The grip loosened.

"Good boy," Roy said, letting go altogether and straightening up. Marvin never doubted the threat.

"Roy was a tremendously powerful man. He was born with gorilla strength," Marvin recalls. "The way he looked at me, I believed him. He had very cold eyes. Terrifying eyes."

Marvin kept that promise to keep his mouth shut even during his emotional reunion with his mother that same day.

"The only place my mother was allowed to see me was at school and, bless her, my mother came to see me at school every day. I soon figured out that she was either going to be waiting for me when I got to school or waiting for me after school or she would be there during one of my two recesses. So if she wasn't waiting for me when I got there, at recess I would go out to a spot in the fence around the schoolyard and see if she was there. If she wasn't there at recess, I knew she would be waiting when I left school. Every day for two years. She asked how I was and what I was doing. I told her only about the good things. None of the bad."

About the only good that came from the nightly abuse was that Mama Pasquale continued to treat Marvin as the baby of her brood and protected him from the others, including Roy. Mama Pasquale wouldn't let Roy lay a finger on Marvin, even while ignoring Roy's torment of the other kids. Marvin took advantage of it. Sometimes he would deliberately provoke Roy or one of his tough friends when Mama Pasquale was there. Then he would watch the boys stew, unable to throttle him.

Mama Pasquale's fussing over Marvin, as well as her unwillingness to go a single night without their disturbing bedtime ritual, meant that Marvin was chosen to go on a special overseas trip, a rarity for the working poor in the postwar period. Soon after the war in Europe ended, Mrs. Pasquale wanted to pay a visit to her native Sicily to see how her family was faring.

"I remember having fun on the way there and being treated very nicely there. We stayed in Palermo. There was a Pasquale cousin there my own age. We played together and had fun. We were there for eight days and I've not been back since. It was just the two of us who went. Just me and her. Her youngest son, Rudy, squawked about not getting to go. Rudy was very jealous of the attention she paid me. I think the older ones understood why.

"The Pasquales, the Old Lady, they were not mobbed up in Sicily, as far as I knew. I found out later on that the young cousin I played with, who was my age, became mob. I had an encounter with him years later."

* * *

Each Sunday morning, Marvin—or Mario, as everyone in the house now called him—would go with Mama Pasquale to the nearby Catholic church for Mass. While the other children lazed around at home or roamed the streets making mischief, Marvin was busy crossing himself and kneeling in the large sanctuary of St. Alphonsus Roman Catholic Church. He almost became an altar boy until the priest heard him sing and graciously declined Mama Pasquale's request.

The troubled son of eastern European Orthodox Jews had, with ease, become the perfect Italian-Catholic boy. Marvin had become Mario. His masquerades had begun.

CHAPTER 4

TORONTO, 1945

Sliding a nickel across the counter of Shaeffer's Grocery Store at the corner of Ossington Avenue and Harrison Street, an 11-year-old Marvin then greedily hopped to the back of the store and reached into the cooler, grabbing a brown glass bottle inside. The diamond-shaped label announced his pleasure: Orange-Crush Soda, 6 fl. ozs. Popping the cap on the metal opener at the side of the cooler, he listened for the swish of fizz that he loved before guzzling down the soda.

These were good times for Marvin, as he burned through the money he made from his newspaper route, although there was only 25 cents left over each week after Mama Pasquale took half off the top, another angle she worked to maximize profit from her foster kids. The rest of his money would go toward Saturday movies at The Pix, the cinema on Ossington Avenue. Usually it was a child-friendly serial, such as Tarzan the Ape Man, but sometimes Marvin managed to catch more adult-oriented fare. One movie in particular, a gangster flick, caught his imagination. Surprisingly for such an immature kid, it wasn't the squealing tires or staccato machine-guns of the movie that engrossed him as he sat mesmerized in the flickering black-and-white glow of the old 454-seat cinema, but the cool dialogue and suave, but tough, gangster anti-hero personalities.

One scene struck him dumb, although he can't remember the name of the movie. A gangster pulled a huge roll of cash from his pocket, peeled off the top note and tossed it on a barroom counter, saying: "Keep the change. Drinks are on me."

"I thought, What a cool thing. I want to do that," Marvin recalls. As he goofed off at Shaeffer's, he would, improbably, get his chance.

* * *

Shaeffer's was a block away from the Roxton Road home where his parents lived and where he was not allowed to visit, but Marvin still wandered down for an Orange-Crush and to hang out with the local kids.

"In those days, there were little independent grocery stores all over. Ninety-nine per cent of them were owned by Jews. Like now, the variety stores are run by Koreans, back then it was Jews," Marvin says. "They were open seven days a week, but in July and August, groups of them would take turns closing on a Sunday for a holiday, so they could take their family for an outing."

Two 14-year-old boys who lived in the neighbourhood, Les Irwin and another boy named Tommy, developed a clever little racket. In a time before banks had night deposit boxes, store owners would wrap up the money from their Friday and Saturday sales in a paper bag or a cloth and hide it somewhere in the store until it could be deposited in the bank on Monday. The plan was that the two boys would find out which store was going to be closed on a particular Sunday and they would break in, find the cash and make off without anyone knowing until the next morning. They realized, however, that they needed a third partner, a much smaller one, whom they could boost up through a broken window into the store. Les knew Marvin from the days before he was placed into foster care. Les was the one who had coached Marvin on how to beg sympathy from the judge. Marvin was thrilled to join the conspiracy. He felt he had earned the chance because of the times he had sat on the veranda of the Pasquale home as a lookout for Roy when his foster brother got together with his budding criminal cohorts.

One of the first stores the boys hit was their hangout, Shaeffer's.

"So they would break a window, push me up through it into the store and I would then go and unlock the door and let them inside. As Les and Tommy tossed the place looking for the cash—it'd be hidden in a sugar can or a bag under the fresh fruit, or whatever—I'd grab a comic book or a pop or candy bar. As soon as they'd find it, we'd tear out of there. It usually added up to about fifty dollars. Les and Tommy would split that and give me five dollars for my end. Now, five dollars for a kid in 1945 was a lot of money. We had broken into four stores like clockwork that way and I had twenty dollars from it. I went to a bank and had it all changed into one-dollar bills. I had twenty of them and I rolled them all together into a bankroll like I had seen in the movie and I'd carry it around with me everywhere."

One day, after a baseball game, the two teams of local boys retired to the Lakeview Restaurant on Dundas Street West at Ossington, a well-loved diner and local hangout just three doors east of the bank where Marvin's father had pulled his ill-fated heist. By coincidence, on the other side of the diner was a variety store that would soon play a similar role in Marvin's life. The fact that the two young sons of Basil Kiperoff, the Lakeview's owner, were on Marvin's team and mingling with them made staff particularly tolerant of the gaggle of 18 noisy kids crowding into the wooden booths and spinning on the 10 stainless steel stools that lined the long counter. Each of the boys ordered a five-cent ice cream cone to cool off, and Mr. Kiperoff helped scoop out cone after cone. As the boys licked away, Marvin slowly did the math—18 cones at a nickel apiece came to 90 cents—and his eyes lit up as he suddenly saw his chance.

He walked up to the large, heavy cash register near the wooden front door, pulled out his roll of one-dollar bills, peeled off the top bill, tossed it on the counter and put on his best movie gangster voice.

"They're all on me, keep the change."

Mr. Kiperoff handed him the dime change anyway.

"You can't go throwing money away like that," the owner said. "Where did you get that kind of money, anyway?"

"From my paper route," Marvin said. The boys were more impressed.

"Thanks, Marv," they called out. It gave him a big rush.

What should have been—and, for anyone else, would have been—an ego boost and a simple fantasy fulfilled, ended up, for Marvin, ruining what remained of his boyhood.

* * *

Detective Eddie Tong was known on the streets as "The Chinaman" because of his last name and his straight black hair, even though he was a decidedly white cop from Britain. Forty years old at the time, Tong already had 16 years of distinguished service on the Toronto force, most of it doing plainclothes work on the street where he had a vast network of snitches. With his sturdy build, fedora and long overcoat that would have been a cliché on a lesser cop, he was a local legend. Marvin knew Tong from the detective's many visits to the Pasquale house, usually on the hunt for Roy or another of the fledgling gangsters that formed Roy's circle of friends.

When Tong and his partner, Detective Roy Perry, stopped their black police car beside Marvin as he walked home from school one day, the boy didn't know what to make of it.

"Mario, get in," Tong said, using Marvin's foster home name. Detective Perry was at the wheel.

"I can't, Officer Tong, I'm expected home for dinner. If I'm late, I'll get in trouble," he said, quickening his pace.

"Get in the car," the detective growled. With a sigh, Marvin hopped into the back of the car for the drive to the Claremont Street Police Station, an old west-end hub with a tough reputation.

"Empty out your pockets," Tong ordered. Marvin pulled out his bankroll and put it on the desk.

"Where did you get this?" the detective asked, poking at the roll.

"From my paper route."

"No, you didn't. I checked it out, you get fifty cents a week and you have to give half of that to your foster mother." It was a Tong trademark; he rarely asked a question for which he didn't already have a pretty good idea of the answer. Then he took out a roll of quarters from his own pocket and held up the stubby cylinder, rolled tight in brown paper.

"You know what this is?"

"Yeah, it's money," answered Marvin.

"There are forty quarters in this roll. I'm going to ask you something forty times. If you can say, once for each of these forty quarters, that you didn't break into the grocery stores, you can take them home with you. OK?"

"Hey, that's great."

"Did you break into the grocery stores?" Tong asked.

"Nope," answered Marvin.

Bang. The detective, gripping the heavy roll of quarters in his fist, smacked the startled boy in the face. He waited a few seconds.

"Did you break into the stores?" Tong asked a second time.

"No," Marvin whimpered.

Bang. Another smack. Pause.

"Did you break into the stores?"

Marvin started to cry.

"Yes, yes, I did. I broke into the stores," he blubbered.

"Who was with you?" asked Tong. Even at that age, Marvin knew the code of the neighbourhood toughs. No snitching. It was drilled into every kid on the street and in the schoolyard. He also knew that Les and Tommy would beat him worse than any cop if he ratted them out.

"You can hit me all you want, Officer Tong, but I can't tell you something that isn't true. There weren't nobody with me, it was only me."

Tong looked at Perry. They already had all they needed to settle this case.

"I'm sorry I hit you, kid," Tong said, in a softer tone. He ruffled Marvin's hair. "You have every right to break into those stores. You can break into as many as you want, it's OK. They make enough money; won't miss it a bit. Just don't tell who-ever's with you that I told you this. And don't tell your foster brother Roy. This is just between you and me. Understand?" Marvin nodded. Then Tong banged the roll of quarters open on the edge of his desk, pulled one out and flipped it to Marvin.

"This is because I hit you."

Marvin walked out feeling pretty good, despite his sore face.

"I leave there figuring that everyone's got this guy pegged

wrong. This cop is OK, I think," Marvin recalls. "He's letting us keep up what we're doing with the stores and he even gave me a quarter. The Chinaman's OK."

* * *

That Sunday, Les, Tommy and Marvin gathered for their fifth grocery job. The target was another store the boys knew well, next to where Marvin had bought the ice cream cones, a gesture that clearly had made its way to Detective Tong. The store was half a block from Marvin's father's bank heist.

The job went smoothly at the start. Marvin was boosted through a window; he unlocked the door and let Les and Tommy in. As the older boys looked for the money, Marvin grabbed an ice cream from the store's freezer and a copy of Captain Marvel Adventures, his favourite comic. He hoisted himself onto the front counter and was happily licking and reading when he looked up and saw detectives Tong and Perry stroll through the front door. Marvin, completely fooled by the cops earlier, gave them a cheery greeting.

"Hey, Officer Tong," Marvin called out. Les and Tommy looked up in panic.

"Don't worry, guys, it's OK," Marvin called to the boys. "Officer Tong said we could break into stores all we wanted. We're OK."

Les rolled his eyes and shouted—"You little bastard"—as he took a run at Marvin, trying to swing a punch as Tong and Perry grabbed him and held him back. Perry started laughing. Case closed.

"We were all charged. I felt like an idiot afterwards but I was just a dumb kid. What the hell did I know? They pulled one over on me."

* * *

After their arrest, Marvin, Les and Tommy were held in Toronto's Don Jail waiting for trial. Along with other juvenile delinquents they were kept in an area away from adult prisoners. The boys were allowed to play floor hockey, and on Marvin's second day in jail he took a knock in the face during a game, giving him a bruise under his eye.

Marvin, Les and Tommy soon had their day in court, appearing before Judge Harry Waisberg, who would go on to lead the 1974 Royal Commission of Inquiry into the influence of organized crime over the construction industry.

For his court appearance on the grocery store burglaries, Marvin was provided a lawyer by the Canadian Jewish Congress. Before court, Marvin asked the lawyer what was the worst that could happen to him. A year in reform school, the lawyer said. But, he added, since this was Marvin's first charge, he could probably get him a lot less; maybe just the strap.

Marvin's mind was racing. Instead of fear at the notion of incarceration, he saw reform school as a way out of the Pasquale home and an end to his nightly ordeal. If he could get a short stay in reform school, he thought, by the time he got out, the Children's Aid might find a Jewish home for him. They might even let him move back with his parents.

Marvin was announced in court as Marvin Elkind, "alias Mario Pasquale."

"Judge says to me—and remember, the whole time I'm thinking to myself, this is a hell of a way out of the foster home—he says to me: 'What happened to your eye to make you look so ugly?'"

Marvin replied, "I was playing floor hockey—what's your excuse?"

It was a gambit to ensure a short stint in reform school. The audacious lip, however, did not go down at all well with Judge Waisberg, who heard the facts of the case from Detective Tong and issued his sentence: all three to be sent to Bowmanville reform school until the age of 16.

Marvin was dumbfounded. Having been told the worst he might get was a year, he quickly counted and realized he had just been handed a five-year sentence. Tong was also shocked. He stood up in court to speak.

"Your Honour, this is not right," he said. "He didn't really know what he was doing, plus, he's here for the first time and you've just given him the longest sentence."

"What are you talking about? I gave them all the same sentence," the judge said.

"Well, he's only eleven, so he'll be in for five years before he gets out. The others are only going to be in for two. That's not right."

"Detective Tong, when you arrested these boys, were you doing your job?"

"Yes, Your Honour."

"Then please let me do mine." Case closed.

Marvin had outsmarted himself. Instead of a short reform-school stint, followed by a safer place to live, he was embarking on another misadventure that would make him look back almost fondly at the weirdness of Mama Pasquale. The downward spiral continued. Marvin's life kept lurching from bad to worse.

CHAPTER 5

BOWMANVILLE, 1945

On May 8, 1945, people gathered around their radios to listen to Winston Churchill and Harry Truman announce the unconditional surrender of Germany. Churchill declared it "Victory in Europe Day," saying: "We may allow ourselves a brief period of rejoicing." And rejoice they did. Celebrations erupted in public squares across Europe and North America. In Toronto, ecstatic citizens gathered along Bay Street, where office workers tossed so much paper out the windows it looked like heavy snow.

The mood was different an hour's drive east. The end of the Third Reich brought disappointment to the occupants on 110 acres of farmland in Bowmanville. Dressed in military uniforms, most decorated with the Iron Cross and various medals of the Nazi regime, a group of German officers was being held behind barbed wire dotted with guard towers at a prisoner of war camp.

Camp 30 had started life in 1925 as a reform school, a prison for boys deemed "incorrigible." But, war being war, in 1941 it was commandeered to house German officers captured during the Second World War. The Germans had made some colourful attempts to escape over the four years of their internment, including once, when they dug a tunnel under the wire. The bid failed when the removed soil, which the Germans hid in the rafters of a camp building, collapsed through the plaster ceiling. But many prisoners seemed content to wait out the war in relative comfort. When the Red Cross asked prisoners if there were any problems, the camp's origin as a reform school was clear. Generalleutnant Johann von Ravenstein, who had been second-in-command under Field Marshal Erwin Rommel, the "Desert Fox," replied: "Just one: the urinals are too close to the ground."

On VE-Day, as cheers rang out across Canada, the German officers were moved north to Gravenhurst while government workers started winding up the barbed wire for the return of troubled boys, for most of whom the low urinals would not be a problem. That it had been a PoW camp was something of a thrill to some of the new inmates. For others, it foretold the isolation of the place.

Marvin, in June of 1945, had no knowledge of the war connection. He was told of it as a warning by guards who were ex-military men. They had watched over the Nazis and would continue to work there guarding the kids.

Marvin had turned 11 just three months before.

"Bowmanville reform school was hell on earth," he says. "No female employees were allowed as they might show compassion. Only males. And they didn't show any."

* * *

Arriving at the Ontario Training School for Boys after a long drive, Marvin and other new inmates lined up at the administration building, where they were told the many rules. Then they were led to another building and told to strip. All inmates went through a series of showers, five of them, one after another, as part of a hygiene program.

Standing naked in the showers, with guards and inmates looking, Marvin immediately stood out. Being a Jew, he was circumcised. It was rare for non-Jews to be circumcised then and few Jewish boys had come through the reform school system. Marvin shuffled along from shower to shower and stood wet, naked and miserable. There to meet him was an older inmate whose job was to hand out towels. Michael Cavanagh, who went by the name of Malcolm, was still a teenager, but the hulking, homely kid looked 30.

"You're a Jewish boy," Cavanagh said, handing Marvin a towel and looking down. "I've been in reform schools for five years and only once before did I see a Jewish kid and the other guys always knocked the hell out of him. Do you know how to fight?"

"Yeah," Marvin said, grabbing the towel and clutching it around his waist.

"Do you want to not be bothered by the other boys?"

"Yeah." He was listening carefully now.

"I'm the captain of the boxing team. We can use a kid your age. Know anything about boxing?"

"Yes, I do. The foster home I lived in was big into boxing."

"You'll like it," Cavanagh said. "The boxing team, we take care of each other. If you come onto the boxing team nobody will bother you. Get dressed. I'm going to take you over to the gym."

Cavanagh introduced Marvin to the Sergeant who coached the team and Marvin signed up. Just as Cavanagh promised, the other inmates left him alone. Good thing, too. In class, students were studying *The Merchant of Venice*.

Marvin fell in love with boxing, the beginning of an enduring passion.

* * *

It made a splash among the kids gathered in Toronto's Mutual Street Arena—even in the edgy world of amateur boxing—when Marvin arrived for a boxing tournament accompanied by a uniformed Bowmanville reform-school guard. But even with that sign of toughness, Marvin, with his short frame and gentle face, still looked like a pushover.

"Elkind," Ted Reeve called out in the noisy hall before the 1946 youth boxing tournament began. Reeve was a sports-writer for the *Toronto Evening Telegram* and a former pro athlete who ran the competition. When Marvin scurried up in a white bathrobe the school had given him as his boxing robe, Reeve shuffled through a pile of papers and looked at him briefly before declaring, "You're out of the tournament."

"Why?"

"You don't qualify. You haven't had ten fights yet," Reeve said.

"I've had about forty."

"Where?"

"All in Bowmanville reform school. Here's the coach, ask him," Marvin said, pointing to the guard.

"Anyways," said Reeve, "you have to be twelve years old to compete."

"I am twelve."

Reeve got a chuckle out of it, this small kid with an angel's face coming from juvenile detention to fight. With a news-man's eye for a headline, Reeve introduced Marvin into the ring not as Marvin Elkind, not as Mario Pasquale, but as Baby Face Nelson, the same bank robber who had pulled the big heist the day Marvin was born. Marvin won and the moniker stuck as his fight name.

Just as when the kids on the playground had stopped picking on him when they knew he was with Roy, Marvin saw how hanging around with the boxing team protected him in reform school. The value of always standing beside the toughest guy around was a lesson that never left him.

Being on the boxing team, though, could not protect him from school staff.

* * *

Bowmanville's policy was built around liberal application of corporal punishment.

"If you misbehaved or didn't do your homework or whatever else, the teachers at the school had the right to give you a demerit," Marvin recalls. "The guards could give you demerits. If you did anything wrong you got demerits. Anybody that had demerits, the next morning you went to 'court' before breakfast. Court was the superintendent's office and whenever your name was called you went in. There would always be a big lineup of kids. And you had the right to defend yourself, to plead your case, but no one would ever win their case. Nobody ever won. Nobody. It was a joke. You would then be sentenced to so many strokes of the strap. It was called S and S—stripped and strapped. You would report to the punishment room at night, just before bed, in your pyjamas. You would be taken into the punishment room and you'd take off your pyjamas.

"You had a piece of paper from the super with you saying how many strokes of the strap you were to get. Two guards did it. Both of them were huge, big guys. You bent over a table, and one guy from the other end of the table would grab your wrists—and every time you'd swear he was breaking your wrists—and while you were bent over the table with one guy holding your wrists, the other guy would apply the strap, a thick leather strap."

Cavanagh, Marvin's boxing friend, had more advice.

"If you want to be a hero with the other kids, you never cry. You show that you're tough and you don't cry when you get the strap and I'll teach you how," Cavanagh said, telling him to turn his pain into hate. For Marvin, it worked. From the first time he was strapped to the last. About a year after he arrived, he was putting his pyjama bottoms back on after another strapping when the guard seemed frustrated by Marvin's refusal to cry.

"Well, what did you think of that?" the guard said.

"Thanks for not strapping me," Marvin said, refusing to admit he was in pain. The frustrated guard punched him, breaking a front tooth.

"As far as I remember, I bled every time I was strapped. But I never cried. I didn't let them see me cry," Marvin recalls. "I left that place and I could never cry about anything. My mother and my wife, years later, wanted me to go to a shrink because I couldn't cry."

Perhaps two dozen times, Marvin and Cavanagh escaped. Getting out was not difficult, just a climb over a low fence. Trouble started on the other side. The camp was miles from anywhere and they wandered along dirt roads hoping they were heading toward town. During one poorly planned break-out, Marvin and Cavanagh walked for what seemed like forever in the pouring rain and were soaked and freezing when they came to a gas station. A police car was parked outside and they were glad to see it. They ran to the cop and gave themselves up. The cop had no idea what they were talking about. He called the school and was told no students were missing. Their getaway had gone completely unnoticed. It wasn't until the shivering boys insisted the school do a head count that it was confirmed two inmates were gone. Marvin and Cavanagh were returned and got another strapping.

Marvin was sad when Cavanagh was released. Years later, when he tried to reconnect with him, he learned his hulking saviour had been executed in 1956 in California's San Quentin prison for murder and robbery.

* * *

In his fourth miserable year in reform school, Marvin met a new social worker assigned to his case. Fern Alexander was just 25, but to 15-year-old Marvin she seemed ancient. She was, however, the first female official he had ever dealt with in custody. Fern came and interviewed Marvin and was struck by the harshness of his sentence at such a young age. She looked at his school record, where they tallied the number of times he had been sent for a strapping: 175.

"She took pity on me," Marvin says.

She soon became an advocate for him, the first since his mother's weak protestations. Fern lobbied for his early release. She offered to act as Marvin's legal guardian as well as parole officer while he lived at his grandparents' house on probation, and a judge agreed.

* * *

Decades later, there was a police investigation into the abuse of boys at the reform school. After interviewing former inmates, authorities decided to arrest the captain of the guards. Marvin was elated when he heard.

"I'll give you an example of how evil he was. While the kids were out playing in the field at the reform school, he would come out and point to four or five kids for no reason and tell them to stand against the fence. He then made us pull our pants down and bend over and, one by one, he would shove his baton up the ass. I still shiver about that. We used to talk about killing him."

Marvin was asked to testify at the trial. He didn't want to. He was sure nothing would happen to the guy. Fern Alexander reached out to him and convinced him it was his duty. Marvin went to Belleville, Ontario, for the hearing. It was the first time he took the stand to testify against anyone. To his surprise, the guard was convicted and sentenced to jail time. At the end of the trial, the guard's daughter confronted Marvin.

"You should be ashamed of yourself. Don't you realize he's an old man?" she said.

Marvin was quick to reply: "Don't you realize that when he did that we were little kids?"

***

Out on probation in Toronto, Marvin still had poor impulse control. Shortly after his release, he and three friends were walking past a cigar store when he spotted a parked car with its motor running. Let's go for a joyride, Marvin said, and they all climbed in, Marvin behind the wheel. After a few blocks, he pulled over and they ran off.

One of the boys was overwhelmed by guilt and told his parents, who called police. Officers came to Marvin's grandparents' house that night and arrested him in his pyjamas. At the hearing, Marvin was almost sent back to Bowmanville, the judge saying he couldn't let the incident go unpunished.

"Believe me," Fern told the judge sternly, "I will not let him get away with this. He will be well punished." The judge eyed Fern for a moment, then agreed to release Marvin into her care.

"Marvin, thank the judge," Fern said.

"Thannnnks, Judge," Marvin said in a goofy voice. At that, Fern slapped him and told him to thank him properly.

"Thank you, Your Honour," Marvin said timidly. As Fern pulled him out of the courtroom by his ear, the judge couldn't help himself: "I think I would have done him a favour by sending him back to Bowmanville."

Despite the joyride, Fern was making progress with Marvin. She went to his grandparents' house at 9:05 each night to make sure he obeyed his curfew. She got him a job at Tip Top Tailors, a clothing manufacturer near the Toronto waterfront.

"I hated that job. The number of times I thought that I should do something so I could go back to the joint," Marvin says. "They were teaching me how to be a presser and it was the summer. That room was so fucking hot. I really hated it. Sweating there with all these old Jews. The foreman used to come around saying the sleeve wasn't pressed right or this or that. There were so many times I felt like whacking the guy right in the mouth. I really hated it but I had to do it so I did it."

Although forbidden to see Roy Pasquale, Marvin did, on the sly. By then Roy was loansharking and running other rackets.

After a year, Marvin turned 16 and his sentence was complete. He appeared once more before Judge Waisberg. Fern knew Marvin wasn't ready to be on his own. She asked the judge for another year to work with him, but the judge said he didn't have the authority. He told her that if Marvin agreed to remain under her supervision, he could order it. All eyes turned to Marvin.

"I was sixteen, but an immature sixteen. I was street smart but immature in all other aspects," Marvin says. "The judge says, Do you want that?"

"I said no." He is ashamed of his foolishness today.

"I didn't appreciate Fern as much as I should have. It's the first time I can really remember someone being protective of me, and that made me feel good. But when I had the chance to be on my own, I chose that. I was a kid and here was this broad telling me what time to be in, when to go to bed, what time to get up, making me do this job I hated, punishing me when I did something wrong. What kid wants that? Hindsight being what it is, had I stuck with her for the extra year, my whole life would have been different."

Immediately after severing the tie with Fern, Marvin committed three acts of colossal stupidity. He quit his job. He left his grandparents' house. And he hooked back up with Roy.

"Thus started my grand demise," Marvin says. "Or whatever you want to call it."

CHAPTER 6

The summer's afternoon heat forced owners of the small shops along Dundas Street West to prop open their front doors to let any stray breezes inside. Marvin strolled along, absent-mindedly looking through windows and doors as he returned to work from a long lunch. It was three months since he had left Fern and sought refuge with his former foster brother Roy Pasquale. The day his probation ended, Marvin had abandoned the job he loathed at Tip Top Tailors, packed a few things and shown up on Roy's doorstep. By then Roy had left his domineering mother's chaotic house and had bought a place a half-dozen blocks east.

Roy put Marvin up in an apartment he had illegally subdivided on St. Clair Avenue West, above a menswear store called Dover's. The upstairs was already crowded. A Toronto cab driver and his young family lived there and another man was renting a bed. Marvin squeezed into a separate bedroom but everyone shared one washroom. Roy had learned from his mother how to maximize space. Marvin didn't pay rent, instead working unpaid for Roy. For a 16-year-old rebellious kid looking for freedom after so many years of abuse, it seemed a dream arrangement, but Roy was getting the better part of the deal, as he usually did. Roy was emerging as a major loan shark and serious racketeer.

Marvin became his henchman.

And it was as Roy's henchman that Marvin knew precisely what he had to do when, by chance during his saunter along Dundas Street that afternoon, he looked into Belkin's, a small tailor shop specializing in made-to-measure suits. Inside, framed by the open door, was a used-car dealer who had borrowed a large sum of money from Roy and long ago stopped paying it back. Roy had been searching for the deadbeat for months, and there he was, standing in Belkin's while the tailor pulled out a long bolt of fabric, helping him choose material for a new suit. Marvin jogged a few doors along to a drugstore with a pay phone and called Roy.

"Guess who's in Belkin's," said Marvin, panting. When Roy heard his most wanted man had reappeared, he erupted in excited rage. Roy knew Belkin's well. The beige suit he was wearing had been cut and stitched at Belkin's not long before. The tailor had also borrowed money from Roy, and had missed a payment. Roy had taken the amount in suits instead.

"Keep an eye on him. I'll be right over," Roy ordered. "If he tries to leave, stop him."

In almost no time, Roy pulled up in his Cadillac. By now the man was standing with his back to the door as the tailor measured his inseam. With Marvin following on his heels, Roy stormed in, shouting.

"Where's my money, you bastard."

The besieged man then sputtered words that almost everyone in that sort of position says. They were words that Marvin would hear over and over and over in the years to come.

"I'll have it for you tomorrow, I swear."

Roy didn't even seem to hear. He continued to march forward, pulled a pistol out of the pocket of his suit jacket and smashed the man in the face with its handle. Again he lifted the pistol and brought it down on his head. And again. It was a pistol-whipping of consequence, given Roy's incredible strength and intense rage.

"And as soon as I'm done doing this," Roy snarled between blows, "I'm going to put a bullet in your head, you bastard."

It was then that Marvin became worried. He had known the man would get a beating from Roy before he even placed the phone call—it was the way the business ran—but murder was something else. The way Roy said it, the throaty growl in his voice, Marvin believed he was serious. Marvin acted on impulse. As Roy bent down and raised the pistol high over his head to bring it smashing down on the man again, Marvin, standing behind, reached out and snatched the gun out of Roy's meaty fist. He turned and dashed out.

Marvin hid for two days waiting for Roy to cool down.

"You did a good thing, Marv," Roy said when Marvin eventually phoned. "I'm happy for what you did. I would have killed that guy and I wouldn't have got my money. Come back—and bring my gun."

It was another lesson in his on-the-job training: try not to kill your customers; it means they can't pay you back. This was Marvin's new life.

* * *

When the occasional shopper wandered through the door of Romik Carpet on Perth Avenue at Davenport, looking to buy floor covering from its sparse selection of samples, the salesmen were happy to ring up a sale, but they didn't go out of their way to attract customers. Romik, a portmanteau of the names of Roy and his partner, Mickey, was a front for Roy's burgeoning criminal empire. A commercial front was a necessary extravagance for gangsters who needed to legitimize their illicit income, employment record and have a plausible reason to maintain office space. It also helped when it came to laundering criminal proceeds. The real money was made upstairs from Romik's meagre showroom, in an apartment that Roy had converted into a private office. He moved a huge glass-topped wooden desk inside and set it up with erect pens in black holders, in imitation of a bank counter.

From his Romik office, Roy kept track of the money he had out on the streets in loans. His interest rate was five per cent per week. His partner, Mickey, carried the large roll of cash ready for fresh loans—they called it the "BR," for bank roll—and a gun to keep it safe.

This is where Marvin reported to work.

"Every day I worked for Roy. Every day," Marvin recalls. "Roy was loansharking so I went around collecting money for him. I would pick up money for him, I would deliver money for him, went around meeting guys he owed money to and paying them. And Roy was fencing—buying and selling stolen merchandise—so I would help with that, too. Every day, picking up booze, picking up money, getting his car washed. I was on call twenty-four hours a day."

Marvin followed Roy from job to job at first, learning the ropes of gangster life. He learned the art of collecting money from deadbeats.

"This was my first real work as a collector. At first I was just a second pair of hands and legs there to help and looking out for coppers. I learned how to get people where they didn't expect you to be coming in. I learned how to make people think you were just coming to talk about something else. I learned a lot."

But what Roy really wanted was a driver. Marvin had just turned 16 and although he knew the rudiments of driving, as he had shown during his under-aged joyride, he did not yet have his licence. Roy sent him to get it.

Marvin arrived at the province's licencing bureau in Roy's beautiful, brand-new, boat-sized Cadillac. Black. The perfect gangster's car. Marvin waited beside the car for one of the driving examiners, whom he watched scurry from one learner to the next

"Where'd you get a car like this?" the examiner said as he approached Marvin, running his eyes up and down the black beauty.

"I come from a very wealthy family. My brother is Roy Pasquale," Marvin said, by now understanding the combined force of a bribe and a threat.

"Pasquale Bros. Food?" the examiner asked, mentioning a well-known downtown food company.

"Yeah," Marvin said, knowing it was a lie. Roy had nothing to do with the company nor was he part of that family, but Marvin saw his opening. "After this is over," Marvin quickly added, "contact me and if you need anything I'll either give it to you for nothing or at cost."

"Hey, OK," the examiner said as they set out through the downtown streets. In those days, there wasn't a written portion to the exam. Instead, the in-car examiner would ask a driver questions to be answered verbally. As they drove, the examiner asked his first question. Marvin got it wrong. The examiner told him what the correct answer was. Then he asked the same question again. This time Marvin got it right. Five times he asked a question. Five times Marvin got it wrong. And five times the examiner gave him the correct answer and asked him a second time.

Then Marvin hit a parked car on the side of a crowded side street. The examiner got out for a second, looked and climbed back in.

"Ah, you didn't do much damage, let's get moving." Arriving back at the testing office, the examiner handed Marvin his licence.

Roy was so happy to have a driver he didn't seem to notice the dents.

* * *

Roy Pasquale hosted high-stakes poker games at his house long before the game became a mainstream pastime. Customers had to pay to play, buying a seat at the table from Roy, who also took a percentage off every pot. He also sold the players booze as they played. Roy always ran the games but never played. Roy kept Marvin scurrying about, waiting on the players, because keeping them happy meant keeping them at the table losing their money. One night, the game was going smoothly until Bertie Mignaccio, four years Roy's senior, ordered a glass of Scotch. Roy was a big rye drinker and suddenly realized his faux pas: he had no Scotch on hand—but he knew where to get it. He called Marvin over.

"Go to Mrs. Volpe's and buy a bottle of Scotch. And while you're at it, stop off and get more cigars," he told his protege, handing him a $100 bill and adding one last instruction: "Bring me back the change."

In 1950, a hundred dollars was a lot of money, especially to a poor kid like Marvin. He stuffed the bill in his pocket, hopped into Roy's Cadillac and headed out. On his way to Mrs. Volpe's he drove past a friend from boxing, Paulie Bagnato.

"Hey Marv, where you going?"

"I'm going to buy a few things for Roy, come with me."

They drove on and spotted another friend, Willie Barboie, who Marvin boxed against, and he joined them, too. Then a fourth boy, another boxer, named Sonny Forbes, climbed into the car. They all trained at the same gym. Someone then shouted out an idea.

"Hey, why don't we go over to Niagara Falls, New York. We can get into this strip club there called the Glass Bar. The reason they call it the Glass Bar is they have a big glass bar and the broads dance right on it."

"Yeah," said Marvin excitedly, forgetting what he was supposed to be doing for Roy. "I got a hundred dollars and a full tank of gas. Let's go."

He drove southwest and across the border into New York. Although underage, Marvin was buying beers for himself and the boys as they enjoyed the show, draining the club of their Canadian beer. Then Marvin saw an old friend of Roy's. Marvin thought Roy would get a kick out of the news so he wandered to a pay phone to call him.

"Roy, you'll never guess who I just saw here at the bar," Marvin said jauntily.

"Marv, where the fuck are you?"

"I'm here in Niagara Falls, at the Glass Bar."

Roy exploded with anger, spewing threats and profanity. Marvin suddenly remembered the poker game, the Scotch and Roy's $100 bill that was now almost gone. He hung up the phone, rounded up his friends and hustled home, fretting about what Roy would do to him. After dropping off his friends, he drove toward Roy's house, turning the headlights off when he came to Roy's block so his foster brother wouldn't see him arrive. He left the car and ran off to his grandparents' house. The next day he called Roy.

Roy again started screaming. Marvin hung up. Same thing the second day and third. By the fourth day, Roy had finally mellowed.

"All right, come over, come back," Roy said. "Let's forget it."

Roy was incapable of hiding his emotions. Marvin was sure Roy had calmed down. He returned to face him.

"Where's the hundred?" Roy asked.

"It's gone."

"OK, you can work it off."

Roy opened a page in his book for Marvin, noting the $100 debt, and started calculating the juice, the exorbitant interest rates loan sharks charge.

When not scurrying about for Roy, Marvin spent his time boxing, working out in a local gym, and finally making the move from the amateur ranks to the pros in order to earn money to start paying off his debt to Roy. At Roy's usurious rates, it would take him a while.

CHAPTER 7

NEW YORK, 1952

Stumbling through the doors at the top of a long set of stairs into Stillman's Gym, New York's famously dodgy boxing club at Eighth Avenue and West 54th Street, Marvin was hit by an oppressive odour but a comforting sound. Under the vaulted ceiling of the barn-sized gymnasium, he surveyed Midtown Manhattan's legendary palace of punishment.

Past a balcony on the second floor, boxers of every ability dripped sweat as they pounded away on the heavy Everlast punching bags, each hung by four chains, or skipped rope in rapid, tiny jumps. Downstairs, two raised, regulation-size boxing rings dominated the room, surrounded by boxers doing push-ups or shadowboxing, shuffling their feet and pumping their fists before stepping inside the ropes, hands tightly taped and gloves laced firm. Rows of wooden chairs were at ringside, sometimes filled hundreds strong with the exotic creatures attracted to the compelling blood sport: writers, retired boxers, wannabe boxers, gangsters, bookies, cops, fans, gawkers, celebrities. When the action in the ring got dull, someone started a poker game. The notoriously crusty owner, Lou Stillman, belittled and berated everyone in the joint, no matter how famous they were, and walked around with a gun in his belt. Despite having no particular talent himself for boxing,

Lou was lord of these rings and ejected people who rubbed him the wrong way, issuing lifetime bans for trifling incidents. He refused to clean the place. Given the nasty habit by regulars of spitting on the floor, it was an unpleasant experience for many first-time visitors. The smoke, sweat and filth gave off a stench that clung to everyone. The sound was a muffled hubbub of low grunts, high-pitched squeaks from shuffling shoes, thuds from bags and bodies being pounded and the swishing of jump ropes, all of it cut at regular intervals by the loud, sharp ding of the ringside bell.

Marvin loved it.

* * *

Marvin's passion for boxing never waned after reform school. Religiously, he followed the professional matches and title bouts. He also kept his own gloves in the ring. It was a passion shared by Roy and Roy's younger brother, Rudy. Marvin knew Rudy well from his time in the Pasquale home as a foster child.

This was a time when every working-class neighbourhood had at least one boxing gym and most boys dreamed of climbing into the ring for a title bout at Madison Square Garden. The big fighters were household names and national celebrities.

"Going to the boxing gym was my playground, my group home, my refuge. I was always accepted at the boxing clubs," Marvin says.

At Roy's urging, both Marvin and Rudy boxed professionally. Roy, of course, was their manager.

Marvin started his professional career, the first of 77 middleweight fights over the next 22 years, with a win in 1950 at Toronto's Palace Pier, a big dance hall on Lake Shore Boulevard West where condo towers of the same name stand today. It was a battle between two boxers taking their first stab in the professional fight game: Marvin "Baby Face Nelson" Elkind and Joe Sitko. Marvin won with a knockout. He was thrilled with that win for about 40 years until, by chance, he bumped into Sitko. Marvin asked how he was doing, and Sitko said that when he was knocked out in his first fight he realized boxing wasn't for him, so he quit and got a job with the railway. He had just retired with a nice pension and was living comfortably in a pleasant part of Toronto. "Damn," Marvin told him, jealously, "why didn't you knock me out?"

Out from under Mama Pasquale's authority, Marvin reclaimed his Jewish identity. For his boxing appearances, he had a white Star of David embroidered on the back of his royal blue robe. People were confused. Was he Jewish? Was he Italian? Was he Marvin? Was he Mario? No one was sure.

"My record when I boxed was 50-25-2. Fifty wins, twenty-five losses and two draws. It's not so good," Marvin says.

Rudy Pasquale showed more promise, fighting under the name Rudy Pascal. In Toronto he tore through competitors, even winning a Canadian championship title, although that match was rigged. It was part of Roy's sick plan to squeeze maximum profit out of his brother's body. Securing the controversial title by buying off the more experienced opponent, Roy then took Rudy to New York, where the prizes were bigger and fame more quickly acquired. Marvin moved to New York with them, arriving in March 1952.

* * *

In New York, Roy tried to replicate the success he had had in Toronto, buying a home, turning it into a boarding house and packing it with fledgling boxers, including Rudy and Marvin.

Roy's place was convenient for them, near both Stillman's Gym and an even more famous institution, Madison Square Garden. Roy also tried to expand his criminal contacts, seeking out major players and trying to hook up with them.

Marvin headed to the dingy chaos of Stillman's Gym, where he met the boxing greats: Joe Louis, Rocky Marciano, Willie Pep, Sugar Ray Robinson, Jake LaMotta and others. He also met Stillman's niece, Irene, whom he started dating. Being Jewish and being nice to his niece gave Marvin an in with the proprietor and his general disdain for humanity. Stillman seemed to like Marvin and gave him a bottom-rung job. His main duty was to scrub down the canvas ring floor and the sides of the ring of all the blood, spit and sweat—just about the only areas Stillman kept clean. He would also be called in to spar with paying customers. Marvin wasn't paid much but, like his arrangement with Roy, neither did he have to pay for use of the gym for training or sparring.

Marvin landed 52 fights in New York, most of them in St. Nicholas Arena. Many of them went poorly. One match in the summer of 1953 saw him paired with a much tougher fighter. Ernie Durando was nicknamed "The Rock" because of the strength of his punches. Boxing fans joked that he packed bricks in his gloves. The New Jersey native had eight years and four inches over Marvin, but Marvin accepted the match because he was promised that Durando would not go all out on him. Unfortunately, somebody forgot to tell Durando that.

When Marvin finally stayed down, sprawled out in the centre of the ring, he was unwilling to move. The referee came over, and Marvin said he couldn't get up because he was ashamed—he felt warm liquid filling his trunks and thought he had soiled himself.

"That's blood, boy. Nothing to be ashamed of," the ref said.

He staggered out of the ring and was taken to New York's Mount Sinai Hospital. Doctors there were perplexed when they found rectal bleeding. Not only that, but there was scar tissue, and they asked Marvin if he had been injured there in the past. Marvin told them about the reform school guard and his perverted way with a baton.

"I had one side of my face, the right side, completely turned around. The eye swollen shut, everything. My nose was broken in three places, I could hardly breathe," Marvin recalls. "My mother flew to New York to see me in hospital. I had no idea she was coming, she just walked into the hospital room. I was in a room there with three other guys and she came in, looked around and said, 'I must be in the wrong room.' I couldn't really talk. I was slowly waving my hand back and forth at her from my hospital bed and one of the other patients says to her, 'Lady, I think that guy knows you.' She didn't even recognize me. My face was so distorted my mother didn't know who I was. That was a very bad time."

Roy asked him why he hadn't stayed down earlier. Marvin looked at him incredulously. Every time during that fight when Marvin had looked up, and each time Marvin had gone back into his corner between rounds, there was Roy screaming at him: "Marvin, you've got to keep going."

* * *

Rudy Pasquale wasn't doing any better. While he had been a promising young fighter in Toronto, he was in over his head in the rings of New York. Part of his problem—a big part—was his brother. Under caring and careful management, easing him in over a year of appropriately escalating fights to gain experience, Rudy might have been somebody. But Roy wasn't a caring or careful manager. All he considered was the size of the prize purse.

Roy announced the Canadian champ was taking on all comers. Fighters lined up for a crack at him. Every boxer likes to pound the snot out of a foreign champ. It allowed Roy to arrange big fights for Rudy in New York. While it was good for business it was disastrous for Rudy's health. Over and over he was mercilessly beaten. Rudy would be in hospital while Roy was counting the money and booking a rematch.

"I'll tell you this right now: with that family there was no such thing as brotherly love, motherly love, fatherly love, no fucking love at all—except the love of money. Roy ruined him."

* * *

While both Marvin's and Rudy's careers were tanking, Marvin held onto his job at Stillman's. One regular customer who loved to watch the fights but never put on the gloves himself was a Jewish man named Isador. He looked refined— by Stillman's standards—and had a bit of money, so Marvin made sure he was his friend. Marvin let him in for free to watch the big boxers spar.

"I used to always take good care of him. I liked him, and he would always throw me a few bucks—which was why I liked him," Marvin says.

Isador, Marvin learned, worked as a maître d' at the Copacabana, a nightclub on East 60th Street, near Central Park. It was famed for its mob ties and for hosting top performers of the day, including Frank Sinatra, Sammy Davis, Jr., Harry Belafonte, Dean Martin and Jerry Lewis. Most people just called it the Copa. Isador saw in Marvin the qualities of a good busboy—servile, not afraid to hustle, unfailingly polite. One day he pulled Marvin aside.

"You know, I can get you a job as a busboy at the Copa—evening and weekend work," he said. "The salary isn't big but the tips are good."

"I'd like that, thanks," said Marvin.

That's how 18-year-old Marvin found himself working at the most glamorous nightclub in America.

* * *

Wearing a crisp white button-up shirt with a small black bow-tie around his 17-inch neck, and black pants loosely covered by a large white apron, Marvin hustled around the linen-topped tables and oversized fake coconut palms of the Copa.

He was inexperienced with the club scene, having squandered most of his evenings and weekends in New York hanging around with other teenagers he met through boxing, sitting in delis and cafés, usually watching boxing live or on TV. But he was a natural for this job. He was already an expert at getting himself accepted and keeping people happy. He really liked the job, too, mainly because he didn't have to worry about spilling food or drinks or mixing up customer's orders. By the time he had to carry the dishes, they were empty. The waiters, who wore white gloves, had to be much more precise. He also found it easy to spot what had to be done to help people enjoy themselves. All he had to do was stay alert. And smile. His big apple cheeks were soon instantly recognized and appreciated by the regular customers. He loved mixing, however peripherally, with celebrities. He also learned who the biggest tippers were and gave them more than their fair share of attention.

"You didn't have to be a genius for this job. You just had to kiss everybody's ass, and I was very good at that," he says. "A lot of it had to do with a bit of a weakness in character—I found it easy to kiss their ass."

To work at the Copa, employees had to be members of the International Brotherhood of Teamsters, the powerful labour union, and Marvin joined without a thought. He always liked joining things.

* * *

There was one particular group of regulars at the Copa that the waiters and other busboys tried to avoid. A helpful colleague pointed them out to Marvin, the new kid, as a warning. Marvin watched the boisterous group for a few minutes and knew they would be his favourites.

There often and usually sitting together were: Anthony "Fat Tony" Salerno, a budding mobster of significance who would later become the acting boss of the Genovese Mafia Family and an underground financier of unsanctioned bare-knuckle boxing matches; Frankie Carbo, a Lucchese Mafia Family soldier and notoriously shady boxing promoter; Frank "Blinky" Palermo, a mobbed-up boxing manager who had a piece of some of the biggest names in the game, including Sonny Liston, and who organized some outrageously rigged matches; and Anthony "Tony Pro" Provenzano, a captain in the Genovese Family and a leading member of the Teamsters union in nearby New Jersey.

Marvin knew Blinky and Carbo a little from boxing. They were regulars at St. Nicholas Arena, Madison Square Garden and Stillman's.

Other busboys hated to go near their table because the men were belligerent and sarcastic. They yelled and belittled, but they tipped well, so it was Marvin's kind of table. Whenever they strolled into the Copa, Marvin rushed over. Even if they didn't sit in his section, he would make sure their table was clean and water glasses brimming. He knew they would insult and intimidate him, but it wouldn't hurt him. After all that he had been through, Marvin could care less about a wisecrack. He even found many of the jibes hilarious, especially Tony Pro's, and shamelessly stole their one-liners.

Most high rollers at the Copa would buy a bottle of liquor for everyone at the table to share rather than ordering individual drinks. Sometimes Marvin would swipe a bottle of Scotch that had been brought out from behind the bar, meant for another table, if it was left unattended for even a moment. He would stuff it under his apron and bring it over, free, for the gangsters. They loved that. To these guys, the only thing better than a good bottle of Scotch was a stolen bottle of Scotch, even though they paid out in tips to Marvin what it would have cost to buy it. It was the way they worked and Marvin knew it.

After a few months at the Copa, more than a few regulars joked that Marvin and Fat Tony looked like father and son. They both had fat, round faces, heavy cheeks and a wide neck. The biggest difference, besides their 23 years, was that Marvin always smiled. Marvin loved the comparison. Taking his cue from the remark, he started smoking cigars, just like Fat Tony did. He liked the image of his new affectation and became a heavy cigar smoker, chomping through five or six a day for many years to come. It got to the point where Marvin always had a cigar either stuck in his yap or held conspicuously in his hand, usually his left, to draw attention to the pinkie ring he started wearing, another nod to his adopted gangster chic. Even Roy approved.

"You've given yourself a nice trademark," Roy said to Marvin one day. He even sounded jealous.

But Marvin, just as he was getting the taste for cigars, was jerked out of the comfortable, hard-to-screw-up job he loved.

* * *

Marvin spotted Fat Tony and Tony Pro entering the Copa one Wednesday night in June 1952. The pair walked past the uniformed doormen and were greeted by beautiful hostesses. As the men were led to a table, Marvin was already hustling over to greet and smile, fill their water glasses and do his thing. Hours later, as Marvin moved past the table, Tony Pro called out to him.

"Hey, little Jew boy, get over here."

"Yes, sir?"

"Friday's your last day here. We already spoke to the owners."

Marvin was stung. He enjoyed the job and loved the money. He also thought he was doing a good job and couldn't figure out why he was being fired.

"What'd I do?" he asked in dismay.

"Nothing. As of Monday, you're Jimmy Hoffa's driver."

"I'm what?"

"You heard me, Jimmy Hoffa's driver. It's going to be good for you, too, because you'll get the same salary as a truck driver. You're already a Teamster, we're just moving you. You'll be making more money than you are here and you won't have to pick up people's dirty dishes."

"I don't wanna be Jimmy Hoffa's driver."

"Kid, nobody's asking you."

Marvin suddenly saw his simple, low-stress life in New

York crumbling. With a sick, sinking feeling, he tried to weasel out of it.

"Look, I'm a Canadian . . ."

"That's exactly the idea," Tony Pro said. "Hoffa's driver has been drafted and you being a Canadian, we don't have to worry about that. So I'm making you his new driver." Whoever had been behind the wheel before had been unlucky enough to have been picked in the Universal Military Training and Service Act, known as the draft, for the battlefields of the Korean War.

"I don't even know the city," Marvin protested.

"You don't have to know anything about the city because Hoffa is a creature of habit. We'll take you out on the weekend and teach you everything you have to know. Saturday morning, someone will pick you up. Be ready."

CHAPTER 8

"Good morning, Mr. Hoffa."

Marvin hopped out of the Cadillac Fleetwood Brougham the moment he saw Jimmy Hoffa emerging through the door of the arrivals area at LaGuardia Airport on a Monday morning in March, Marvin's first day as driver for the already controversial figure within the International Brotherhood of Teamsters. Marvin had been waiting for more than an hour, not because Hoffa was late but because out of fear Marvin had left ridiculously early. He recognized Hoffa from a photograph shown him by Tony Pro.

"You're off to a good start," Hoffa said as he climbed through the open door and into the back seat.

Marvin pulled out of the airport and started heading toward the Teamsters' New York office at the Loews Midtown Hotel. Thankfully, Marvin knew the place well as it was right across the street from Madison Square Garden; all the big boxing matches were held at the Garden and the out-of-town boxers and fans all stayed at Loews. Not far into the journey, Hoffa told Marvin to pull over and two men joined him in the back. They were large Teamsters, both Korean War veterans, acting as Hoffa's bodyguards. One of them, a grinning Irishman, was named Tommy Corrigan. In the rough-and-tumble of high-level union politics, many of those around Hoffa were hired for their ability to crack heads.

"There are rules and there are cardinal rules," Hoffa said, giving Marvin the drill. "If you break a rule, one of two things is going to happen. Either I'm going to yell at you or these boys here are going to beat you. If you break a cardinal rule . . ." He paused.

"Turn around," Hoffa snapped. Marvin twisted around in his seat to face Hoffa.

"If you break a cardinal rule, you will not be around to see the morning. You don't get a second chance. Now, the cardinal rules," he said, starting to count them off on his fingers as Marvin turned back to face the road, "are complete obedience, complete loyalty, whatever you hear in this car stays in this car. The rules: I don't want to hear that there was a snowstorm, rainstorm, earthquake, flood, whatever—no excuses—I never want you late."

* * *

Two days earlier, on the Saturday, Marvin had been picked up at Roy's boarding house by Tony Pro and Fat Tony. He nearly wasn't there to meet them. He had counted his money the night before and found he had enough for train fare to Toronto and had even phoned his mother and told her he was coming home. Roy also didn't want him taking the job; he didn't want to lose control over Marvin. But when Marvin told Roy who had set him up in the job, Roy backed off: "Can't argue with them," he said. So Marvin didn't.

Tony Pro and Fat Tony took Marvin to a menswear store named Little David's where they bought him two blazers, six pairs of slacks, a beige coat, a peaked cap, a dozen sportshirts and two pairs of shoes, one black, the other oxblood. No ties. Hoffa didn't like his staff wearing ties; it was bad for his blue-collar image. They even asked him if he needed underwear. He said he didn't. They then took him to a jewellery store called Anthony's where they fitted Marvin with a gold rope chain necklace. Afterwards, they had Marvin drive their car as they showed him the places Hoffa typically needed to get to. There weren't many. Later they moved Marvin into a room at Loews Midtown Hotel, where the Teamsters' organizing office was and where Hoffa stayed when in the city. Marvin's breakfasts were free at the hotel. It didn't seem such a bad deal.

Later, when he was hanging around in the hotel, a woman who worked there spotted his gold chain.

"Oh, I see you're one of Jimmy Hoffa's guys."

He asked how she could tell and she said all of Hoffa's guys had the same gold chain around their necks. Marvin hadn't noticed. The woman said it was a mark that they were Hoffa's slaves. "Slaves in chains," she mocked.

One day Marvin asked one of Hoffa's bodyguards about the necklaces. "Mind your own business," he replied.

Even with that negative connotation, Marvin still wears the necklace today, fingering it when he speaks of it; he cannot see it without a mirror because his chins block his view.

Despite the stress of the new job, Marvin, as always, coped well. He worked hard to fit in. He was never late and always, always, always called his boss "Mr. Hoffa." Hoffa spent the weekends at home with his family in Detroit. Marvin would pick him up at the airport most Mondays and take him back to the airport on Fridays. At 6 a.m. on weekdays, Marvin would drive the Cadillac to a garage a block from the hotel where it was washed and searched for hidden microphones. He would be waiting for Hoffa at the hotel by 7 a.m.

Hoffa, as Tony Pro had said, truly was a creature of habit. He ate most meals at Manny Wolf's 49th Street Chop House, a steakhouse in a historic wooden two-storey building on the Upper East Side. Manny Wolf's was the sort of place that makes vegetarians wither. Anything went at Manny Wolf's as long as there was no violence, not even an argument. If customers didn't give police a reason to come, they could do whatever they wanted.

Sometimes Marvin would sit at Hoffa's table with other Teamsters, including his bodyguards. Other times he would sit by himself at a small table by the kitchen door, where waiters and staff sometimes joined him. He was never asked to pay.

The job also meant his nights and weekends were wide open because Hoffa was something of a monk when it came to Manhattan nightlife, despite no end of places to tempt.

"Mr. Hoffa never drank. Never smoked. Never chased women. Never smiled. He was very serious. Tony Pro would be cracking jokes and everybody would be breaking up but Hoffa wouldn't even crack a smile," Marvin recalls. "I didn't see him smile the whole time I was with him."

"Marvin, take me home," Hoffa said at the end of most workdays, meaning take him back to the hotel. "By nine o'clock I will be in the tub, then to bed. Got a big day tomorrow. Have the car out front at seven tomorrow."

Marvin soon learned there were a few rules not laid out by the boss on his first morning. Soon after he started, Marvin was driving Hoffa, Tony Pro and another Teamster. The men were talking away in the back when suddenly Hoffa raised his voice to get Marvin's attention.

"Marvin, you know we're a brotherhood. We're all brothers here. Even though we're executives and you're a driver, if you feel you have something to add to the conversation when you're driving, just turn around and say it. Don't be scared, we're all brothers."

"Thank you, Mr. Hoffa. I will."

Less than a week later, Marvin was driving surprising cargo. In the car with Hoffa were Tony Pro, Fat Tony and Vito Genovese. Genovese was the underboss of the New York Mafia family that would soon bear his name, once he ousted his boss. Marvin knew who he was because Hoffa introduced him when he picked him up. As the men talked in the back, Marvin had a thought about what they were saying and, remembering Hoffa's encouragement, cocked his head a bit toward the back and cut in.

"You know, Mr. Hoffa, I've got some ideas on that," Marvin said.

"Who's asking for ideas? You're our driver, shut up and drive," Hoffa snapped. So much for the brotherhood.

In no time Marvin figured out exactly how to play it. Unless asked, he kept his comments to "Yes, Mr. Hoffa," or "No, Mr. Hoffa." When he was yelled at by Hoffa or one of Hoffa's cronies, whether from the union or from the mob— and sometimes it was both—Marvin acted as if he didn't hear it. Tony Pro, especially, liked to bully Marvin.

"Marvin, what are you playing at? What are you doing making the turn like that? Want a whack in the mouth?" Tony Pro yelled once when the car jerked a little.

"No, sir, I don't. Sorry, sir," Marvin replied, even though he was pretty sure that if it came to it, one-on-one, he could tear Tony Pro apart. He knew, though, that such a duel would never be one-on-one. Tony Pro had his own "brotherhood."

* * *

It was a period of growth and transformation for the Teamsters. When Marvin started driving for Hoffa, it was the year the union's long-time president, Daniel J. Tobin, who had held the reins for an incredible 45-year run, was ousted by Dave Beck. Beck, however, couldn't do it alone. Hoffa, who was then a youthful firebrand of a leader from Michigan, had been working obsessively to expand both Teamsters membership and his own influence. In a tense standoff between Beck and Tobin, Hoffa tilted the balance of power to the newcomer, pledging support from the three regional groups he controlled: Central, Southern and Eastern conferences. In return for his convention-floor rescue, Beck made Hoffa a national vice-president. At 39, Hoffa was the youngest to be made a VP. And with the new president so deeply in his debt, he was allowed to operate pretty much as he pleased, without supervision and with little restraint. He started spending most of his time away from his Detroit base. When Hoffa spoke, it was with the voice of almost 650,000 Teamsters, even though he was far from being the household name he would soon become. One of his early priorities, besides leading the charge toward centralized bargaining, was to thoroughly organize New York in his favour. To control New York meant working with the city's five Mafia families.

The Teamsters were gaining a reputation as the most corrupt union in America. Hoffa didn't help. He was already being questioned about the management of union health and welfare money in his Michigan base, which he had turned over to gangsters, and he seemed oblivious to the bad optics of consorting with known racketeers in New York.

As Marvin drove Hoffa and his union allies around the city, dozens of mobsters, dodgy businessmen and characters who were both would climb in and out of the back seat of the

Cadillac. Besides Fat Tony and Vito Genovese, Hoffa also greeted, while Marvin was at the wheel, Sam Giancana, who, within months, would be named boss of the Chicago Mafia Family, and Alberto Anastasia, an old longshoremen's union leader on New York's waterfront, who was boss of what is now the Gambino Mafia Family. Hoffa and Fat Tony didn't like Anastasia but recognized his power and position. They called Anastasia "a heat score"—meaning someone who draws too much police attention. Anastasia was in Hoffa's car at least six times, Marvin says, but Hoffa warned Marvin never to talk to him. Roy Pasquale did some muscle work for Anastasia, who had called Toronto first to check him out. Roy idolized Anastasia for his cold-blooded style, but Anastasia was on the wrong end of cold-blooded action in 1957. As he sat in a barber's chair at the Park Sheraton Hotel, he was shot dead.

Marvin's encounters with many of America's best-known and most powerful gangsters were, at the time, a source more of fear than of opportunity. Marvin was happy to exploit his Teamsters connections, but he remained an immature young man of modest ambition. He was more interested in women than power.

***

Marvin was waiting for his girlfriend, Irene, to finish work one summer afternoon so they could go to one of the resorts on Coney Island for a night of dancing. Marvin was wearing an International Brotherhood of Teamsters T-shirt as he lounged in his car, a two-door Ford, pale green with a yellow top. Marvin babied it as one of the few possessions he couldn't wear or fit in his pocket. As he waited, he spotted a beautiful woman. He climbed out and sauntered over.

"I'm a big shot with the Teamsters. I don't know what you do but I could probably do a lot for you. Let's go for a drink."

This was Marvin's idea of union corruption.

"How old are you?" she asked.

"I'm 18," he said.

"Leave me alone, little boy."

Marvin was undaunted, "Who you calling 'little boy'?" he shot back, patting the woman's rear.

She reached into her purse, pulled out a police badge and shoved it in his face. "You just assaulted a police officer." Marvin was aghast. In the early 1950s, he had never heard of female police officers in Canada, other than the matrons who issued parking tickets. In New York, he learned, the force was more progressive. He was let go, after a couple of her male colleagues slapped him around a bit to teach him a lesson.

"What do you say now, tough guy?" one of the male cops asked.

"I apologize."

While Marvin's desire for romance brought that run-in with police, his boss's insatiable desire for power brought others. By this time Hoffa was spending a lot of indiscreet face time with gangsters, while becoming an increasingly polarizing figure within the labour movement. The notoriety had a direct impact on Marvin. One morning, Marvin glanced in the rear-view mirror of the Cadillac to see the flashing lights of a New York City Police Department cruiser behind him. He pulled the car to the curb and rolled down his window.

"Morning, Officer, can I help you?"

"You were speeding."

"No, I wasn't. I am driving this thing like a baby carriage," Marvin said, gently patting the large steering wheel in front of him.

"Yes, of course, we must have made a mistake. And who is that in the back?" the officer said, craning to look in the back seat. "Is that Mr. Hoffa?"

"Yes, it is," Marvin said.

"Morning, Mr. Hoffa," the officer said.

Hoffa remained silent, as if he hadn't heard or seen a thing. He refused to even look up. The moment the cop turned toward his cruiser and Marvin was rolling the window back up, Hoffa spoke.

"Drive on."

From then on, traffic stops just like that became a regular part of Marvin's week. Hoffa told him never to drive a lick over the speed limit and never to give the cops any lip.

"Don't give them any reason to cause a problem," Hoffa said.

Marvin started to enjoy the adrenalin rush that came from driving someone like Hoffa with all the cloak-and-dagger meetings in the back of his car. He liked being on the inside and part of the action. He liked the feeling of belonging, even in Hoffa's violent, dangerous gangster-unionist milieu.

*   *   *

Despite Hoffa's gruffness and other failings, he showed concern for Marvin on personal matters. One Friday in late summer, when Marvin was driving Hoffa to the airport, the boss asked him about his plans for Rosh Hashanah, the approaching Jewish High Holiday.

"I hope you're going to be home for the Jewish holidays to celebrate with your family," Hoffa said.

"No, Mr. Hoffa, I won't be able to. I don't have money or holiday time left," Marvin answered. Hoffa was angry.

"You're a single man. You get paid like a trucker. What do you do with your money?" he bellowed. Marvin started to explain his lifestyle, the fact that he had to buy a car and the drinking and how he wasn't good with money. Hoffa cut him off.

"I will be very disappointed if you're not back in Canada for the Jewish holiday with your family."

After dropping Hoffa off and returning the car to the Teamsters office, Marvin was told to tell the secretary when the Jewish holidays were so she could arrange an additional week of vacation and airfare for him to return to Toronto. Hoffa had made a call from the airport. Hoffa was a big supporter of Israel and spent eight days visiting in 1956, laying the cornerstone of the James R. Hoffa Children's Home of Jerusalem, a charitable shelter for impoverished kids built with money raised by Hoffa and his wife. It was a softer, generous side that few saw.

"He was a very intimidating man," Marvin recalls. "And he did it on purpose sometimes. But I respected Mr. Hoffa, I really did. That's a fact. I also feared him, that's also a fact. I feared him because of things I heard in the car, conversations he had about people he was upset with and then I would see what happened to them. So I also feared him. When you're doing the driving for someone, you can learn a lot because you're always around but nobody thinks about you being there. It was not a job for the faint of heart. He scared the shit out of me but he didn't harm me; in fact, he only did me good."

* * *

Just as Marvin's New York life was getting more exciting—with its harrowing boxing matches, the bizarre job driving

Hoffa, meeting gangsters, and a budding romance with Irene—it was winding up for Roy and Rudy. It wasn't easy cracking into New York's crowded underworld when you had no history there. Roy had tried to exploit his link with Marvin to meet up with Hoffa, but Hoffa had dismissed him, saying Roy must be a lightweight if he needed to go through his driver to meet him. And Roy had drained whatever value he could out of Rudy. They decided to return to Toronto. Roy expected Marvin to come with them. Marvin would have gone, but when he mentioned to Hoffa that his brothers were moving back—before Marvin could even get to the part about him joining them—Hoffa interrupted.

"You're doing a good job as my driver, Marvin. I'm not interested in looking for another one." He said it so firmly that Marvin didn't feel he had an option. And once again, Roy couldn't argue.

CHAPTER 9

MIAMI, 1954

A 20-year-old Marvin was wrapped in the soothing swelter of the vibrant city of Miami. Continuously warmed by the Gulf Stream, it had such a growing Latino vibe he felt as if he were back at the Copacabana, but this time the palm trees were real. Marvin had little time for sightseeing, though. He was here to fight in a match that promised one of his bigger payouts. Jimmy Hoffa had given him time off to travel to Florida for it. It was one of the fringe benefits of driving for him. Hoffa made allowances for Marvin's boxing career partly because he was a fan of the sport but also because he liked having a guy with a good left hook near him. But as Marvin left for South Florida, Hoffa gave him one last instruction.

"You might get a visit down there by someone. He's important to me, and if you do, I'd like you to co-operate. He might not come, in which case just forget it. But if he does, listen to him very carefully," Hoffa said.

Marvin had no idea what the boss was talking about and just hoped no visitors came to complicate his life.

At the Fontainebleau Hotel, which had just opened, drawing both rave reviews as the most luxurious hotel on Miami Beach and police suspicions that it was run by the mob, Marvin changed into his boxing trunks and slipped on his blue robe with the white Star of David on the back. Among the many attractions at the sprawling oceanfront property were fight nights. Marvin sat on a table set up in a noisy dressing room, a side room to the hall where the regulation ring was built. The tables were in greatest demand after matches, when beaten boxers needed to lie down. Boxers like Marvin didn't get a private changing room; those were for title holders and contenders. And so everyone else crowded onto the benches and tables in two communal rooms, one each for fighters on opposing sides of the fight card, since boxers don't dress in the same room as their opponents. Marvin was here with his trainer, Joey Bagnato. Joey was one of 24 Bagnato children, only 12 of whom had survived, seven of them boys, most of them involved in boxing. One brother, Vince, was the best-known fight promoter in Canadian boxing; another, Paulie, was one of the youngsters who had gone with Marvin to the Glass Bar in Niagara Falls years before. Joey Bagnato was a former Canadian lightweight champ who had retired from the ring but stayed in the game as a trainer. Joey was helping Marvin tape his hands before the fight when two large men walked in and each flashed open his suit jacket to reveal a gun tucked into his waistband. The room went silent.

"I want everyone out of here except the little Jew boy and his trainer," one of them said, motioning to Marvin and Joey. Even a roomful of boxers don't argue with a couple of heavies packing heat.

Once Marvin and Joey were alone with the thugs, another man casually walked in, looking around. He was short, dapper, smoking a cigar. He spoke to Marvin in Yiddish: "Young boy, have no fear." He seemed to want Marvin to know that he was Jewish as well. Then he switched to English.

"Do you know who I am?" he asked.

"I think you're Mr. Lansky," Marvin said, speaking of Meyer Lansky, the famed Jewish-American mobster who had helped Lucky Luciano put the "organized" into "organized crime."

"Did you know I was coming to see you?"

"I knew someone might be coming, didn't know who. I was told that someone important might come see me."

"Do you still think someone important came?"

Marvin answered honestly, "Yes, I do."

"Do you know where you are?"

"Yeah, Miami."

"Who do you think owns this city?"

"I'm guessing you."

"Do you know who you're fighting tonight?"

"Yeah, this guy Rocky."

"Do you know who owns Rocky?"

"I'm guessing you."

"What do you think of him?"

"Well," Marvin said, looking up at Lansky and talking tough, "he's a feather puncher. I'm pretty sure he can't knock me out, but he's fast. If I can get in close to him, I might be able to knock him out."

Lansky listened and nodded for a moment.

"It would be very meaningful to me if Rocky might be able to knock you out," he said, looking into Marvin's eyes.

Marvin was silent for a moment, thinking.

"How much are you getting paid for this fight?" Lansky asked.

Marvin said his share was $500. Lansky pulled out a large roll of cash, counted out bills, folded them and tucked the wad into the pocket of Marvin's robe.

"There's an extra five hundred dollars. When you get back

to New York, buy your mother something nice and send it to her. If you don't go down, you might not see her again," Lansky said. "Now, what do you think?"

Marvin felt the money weighing down his robe—few things grabbed his attention more—and looked at the bulge, resisting the urge to count it. He then looked back at Lansky.

"Do you have a particular round in mind?"

Lansky smiled, turned and started to leave, calling back with a wave of his cigar: "Doesn't matter—as long as it's in the first three."

* * *

For the 20 minutes before his bout, Marvin and Joey Bagnato discussed how to do this. They knew Rocky wasn't the hardest puncher, and Marvin, while not a title contender, was built like a tank. He was squat and muscular, weighing 160 pounds with a 17-inch neck. It could be tough to go down without getting hurt or unmasked as taking a dive. Lansky probably wouldn't like that.

Joey told Marvin to tumble in close to him to take the hit, so his opponent wouldn't get too much swing on it. If he tucked in close and took a couple of blows, he could fall down and make it look legit. The two of them practised it a little in the dressing room.

At the sound of the bell, Marvin and Rocky danced out into the middle of the ring, jabbing and swinging at each other. Then Marvin went in close to take a hit and get it over with. But Rocky didn't throw the punch. The bell rang, ending the first round.

In Marvin's corner, Joey gave him water, a towel and advice: get back in there and take the punch. At the start of the second round, Marvin hopped over to Rocky again and after a little sparring fell in close, bracing himself and exposing his head. Rocky still didn't throw the shot and the bell sounded the end of the second round.

Back in his corner, Joey had only one thing to say, "Marv, if you don't go down this round, don't look for me to be in your corner when you get here. I'll already be gone."

In the third round, Marvin grew desperate, repeatedly sticking his head out for Rocky to land a blow hard enough for a convincing performance. With little time to spare, as the third round ticked down, Marvin finally felt a brush from Rocky's glove glancing his cheek. Marvin couldn't wait for a second chance. He dropped. As the referee hovered above him, counting, Marvin pretended to struggle. At the count of seven he dramatically tried to get to his feet before collapsing back down and accepting the 10 count, giving Rocky—and Lansky—a third-round knockout.

Afterwards, as Marvin got dressed, Lansky appeared once more. This time, he was grinning.

"When you're done being a driver and you're too old to box, you can go into acting."

* * *

Meyer Lansky was another in Jimmy Hoffa's constellation of mob friends who skipped through Marvin's life while he drove for the Teamsters boss. Within Hoffa's circle, it was becoming increasingly difficult to separate the labour activists from the racketeers and union business from mob business. To Hoffa, it seemed to be one and the same in a dangerous balancing act that grew more difficult once the government decided to bring him down.

Lansky, while involved in building casinos in Cuba and Las Vegas, still looked for every avenue to make some dough, even going so far as to personally rig boxing matches. When boxing was as big as it was back in 1954, profits from making the right bet were enormous. And, for someone in Lanksy's position, as the proprietor of a nationwide syndicate of bookmakers, making sure the wrong boxer fell ensured that large sums were cheated out of customers. Such small payouts to guys like Marvin were—even for a man of Lansky's notoriety—big business.

* * *

In 1956, Marvin found he was no longer of use to Hoffa. Hoffa's work in New York was largely done. He was just months away from securing the presidency of the Teamsters from Beck at the national convention in Miami Beach. Most of his time now was spent in Washington, D.C., where the Teamsters had moved its headquarters. Beck was in trouble legally as well as politically within the union. He had been forced to testify before a United States Senate committee investigating labour racketeering and, under aggressive questioning by Robert F. Kennedy, had taken the Fifth Amendment—invoking his right not to answer for fear of self-incrimination—an outrageous 117 times. Beck was indicted for embezzlement and labour racketeering and declined to challenge Hoffa for the union's top spot. Besides, with the Korean War armistice, the threat of losing another American driver to the draft diminished considerably.

Marvin wasn't complaining. He was anxious to get back to Canada. He had made several trips to Toronto while away in New York, celebrating many of the Jewish holidays with his mother, stepfather and brother and sister, even attending Camp Shalom on Lake Muskoka, a "traditional Zionist camp" where he frolicked with other young Jewish men and women, including future Canadian senator Jerry Grafstein. Marvin had become something of a social acrobat, crossing from the rough world of boxing and mobsters to the genteel world of Toronto's Jewish establishment. But, as he had done all of his life, he twisted himself to fit acceptably into both but never perfectly into either.

With Roy and Rudy back in Canada, Marvin put in to the Teamsters for a transfer. There wasn't a driving job available in Toronto, but he was offered a post in Montreal. It wasn't home but at least he would be back in Canada. The transient world of New York boxing and his solitary job with Hoffa left him without many friends and his relationship with Stillman's niece remained casual. Marvin was lonely. That was something he never liked. Marvin's new job was with another shady guy involved in both unions and the mob; his new boss was becoming as notorious in Canada as Hoffa was in America.

***

In the years to come, Marvin would think about his old boss many times. It was impossible not to, once Jimmy Hoffa disappeared, sparking one of the most enduring modern mysteries. As Hoffa became a pop-culture emblem, in death even more than in life, Marvin would marvel at the time he had spent with him in the car.

Marvin is certain he knows what happened to his old boss and where his body was hidden.

After Marvin left him, Hoffa's life continued on a trajectory of confrontation. He became the general president of the

International Brotherhood of Teamsters in 1958. In 1964, he was convicted of jury tampering, attempted bribery and fraud, and sentenced to 13 years in prison, eventually stepping down as president. In 1975, Hoffa was fighting to regain control of the union. The executive tried to dissuade him by offering him a lifetime pension, but, as Marvin says, Hoffa craved power and influence more than money.

On July 30, 1975, Hoffa was back in his Detroit base when he left for a meeting with Anthony Giacalone, a Mafia boss from Detroit known as "Tony Jack," one of the union's main contacts with the Mafia, and Anthony Provenzano, known as "Tony Pro," the Mafia captain and Teamsters leader who had made Marvin Hoffa's driver two decades before. Hoffa has not been seen since. He was declared legally dead but his body was never found.

"It was his own people who did it. Mr. Hoffa gave them no choice. He was very close with Tony Jack and everybody knows that he provided the trigger man. Tony Jack told me. He didn't say 'Marvin, I provided the trigger man.' But he told me in another way," Marvin says.

Ten years after Hoffa disappeared, Marvin was at a four-day Teamsters conference at the newly opened Omni International Hotel in Detroit. He was there as an errand boy and security man. Tony Jack was among the delegates.

"Let's take a break, let's get out of here," Tony Jack said during the meeting. An entourage of intimates got up with him. The hotel was across the road from the Renaissance Center, but the two were connected by a long glassed-in walkway that stretched across the 10 lanes and wide centre median of East Jefferson Avenue. Marvin walked beside Tony Jack because he was carrying his orange juice and standing ready to light his cigar.

When Tony Jack passed the middle point of the bridge, facing the Renaissance Center, he nodded toward the huge tower's foundation.

"Say good morning to Jimmy Hoffa, boys," he said.

Marvin is sure Hoffa's body rests in the concrete footing of the Renaissance Center, which was under construction at the time of his disappearance. The story Marvin heard from Detroit mobsters is that after Hoffa was snatched and killed, practically every union carpenter in and around the city was called in to rush the construction of wooden forms needed for pouring concrete at the Renaissance project. As soon as the forms were in place, the concrete flowed, tons of it; ahead of schedule. Never before or since has he heard of his union brothers working so diligently to get a project done.

"There was a mad rush to get the concrete poured," Marvin says. At some point, he says, someone slipped Hoffa's body into the wet cement, where it was encased beneath what is now Detroit's most visible landmark.

CHAPTER 10

MONTREAL, 1956

When Marvin was told who he would be driving for in Montreal, he called his foster brother Roy. Roy knew a little something about everyone.

"Hey, Roy, they're sending me back to Canada, but not to Toronto. Montreal. I'll be driving for this guy Vic Cotroni," Marvin said.

"There are three Cotroni brothers, Vic, Pep and Frank," Roy said. "And you're driving for the best one."

Montreal was emerging as a glistening jewel in the underworld. Gangsters there were early leaders in organized gambling, loansharking, prostitution, bank robberies and drugs. Brothels and nightclubs were the focus of a lively nightlife tolerated by authorities. Graft was a way of life. The Cotroni family arrived there from Italy in 1924 and Vic started to specialize in vice crimes. Soon he was a force within the city, which itself was becoming one of the most important in world crime. From the early days of the French Connection, the famed drug-trafficking network, European heroin was flooding New York and other major cities through the port of Montreal. The growing importance of Montreal attracted the Mafia, and the city soon fell under the influence of New York's Bonanno Family.

Cotroni co-operated with the Bonannos and reaped his reward, running the city as a branch office of the New York boss. It gave Cotroni the strength to suppress local rivals.

By the time Marvin arrived in Montreal, 60 per cent of America's heroin was passing through the city. It made its way south, across the border to New York City, or west to Windsor and smuggled across the river into Detroit. Teamsters truckers were involved in the cross-border flow, and Jimmy Hoffa was accused of giving some of the smugglers cover jobs with the Teamsters as a way to explain their travels. That might account for the contact between Hoffa's people in Detroit and Cotroni's people in Montreal. Marvin didn't see any significant drug trafficking by the Cotroni brothers or the Teamsters when he was in Montreal, but he did, on a regular basis, see reams of stolen fur coats being secretly loaded onto Teamsters trucks, heading for a major fur retailer in Toronto.

* * *

For three decades, Montreal was as much Vic Cotroni's as it was the mayor's. With one brother, Pep, heading the drug-trafficking wing of the family, and another, Frank, acting as the strong-armed street boss, Vic Cotroni was insulated from the overt violence and seedy drug dealing. He was becoming untouchable by authorities and even managed to keep up a facade of respectability.

"Vic and Frank Cotroni were involved pretty much in the same things, but Vic handled them with class," Marvin says.

Like any successful mobster of the day, Vic Cotroni was involved in labour racketeering. Mob muscle helped to pressure workers into joining the unions that Cotroni had deals with. Mob muscle was used to bolster picket lines during strikes that Cotroni supported and to protect scab workers during strikes that Cotroni did not.

Technically, Marvin was still working with the Teamsters union when he started work as a driver for Vic Cotroni. On paper, he was a truck driver and earned a truck driver's salary. But the only haulage Marvin did was moving Cotroni and his friends. Just as it had been with Hoffa, Cotroni was on the rise when Marvin joined him, a powerful figure who had not yet become a household name. In Montreal, Marvin wasn't handed the keys to a Cadillac, as he expected, but to a Buick. Although Hoffa had tried to maintain the veneer of working-class roots by insisting Marvin not wear a tie, Cotroni did Hoffa one better.

"Vic was a modest guy. I didn't drive him in a Caddy. It was in something called a Buick Roadmaster. It was as big as a Caddy but much less flashy. Vic always liked the idea that he could say to people that he drives in a Buick. Driving it didn't have the same feeling as a Caddy, though," Marvin says.

The idea of driving for a mob boss didn't frighten him.

"Nervous? Not since I got over the nervousness of driving Mr. Hoffa. Once I conquered that, I was fine for anything else. If you treated Vic with respect, he treated you with respect right back. It wasn't hard to treat Vic with respect.

"He was very soft-spoken. Vic, when he talked, you used to have to strain your ear and lean in close to hear him. I didn't want to insult him by asking him to repeat himself. His brother Frank talked loudly. When he started up, you'd move away from him."

* * *

Vic Cotroni liked having Jimmy Hoffa's former driver work for him. It gave him confidence in Marvin's abilities—he was by then an experienced driver—and his trustworthiness. Cotroni also got a chuckle out of the connection. As Hoffa became more notorious, Cotroni would often introduce Marvin to the men climbing into his car or in restaurants or at parties where Marvin drove him.

"This is my driver, Marvin, he just spent four years driving for Jimmy Hoffa," Cotroni would say.

Marvin loved the association, too, and told war stories, always making sure he sounded like he knew far more than he did. It made people more respectful toward him. He craved respect.

Marvin would pick Cotroni up at the mobster's well-appointed home in Mount Royal, a pleasant suburb of Montreal not far from downtown, and drive him to an office on Décarie Boulevard. "They had a little lounge there and I would just hang around there and drive him anywhere he wanted in the day and drive him home in the evenings. His office was above a place called Champs Showbar," Marvin says. It was a strip club, music bar and restaurant controlled by the Cotroni organization and run by Jimmy Orlando. Orlando was famous from his days of playing NHL hockey with the Detroit Red Wings in the 1930s and '40s. On ice, he was the team's enforcer, brawling his way to two Stanley Cups and tagged as "the bad man on ice." During the Second World War, however, Orlando lost his taste for fighting and was arrested as a draft dodger. He fled to Canada but, unable to travel south of the border, his NHL career was over. Among the onstage talent at Champs was Orlando's mistress, the famed burlesque performer Lili St. Cyr, whose titillating shows, one of which involved her taking a bubble bath on stage, made her one of the best-known women in the city. There was titillation off the stage, too.

"They had strippers and waitresses who were also hookers. The girls were for rent and people did their arranging through the maître d', Buncy. They would make the arrangements and whatever it was going to be for the evening with the girl would go right on your bill, alongside the dinner and drinks. They would make their arrangements, either for any girl or they would pick a specific one. A lot of the regulars got the girls on credit, but they would be charged interest on it and the guys would find themselves owing to the Cotronis. For some guys that became a real problem. I spent a lot of time there at Champs. I would be there, and it was open for lunch and Vic's office was right upstairs, so whatever I ate or drank at Champs I didn't pay for."

Despite—or perhaps because of—his interest in burlesque clubs and prostitution, Cotroni made friends in high places. As Marvin drove Cotroni around, he was amazed to find out who the mob boss counted as his friends. Wealthy businessmen, police officers, politicians, journalists, civil servants and border agents were all on the Cotroni payroll. While Hoffa was a unionist who met constantly with gangsters, Cotroni was a gangster who met constantly with businessmen and unionists. In Marvin's world, everyone seemed to be something other than what they were supposed to be.

* * *

One of Cotroni's most important friends, says Marvin, was Hilaire Beauregard, the director of the Sûreté du Québec, the provincial police force, a position he held until 1960. Marvin once picked up Beauregard and a few other people at their homes and drove them to Cotroni's house for a dinner party. Other times, Marvin drove Cotroni and the police boss to the

Sabre Club, a private club in Montreal offering steam rooms, card games and massages. It was a gentlemen's club, and not, as many mob establishments were, a front for prostitution. Inside the discreet confines of the Sabre Club, Cotroni and Beauregard chatted quietly with each other, sometimes inviting others into their confidence. Other times, Cotroni and Beauregard would eat meals together at popular restaurants, seemingly unconcerned about being seen fraternizing with each other.

"Vic Cotroni was very close with Beauregard. They were good friends. Mr. Cotroni helped him with his family's snack-food business. He helped him get concession rights to sell their snack food at any place they wanted. They spent quite a few evenings at the Sabre Club, and whenever Vic went there I had a choice of just waiting in the lounge or to go in and use the facilities. I would use the facilities," Marvin says. "Frank Cotroni would be there as well. I got to know Frank, I had no choice. But it was clear that I was working for Vic. I didn't like Frank, so I didn't make too much of it. Frank was a big fight fan. That gave us something to talk about."

Beauregard also sometimes joined Cotroni in the car when Marvin drove them to the United States with another important friend, a businessman who owned a large clothing manufacturing company through which Cotroni would launder his money, Marvin says. The businessman also owned a large, luxurious yacht moored in Plattsburgh, 60 miles due south of Montreal in New York State. Marvin would drive money back and forth between the businessman and Cotroni. He would drive Cotroni to meetings with the businessman at exclusive restaurants, private golf course clubhouses and gentlemen's clubs around Montreal. And also to the businessman's yacht.

"The yacht was on the American side, and whenever they had meetings there, they told me a certain time they picked to have it because, when we went, at the American border crossing, I was always told which lane, which customs station, to go through and I used to go and pull up and open the window and the guy inside would just nod and I drove through. It was always the same guy and we were always just waved through immigration and customs. We were never stopped and never questioned. Coming back into Canada was also never a problem, either. We always had a nice dinner on the yacht. It was a beautiful yacht there."

Another man Marvin drove Cotroni to see several times was William Obront, a financial whiz. Like Meyer Lansky, Obront manipulated businesses and juggled accounts. The Montrealer controlled dozens of companies, including a slaughterhouse and meat company that was responsible for serving—as later investigation discovered—diseased horse-meat to visitors at Montreal's Expo 67, where he controlled the massive fair's only meat storage facility. Another customer for his meat was the Canadian Army.

"Willie owned an abattoir, that was his business, he was in the meat business. When we used to have to go see him, Vic would say 'Let's go see The Butcher.' He always called him The Butcher. He would meet with him for a couple of hours while I waited in the car. I sat and read the paper." Others Cotroni often met with included the owner of a successful limousine company and the owner of a major supermarket chain. "What they were doing, I don't know. Teamsters used to do a lot of driving for them."

Like Hoffa, Cotroni had a short list of favoured destinations. He ate many of his meals at Moishes steakhouse, an old revered steakhouse that served meals not unlike what Hoffa ate at Manny Wolf's. Cotroni also liked Chinese at Ruby Foos, at the time the largest restaurant in Canada and a landmark on Décarie Boulevard that attracted a bustling mix of tourists, hockey stars, prime ministers and Montreal regulars.

But it was not like driving for Hoffa. There was never interference from police as Marvin drove Cotroni around town.

"No comparison. Never. Ever. None. Not once. No police. There was no question that the police stayed away from Vic. I never once got stopped by a cop when I was driving him. I never once got asked any questions. In fact, he seemed well taken care of."

Marvin liked working for Cotroni but was always looking to get back to Toronto. He would soon get his chance.

CHAPTER 11

TORONTO, 1956

Marvin heard from Vic Cotroni that the Teamsters were coming to organize Canada, based in Toronto, and with that news saw his chance to move back home. He was even more hopeful when he heard who would be leading the drive. Thomas William Corrigan, known as Tommy, had been in the back seat of Jimmy Hoffa's car many times back in New York when Marvin was at the wheel. A boxer with wartime experience, Corrigan was one of Hoffa's strong-arm goons, although he harboured grander ambitions. Marvin had seen Corrigan carry a gun several times when he was watching over Hoffa.

Just five years older than Marvin, Corrigan seemed a generation beyond him, with his swagger, confidence and brashness. Corrigan was a product of Hell's Kitchen, a crowded Irish slum on the west side of midtown Manhattan that was the inspiration for *West Side Story*, the Broadway musical of love and gang violence. Corrigan grew up fast and hard, acquainted with using his fists and his foul mouth. After a stint in the U.S. Army in Korea, he returned to New York, where he divided his time between an undistinguished welterweight boxing career and working for Hoffa and the Teamsters as an enforcer before moving to Chicago. Corrigan was then given free rein to organize Canada for the Teamsters. At first making extended visits to Toronto, he later made the city his home, becoming a permanent Canadian resident, although he would never shed his Hell's Kitchen persona with its "dese guys" and "dem guys" vernacular.

When Marvin called Corrigan, he reminded him of their link to Hoffa and asked if he could find work for him in Toronto. Corrigan answered right away.

"Yeah, I have an opening for you."

Marvin saw it as a great opportunity. He had worked for Hoffa and hadn't screwed it up. He had moved with gangsters in Montreal and been the master of discretion. He had strong-arm experience from his time with Roy. He had proved his loyalty and toughness. Now he was coming home to help build a new union outpost. He figured Corrigan wanted him as one of his senior organizers. Now, Marvin thought, he really could mimic Fat Tony Salerno, not only with his cigars but as a union fat cat. He called his mother with the news.

Arriving back in Toronto, Marvin went straight to see Corrigan. Corrigan told him to rent an apartment nearby and if he had any trouble getting a lease to let him know and he would guarantee it with the landlord.

"That's great. What will my job be? What do you want me to do, Tommy?"

"What do you mean, what will you do?" Tommy said. "You're going to drive for me and do errands. What else would you be able to do?" Marvin's dream of being a union boss vapourized. He was stung by the slight but didn't argue. Neither would he forget it.

* * *

If Marvin thought he had escaped the coarse criminal life under his foster brother Roy for a proper job with an international union, he was mistaken. Not only was Marvin still a driver and errand boy, Corrigan kept Marvin ensnared in a criminal milieu. Corrigan would meet with success as a union organizer, becoming an international representative for the Teamsters; president of Teamsters Local 847; recruiting more than 10,000 members in Canada; and controlling the Canadian operations of two other obscure unions—the Textile Processors, Service Trades, Health Care, Professional and Technical Employees International Union and the International Union of Allied Novelty and Production Workers—but he wasn't a true labour activist.

Tommy Corrigan was an anomaly in labour circles. A fierce capitalist and staunch entrepreneur with right-wing views, he was far from the stereotype of the hard-left socialist firebrand fighting for workers' rights. He had all of Hoffa's bad traits—the scheming, conniving and swindling—without the good, Hoffa's commitment to workers' bargaining rights. For Corrigan, labour activism was an audacious con in which he wielded the power of the union not for the benefit of members but for himself. He was a gangster who had grabbed hold of the union as a tool for fraud, extortion, theft and other shady deals. The union was his commodity to sell and barter in cozy relationships with business owners and as a way to enrich himself through pension and health and welfare funds. For the workers, it was the worst of both worlds, a world in which their union boss was closer to management than to its members. It was a particularly effective con, one that created a perfect front for his activities, his income and his associates and gave him entree into Toronto's social circles as a "labour leader." He attended the most elite black-tie charity galas. He mixed with the leaders of civil society without shame. To those who knew Corrigan outside those social circles, however, he didn't hide his thuggery. It was widely said that Corrigan had married into the mob, and underlings speak of his family ties to one of the most powerful American Mafia bosses, although evidence of it remains elusive. As if to prove it, Corrigan spoke excellent Italian, for a poorly educated Irishman.

"The big difference between Jimmy Hoffa and Tommy Corrigan is that money was not that important to Mr. Hoffa. He loved the power—the power of running the union—and he wanted to say he made lives better for his people. Corrigan just wanted to be rich and didn't care who he screwed doing it," Marvin says. He then offers the perfect assessment of Corrigan: "He looked out for himself an awful lot."

* * *

Marvin was so used to surprises that it didn't seem the least bit odd to him that, although hired by a union head office, who signed his pay cheques, he was in fact put to work for a private waste-management company collecting unpaid bills, delivering envelopes of cash as kickback and driving company owners and managers about town as they were courted for their private garbage and scrap-metal collection and recycling business.

Corrigan was a silent partner in the company alongside two owners of contrasting temperament: Murray Wortsman, a tough-minded Jew, and Sam Salla, a mild Arab. Corrigan made sure that they got major clients. Companies liked keeping the Teamsters boss happy if it meant he kept his unions out of their business or content with substandard contracts. Corrigan secured the business of some of the largest corporations in the area, including an international fast-food chain and a household name in appliances and technology. That last contract was a huge moneymaker for them, as a senior company executive gave them the right to haul away all of its scrap metal and recyclables at a favourable rate. The stuff was worth a small fortune. In return, on a regular basis, Marvin drove to the company's head office and delivered an envelope of kickback cash.

Marvin's work grew more complicated when Corrigan realized his business partners were cheating him. One afternoon, Corrigan called Marvin and told him to pick him up right away. When Marvin arrived, Corrigan had him hurry to the recycling firm's office. Together they went in and grabbed the company's accounting books, pushing back all protesters. Their next stop was a downtown law office where a lawyer was waiting to look over the books. Marvin was told to hurry because it was almost closing time. When they got to the office building, two men had the only elevator on hold and were about to load it with furniture. Tommy told them he needed to get to the ninth floor right away, he would take the elevator and send it right back down for them.

The workers said no. Tommy handed Marvin the accounting books.

"Don't drop them," he told him as he turned toward the men and punched them to the marble floor, kicking them once, maybe twice, before getting into the elevator. Corrigan and Marvin caught the lawyer just in time. The examination proved Corrigan's suspicions. The lawyer told him his partners owed him about $250,000. When Corrigan confronted them, the mild-mannered Salla said they would pay, and the toughminded Wortsman said they would think about it. A week later, Salla was found dead. Marvin says he was poisoned. Wortsman was still uncooperative.

Wortsman belonged to the same synagogue as Marvin. After Salla's death, Corrigan told Marvin to find out when Wortsman was going to be there. There was a men's group dinner planned for the following Tuesday and Wortsman was to emcee it, Marvin told him. On that Tuesday night, while the businessman was in front of a crowd cracking jokes, Marvin was driving Corrigan and a friend named Stan, who was an auto mechanic, slowly through the parking lot of Beth Sholom synagogue on Eglinton Avenue, not far from where Marvin's mother and stepfather had moved.

"Stan knew everything about cars, including how to get in them. So we found Murray's car in the parking lot and, while everyone was inside, Stan unlocked the door of Murray's car and Tommy put a grenade on the passenger-side seat. Left it lying there, a live grenade. The next day Murray called and said he would pay," Marvin says.

Another time, Marvin drove Corrigan and an associate of his from New York to pick up a wealthy Toronto businessman. Marvin knew the businessman and greeted him with a smile. His reception from Corrigan in the back seat wasn't as warm. With Marvin stealing peeks through the rear-view mirror as he drove, Corrigan confronted the man over a perceived debt.

"You owe us ten grand," Corrigan said.

"Well, I don't have it," the businessman said.

Corrigan pulled a gun out of his coat, resting it casually across his lap, and said, "Tell me again that you haven't got it."

The next answer was different, "Have your driver take us to my house."

Marvin drove to the Bridle Path, the most affluent neighbourhood in Canada, filled with multimillion-dollar mansions on large manicured lots. Marvin went into the man's house with him as Corrigan and his colleague waited in the car. The businessman asked Marvin to wait outside a room. A few minutes later, he emerged with a large envelope filled with high-denomination bills. Marvin took it to the car and passed it to Corrigan, who counted it, before saying, "Let's go."

* * *

It was a pleasant vacation in the Caribbean and a vastly wealthy Canadian businessman had struck some amazing deals on high-end gold jewellery for himself and his family. Back in Toronto, he showed off the haul along with his tan. He spoke freely to his friends of having not declared it at the border, saving himself thousands in duty and taxes. Too freely.

A disgruntled employee took offence to his boss parading the expensive baubles and bragging about his duplicity. He turned his boss in, ratting him out to the border agency, which sent agents to his home to collect their share. The businessman was furious, not only at being made to pay duty, tax and fines, but at the betrayal. He moved in unsavoury circles, including with Corrigan, and let it be known he wanted to know who had turned him in and that he would pay for the information.

It was Marvin who uncovered the fink. One day, at his daily meeting with Corrigan at a coffee shop, he mentioned it.

"Let me pass the name on for you," Corrigan said. "I'll do better for you because I'm close to him." So Marvin told him the identity of the fink. A few days later, Corrigan handed Marvin a $500 reward.

"That's it? I thought he'd really pay out for that tip," Marvin said.

"He did. There's five hundred practically for nothing. It's a good take," Corrigan replied.

About two months later, Marvin walked into a restaurant

and saw the businessman. Marvin had met him two or three times before and saw this as an opportunity to ingratiate himself to him, to remind him of the favour he had done. Marvin greeted him at his table.

"Were you happy with the work I did for you with the jewellery?" Marvin asked.

"It was you? Tommy just said it was one of his boys," he said.

"Yeah, it was me."

"Well, it was great to take care of you for it, Marvin."

"Sure," Marvin said. He hesitated, then couldn't stop himself from adding, "I just thought you'd take care of me a little more."

"What, five thousand wasn't enough?"

"Five thousand? It was five hundred. Tommy gave me five hundred."

"Well, I gave Tommy five thousand to give to you."

When Marvin saw Corrigan the next day, he immediately brought it up.

"I bumped into our mutual friend," Marvin said.

"Yeah, he told me."

"Well, he gave you five grand to give to me."

"Kid, it's not my fault you're stupid." And that was that.

Marvin may have left Roy, but he hadn't travelled far. And although his union job wouldn't deliver him from a life on the shady side of the law, in Toronto he soon found one source of salvation.

CHAPTER 12

TORONTO, 1957

The engine roared into overdrive when suddenly there was no longer any road underneath to slow the car down. The wheels, now useless, spun noisily as the car shot up and out, flying 25 feet from the shoreline before splashing down into Toronto Harbour on Lake Ontario. The car began to sink as the driver wriggled free.

The splash caught the attention of a yard worker at the coal-fired waterfront power station at the western end of Unwin Avenue near Cherry Beach. He shouted and whistled to a crane operator who was closer to the water. The crane man, Ole Timgren, ran to a life-preserver on the dock and gave the ring a mighty toss toward the disappearing roof of the car. The rope snagged on its post, but it was just long enough to reach the car. As the injured driver clutched at the ring, his lungs burning, a boat that had been clearing dead fish from the shoreline—a byproduct of the coal plant—headed for him. The crew hauled the man aboard. Panting for breath, he told them no one else was in the car.

That the man tossing the life-preserver was the brother of Ray Timgren, a former Toronto Maple Leaf who had won two Stanley Cups with the team, made the rescue even more noteworthy for Toronto newspapers.

The next day, as police tried to figure out how to pull the car up from the murky bottom after the city's heaviest tow truck had failed to budge it, Marvin, who, three months earlier, had turned 22, was reading about the dramatic rescue in the newspaper. He recognized Ray Timgren's name, but what surprised him even more was the name of the driver. Samuel Geist was still in hospital, explaining how he thought his car had been in reverse when he slammed down the accelerator and was terrified when he shot forward into the harbour. Geist's name meant more to Marvin than the hockey player's.

* * *

On a blisteringly hot day in June, a few weeks before Sam Geist's watery plunge, Marvin had driven out to visit his mother, Beatrice, at the lavish new house she and Morris had moved into. On his way back, with the car windows wide open to catch the breeze, he cut through Cedarvale Park along a small driving path where he noticed two young women, carrying books and wearing school skirts. Always with an eye for the ladies, Marvin pulled up beside them.

"It's too hot to walk. Can I give you girls a lift?"

One girl, Hennie Geist, shook her head. Always a cautious, level-headed woman, she knew better than to climb into the back of a stranger's car, even if the stranger had a charming smile and apple cheeks. The other girl, however, recognized Marvin.

"I know you. You know my father," said Honey Persofsky.

"Yeah, I know him," Marvin said.

Marvin was no longer a stranger, so the two women climbed into the car and he drove them back to Vaughan Road Collegiate, with Marvin trying to lay as much of his good-natured charm as he could on Hennie and Honey, but

especially Hennie. Afterwards, Marvin could not stop thinking about the strikingly cute, diminutive young woman with
the round face, dark almond-shaped eyes and long lashes. Just
16 years old and standing five feet tall, here was a girl Marvin
could have on his arm and still tower over by five inches. Her
straight sensibility and firm but demure nature only added to
her allure for Marvin. Obsessed with Hennie, Marvin called
the Persofsky home and asked Honey for Hennie's phone
number. Nervously, he called Hennie and asked her to go to
the movies with him on Saturday night. Marvin was delighted
when she said yes.

He was crushed on Friday, however, when he called back
to confirm the time to pick her up. She was embarrassed.

"My father knows who you are and said I can't go out with
a gangster," she told him, already displaying the frankness she
maintains to this day.

Marvin called her again the next week and was told
the same thing. The following week as well. And the next.
Hennie's school year ended and she got a summer job downtown. Marvin would visit her on her lunch break without her
parents knowing. They chatted over sandwiches, but Hennie
would not date Marvin against her parents' wishes.

Then he read in the newspaper about Hennie's father's
crash. He stared at the newspaper, drawn first by the headline—"Drives off end of dock; lifebuoy, scow save man"—then
by the hockey player's name and, finally, unexpectedly, the
poor driver's last name. Marvin read the 200-word story a
second time, and a third. The injured driver had the same last
name as Hennie. He lived on the same street as Hennie. And
he was a furrier, the same as Hennie's father.

***

Hennie was distraught when Marvin phoned her that day. Not only was it her father that had barely escaped the crash, but his condition was worse than the newspapers made it sound. His being in hospital put the family in a bind.

Her father helped run a fur company, but his relationship with his partner had been under strain. In tears, Hennie told Marvin that the partner had paid the family a visit but, rather than sympathy, he had brought a message: if her father wasn't able to work, he would have to hire someone to take his place. With no money in the bank, the family didn't have enough to get by.

"I don't know what we're going to do," she told Marvin.

Marvin had an idea, though he said nothing of it to Hennie. He headed to Romik Carpet, up to the office where Roy sat behind his big desk.

"Roy, I want to borrow five thousand dollars," Marvin announced.

"What the hell do you want that kind of bread for?" It wasn't a question Roy often asked, since he cared little about why his customers wanted money, only that they were capable of paying him back. When Marvin told him about Hennie and her father and the family's plight, Roy had two words to say.

"You're crazy."

"Roy, I'm in love with this broad."

"You're not in love with her, you just want to marry a straight girl. You're kidding yourself."

"No, I'm in love," Marvin insisted.

"Well, you've got to pay it all back—with the juice. Plus, you got to do some work for me for free."

It had been a mistake for Marvin to open up to Roy. Instead of giving Marvin a break as a friend and former foster brother, or as a man who wants to help love flourish, Roy smelled Marvin's desperation and knew his judgment was impaired by hormones, so he tacked on the employment condition, a renewal of Marvin's indentured servitude.

Marvin took the $5,000 to Hennie's house. Her mother refused to take it. She said she knew the kind of people he worked for and there was no way the family could pay back that kind of money.

"This is not a loan, it's a gift. From me and only me," Marvin insisted.

Marvin started visiting Sam Geist in hospital, getting to know him and working with him in therapy handicrafts. It did not take long for the Geists to warm to the friendly young man who seemed so dedicated to their daughter and showed a heart big enough to match his cocky self-assurance. Eventually Hennie was given permission to date him.

When Marvin got his date, he and Hennie took their seats in one of the two balconies in the colossal Shea's Victoria Theatre at Victoria and Richmond streets to watch Yul Brynner in the newly released musical *The King and I*. Marvin tried to kiss her in the darkened theatre when the movie took its romantic twists, but Hennie wouldn't have it. It made Marvin even crazier for her. He always had a thing for wanting what he couldn't have.

"He was very nice and very friendly and we just hit it off," Hennie says.

Marvin's relationship with Hennie blossomed, but what she didn't know was that her boyfriend was quietly toiling away for Roy, working to pay off the money he had given to her family.

"I paid Roy. And I paid him. I paid him and I paid him and I paid him. And then I paid him some more," he says. Eventually Marvin would have enough. He would do one last job for Roy and then consider the debt repaid. But that would come years later, after Marvin and Hennie's big day.

* * *

On February 16, 1958, a 19-year-old Hannah "Hennie" Geist, pretty in a white gown, veiled and tightly gripping a delicate bouquet of flowers, walked with measured pace down the aisle of Beth Sholom synagogue in Toronto. She smiled broadly and batted her long dark lashes as she went, enjoying the moment but feeling uncomfortable as the centre of attention. At the altar, she was greeted by the 23-year-old Marvin Elkind, wearing a starched white shirt, a thin black bowtie, black tuxedo and white boutonniere. On his head was a white yarmulke.

Had there been no roof, his smile would have been visible from outer space.

The nuptials were a sprawling affair, with a lavish reception and mountains of food, including an intricate three-tiered wedding cake. On orders of his mother, none of the Pasquales were invited, and Marvin was happy to oblige. He would have been nervous about Roy upsetting the perfect day. After the ceremony, Marvin sought to recreate the swinging vibe of the Copacabana, bringing in the Benny Louis Orchestra, a 14-piece ensemble that included Rick Wilkins, who went on to become one of Canada's foremost musical arrangers, working with the Jackson Five, Oscar Peterson and Anne Murray on her hit *Snowbird*.

Marvin's wedding cost a bomb. Many wondered where the money was coming from. Although Morris was well enough off because of the payout for his menswear shop, traditional families looked to the bride's parents to foot the bill. But the Geists, especially after Hennie's father's accident, did not have the means for such an extravagance. Marvin's mother was impressed by the festivities but was mortified to think that Marvin had stolen the money or done some unspeakable service for it. What she didn't know was that Marvin had learned a few things from his years driving Jimmy Hoffa: he had borrowed the money from the Teamsters pension fund—and never paid it back. Tommy Corrigan had given Marvin the cheque and, in return, Corrigan and his wife had been given pride of place at the wedding. Marvin had to add just $200 of his own to pay the bills. Fun aside, he has never forgotten the importance of the marriage. Marvin considers it the best decision he ever made.

"She's been a saint. It has not been easy living with me over the years," Marvin says.

Marvin invited his old boss, Jimmy Hoffa, to the wedding. Hoffa declined but as a gift he sent Marvin two airline tickets to Miami for a honeymoon and a suite at the Di Lido Beach Hotel: "It was tremendous. We were going to go to Niagara Falls but he sent us to Florida. Not too bad."

Afterwards, Marvin and Hennie moved into Marvin's one-bedroom apartment on Bathurst Street. Two years later, a daughter arrived. When Hennie became pregnant with their second child, they looked for a bigger place. A new building was under construction nearby, with Teamsters doing the flooring. Marvin used that contact to get a decent apartment at a good rate.

* * *

There were family losses as well as additions.

Morris Elkind, Marvin's stepfather, may not have had much interest in having Marvin as a son, but he loved the idea of having grandchildren. The birth of Marvin's first daughter—Morris and Beatrice's first grandchild—helped to thaw Marvin's relationship with Morris. On November 24, 1961, Marvin sought to strengthen their bond and picked Morris up, telling him he wanted to take him out for the day. For lunch, they went to Morris's favourite spot, The Bagel, a deli on College Street. Morris ordered the wurst and eggs with a bagel, Marvin a plate of fried onions and a bagel.

Because it gnawed at the both of them, they just couldn't avoid talking about the past. It didn't go well. Morris told him how humiliated he felt about Marvin's past. Marvin said he was angry that Morris had given him up as a child. Morris blamed Marvin, saying if he hadn't been such a rotten kid it wouldn't have happened, while Marvin said it was Morris's fault, he hadn't had the patience to deal with his acting out. It grew heated, so much so that staff and other customers asked them several times to quiet down. Eventually Morris got up to leave.

"I'm not getting back in your car," Morris shouted.

"Who's asking you to?" yelled Marvin.

Morris stormed out. He took the streetcar to his brother Harry's house. Harry started to drive Morris home but soon diverted to St. Joseph's Hospital.

Marvin had just returned home, still fuming, when the phone rang. Morris had had a heart attack and died, he was told. He was 55 years old. Marvin was devastated, feeling both sad and deeply guilty. The circumstances of Morris's death did nothing to bring Marvin closer to his family.

"It was all my fault," Marvin says, shaking his head. "We were getting along terrifically until we got on that subject."

When Morris's estate was settled, Marvin found he was cut out, not getting a piece of the family's menswear business.

It upset him, but he didn't fight it. He didn't want to make things worse.

* * *

Marvin knew he was far from the perfect son but vowed to be a good husband and a good father to his two daughters. As children, the girls shared their father's elfin face, all big smiles and bright eyes. His home today is decorated largely by photo portraits of them as children and as adults.

"The one great thing I've had in my life has been my wife and my two daughters," Marvin says. "I guess that's three great things."

After his rootless childhood and adolescence, always longing and never belonging, Marvin was determined to provide some stability in his own domestic life. As he matured and settled with a family of his own, his life outside the home remained anything but stable. He saw his dubious line of work as the only means of giving them the house they wanted and the things they needed.

CHAPTER 13

LOUISVILLE, KENTUCKY, 1958

Marvin took U.S. Route 25 south of Toledo, Ohio, tearing along the highway until shooting out southwest near Cincinnati. With him in the car for the 12-hour drive were three seriously mobbed-up men. Red LaBarre, Freddie Gabourie and Frank Pucci were terrific mechanics, meaning they could work a crooked dice game or card game to ensure they always came out on top. Having honed their cheating skills in Hamilton and Toronto and surrounding cities and towns, they went on road trips in search of fresh hunting grounds.

Their target this month was Louisville. Built along a bend in the Ohio River, the city was famous for the Kentucky Derby, the thoroughbred horse race. Marvin and his gangster friends were heading not to the racetrack but to a high-stakes casino dice game above a strip club. Roy was bankrolling the excursion and offered Marvin as their driver to keep an eye on his investment. Marvin was still weaving work in for Roy with his work for Corrigan, while also trying to land work of his own. In Louisville, the gang split up so that they would arrive at the dice game separately. Inside, their smooth talk and fast hands worked wonders, as they slipped loaded dice in and out of play, raking in the dough while never showing they were together.

Freddie Gabourie wore a new cabana jacket he had just purchased. It was another stylish turn for a man with movie-star looks. Suave and well-mannered, he drove the other gangsters' wives and girlfriends crazy. He would stand whenever a lady got up from a table and the women would smack their own men, asking why they couldn't be more like Gabourie. His newest jacket, though, had nearly vertical slit pockets, like giant buttonholes, that were unfamiliar to a man more accustomed to horizontal or patch pockets. The cheats were on the verge of walking out winners when it was Gabourie's turn to swipe the table's dice and slip a doctored set into the game. He tried to drop the dice into his pocket, but he hadn't practised with the unfamiliar slits and they just tumbled on down, clattering on the floor. It took a second for everyone to figure out what was going on. They looked at the dice on the floor and up at Gabourie still clutching a set in his hand. The crowd went crazy.

"We lynch 'em round here for that," someone yelled.

Marvin saw the trouble immediately and slipped out the door and down the steep stairs. He ran to the car, got it started and drove round to the front of the strip club. He unlocked the doors and waited to see who was first out the door: if it was LaBarre, Gabourie and Pucci, he would give them a fighting chance to jump in before roaring off; if it was anyone else, he would floor it, heading north as fast as he could.

Inside the club, LaBarre and Pucci also acted quickly. Nobody knew the men were together, so the two Canadians roughly grabbed Gabourie, one on each arm, acting angry and menacing.

"We'll fix this cocksucker," LaBarre yelled to the crowd as he and Pucci hustled Gabourie toward the door, making like they were going to give him a vicious lesson in southern justice.

As soon as they were near the door, they let go of Gabourie and all three of them ran for it, sparking a sudden rush after them by a wild mob who realized they had just been duped twice. The trio stumbled down the stairs, launching themselves out the door. With relief, they saw that Marvin had not abandoned them. They tumbled into the car and Marvin floored it just as the mob reached for the open door. LaBarre's feet were still dangling dangerously out the door as Marvin's spinning tires threw up stones and dust, forcing back the lynching party.

Marvin couldn't hear the engine for all the laughing.

It was another night in the strange and dangerous world of the professional cheats. Another time, in the early 1960s, they rode the train from Winnipeg to Toronto for the Grey Cup football championship, setting up makeshift dice tables and cleaning out the travelling Winnipeg Blue Bombers' fans along the way. Kentucky and the Grey Cup, though, were special occasions. More typically, their cheating was done closer to home.

* * *

Like most mob-controlled joints, the Arabian Village on College Street, a busy thoroughfare in Toronto, looked legitimate from street level, but those in the know headed upstairs where the real money was made. It was one of the best dice parlours of the early 1960s. Large casino-style craps games moved major sums in an illegal gambling den that attracted a diverse crowd.

Marvin and Howard "Baldy" Chard, another boxer, were the bouncers. Marvin was stationed downstairs and anyone wanting to go up needed to get a ticket from him. If anyone questioned his judgment, Marvin whistled for the frightening Baldy, who would stand behind Marvin with his arms crossed, revealing forearms like tree trunks. That usually set-tled any disagreement.

Upstairs, each night, the $2,000 house bank—a huge roll of folded cash—was pulled from the trouser pockets of John "Johnny Pops" Papalia. Papalia was a burgeoning mob pow-erhouse who lived in Hamilton, a steel town an hour's drive southwest of Toronto. It was testament to the hard men of Hamilton—and Papalia's particular talent as a gangster—that such a physically unremarkable guy in a city subordi-nate to Toronto in almost every measurable way could become the heart and soul of the mob in the province. As a teenager, Papalia had been pals with Roy Pasquale, and the two had embarked on an unrelenting crime spree. Roy and Papalia even robbed a bank together, the same branch at Dundas and Ossington that was Marvin's father's undoing. This heist went better, with Roy and Papalia—along with their buddy Pasquale Giordano, a boxer who fought under the name Patsy Gordon—walking in with guns and dashing out with a small sack of cash.

Marvin knew Papalia well from his time at the Pasquale home. He was one of the ill-tempered lads hanging around whom Marvin liked baiting whenever Mama Pasquale was there. He loved watching Papalia seethe as his foster mom sternly warned the older boys to keep their mitts off Marvin. Marvin would also sit on the Shaw Street veranda watching for cops while Papalia, Roy, Patsy, future mafioso Paul Volpe and others conspired together inside. While there was no fondness between Marvin and Papalia, there was great familiarity. In the underworld, one easily passes for the other. It meant Papalia trusted Marvin to work the door at the Arabian Village, and Marvin, well, he worked for anyone who paid in cash.

Waiting for the customers upstairs was the mobster's inner circle: Gabourie and LaBarre, the famed dice mechanics, along with Jackie Weaver and others on Papalia's payroll. Everyone Marvin let through the door to the upstairs room was mercilessly fleeced.

"They cheated the shit out of everyone," Marvin recalls. Not just in the Arabian Village. The busy little gang found ways to pull similar stunts at venues across the province.

* * *

It was a quick swap, a C-note for a caterer's list. The hundred-dollar bill was quickly pushed into the pocket of the food-service employee and the list of upcoming parties was folded and stuffed into the breast pocket of one of Papalia's gambling mechanics.

Marvin would often drive a crew of Papalia's guys, including Gabourie, LaBarre and Weaver, to the biggest stag parties. Whether it was a party from the lists bought from the top caterers or something they heard through the grapevine, the group was thrilled to hear of upcoming nuptials, but the only romance they cared about was their love of winning. For more than a decade they would present themselves at stag parties, give the guy running it another C-note, saying, "Here's a present for the bride and groom," and then offer to run the casino at the party so he could enjoy himself. The gangsters loved the crowds at stag parties. Wealthy, feeling a little wild and often drunk, they were usually unsophisticated gamblers. Marvin and Papalia's boys gave them a night to remember, especially the morning after, when, nursing a hangover, they realized how much money they had lost to the strangers.

One time in the early 1960s, they showed up ready to roll at a large stag packed with well-heeled guests, but when they asked for the guy in charge they found it was organized by Joe Pancer.

Joe was an experienced gambler known as "Joe the Goof"; the nickname had sprung from his obsession with silly bets. He would bet on anything. In a bar, he would turn to a guy next to him who was about to light a cigarette and say, "I'll bet you a hundred dollars your lighter won't start the first time you flick it." Despite the crazy bets, he somehow managed to make a lot of money. Joe knew exactly what Marvin and his friends were up to when they arrived, uninvited in their suits and smiles. They were ready to leave when Joe stopped them and laughed.

"What the hell, go ahead. I'll just play gin rummy tonight."

With the go-ahead, the boys slipped Joe a few bucks and set up shop. It was an especially good take, since the crowd was as loaded as the dice. It was the political establishment in the room that night, including Smirle Lawson.

For 25 years, Smirle Lawson was the province's chief coroner, but before taking that office he had been an unlikely sports hero. As a hard-charging halfback, Lawson was one of the stars of the first Grey Cup, leading the Varsity Blues to football glory in 1909 with a 50-yard touchdown run in the final moments of the game. A hint of his mischievous streak came from revelations that his surgery professor in medical school had promised him a perfect final grade if he scored three touchdowns, which he did. After graduating, Lawson joined the Toronto Argonauts and led them to their first Grey Cup win in 1914. He became chief coroner in 1937, and had many important friends, becoming the centre of a powerful civic cabal that included Toronto's chief of police, John C. Chisholm, until the top cop killed himself in an unmarked police car with his service revolver in 1958.

Another friend was Lionel Conacher. Like Lawson, Conacher had been an Argos captain. He was an athlete of singular success: he took the Canadian amateur light heavy-weight boxing title in 1920; he then won a Grey Cup championship in football in 1921, a Triple A championship pennant in baseball in 1926 and two Stanley Cup championships in hockey in 1934 and 1935. After retiring from pro sports, he became a politician, provincially and then federally. Conacher and Lawson were close in the football fraternity. Conacher's brother, Charlie, also became close with Lawson. Charlie Conacher played for the Toronto Maple Leafs and also won a Stanley Cup, in 1932. Another close friend was Judge Walter T. Robb, who chaired the Ontario Liquor Licensing Board. That was an immensely powerful position, since the issuing of liquor licences allowing alcohol to be sold was huge business. Judge Robb had played lacrosse with Lionel Conacher and always had time for Lawson and the Conacher boys.

Most of them also liked to play the sorts of games that Marvin and Papalia's gang ran. Members of this cabal helped each other in unofficial ways, and Marvin watched as his circle worked with Lawson's circle, focusing primarily on Judge Robb. With his control over liquor sales in the province, Robb was one of Ontario's most sought-after men.

"In those days, getting a liquor licence was like printing money. Very few places had them. They were difficult to get and you had to get to Judge Robb," Marvin says. "You just couldn't go to Judge Robb yourself and pay him off. You had to go through somebody. Smirle Lawson was one of his contacts. Charlie Conacher was one of his contacts. So if you wanted a liquor licence in a bar or something, you would get to Judge Robb through these certain guys."

Marvin's strange journey continued, taking him ever deeper into the underworld. At the same time, he was becoming a bit player in, and witness to, an incredible hidden machine of corruption, swindles and favours that stretched beyond the jaded gambling dens into city hall, the police force and the provincial government.

Marvin's obsession with boxing got him in tight with Baldy Chard; his relationship with Roy Pasquale got him in with Johnny Papalia; his work with Papalia's gang put him in with cops, financiers, bankers, celebrities and some of the city's dodgy political elite. He watched, listened, learned. Each link led him to another connection and suddenly men were within reach who, really, should have been nowhere near guys like Marvin.

* * *

The money totalled $5,000—to the penny—and was counted twice before Roy let it go. Marvin neatly stacked the bills inside his portfolio bag, a leather case with a zipper but no handle that he tucked under his arm for safekeeping.

"I'm doing this for you and then that's it. We're even," Marvin said. He was finally putting his foot down and closing his account with Roy for the money he had borrowed to give to Hennie's family.

Roy had bought land near Lake Simcoe for which he had paid an insignificant amount. It was a large swath of under-utilized agricultural property. He knew that as development increased in the area, getting the land rezoned from strictly agricultural use to residential or commercial use would raise its value many times over. When one of Roy's regular loan-shark clients, a man who worked for the ruling Progressive Conservative Party in the province, was having trouble paying Roy back on time, Roy offered him an alternative. Instead of paying the loan, all he had to do was use his political connections to get Roy's land rezoned. It must have been easy for him, because not long afterwards the property was rezoned to residential, and Roy sold the land for a thousand times what he had paid for it. In return, Roy needed to pay the political contacts $5,000. When Roy told Marvin to deliver the cash, Marvin asked what he was getting out of it. Roy said zero. In that case, said Marvin, this would finally erase his own debt to Roy. Roy reluctantly agreed.

Marvin took his bag of cash to a law firm in Toronto. Inside the office of Abe Singer, Marvin said he had a delivery from Roy Pasquale. With the lawyer was Allan Grossman, who had made the leap from city to provincial politics, becoming a member of the provincial legislature in a vote that saw him defeat the last elected Communist in Ontario. At the time, Grossman was the minister of trade and development. Singer counted the money as Grossman watched. Marvin took his empty bag back and wished them both well.

Marvin felt a tremendous sense of relief. After 15 years, his debt to Roy was finally paid in full.

* * *

Through the 1950s and into the 1970s, Marvin floated through this secret backroom world of shysters, cheats and mobsters who mingled with businessmen, financiers, union bosses and members of the political machinery. He hovered along the edge of that delicate, dangerous territory where the underworld and the upper world met. And he walked that line, wearing his big grin, carrying his fat cigars and starting to think he was really a somebody, but never truly believing it. It led Marvin to dream he was on the cusp of something bigger, if only he could somehow find a firm footing, his niche, in this inglorious swirl. He knew he was capable of being more than muscle, if only he could get others to let him use his brain.

CHAPTER 14

DETROIT, 1967

The lineup outside the movie theatre in downtown Detroit already stretched out the doors and down a city block by the time Marvin and Hennie arrived. The main attraction was *The St. Valentine's Day Massacre*, the just-released Roger Corman film about Al Capone. It was classic gangster cinema—a genre Marvin always enjoyed—filled with quick-talking mobsters dabbling in murder, extortion and fraud. Jason Robards's Capone helped immortalize mobsters as linguistically challenged thugs in snappy suits with lines such as: "That no good louse." The film's graphic violence would soon prove too real for Hennie, as she took her place in line alongside Marvin on a Sunday evening in late July.

***

Marvin and Hennie were staying across the border in Windsor while Marvin conducted a little business he didn't much talk about with his wife. Their accommodation was the Elmwood Casino, on Dougall Avenue.

The Elmwood was the hottest nightspot in the city even though, despite its name, it didn't offer gambling. Its large Vegas-style signs promoting international stars brought in the crowds for the restaurant, lounge and motel rooms. The acts that had started out at the Copa years before passed through the Elmwood—Milton Berle, Sammy Davis, Jr., Sid Caesar and Jimmy Durante among them. Marvin and Hennie spent their day poolside. In the evening, they headed across the border for a movie, leaving their daughters, six and four, with a babysitter.

"We get there and it was all black people lining up for the movie. We were the only white people there. We noticed it, but didn't think too much about it. I bought the tickets but the tickets used up all of the American money I had with me. We went inside and I lined up at the snack bar and ordered a hotdog and a drink. But when I went to pay they wouldn't take Canadian money. I said I'd pay the difference but they refused. A black guy next to me in line said, 'Where you from? Canada?' I said 'Yeah.' He said, 'Here, let me treat you.' And he paid for my hotdog and drink. It was very nice of him. We saw the show and had a real nice time and went back to the Windsor hotel," Marvin says.

The next day, Monday, July 24, Marvin went to his business meeting in Detroit. He took Hennie and the girls across with him, dropping them at the same theatre to see the family matinee of *Snow White and the Seven Dwarfs* while Marvin met at an office tower not far away.

Marvin let out a low whistle of approval as he looked around the office of David Auer. The opulent surroundings boasted not only a private washroom with a shower, but a sauna. There was even a small pool on the balcony. Marvin loved it. For Auer, crime paid—at least until 1983 when police found his body in the trunk of his silver Mercedes in a motel parking lot in Pontiac, a suburb of Detroit, beaten and strangled. But before that messy end, Auer was living large, running a mortgage and financing scam. His specialty was drafting documents that could be used to obtain a phoney mortgage from a bank. Clients like Marvin would pick out a building with a commercial storefront and apartment above it—any place would do—and Auer would draft documents showing ownership. The documents could then be used as collateral at certain banks to obtain a mortgage for 10 per cent of the building's value. Marvin used the address for Roy's Romik Carpet. Marvin had done it once before and it worked like a charm. He dealt with a branch of a major bank in Toronto where the manager was in on the deal. The manager and Auer both took a hefty cut. By the time Marvin had paid everyone off, he was left with $2,500 in profit.

As Marvin sat with Auer and the financier's right-hand man in the sumptuous office hammering out the details, they were interrupted.

"They've started! They've started! It's really going out there," a man shouted as he ran in, panting.

The men rushed to the window.

Marvin was perplexed, "What the heck?"

"The blacks have started rioting. They're tearing apart downtown," Auer said.

Marvin looked out the window. On the street below he saw a crowd of African-Americans running through the streets. Some were throwing rocks through store windows and looting. Fires were burning in the street. It was a full-scale race riot. Racial tension in the city had been escalating for years as a result of economic inequality, accusations of racist police brutality, a shortage of affordable housing and rising black militancy. The spark for this particular riot came the night before Marvin's meeting, when police raided a blind pig, an unlicensed bar, where black patrons were celebrating the return of two Vietnam War vets. After the police roundup, gathering crowds grew increasingly upset with the treatment. Anger and looting spread. Marvin had no idea of the discontent in the city, and his pleasant time at the cinema the night before had betrayed no sign of the problems so glaring on the street below. He was mystified, but all Marvin could think of right then was his wife and daughters somewhere out there, alone in the middle of the mayhem.

Nothing matters more to Marvin than his family. As important as this deal was to him, the phoney mortgage would have to wait.

Dashing out of Auer's office, Marvin found his car intact and roared through the crazy streets, swerving around the fires, bricks and rioters. As he approached the theatre he saw Hennie and his tiny daughters standing outside, huddled together on the sidewalk surrounded by three cops, their batons raised menacingly to the rioters nearby. Marvin pulled over and jumped out to open the back door as his family jumped inside.

Marvin turned to the cops. "I want to thank you for . . ." he started.

"Don't thank us, get the hell out of here," a cop shouted back as the officers retreated to where their colleagues were congregating.

Marvin turned toward Canada. As he drove, cop cars streamed into the city in the other direction. When he approached the border, officers holding shotguns stood guard along the roadside. They took one look in the car and waved them through without asking them to stop. On the Canadian side, the border agents asked them if they had just come from Detroit. Marvin nodded.

"Well, welcome home."

Indeed. By the time the riot ended days later, after tanks

and the National Guard were sent in, 43 people were dead, almost 500 were injured and more than 2,000 buildings were ransacked or destroyed. And at least one crooked mortgage deal had been scuttled.

The phoney-mortgage scam was another manifestation of Marvin's unscrupulous life. But his fraudster side was a closely guarded secret. To those outside Marvin's underworld cabal, it looked for all the world like he had gone straight: he was a husband and father; an active member of the Jewish community; a member of the Teamsters union who routinely accompanied its national president; and a businessman who ran a high-end menswear store in downtown Toronto. It was a masquerade for Marvin, another sign of his uneasiness with who he was. Along with his blue-collar driver's job and career as a thug, Marvin had gone into his stepfather's trade after all.

* * *

The Coach Room had an intentionally refined, old-fashioned feel, with plush carpeting and leather chairs dotted about the 2,000-square-foot menswear store on Eglinton Avenue near Avenue Road. The front half of the store displayed fine shirts, socks, ties, belts and such. Up a few steps, the back half offered suits, sports jackets, trench coats and other outerwear. The stock wasn't cheap. It was at the cutting edge of men's fashion, a stride and a half past the Everyman apparel offered at Elk's, his family's chain of stores.

"Some guy would come in and want a certain type of shirt, a high-class shirt that Marvin didn't have, and he'd fly to New York to pick some up," a former client says. Marvin admits he was running an unsustainable enterprise.

"I liked the idea of getting things for people you couldn't

get anywhere else in the city, or in the country," Marvin says. He doesn't think he was driven by bitterness over being cut out of the family's clothing business. He says he wasn't in competition with Elk's, and his drive to be a small-business titan had nothing to do with proving to his family that he could be a success in the trade. But you have to wonder.

On weekdays, Marvin worked for Tommy Corrigan, his Teamsters boss, but on Saturdays he transformed into the congenial proprietor of The Coach Room, helping wealthy clients find high-thread-count shirts, well-made suits with the latest cut and all the appropriate accoutrements. Meanwhile, he was using his position as a young businessman to enhance his standing within the Jewish community.

"It was a high-class store, people knew it, so I had no trouble getting on the community committees. A lot of the people involved were my customers," Marvin says. "I liked the idea of the publicity. I liked being in the papers, the society pages. I would be in wedding parties and at the head tables at the big dinners. I enjoyed it while it lasted."

Through the early 1960s, Marvin became a minor fixture in the social pages of the Jewish press and even the *Toronto Daily Star*'s "Social Whirl" column. His talent as a talker—good-natured, witty, outgoing—made him a natural master of ceremonies and he emceed his way into the news as the congenial, smiling host of B'nai Brith dinners and annual meetings, sitting with Hennie at the head table as the large Jewish organization's new executive was installed in 1961, becoming a member of the United Jewish Appeal Welfare Fund leadership development group in 1962, the same year he was named "man of the year" and installed as a warden in the B'nai Brith's Circle Lodge. That year also, his smiling apple-cheeked face made the front cover of the *Canadian Jewish News* for a story about key fundraisers in that year's United Jewish Appeal. Marvin and Hennie also took a leadership role in Beth Sholom synagogue's Young Married Couples group, sitting with the rabbi at the head table for the annual dinner and dance. In 1964, Marvin was elected to the synagogue's board of governors. Marvin had finally buried "Mario Pasquale," finding a sense of identity in his Jewish heritage.

He and Hennie holidayed in Florida with John Bitove, Sr., and his wife, before the businessman became a huge restaurant and food-service magnate. Marvin would attend Toronto Argonauts games and Maple Leafs hockey and Maple Leafs baseball games with Bitove, Corrigan and others. Marvin even became a minority owner of the Toronto Rifles football team, the first professional American football team to be based in Canada, competing in the short-lived Continental Football League.

It wasn't something Marvin could sustain. Like so much in his life, it was a facade.

CHAPTER 15

Shortly after 5 p.m. on June 14, 1965, a cheque for $5 million, payment for a loan from an institutional lender, bounced. The shortfall put Atlantic Acceptance Corp. Ltd. officially in default. The news that the company had been placed in receivership was big news the next morning.

Atlantic Acceptance had experienced spectacular growth after C. Powell Morgan took the presidency in 1958. In five years, the company's assets had grown to $133-million from $11-million, at least on paper. A stock-market darling, Atlantic Acceptance was on the cutting edge of aggressive corporate financing, acting as a bank without the regulatory oversight banks had to comply with. It attracted investment from Princeton University, the United States Steel Fund, Ford Foundation, the Carnegie Foundation Pension Fund, private New York investment firms and other venerable institutions.

Before the cheque bounced, Atlantic Acceptance shares were selling at $20.37; two months later they had plunged to 65 cents. Its debts were $115 million. Atlantic Acceptance's downfall was described as a blow to the free enterprise system, the biggest stock collapse in Canadian history. The scandal only got worse. Failure rippled outwards—companies that had money tied up in the firm faltered and collateral bankruptcies piled up. From department stores to aluminum siding companies, used car dealers to the Canadian Bar Association, investors suffered. Powell Morgan resigned as chairman of Atlantic, and of Commodore Business Machines; it was Atlantic money that financed the technology startup that would go on to revolutionize personal computers. But the future tech giant was almost destroyed along with Atlantic.

It took a while for regulators to figure out the problems. Atlantic was borrowing huge amounts and comingling the money with revenue from disreputable and fraudulent sources to lend in a credit financing business that later collapsed. Many aspects of Atlantic Acceptance were a systematic and purposeful fraud. Some of the money was loaned to co-conspirators at no or low interest. Other loans were deemed uncollectible from the moment the transactions were completed. Tangled up in the labyrinth of shady firms, hidden ownership and shuffled accounts was The Coach Room, and its proprietor, Marvin Elkind.

Marvin's veneer of respectability was being stripped away.

* * *

Marvin was at The Coach Room when four men in suits—definitely not purchased at his fine store—entered. Instead of a shopping list, they presented Marvin with a search warrant. Marvin wasn't surprised. He knew the business couldn't continue with everything that was going on with Atlantic Acceptance and Powell Morgan. He left the RCMP officers to rifle through the place, seizing account ledgers and receipts. The store's bank accounts, he learned, had already been frozen by court order.

The next morning, Marvin was at home when he answered his door to see the same officers on his front porch. They had a second search warrant. The officers were especially gentle during this search. Marvin's daughters were playing in the house while they gingerly poked around.

Once again, the life Marvin was getting comfortable with was torn away.

He had got involved in the store through Tommy Corrigan, who was in on the shady deals and was a friend of Powell Morgan's. Marvin was a natural to front the store because of his experience in menswear, and he threw himself into fulfilling the fantasy of being a successful businessman, without having to worry about profit margins. He also went in on side deals whenever the opportunity arose, such as it did with the phoney mortgages with David Auer in Detroit, a connection he made through Atlantic Acceptance. As the proprietor of The Coach Room, and with help from guys like Corrigan, Morgan, Auer and the crooked Toronto bank manager, Marvin had had no trouble getting loans to jet off to New York on a whim to buy shirts for upscale clients. In the end, however, those customers would turn on him. After the fraud was uncovered, the paperwork showed that payment from each sale had been declared an uncollected debt. Each of Marvin's customers was sent a notice by the bankruptcy trustee demanding payment—for merchandise they had in fact paid for. It crippled Marvin's social life, to say the least. There would be no more mention in the social pages.

As the investigation continued, it was revealed that Marvin's ownership of The Coach Room was a sham. The money for its stock and expensive fixtures had come through Atlantic Acceptance.

"It was one hundred per cent a scam," Marvin says. "It was a front. All of the money from sales at the store went to Morgan's company, and the sales were listed as financing, and each bill was written up in the books as a receivable that was non-collectible." It was, in essence, a retail version of a Ponzi scheme, with one fraud generating money that was pushed into another. One company filled Marvin's store with fixtures that were worth less than $10,000 but billed for more than $40,000. The store then used the fixtures—on paper worth $40,000—as collateral for mortgages and loans. Then, once the store was running, each and every sale became part of the swindle, Marvin says. If the store did $5,000 in sales in a week, each of the already-paid receipts was sent to Atlantic and listed on the books as an unpaid debt to be written off. The money was kept and skimmed or used to finance other projects and schemes. It took some time for police to wrap up the loose ends of the Atlantic Acceptance evidence. Most of the big fish, as usual, skipped blame. Some, such as Atlantic's chartered accountants William Walton and Harry Wagman, and frontmen like Marvin, were easier pickings.

Atlantic's affairs took years to fully sort out, but by the summer of 1965, front-page headlines already screamed scandal and a Royal Commission was formed.

Things grew more mysterious when, less than two weeks after the commission of inquiry was announced, a Canadian Pacific Airlines plane carrying Atlantic's senior auditor, who was scheduled to be a key witness, exploded after taking off from Vancouver airport, killing all 52 people on board. The RCMP launched a probe into whether the auditor's presence on the plane was a factor. Then, in 1966, Morgan himself died, of leukemia, with the answers to most questions dying with him.

* * *

Justice Samuel Hughes, presiding over the Royal Commission Appointed to Inquire Into the Failure of Atlantic Acceptance, started public hearings in March, 1966. The estimates of losses by investors ranged from $50 million to $75 million. The commission waded through the complicated wheelings and dealings, submitting its findings in a massive report.

"Morgan and Morgan alone drove Atlantic forward to catastrophe," Judge Hughes wrote, "and like all well-known swindlers of history, he did so with a fatalistic and cynical disregard of those principles of fair and honest dealing which have been generally accepted and adhered to for generations in both the civilized world and the savage world." Judge Hughes was right about Morgan being a great swindler, but he got it wrong when he pinned all of the blame on the dead boss.

For Marvin, the ramifications of the scandal were calamitous. He was charged with fraud, disposal of assets to defraud creditors and failure to disclose to the Trustee of Bankruptcy, contrary to the Bankruptcy Act.

* * *

Once arrested on such serious criminal charges, Marvin headed to the one lawyer he felt he could fully trust.

Harvey Salem was a childhood friend, one of the few he had outside of the foster-home/reform-school/boxing-club axis that had so marked him. Even so, the first time Marvin and Harvey met, when the boys were seven or eight, Marvin had put Harvey on crutches. It was at a summer cottage north of Toronto where both families were on holiday. The boys were playing on a dock when Marvin pushed Harvey into the water. Harvey's foot scraped along a piece of wood sticking out from the pilings, tearing the flesh from his heel. The foot was wrapped in plaster and Harvey spent most of the holiday on crutches. Rather than creating a rift between them, it built a bond. Marvin felt so bad, he spent every day with Harvey, bringing him comic books and telling him jokes. When Harvey's foot was a little better, Marvin taught him how to ride a bike. Their friendship continued when they returned to Toronto, although they moved in different social circles and went to different schools. Growing up, they kept in touch, off and on. Harvey lived near the Elk's store where Marvin sometimes worked, and on his way home from school he sometimes stopped in to kibitz. At Christmas, Harvey worked there, too. Morris Elkind called him "Whipper," after wrestler Whipper Billy Watson, because of Harvey's accomplishments on the varsity wrestling team. Harvey saw first-hand the animosity between Marvin and Morris, when Morris told Marvin, "When I die, you die"—the implication being that Marvin was such a screw-up that he was incapable of looking after himself. It was that sentiment, Harvey thinks, that drove Marvin to act so recklessly to make The Coach Room a glittering gem, against all the rules of supply and demand. Harvey had recently graduated from law school when Marvin was charged, and Marvin's case was among his first.

"Marvin was suffering from megalomania, a serious mental illness," Harvey says. "The whole gist of this illness was he felt he could do no wrong, that anything he did would turn out OK and make more money. He was fixated on making a better deal than Elk's menswear. He was higher end than they were, but that was his goal, I think. He had a good defence, but firstly, he had no money and we were looking at a lengthy trial and I couldn't do it for nothing. And secondly, he would have had a mental breakdown. He just couldn't have handled a trial. So we made the best deal we could."

Marvin was devastated to learn that there was a fink in his case. One of his friends, a man with whom he had socialized and travelled, whose family had spent time with his family, was cooperating with authorities in exchange for a walk. The fink had had a business relationship with Atlantic and The Coach Room. Marvin felt the sting of betrayal and a surge of disgust.

"I felt like I wanted to kill him," Marvin admits, shrugging at the irony.

Did he consider cutting a deal himself, ratting on Corrigan or testifying against the others in the various financing swindles? No way.

"I still considered myself to be an honourable gangster in those days."

* * *

Not even a guilty plea came easily for Marvin.

He had agreed to plead guilty to the charges and was awaiting his sentencing hearing when he received unexpected news. The judge presiding over his case had been arrested. His Honour was accused of cutting secret deals with prostitutes appearing in his court: the girls could avoid jail in exchange for a little private community service. The figurative disrobing that followed the literal disrobing meant Marvin's sentencing was delayed as the judge's cases were reassigned. When Marvin's rescheduled sentencing arrived, he once again heard odd news. This second judge had also just been arrested. This time, the judge was accused of tipping off gambling boss Vince Alexander to impending police raids on his gambling den. Marvin again realized what a small world he lived in. He knew the gambler well. He was a good friend of Roy's.

When Marvin had his sentencing hearing reslated for a third time, he was facing one year to five years in prison. When

Marvin arrived in court, Harvey Salem told him he had more bad news. His case was being heard by a judge notorious for meting out stiff sentences. Lawyers called him "the hanging judge." Harvey told Marvin to brace himself for the maximum. As Marvin was contemplating that, Harvey spoke to the Crown attorney, Patrick LeSage. LeSage knew about the unfair delays Marvin had faced. He also understood the ramifications for Marvin of appearing before the hanging judge and LeSage became unavailable for Marvin's hearing, meaning it would be postponed yet again, the next time to Marvin's benefit. It was an appreciated gesture that Marvin never forgot. After LaSage was appointed to the bench, and he presided over the sensational 1995 trial of serial sex killer Paul Bernardo, Marvin went to watch him in action for old time's sake.

In December of 1969, Marvin once again went to the Toronto courthouse for sentencing on his fraud conviction. This time the judge wasn't a lecher or a snitch or a hanging judge. In fact, as Marvin sat in court, some good news was whispered to him. With him, as a character witness, was Marvin's rabbi, David Monson. Monson had known Marvin since reform school, when he went to Bowmanville to teach him Hebrew, since it was not part of the school's curriculum. Later he officiated at Marvin's wedding. Monson was a politically active philanthropist and a close friend and confidant to John Diefenbaker. When Diefenbaker was prime minister of Canada, Monson had helped this judge get appointed to the bench.

"You'll be OK," Monson assured Marvin.

The rabbi was right. Marvin was given the minimum sentence of one year.

CHAPTER 16

TORONTO, 1969

It was with foul memories of his reform-school abuse that Marvin got set to enter Mimico Correctional Centre, a west-end Toronto jail. He was tougher now, at 35, with considerable street smarts and fighting experience. Still, if there was one thing he had learned from being with mobsters for most of his life, it was: don't leave things to chance when you can rig them.

Marvin knew the provincial jails were overseen by Allan Grossman, whom he had met when delivering Roy's bag of cash for the rezoning of his Lake Simcoe property. Grossman was now the minister of reform institutions. Marvin paid him a visit.

"What kind of work do you want to do inside?" Grossman asked.

"I'd like to work in the clothes room," Marvin said. When inmates arrive at jail, they are wearing what they wore at their last court appearance. In the clothes room, inmates take the arrivals' clothing, tag and store it, then hand out prison uniforms. It was the softest job in the joint, unless you could do office work, which Marvin couldn't.

"I'll see to it," Grossman said.

* * *

On December 18, 1969, Marvin returned to jail. He was pleased to see that the 25 years since reform school had done much to improve the system. Grossman, in fact, was responsible for many of the changes. In his years as minister, Grossman had become a world leader in the movement for progressive penal change, and the inmates approved. His initiatives of temporary absences and banning of the strap made him the best-loved politician in the jails.

"He was very popular with the inmates because of his changes. And because he was Jewish, Jews became very popular inside as well," Marvin says.

On March 13, the morning of his 36th birthday, Marvin walked into the dormitory to find a strip of toilet paper draped across the wall with a message from fellow inmates: "Happy Birthday Marvin, You Big Fat Heeb." That's a downright affectionate greeting in the joint. They even had a cake for him. Although Marvin made many friends inside, he went out of his way to ingratiate himself to one particular man who also was locked up.

* * *

Harold Ballard was executive vice-president of the Toronto Maple Leaf hockey team and Maple Leaf Gardens, the arena where they played. Ballard was the embodiment of controversy and bombast. He seemed not to care how much public criticism he provoked as long as he got his way.

In 1969, when Ballard took a piece of the Leafs, he was all about business. He turned the Carlton Street arena into what was dubbed the Carlton Cashbox after cramming saleable seats into every nook and cranny, selling ads on any flat surface and boosting concession prices. When he removed a large portrait of the Queen to make room for more seats, he quipped: "She doesn't pay me, I pay her." It wasn't what Toronto was used to under team founder Conn Smythe, who had brought the club to its golden era, evidenced by Smythe's name etched on the Stanley Cup 11 times.

In 1961, Smythe sold his controlling interest to his son, Stafford—or so he thought. Ballard had fronted the money for Stafford's purchase and the majority ownership was split three ways between Stafford, Ballard and newspaper baron John Bassett. The deal sparked years of controversy, with the power struggle regularly featured in the news. The size of the headlines grew substantially when both Stafford and Ballard were charged with income-tax evasion and other infractions after investigators found that team money had been used to renovate their homes and cottages.

Ballard was in his 60s when he was pulled from the club's front office and incarcerated. Although he was a strong personality, it was a hard adjustment. Marvin stepped in to make it a little easier.

"As soon as I found out Ballard was inside the joint, I went right over to see him. I became Ballard's 'kiss-ass' boy. I made his bed, got him coffee, looked out for him, things like that," Marvin says. It was like being a busboy back in the Copa, with just one customer and less dishware. "Some of the other inmates were upset that I got to Ballard first because they wanted to be Ballard's kiss-ass. He was rich and famous. Everyone knew him."

Marvin had keen radar for the rich and powerful and always looked to connect with anyone who might be useful. He never dreamed Ballard would return the favour so quickly.

Before going to jail, Marvin had set aside as much money as he could for Hennie and their daughters, adamant that his wife should not have to work outside the home. He was a traditionalist that way. One Sunday, when Hennie came to visit, she told him that an unexpected bill had come in for $500 and she would be out of money before his release. Marvin told her to pay the bill and he would think of something. He left the visitor's room visibly upset.

"What's wrong?" Marvin looked up to see Ballard. Marvin told him about the family's money trouble. Ballard walked away. Marvin figured Ballard was disgusted with his lack of financial acumen. However, during the next visit from Hennie, Marvin's wife had more news: the day after her last visit, a courier from Maple Leaf Gardens had come to the door with a cheque for $500. Marvin went to Ballard.

"Thanks so much for what you did. You saved us. I swear, I'll repay every cent when I get out," Marvin told him.

"Marvin," Ballard said, "did you ask me for a loan?"

"No."

"So don't insult me."

The give-and-take between Marvin and Ballard continued when they got out of jail. Whenever Marvin needed hockey tickets, Ballard came up with them. Years later, Marvin also worked security at one of Ballard's marriages. Ballard gave him one explicit instruction: keep his kids out of the place. Ballard was not getting along with his two children from a previous marriage and they did not approve of his choice for a new wife. Ballard didn't want them to upset his bride. The wedding, simple by Ballard's standards, was in his private quarters inside Maple Leaf Gardens. Marvin stood outside the apartment door. To get to it, a person would need to get past official Gardens security and find his way to his quarters. Ballard knew his kids could do that. Marvin stood guard, wearing his best suit, greeting guests warmly and giving them his big grin and a once-over to see who they were.

Sure enough, Ballard's son and daughter showed up, dressed for a wedding but not wanting one. Marvin recognized them and politely stopped them.

"Look, your dad doesn't want you here," he said. "You'll have to leave." It was the perfect mix of diplomacy and might. He spoke pleasantly but there was enough menace in his look that the children listened to him where they had ignored Gardens security. They left without making a scene.

* * *

Marvin was paroled on April 18, 1970. Hennie and their two daughters still lived in the apartment they had gotten with the help of Tommy Corrigan. But after 11 years, they wanted to break from the gangsters who had such a grip on Marvin.

Marvin and Hennie started looking for a home that would give them more living space and, since they wanted to do it without help from any of Marvin's crooked friends, more breathing space. They rented a townhouse in north Toronto and loved it. After two years, however, the owner wanted to sell. Marvin was given first dibs, but his application for a mortgage was turned down. The fraud conviction didn't help. Marvin was forced back to Corrigan, but his boss wasn't interested in spotting him that much money, so Marvin went to see Giacomo Luppino.

Giacomo Luppino was the wise old man of the mob in Ontario. As if to show off his ferocity, when he arrived in Canada from Italy he carried in his wallet the leathery ear of a rival, which he had hacked off in public as a lesson to others. He also had the ear, metaphorically, of Stefano Magaddino, the powerful mob boss across the border in Buffalo, which boosted his influence considerably. Luppino and his five sons became a major Mafia power based in Hamilton. Giacomo Luppino knew Marvin from his work for Papalia and Roy and agreed to secure the townhouse mortgage; he even charged Marvin conventional rates. But being in debt to the Luppinos came at a cost.

Marvin had tried to move into the house without help from gangsters, but the continued reliance on mob money kept him tightly tethered. Luppino soon asked for a favour. He handed Marvin six large manila envelopes, all sealed and bound together by tape. Marvin had no idea what was inside. Luppino told Marvin to take them to his son-in-law, Paolo Violi, who had succeeded Vic Cotroni as the boss of the Mafia in Montreal. Marvin arrived at Violi's café and gave Violi the package. Just then three little girls came into Violi's shop. One ordered an ice cream cone.

"Aren't you girls going to order something?" Violi asked her two friends.

"No, sir, we don't have any money," they said.

Violi scooped out three ice cream cones and gave them to the girls, declining to take money from the first girl. Marvin was impressed. Violi put on a suit jacket, grabbed a large shopping bag and asked Marvin for a ride. Just a few blocks from the café, Violi told Marvin to park outside a shoe-repair store and to come with him.

"You have my money?" Violi asked the old cobbler.

"I need two days," the old man pleaded. "Just two days."

"You're already two weeks late," Violi bellowed as he pulled a baseball bat out of the shopping bag and started swinging it about the store, smashing machinery and cabinets as the shopkeeper slumped to the floor in distress, burying his head in his hands and weeping.

"Paolo, how much does the guy owe you?" Marvin said, interrupting the demolition.

"Fifty bucks," said Violi.

"Stop this, I'll give you fifty myself right now."

Violi took a few more swings about the store.

"You don't understand," Violi said. "It's not about money, it's about obedience." Marvin felt sick.

"I've seen many cruel things, before and since, but that was one of the worst," Marvin says. It was not long until Marvin himself owed money to the Luppinos. He was behind in his mortgage payments.

"I really liked Old Man Giacomo. He was a tremendous man," Marvin says. "I used his weakness to my advantage and that was children. He loved children. Family was very important to him. I went there on a Sunday and I had one daughter holding one hand and the other daughter in the other and Giacomo was there raking the lawn and working in his garden. There was the big boss of the mob, out raking the leaves in his yard, wearing an old grey sweater and a felt hat. And Mrs. Luppino came out with cookies for the kids. I said all I needed was three months when I didn't have to make payments and then I could sort it all out. Luppino said he would agree if he got a kiss on the cheek from my kids. My two little girls go up and they each gave him a kiss on the cheek, one of the girls on each side. He said he'd give me six month's break. I'd asked for three but he said he'd give me six months, three for each kiss.

"I always came away with what I needed from him when I came with my kids."

CHAPTER 17

VANCOUVER, 1970

Harold "Harry the Hat" Walker didn't wear a lot of hats. He got the nickname because he shared a name with a well-known baseball player who was called Harry the Hat for his tic of adjusting his hat between pitches. Unlike his famous namesake, this Harry the Hat owed $5,000 to Roy Pasquale.

Harry the Hat was moving from Toronto to Vancouver, but because he had been a good customer and come to Roy to tell him he was relocating for a better job, Roy was OK with it. Harry the Hat gave Roy his new phone number and headed west. Roy kept in touch, but his confidence slipped. Roy called Harry and said his money was due; he needed it paid in full. Harry, a model of frankness, explained his dilemma: he had the money but was involved in a deal in Vancouver and owed the same amount to a loan shark there. The man trying to collect the cash in Vancouver was Les Irwin.

Roy knew Les from the old neighbourhood. So did Marvin. Les was the boy who had got Marvin involved in the grocery-store burglaries. Roy and Marvin also knew Les from boxing. Les had been a pro fighter before retiring from the ring, but he had not relaxed his fists. Like many ex-boxers with few skills other than a menacing look and a powerful punch, he went to work as a collector. Les boasted, "I'm an arm and leg man." And he was, with renowned proficiency at breaking one or the other and often both. He made his collections with a baseball bat—sliding the long bat's handle up the sleeve of his suit jacket and concealing the business end in a shopping bag carried in the same hand. But that's where any subtlety in his craft ended. He once strode into a busy bar, hauled a stock promoter from his stool and whipped out the bat, smashing the man's head, arms and legs. Collecting from small-time stock promoters was Les's specialty, and when the markets in Vancouver heated up, he saw his future in the west. Like most collectors, he was paid on commission. If he didn't retrieve the money, he didn't get any for himself. It kept him highly motivated.

"Les is out here and you're out there. You see my problem," Harry the Hat explained to Roy over the phone. Roy knew exactly what he meant. Les, potentially looming with his bat around any corner in Vancouver, posed more of a threat than Roy, as fearsome as he was, who was behind his desk in Toronto.

Roy asked around for Les Irwin's phone number and called him.

"I need you to lay off Harry the Hat," Roy told him.

Les laughed. Roy packed his bags.

* * *

Marvin and Roy took the train from Toronto to Vancouver. Marvin's ticket was paid for by Roy and he didn't mind the better part of a week sitting on a train, but he was curious why they didn't just fly. Roy mumbled something unconvincingly about the scenic route.

Once in Vancouver, on February 15, 1970, Roy borrowed a car from a friend and told Marvin to phone Les.

"When you get ahold of Les, don't let him know that I'm here," Roy said. "Tell him you're here alone and want to get together."

"Well, Roy," Marvin said, "I don't want you doing anything to Les." Marvin was still sentimental about the guy he had looked up to so long ago.

"I'm not going to. I'm just going to talk to him."

Marvin called up Les and said he was in Vancouver.

"Who did you come out with?" Les asked.

"I came by myself."

"What do you want to do, want to get together?"

"Yeah."

Les picked a spot to meet, a parking lot near the newly built Pacific Coliseum, the hockey arena in Hastings Park, and told Marvin to look for his dark brown Lincoln. When Marvin and Roy were getting into their borrowed car to head out, Marvin saw Roy had a long thin package in a shopping bag.

"What's that?" Marvin asked.

"It's a fishing rod I'm giving Les as a gift, a peace offering."

Marvin pulled into the parking lot and spotted the Lincoln. Roy told Marvin to go over and tell Les that he had come with him, that he came in peace. Marvin joined Les in his car. After greetings, Marvin broke the news.

"Listen, Les, Roy is in the car."

"You didn't tell me."

"Well, he told me not to. But he came out to make peace with you so that you two can work together and you get your money for collecting from this guy and Roy gets his, too. You can both win. And to prove his good faith, he brought you a gift. He brought you a fishing rod."

"Oh, OK," said Les.

"I'll go get him."

As Les sat in his car, windows open, Marvin returned to Roy's car and told him Les was waiting. Roy handed the shopping bag to Marvin.

"Bring it."

At the Lincoln, Marvin did the introductions, "Les, you know Roy. Roy, Les."

"Hand me that," Roy said, motioning to the bag in Marvin's hands. "And go back to the car."

* * *

Marvin was walking back to Roy's car when he heard the bang. He ducked instinctively and twisted around. He couldn't see Les, but Roy was barrelling back toward Marvin and the car, holding a sawed-off shotgun in his hands, stuffing it back in the bag as he strode.

"What the hell happened?" Marvin shouted.

"It doesn't matter what happened."

"You said it was a fishing rod."

"I made a mistake."

Two things happened the next day. Harry the Hat showed up at their room in the Hotel Vancouver and paid Roy his money. Then Marvin and Roy headed to the airport for a flight back to Toronto. Marvin realized why they had taken the train out to Vancouver: Roy didn't want to risk taking a shotgun onto a plane. A few days later, they read about a body being found in a Lincoln, most of his head blown off by the force of a shotgun blast. No one was ever arrested.

"I suffered with it a lot. I soul-searched about it a lot over the years," Marvin says. "But nobody ever spoke to us about it."

* * *

Two years after that nasty business in Vancouver, Marvin was back in the city. He had been having second thoughts about his boxing career. With every match, it was becoming clearer that he wasn't going to be a contender. He saw the toll it was taking on his health, and he wasn't making much money from it, either.

But when the wealthy and colourful Vancouver stock dealer and mining maverick Murray Pezim, a manic self-promoter who claimed he had discovered more gold than anyone else in history but detested gold jewellery and refused to wear it, tried to get Marvin back in the ring to fight a boxer Pezim was backing, the offer was too tempting. Pezim rarely took no for an answer. The son of a Toronto bootlegger wanted his boxer to rack up some wins against veteran boxers before moving up to bigger fights. Pezim usually had a lot of money, or the promise of a lot of money, behind anything he did, such as when he bought the B.C. Lions in 1989, when the Canadian Football League team was floundering.

Pezim offered Marvin $1,000 for the fight.

"It's not worth getting my head knocked off for a grand," Marvin said.

Pezim offered $2,000.

"Still not worth it."

Pezim went to $3,000, more than Marvin had ever made in the ring before.

"I'll see you there," Marvin said.

Marvin pulled on his gloves and donned his robe for the last time. Hennie and their daughters travelled to Vancouver to watch, although Hennie was against him taking the fight.

Marvin needed the money, so he took the match, but it was going to be a walk for his opponent. The bookies were giving eight-to-one odds against Marvin. As he prepared for the fight, Marvin told his plight to boxing pal and former world champ Jake LaMotta. Marvin had known LaMotta for years. In fact, LaMotta had been fighting on the same Miami card when Marvin was paid to take a dive by Meyer Lansky. He was one of the boxers who stood outside the dressing room as Marvin chatted with the famous gangster. LaMotta had won the world middleweight boxing title in 1949 by beating Frenchman Marcel Cerdan. He had been given the chance to challenge Cerdan by agreeing to take a dive in a fight against Billy Fox a few years earlier. LaMotta had published his memoir, *Raging Bull*, at the time of his conversation with Marvin in 1972, but had not yet been portrayed by Robert De Niro in the film of the same name.

LaMotta told Marvin his opponent would be overconfident. Maybe Marvin could try the possum trick: falling against the ropes, making like he is finished, hoping his opponent drops his gloves to come in for the knockout. It might make him vulnerable to a surprise attack.

In the ring, Marvin tried his best to beat his opponent but it wasn't going well. He lost each of the first seven rounds of the 10-rounder. Four times, Marvin had to pick himself up off the floor, each time asking himself why he didn't just stay down. In the eighth round, Marvin decided to try LaMotta's trick, and if it failed, he'd just drop and stay down. Marvin was caught by a right and fell backwards, struggling. He stumbled into the ropes, his head rolling and arms dropping. Just as LaMotta had surmised, the boxer moved in, dropping his gloves, ready for a triumphant knockout.

With his own gloves down, Marvin had no defence. He cleared his head enough to time things right, then threw his left hook, by far his best punch, catching him in the right eye. If his opponent had gone down, he would have recovered and still won the match by decision. Instead, he remained on his feet, stumbling to recover his balance by waving his arms. Marvin smelled blood, this time not his own. He had a clear shot at his head and aimed a right uppercut. He started low, right from his knees, driving up—not at his jaw—but at his Adam's apple. His opponent was down and out. They gave him the 10-count but they might as well have counted to a thousand.

It was an unexpected win. The fighter and Pezim immediately wanted a rematch. Marvin said sure, five thousand dollars and he would be there. The poor fighter couldn't find anyone, not even Pezim, to offer that much money for Marvin to climb into the ring. He begged, threatened and pestered for a rematch, but Marvin refused.

"Me winning was a fluke," Marvin says. "If we had the rematch, I think he would have destroyed me. That seemed to me like a good time to quit. I wanted to end on a high note. I ended with a win."

Sometime later, Marvin was talking about the match with LaMotta and George Chuvalo, the Canadian heavyweight champ who had twice faced Muhammad Ali without being knocked off his feet. Marvin told LaMotta how his last opponent was demanding a rematch. LaMotta said he understood. After LaMotta had taken the world title from Cerdan, the Frenchman had also demanded a rematch. The fight was scheduled, but on the way to America Cerdan's Air France flight crashed in the Azores, killing everyone on board. LaMotta said he was sad for Cerdan that he didn't get his rematch.

"But," he said, signalling skyward, "he's up there waiting for me."

"Well, if he's up there," Marvin said laughing, "I guess you'll never have that rematch." Marvin was cracking up at his zinger, but LaMotta wasn't amused. He got up and walked away. Chuvalo told Marvin to apologize.

* * *

Although he had left the ring, Marvin still rattled around with Roy, which meant he made little progress in life. By 1977, he was restless. When he was offered a well-paying job in Calgary, he took it. It was a straight job, too, although it was considered a plus if applicants could handle themselves and have a thick skin. Cadillac Fairview, one of Canada's largest retail property developers, was involved in a new joint venture in Calgary. The company wanted someone at the job site who would look out for its interests.

"In other words, someone to make sure that when the lumber arrived it stayed on that job site and did not go to other jobs being done by the other company," Marvin says. "And I got that job. It was a good job. They gave me an apartment in Calgary and a car. So much of my salary went right into the bank in Toronto for Hennie. It was a good deal. The contract was for a year. The only thing wrong with the job, and I was OK with it, was that the people at the other company labelled me a spy— which I was—so on the job site nobody would talk to me. I ate breakfast alone, lunch alone, nobody ever talked to me."

It was another step toward Marvin's destiny. He was hired as a corporate watchdog, a spy, someone regarded as a fink.

Before heading to Calgary, Marvin wanted to leave some money behind for Hennie, but he had none. Marvin told Roy there was a house for sale in his neighbourhood that was easily worth $35,000, but, he said, he had an in and Roy could buy it for $22,000. Roy drove past the place, gave it the once over, saw the For Sale sign out front and went back to Marvin.

"You're sure you can get it for twenty-two thousand?"

"Yes, I'm sure. I got an in, it's a Jewish guy. I got to give him a deposit, though, five grand, and it has to be under the table." Roy liked crooked deals. He gave Marvin $5,000 to make the deposit. Marvin put most of it in the bank for Hennie and flew to Calgary the next day with the rest. Marvin phoned Roy when he was 1,700 miles away to let him know he had nothing to do with the house. But don't worry, he said, he would pay him back.

"What are you talking about?"

"The only thing true about the deal is that the house is for sale. It still is," Marvin said, laughing nervously. The fact that Roy had killed over the same amount didn't seem to worry him.

Roy went crazy. "Where are you?"

"I'm not going to tell you."

"When are you coming back?"

"I signed a year's contract."

"Here's what you're going to do. When you come back, I want the money and I want interest on the money. I want ten thousand the day you come back."

"I'll give you seven," countered Marvin. They settled on $7,500.

"And," Roy said, before hanging up, "I want you to phone me every week."

Marvin knew he would have the money when he got back. In the meantime, he and Hennie had a buffer in the bank, a rarity. And he did call Roy, every Sunday. He checked in as a debtor and caught up on the gossip as a foster brother. Sometimes when Marvin phoned, Roy's son, Little Roy, would answer. One Sunday, Marvin made his regular call to Roy. Marvin was at a party in Calgary. It was noisy and he had been drinking. The guy who answered wasn't Roy, so Marvin told the boy to get his dad.

"I can't," the boy said.

"Why not? Where's your dad?"

"He died."

Marvin was stunned. He put down the phone, then turned to everybody at the party and called out, "Hey! My foster brother died. It's celebration time!" Not only was he free of Roy, he wouldn't have to pay back Roy's money. It was a night to celebrate and Marvin was good at that.

The next morning, Hennie called.

"Marvin, will you call Roy? He's called here twice. You were supposed to phone him yesterday."

"I don't have to, honey. Roy's dead."

"Dead? I just hung up on him five minutes ago," Hennie said.

Marvin was devastated. In his drunken state he had mis-dialled Roy's number and hadn't noticed that it wasn't Little Roy who answered. He started to really feel his hangover.

Marvin worked through his contract in Calgary, desperately lonely and aching to return to his family and city. When he finally came home, he had more than enough money to pay back Roy, with the interest, and he found a new gig, one that didn't involve his foster brother.

CHAPTER 18

TORONTO, 1978

Baldy Chard asked Marvin to stop the car outside Toronto police headquarters. Marvin was driving his partner in the collection business. Howard Chard, known as Baldy, was hailed for decades as one of the toughest men in Canada and was certainly one of the most feared. He seemed not to feel pain. You could hit him with a sledgehammer, people said, and he might flinch. Baldy was five foot ten and topped 300 pounds, with a build such that his suits needed custom tailoring to cover his odd dimensions. In the boxing ring, he was known for his strength and ability to withstand punishment. Outside the ring, ungloved and unrestrained, he inspired fear even among Mafia bosses.

"What do you need at the cop shop?" Marvin asked.

"I have to see somebody. Just drop me at the front and wait."

That was good enough for Marvin. Although business partners in the gruelling work of enforcement and debt collection, the pair lived by a rule: Marvin didn't trust Baldy and Baldy didn't trust Marvin. They didn't demand too many answers of each other. It was what kept their bond strong for 15 challenging years. Marvin pulled his black Oldsmobile 98, a long boat of a car, to the front of police headquarters on Jarvis Street.

"Keep it running. I'll be right back," Baldy said.

Inside, Baldy asked for Inspector Jimmy Morgan who, shortly before, had searched Baldy's house and got into an argument with the fighter's wife. During the fracas the woman grabbed a kitchen knife and waved it about. As Baldy waited, patrol officers flittered in and out and cops worked behind desks answering questions from the public. When Morgan came down he asked Baldy what he wanted. Without a word, Baldy punched him in the head.

Outside, waiting in the car, Marvin was oblivious. Then he heard a commotion. He looked up to see Baldy running. Baldy's fists were always faster than his legs. Bursting out of the station behind him were six shouting cops, their faces contorted in anger, their batons raised and waving. Marvin checked that his car door was unlocked and got ready to whisk Baldy away. But the cops were gaining with every step. Marvin waited a few seconds more. Baldy wasn't going to make it. Marvin slipped his foot off the brake and gently pulled away from the curb, looking in his rear-view mirror. Behind him he saw Baldy go down, disappearing beneath a heap of blue, with black batons thrashing up and down.

* * *

Detective Morgan was not the first copper Baldy hurt. When he was 18, Baldy had tussled with an officer in Toronto's Regent Park; by the time the fight was over, each man had a bullet in him. Baldy was found guilty of wounding. At the time of that brawl, he had just been released from reform school, having served his sentence for a crime that made front-page news in 1940: Baldy and a friend had broken into the house of an elderly widow during the night and violently snatched her life savings, which she kept wrapped in a stocking around her waist. The woman had no trust in banks and had squirrelled her money away for more than 40 years. But it took less than two weeks for Baldy to squander his half of the $2,500 on booze, gambling and a second-hand car. His buddy was caught using the outdated banknotes—some so old they were issued by the Bank of British North America and were almost a foot in length—at a downtown bar.

Baldy had then looked to vent his aggression in more acceptable venues. One day he walked into a boxing match and demanded that he be allowed to fight. The promoter threw him in the ring cold, and Baldy pummelled an established fighter.

"I'll fight anyone," he declared, when presented to the boxing press. "I am always in street fights. I don't know how it happens, but I'm fighting since I was knee-high to a goat."

Baldy's career stumbled when he got too close to the mobsters and bookies. In 1948, when he was the odds-on favourite to win a heavyweight bout at MacArthur Stadium in Syracuse, New York, he dropped to the canvas after only a minute and 55 seconds. Outraged spectators jeered; nobody, not even his opponent, saw Baldy take a single hit. It was a rigged match that ruined his legitimate career. But he soldiered on, sometimes earning extra money by fighting in unsanctioned bare-knuckle fights. He was Marvin's kind of guy.

* * *

Marvin tried to collect $10 from everyone entering Joey Bagnato's Toronto gym on Easter Sunday, 1965, but it was hard, given some of the rogues slinking in. Baldy Chard and former British Empire heavyweight champion James J. Parker were both tough fighters who had left the ranks of professional boxing but lost none of their testosterone. They disliked each other and, after an argument in a Toronto bar, agreed to settle it, not so much as gentlemen, but as gladiators. A secret winner-takes-all bare-knuckle showdown was arranged.

It was a thrilling prospect that such notorious tough guys were going to go at it in the ring, governed by only the rudimentary rules of no eye-gouging, biting or kicking. Among the 88 people who got in before the gym's steel door was locked was Johnny Papalia. He was joined by other mobsters, gamblers, rounders and well-connected fight fans, not all of whom could be coaxed out of their ticket money by Marvin.

"There were not supposed to be any freebies because the winner was to take it all. There were eighty-eight people there and it was supposed to be a sawbuck apiece but I only collected eight hundred dollars," Marvin says.

Before the match, the two fighters pulled Marvin aside.

"Where's the money?" they demanded. Neither wanted to suffer in the ring while Marvin made off with the cash.

"It's right here, I got it."

Baldy grabbed it from Marvin, counted it and put it in his back pocket.

"What do you think you're doing?" Parker protested.

"If you beat me, you can have the privilege of taking it out of my back pocket," Baldy said.

The difference between Baldy's and Parker's styles was clear. Baldy climbed into the ring in his street clothes, Parker in his boxing trunks and robe. At one point during the fight, the frenzied crowd got too close and someone in Parker's entourage jumped up, waving a gun, to keep people back. He was disarmed by another ex-heavyweight in the crowd.

"Baldy won the fight and the eight hundred dollars never left his pocket," Marvin says.

Parker later offered this assessment: "I had no respect for Baldy. He was a pimp and a stoolie and a bully. But he might have been the toughest guy in the world."

The fight was an instant legend and is still talked about in fight circles, usually with embellishment. So much so that, 36 years later, there was still disagreement over how much money Marvin collected at the door. At a charity boxing event, Parker, reduced to speaking in a whisper because of ill health, said—perhaps jokingly—"Marvin didn't turn in all the money."

Marvin laughed uproariously.

"That's a good laugh, because can you see those two guys, two of the biggest, toughest heavyweights, letting me keep their money?"

Maybe. It is the kind of legend that made Marvin stick out.

Marvin was quick to realize the perfect symmetry of a partnership with Baldy. Marvin had the mouth and Baldy the fists. As Baldy collected titles that meant something on the street—heavyweight champ of Kingston Penitentiary; street-fighting champion of Ontario; toughest bouncer in Toronto—Marvin collected Baldy. As he had done with his foster brother Roy and his reform-school buddy Cavanagh, Marvin always wanted to be with the toughest guy around.

He picked Baldy.

* * *

Marvin and Baldy rented themselves out to people who appreciated their talents. Their clients were typically loan sharks and bookies who hired them to chase down street debts, the kind that can't be collected through the courts.

"We didn't usually bother much with straight people because we didn't want to deal with people that would call the cops," Marvin says. "We liked people who were scared to get the police involved, people who are shady to begin with or have other problems besides just us."

When Marvin and Baldy confronted deadbeat debtors, the threat of bodily harm was clear, but unspoken. Usually, Baldy wouldn't have to use his hammer fists, nor Marvin his left hook.

"I tried very hard not to," Marvin says. "One of the big parts of our success was hardly ever—hardly ever—did we have to do anything to anybody."

Once, Marvin and Baldy tried to expand their business and hired another pair of fists. Benny "Red" Randell was raised in the dreary clouds of the Nova Scotia coke ovens and saw his fists as his only way out of poverty. Randell was instantly recognizable, with a handlebar moustache and hair of such a flaming red that he looked like Yosemite Sam from the old Warner Bros. cartoons. He once went the distance against Willie Pep, a former world featherweight champion. In 1978, he had a private match against the much younger and bigger Toronto Maple Leafs enforcer Dave "Tiger" Williams, after the two had an argument at Lansdowne Boxing Club. Tiger was knocked out in the first round. But so many years of stopping right hooks with his head had taken its toll on Randell's left temporal lobe and, forced from the ring, he needed a job. Marvin wanted to help him. The trouble was Randell was caustic and unpleasant much of the time and uncontrollably angry the rest. He often complained to Marvin that he didn't make him take his medication, to which Marvin would reply, "What am I, Florence Nightingale?" In the 1990s, Randell campaigned for help for brain-damaged boxers. As if to prove the need, he took to dumping the feces from his 170-pound Newfoundland dog at the home of the then-premier, Bob Rae:

on his doorstep, his lawn and over his wife's car. The ex-fighter was dubbed a "poo-gilist." Marvin found that Randell was no better suited to the collection business than to being a lobbyist; both require too much diplomacy.

On Randell's first and last job with Marvin and Baldy, the trio visited the debtor and, as they usually did, quickly settled the bill. As Marvin and Baldy were about to leave, they heard screaming. Randell was beating the guy up.

"What the hell are you doing, Red? He paid us already," Marvin implored.

"This is so he'll know for next time," Randell said. Marvin dropped him from the team.

The setback with Randell notwithstanding, Marvin and Baldy built a reputation on the street as a renowned collection team. Their success was noted by Frank Barbetta, a staff superintendent with the Toronto police.

"Best collection team I ever ran into: Elkind and Chard. One guy makes the threats and the other looks like he can carry them out," Barbetta once declared. It was a wry assessment from the savvy cop. That was exactly how things worked. Few people could say no to Marvin; even fewer when Baldy was within swinging distance.

Although no longer pro fighters, the pair remained rooted in the roughneck world of boxing.

* * *

George Chuvalo, dressed in a brown suit with a tan tie, sat at a paint-chipped table in the corner of Lansdowne Boxing Club, the walls behind him covered from floor to ceiling with boxing posters. Beside him was Charles "Spider" Jones, former three-time Golden Gloves champion.

"Hello, boxing fans, I'm George Chuvalo. Welcome once again to *Famous Knockouts*," he said, as he introduced another episode of his syndicated boxing television series. "And here to help me with the show, as usual, is a former boxer," he continued, setting up one of the wisecracks that were a hallmark of the program, "a man who made a lot of noise in fight circles—when his body hit the canvas."

"I want to ask you a personal question," Spider retorted. "George, how would you best describe your fight style?"

"I have to say, Charles, that I asked no quarter and I gave no quarter."

"Yeah," said Spider, theatrically rolling his eyes to the camera, "I know a lot of bellhops could testify to that."

The slapstick and jokes were a prelude to the main event: the former champs setting up a reshowing of a boxing classic, Rocky Marciano's 1955 title bout against Archie Moore. From 1983 to 1986, *Famous Knockouts* followed this format, with jibes, jokes, skits and even songs in between replays of classic fights. In some of those skits, Marvin made an appearance in the role of the quintessential hustler. Wearing a fedora and smoking a cigar, he would be seen playing cards or running a dice game and generally looking shady. Whenever Marvin's character was onscreen, he was introduced as "The Weasel." At the end of the show, Spider would pretend to go into a panic, patting his pockets.

"Hey! My wallet's gone," he announced.

"And so is The Weasel," said Chuvalo.

The name stuck. So perfectly did it fit the persona Marvin had carved out for himself in his rogue's gallery world, it was impossible not to use it. The weasel, as a breed, is a small, active predator with short, scurrying legs and a thick neck. An omnivore, the weasel has a reputation for cleverness and guile and, when cornered, can be ferocious. A group of weasels is called a sneak.

Chuvalo and Spider didn't think the name out quite so academically. In their world, a weasel was a cunning, sneaky person, someone who is ambiguous on purpose. Someone like Marvin.

"The name was given to me as a character in the skit but also for the fact of my reputation for working both sides of the street," Marvin says. "This was before I worked for the government, just that I was willing to work for anyone who paid me. That, and the fact that I was known for talking my way into trouble and talking my way out of trouble." He embraced the nickname, dismissing the unflattering connotations.

"In the fight game, it did me a lot of good. At fights, when I went to watch big matches, I would be introduced in the audience by the announcer who would say 'We lovingly call him The Weasel.' People remember it. People like it. It's definitely been to my advantage.

"My family don't like it, but they don't like my lifestyle, either. They begged me and begged me and begged me to change my last name. I said I would if they gave me a few bucks. They didn't, so I never did."

From Marvin Elkind to Baby Face Nelson; Mario Pasquale back to Marvin Elkind. And then The Weasel.

Just as "Baldy" was better than "Howard," "The Weasel" was more memorable than "Marvin." Nobody could have known then—most of all not Marvin—that in short order the name would become perversely, deliciously appropriate. In the years to come, when The Weasel had real reason to fear, Baldy remained oblivious to it all and would inadvertently act as his protector.

* * *

The Weasel and Baldy were heading back to Toronto from London, Ontario, one evening in 1980, after successfully closing a large account, a $12,000 gambling debt from a dentist. They had confronted him at his office and the frightened dentist had told them to come back in two hours. When the pair returned, the dentist wasn't there.

"He's left for the day. He wasn't feeling well," the receptionist told Marvin. "But he left this for you." She handed over a large envelope bulging with money. Marvin and Baldy's end was half.

"All right, we can take it easy for a few weeks," Marvin said as he drove back to Toronto.

Baldy leaned back in the passenger seat and sighed: "You know, Marv, nobody has as great a life as you and me."

Marvin was incredulous. "Are you crazy?"

"Marv, look, we just got three Gs each, it wasn't too hard, we can take it easy for a while now. This is the good life."

"What's the matter with you?" Marvin said. "Everybody hates us, we got the cops looking at us all the time, we got people looking at us like we're bad guys, we got people we gotta see that when we walk in their door we never know if they're going to greet us with a twelve-gauge or a baseball bat. We never know what they're going to do when they find out we're looking for them. Anything could happen."

Baldy sighed contentedly.

"That's what makes it so terrific."

While Baldy thought he had the best job in the world, Marvin hated almost every minute of it.

"Why did I stick with it? I had hardly any education. I didn't have any real skills. I had a problem since I was a kid, trouble concentrating. But here I was, able to put a roof over my family's heads, educate my two daughters, do everything I had to do, send them to summer camp, everything that had to be done as a father and husband. I supported them, I can't say in fine style, but in proper style. They always had the clothes they needed, the food they needed and the money to go where they needed. I could not see myself making enough money for that in any other way. But I hated the business and that's a fact."

But with Marvin now moving into middle age, there had to be an easier way to make a living.

CHAPTER 19

TORONTO, 1980

As police rushed through the front door of the swank apartment, unlocked by the building's superintendent, the surprised man inside dived past his expensive furnishings into the kitchen. Wearing only his underwear, he was stopped by the officers as he crouched, a loaded 12-gauge shotgun at the tip of his outstretched hand. Two Toronto police sergeants had come to apartment 806 at 31 Alexander Street, behind Maple Leaf Gardens, on September 1, 1980, with an arrest warrant for fraud conspiracy against Neil Cameron Proverbs.

The Labour Day raid led by Sergeant George Reynolds was routine police work as officers responded to a complaint against the 45-year-old stock promoter for swindling close to a million dollars from a prominent Toronto family. Proverbs's arrest was only the start of a long, painful journey.

When Marvin, at the age of 46, stuck his nose into the matter, he cast a jinx over everyone and everything. As events twisted and turned over the next three years, the arrest would ripple into public outrage, a policing scandal and a political headache. Lives and careers would be ruined. It would thrust Marvin uneasily into the spotlight, landing his name, grinning face and clumsy scheming onto the front pages of the nation's newspapers. But it would also play a pivotal role in his remarkable transformation. The Proverbs case was, in the words of the *Toronto Star*, a sensational story that "even in the realm of fiction would have seemed bizarre." And the paper didn't even know the full story.

* * *

Neil Cameron Proverbs, the son of a prominent businessman and a graceful society mother, was a talented athlete as a youth but took too keen an interest in the shady side of life. In 1957, when Toronto police formed a new morality squad to clamp down on gambling, the first raid they conducted was on a floating dice game. Money went flying as customers scrambled to pocket their winnings before being arrested. Among them was 22-year-old Neil Proverbs.

As Proverbs grew older, he melded the street smarts of his wayward youth with the corporate skills gleaned from his father, which allowed him to mix with a better calibre of victim than most con men. He described himself as a stockbroker, but those who knew his business called him a "stock hustler." He wore alligator shoes with his fine suits and was known at the city's best restaurants. But it was only his face the restaurateurs recognized because each maître d' seemed to know him by a different name. To one, he was Mr. Palmer, to another, Mr. Nelson, and Mr. Davis, and so on. When he paid a bill, it was always with cash.

"Proverbs was a very, very, very, very—and I can't say enough verys—smooth con man," Marvin says. "He dressed like he just stepped out of a fashion magazine and he spoke well. Because he came from a well-to-do family, he had tremendous contacts."

* * *

Marvin says the root of Neil Proverbs's trouble was a swindle the con man strung together around the idea of a chain of drive-through variety stores. Proverbs knew there was an easier way to make a profit than the costly venture of building stores. He met with the son of a successful businessman. Proverbs told him that they would take the company public, selling shares on the stock market, but never actually open a store. To raise the price of the shares, the company would issue press releases that made it appear it was really going places, and then Proverbs and the scion would sell before the trickery was discovered.

"His biggest ambition was always to make money on his own," Marvin says of the businessman. "Everything he ever had before was what his father gave him. I always said that there is one thing about him I always liked: he's the one guy in the world dumber than me."

The businessman gave Proverbs $800,000 to invest in the plan, and then . . . nothing happened, Marvin says. He called the police. After reviewing the matter, police issued an arrest warrant for Proverbs, but no one knew where to find him. Proverbs was always careful, even paranoid. He registered his apartment and car under aliases, refused to have a phone in his home and often imagined he was being followed. Officers caught a lucky break when they spotted him driving downtown. They followed him home, then asked the superintendent which apartment belonged to Neil Proverbs. The super said there was nobody there with that name. Police showed him a photograph.

"That's Nelson Palmer," said the super, giving the name by which he knew Proverbs. Police asked him to let them into the apartment. It was then that the officers stormed through the door and Proverbs reached for his shotgun.

After the arrest, a more careful look at the bogus drive-through deal suggested that the investor might not be the clean-hands victim he portrayed himself as. Evidence mounted that he had known of Proverbs's plan to pump the stock before they dumped it. The investor, however, was related to a powerful government minister and whether at the politician's request or out of cautious courtesy, fraud charges against Proverbs—and any investigation of the investors along with it—were dropped. (Officials later said the charges were dropped because of a lack of evidence after their search of Proverbs's apartment turned up no incriminating documents.)

The cops who had chased down Proverbs were disappointed. If they couldn't proceed with fraud charges, then the gun was what they were left with. As the fraud charge was withdrawn, a gun possession charge was filed.

Then in walked Marvin.

"Even before I was a fink, I had friends on the cops' side. I didn't fink, but I had friends there mainly because of boxing," Marvin says. One night at the fights, Proverbs told Marvin about his legal woes. Proverbs was what Marvin liked to see—a rich guy with a problem. Marvin said he would help, but he needed $4,000 to give to the cops and another grand for himself. If he succeeded in getting the gun charge dropped, the price would double, he said.

Proverbs was intrigued.

* * *

Marvin was giddy when he stuffed the $5,000 from Proverbs in his pocket. At the time, it seemed the easiest score he had made, although, in hindsight, it may have been the hardest.

Marvin didn't offer to share any of the cash with the cops. He did, however, approach a friend on the force.

Pat Kelly was a tough cop on the holdup squad, a tight-knit crew of rough-and-tumble coppers who often scared crooks into going straight—or at least into taking their schemes to a neighbouring jurisdiction. It was thanks to the holdup squad that Toronto was never plagued with the same level of bank banditry as Montreal, which was notorious for its heists. Kelly was known as the toughest cop in Ontario. In his spare time he was a boxer, and had sparred with Chuvalo.

"I knew Pat Kelly quite well from boxing," Marvin recalls. "We became good friends. One time he needed an air conditioner for his house and I got him a hot one for nothing. Just to be his buddy. It never hurts to have a cop owe you something, but I also liked the guy."

Kelly put Marvin in touch with Sergeant Reynolds, the officer handling the Proverbs case. Marvin introduced himself at the police station, saying he was a close friend of Roy McMurtry, the attorney general of Ontario. Reynolds said he was willing to meet with Proverbs if he had information to share on other crimes. That was a time-tested way to recruit finks, offering crooks a chance to save themselves by turning someone else in. In underworld lingo, it's called "body trading." Marvin arranged a meeting at the Royal York Hotel between Proverbs, Reynolds and his police partner, William Bullied.

After introductions, Proverbs asked to be alone with the cops.

"I have a lot of stuff to give, but Marvin can't be around for it," he said.

"Marvin, take a walk," said Reynolds.

Later, Proverbs told Marvin the meeting had gone nowhere. Marvin asked Reynolds the same question and got the same answer. Proverbs, the cop said, had wanted them to go into the hotel's steam room where they would all get naked so he knew there weren't hidden recorders. The cops didn't go for it.

Three months later, Reynolds called him, Marvin says.

"Marvin, I'd like to get together again with Neil Proverbs to see if we can do anything on this, maybe we can start over." The next night, Marvin spotted Proverbs at a boxing match and passed along the message. What Marvin didn't know was that in the intervening time, Proverbs's gun charge had gone to court for a preliminary hearing. Proverbs was upset by what he heard from the stand. Some of the officers, he felt, were skewing evidence against him. His paranoid and conniving mind came up with an outrageous plan to fight back.

CHAPTER 20

TORONTO, 1981

"You're looking here at a combined thirty-seven years of successful lying," said police Sergeant George Reynolds, sitting with his partner, Sergeant William Bullied. He was talking to Neil Proverbs.

"We've tried to hone it to a profession," Bullied agreed.

The two cops, who had been on the force for a combined 37 years, were giggling and laughing their way through a delightful meal. Wine and liqueur glasses littered the table on November 2, 1981, at Capriccio Toscano, an Italian restaurant on Yonge Street, near Proverbs's apartment. Proverbs had invited the cops to dinner after Marvin reconnected them, and Proverbs was certainly paying for it.

It was not generosity behind the hospitality, but an outraged sense of injustice.

The loose talk by the cops came after Proverbs asked about police integrity. He had arranged the get-togethers on the pretext of trading information about a heroin deal in return for leniency on his gun charge. But talk of the drug deal had dwindled, and yet the dinners and luncheons continued. What came from Proverbs was not information but questions, lots of questions: about police, the justice system and how his case could be cooked in his favour. Every word, every bite and every sip was being captured on hidden video. It was all an elaborate reverse sting, the cops would later learn. This time, the crusading con man tricked the cops.

* * *

Proverbs knew the value of planning. First he splurged on meals at Capriccio Toscano. He became a regular, one who ordered large and tipped larger. He blew $10,000 on food and drink just to get him to step one of his scheme. It paid off. The warm relationship he built with the restaurateur meant he was granted his odd request to rig up one of the tables.

Proverbs hired a technician to wire the table near the back of Capriccio Toscano. A brighter light bulb was inserted above the table to make the action easier to capture. A microphone was hidden under the table, another overhead and a third beside the camera. The equipment was put through a few test runs, with the camera at first resting in a nearby wine rack before being set inside a speaker box across the dance floor from the table. To prepare his cover story, Proverbs then went to the library to read up on heroin, so he would sound like he really knew something about a supposed drug deal.

Proverbs, through Marvin, then invited the cops to dinner, although Marvin knew nothing about his plans to videotape the meetings. Proverbs called Marvin a "steer man," a con man's term for someone who steers a mark toward him.

The first meal with the cops was a lunch, on October 22, 1981. Reynolds arrived with Bullied and as the food and alcohol flowed the cops chatted recklessly. They were laughing at how tough and brutal some of their fellow officers were. As Reynolds enjoyed a Canadian Club whisky with ginger ale and cannelloni with mushroom sauce, he was barely able to finish a story for laughing so hard.

Reynolds and Bullied said officers on duty kept a knife or replica gun hidden in case they shot someone inappropriately. They could then toss the weapon under the body to claim self-defence. They laughed about the time one popular officer shot someone in error. Several detectives separately said they needed to examine the victim.

"When it came time to cart him away, there were five or six knives under his body," said Reynolds, giggling. Each of the cops had quietly stuck a weapon there to exonerate their friend, not realizing that others already had.

Proverbs then asked Reynolds if the testimony he had given at his preliminary hearing was slanted against him.

"Yeah," said Reynolds, tilting his hand in a diagonal motion, "sixty degrees to ninety degrees."

Reynolds also said that Marvin irritated him, and called him a "disturbing influence" in the case.

"If not for Marv, you might have been discharged," Reynolds laughed.

At their second meeting, a lunch on October 29, Proverbs probed deeper.

"A lot of people don't realize justice is for sale," he said.

"Oh, of course it is," the officer replied.

* * *

By their third meal, Proverbs had mastered the art of complimenting and cajoling the sergeants into telling more stories. He asked what would happen if someone crossed a police officer.

"You would make about four thousand enemies and it

wouldn't be safe for you to go out and buy a newspaper at night," Reynolds said.

Then Bullied told of how police operate in court.

"We do what has to be done," he said. "Let's be realistic about it: if we did it the way everything should be done, probably no one would ever get convicted."

Reynolds boasted of how easy it was to force a false confession, saying, "You don't have to be overly intelligent to realize that once you sign the paper, the pain stops."

Seven times, Proverbs brought the officers to the same table in the same restaurant: two lunches and five dinners. Each stretched for hours. Altogether, Proverbs would capture 37 hours of secret tape of the officers talking about fixed arrests, fabricated evidence and corruption. The police chief was "crooked"; the attorney general fixed trials; judges conspired with police to determine a sentence before evidence was heard, they said. They impugned officials by saying they engaged in drug use, corruption and incompetence. The way the cops spoke, the justice system in Ontario made Al Capone's Chicago seem a city of angels.

At their last dinner together, on January 5, 1982, they had steak, wine and Hennessy cognac while the officers suggested what Proverbs could say at his trial to "circumvent" the evidence. The cops suggested he testify that he was cleaning his gun in the kitchen and loaded it to test the mechanism. He was then interrupted by distressing news, Reynolds offered. He could say he had forgotten to unload and store the gun. Then, when officers came to arrest him, he had no idea it was cops at the door, he thought it was thugs, so he reached for the gun. Proverbs said he loved it.

As the meal ended and laughter faded, Proverbs became circumspect.

"Events can sometimes happen very rapidly," he mused aloud.

* * *

Proverbs edited the tapes himself, cutting a five-hour highlight reel. Soon after their last meal, he handed a copy to Bullied. The astonished sergeant passed it to Reynolds, who gave it to his boss, who submitted it to the internal affairs unit.

William McCormack, the head of internal affairs, launched a probe. He did not like what he heard and saw and, although he found nothing criminal, there was clear evidence of a breach of procedure. The tapes remained a secret for three months, until a source phoned John Kessel, a reporter at the *Toronto Star*.

"John, there's a man in town with fascinating videotape," the caller said.

Two months later, Kessel and colleagues had gathered enough material from sources to reveal the bare bones of the story, even though they couldn't track down Proverbs or see the videos.

On May 5, 1982, the mysterious "wine-and-dine" tapes made the front page of the *Star*, even as the Falkland Islands war claimed its first British casualties when an Argentine missile exploded into a destroyer in the South Atlantic. On May 17, during a short court appearance for Proverbs's gun charge, Kessel saw the man for the first time. The reporter followed him from court to the Sheraton Centre, walking parallel to him because Proverbs kept turning around to look behind him. In the hotel lobby, Proverbs made several phone calls, each from a different phone booth. He then stopped to talk to someone he obviously knew. After Proverbs left, Kessel gave the friend a note to pass along to Proverbs asking him to call. Weeks later, they finally met for dinner. Proverbs told Kessel what was on the tapes. Then Proverbs, a lawyer and the *Star* began negotiating. In the end, the paper was given a copy of the five-hour edited version of the tapes if they agreed not to publish a photograph of Proverbs—unless another newspaper did so first—and to cover his legal fees if a lawsuit was brought against him because of the tapes.

It was a beautiful scoop for the paper and, from then on, the *Star* covered the "wine-and-dine" tapes as if it were the moon landing.

Almost the full front page of the September 7 edition was devoted to the revelations, including a rare front-page editorial calling for an official inquiry. Another two full pages of details were inside. It was the lead story on the front the next day, too. And when Proverbs's trial started in November, hardly a day passed that month without the story appearing on the front page of one of the city's papers, usually all of them, no matter what happened around the world, even the death of long-time Soviet leader Leonid Brezhnev.

Publicity was intense. Questions were raised in parliament and several police investigations were launched. And throughout the flurry of reports, there were constant intriguing references to an unnamed intermediary who had somehow brought Proverbs and the cops together.

***

What the newspapers didn't know was that Proverbs had pulled one more stunt at his table at Capriccio Toscano before pulling the plug on his wiretapping enterprise.

Marvin was getting ready for a family dinner when Proverbs called him. He needed to see Marvin right away, it was urgent, he said. When Marvin objected, saying he had promised to have dinner with his family, Proverbs told him to bring them along, dinner was on him.

"You're on," said Marvin.

"I want you to enjoy yourself, so take a cab. I'll pay for the cab and I'll pay for your cab home, so you don't have to worry about drinking and driving," Proverbs said.

"I'll do that."

Proverbs greeted Marvin, Hennie and their daughters at the restaurant.

"Marvin, this is important stuff I have to talk to you about, so let's you and me sit over here and your family can enjoy themselves at another table without being bothered," he said, steering Marvin to his special table at the back.

The liquor and wine came and Marvin started sucking back as much as he could; Marvin's favourite brand was gratis. He was sloshed in no time, and Proverbs was asking him about the money he had given him to pass to the cops. Marvin blithely acknowledged it all with a laugh and a raised hand to order another round. He said he had all kinds of political connections and was pals with crooked cops. He said he gave the money to the investigators to grease the wheels of justice. Marvin, Hennie and their daughters, having enjoyed a great meal, thanked Proverbs and went home. A week later, Proverbs called Marvin to say they had to meet again. He explained what he had done, how he had met over and over again with Reynolds and Bullied and had it all on video. Marvin didn't believe him. Proverbs said he would prove it. He took Marvin to a video store where the equipment was set up in a back office. He pushed a tape into the machine. On TV were Proverbs and Marvin, sitting in Capriccio Toscano having the indiscreet conversation they had had the week before.

"I nearly had a heart attack," Marvin recalls.

Marvin went home and made a phone call to a friend in Calgary.

"Got any work for me out there?"

* * *

Every morning while hiding out in Calgary, Marvin left his hotel to buy a newspaper so he could keep track of the Proverbs story. In those days, the only Toronto paper he could buy out west was the *Globe and Mail*, and it arrived a day late. After Proverbs's trial started on November 2, 1982, he scoured the papers for any whisper of his name. So far, there were only oblique references to an "intermediary" or "middleman." With a story this hot, there was no way it could stay that way.

On November 5, when he picked up the previous day's *Globe*, he had no trouble finding the Proverbs story—a bold headline stretched across the entire top of the front page: "Evidence often untrue, policeman admits saying." Marvin got to the end of the front-page story on the courtroom confrontation between Reynolds and Proverbs. Although not a lawyer, Proverbs was conducting his own defence. Marvin turned the page to read the rest. There, near the bottom of the first column, was something approximating his name.

"Under questioning from Mr. Proverbs," the story read, "Sgt. Reynolds said the man, Murray Elkind, had described himself as a good friend of the Attorney-General." Marvin soon learned the other newspapers hadn't mangled his name.

He had finally been unmasked as the mystery man who started the whole mess.

CHAPTER 21

CALGARY, 1982

Marvin answered the knock at his hotel-room door without much concern. Almost nobody knew he was hiding in Calgary and few in this western city knew who he was, despite his name having appeared in the Toronto newspapers.

He was rattled to see Calgary police on the other side.

"Marvin Elkind?"

"Yeah."

"You're under arrest."

"What's it about?"

"Theft, fraud. Don't know much," the cop said. "All I know is there's a Canada-wide warrant for your arrest." Marvin couldn't have imagined the desperation of police facing the embarrassing wine-and-dine tapes. Someone had found an old arrest warrant for Marvin in the police computer, filed years ago by Ontario Provincial Police in Renfrew County, in the picturesque Ottawa Valley. Marvin remembered his judicial odyssey in Renfrew. It stemmed from a side business he would return to when he was short on cash, which was often: aluminum siding.

They called themselves "tin men," going door-to-door convincing homeowners to have aluminum siding installed. The more money they could talk out of customers, the more money they made. The siding deals were a scam. Sure, the work usually got done but the materials and workmanship were not top grade. Typically the homes didn't even need new siding in the first place. And despite what Marvin said on the doorstep, the homeowners were being woefully overcharged. There was no "special, one-time-only deal." Once customers turned over a deposit, there was nothing they could do to get it back. A couple of times Marvin got into trouble over it. Once, in the 1970s, Marvin and Tony Unitas, owner of the Newsboys Boxing Club in Toronto, went to Thunder Bay to blitz the city with doorstep propositions. The trip was a bust and they were ready to return. The day before they were to leave, they finally found a sucker. They quoted the woman $5,000 for a $15,000 siding job, but said to get that deal she needed to hand over a $1,000 deposit. As soon as they had the cash, they dashed to the airport. Three years later, Unitas was promoting a boxing match being sponsored by his gym. The woman in Thunder Bay recognized him on television as the man who had conned her, and she called the police. Unitas was arrested and quickly turned Marvin in to police. They made restitution and paid a fine.

The pinch in Renfrew had not been so dramatic. Police didn't even want to press ahead with charges. Instead, the investigator told Marvin he would forget about the arrest if he got out of town and didn't come back. It seemed a fair deal to Marvin, and he hadn't thought too much about Renfrew since. The unissued warrant, however, stayed on police books. A couple of times afterward, whenever he had a run-in with the law, police would see the warrant in the system and call Renfrew. The answer was always the same: "Will not return." Which meant that Renfrew police would not pay for his return to their jurisdiction to face the charge, so he was always let go. Now, working in tandem with Toronto police, Renfrew was determined to get their man. It was all a setup, of course. Renfrew cops were no more interested in pressing the charges of theft and intent to defraud than they were before. Police in Toronto were simply desperate to get their hands on Marvin, the man who had set their embarrassing scandal in motion—so much so that an OPP superintendent had been sent to Calgary to collect him. The "blue wall" was rising. Superintendent Fern Savage looked every inch a cop—tough, with a thin face. When he confronted Marvin in Calgary, he made no mention of Proverbs or the brouhaha unfolding in the Toronto court. He just said he was there to make a lawful arrest on a valid warrant. Marvin knew better. If the Renfrew cops wouldn't pay to have him driven from Toronto, they sure weren't going to pay for flights from Calgary.

* * *

At the airline check-in desk at Calgary airport, Savage and another cop identified themselves as law-enforcement officers and registered their handguns. The woman at the counter looked at Marvin.

"And does this gentleman have a gun also?" she asked. Marvin and the cops all laughed. No one said he was a prisoner. Marvin had no gun but he did have bags to check in. After his arrest, he had packed his luggage and checked out of the hotel. He had a couple of suitcases and a small carry-on bag. He wrote his name on all of the tags attached to each item and headed to his seat with his escorts. They squeezed into the seats of the small commercial plane, and as the crew and other passengers prepared for takeoff, Savage was surprised by an announcement.

"Would passenger Marvin Elkind please come to the front of the plane." Savage and his partner jumped up, thinking something was afoot. Savage told Marvin to stay in his seat and for the other cop to stick close to their prisoner while Savage went to the front to see what was up. A minute later he returned, carrying Marvin's carry-on bag. He had left it at the check-in counter.

Throughout the four-hour flight and half-hour's drive to an OPP office in Toronto, there was still no mention of Proverbs.

"We're going to the movies," Savage finally said, "but nobody is going to hold your hand." He took Marvin to a room where officers working on pornography cases watched seized tapes. On the screen, Marvin saw the video of him being wined and dined by Proverbs.

When it was over, Savage asked him, "What do you think?"

"That actor looks a lot like me," Marvin said.

Savage wasn't so tough that he couldn't enjoy a laugh, but he then pressed ahead.

"I can give you a lot of trouble on this charge you're facing. But I got options. Want to hear the options?"

"Yeah," Marvin said.

Savage could help Marvin with his Renfrew beef if he testified at the Proverbs trial, he said. Marvin was then grilled about his contact with Proverbs. By the time he was finished, it was the early morning and Marvin hadn't slept since the day before. It didn't take him long to decide what to do; he did what he could to help himself. After all, it was Proverbs who had forced him into this by wiring him up, he reasoned. Proverbs, in essence, finked on him first. A secretary came in and typed up Marvin's lengthy statement. Then a justice of the peace was called, and Marvin swore his statement was true.

But was it true? "Not really," Marvin says now.

Afterwards, Savage took Marvin home to drop off his luggage before the five-hour drive to Renfrew. Marvin spent a night in jail and, the next morning, nobody opposed his being released on bail. Another OPP officer came up to him the moment he was freed.

"Can I give you a lift back to Toronto?"

"No kidding, yes."

The cop didn't take him far. He drove him south to the next OPP detachment. He was told another officer would collect him for the rest of the journey. Marvin was in the detachment's kitchen making a pot of coffee when the second officer arrived. In walked Fern Savage.

"This is for you," Savage said, stuffing a folded sheet of paper into Marvin's hand.

It had a red embossed seal at the bottom and Marvin's name and address at the top, under the words "Criminal Subpoena." It clearly carried the full force of the law, issued in the name of "Elizabeth the Second, by the Grace of God of the United Kingdom, Canada and Her other Realms and Territories Queen, Head of the Commonwealth, Defender of the Faith. . . ." Marvin skimmed to the middle. He was "commanded" to attend court at 10 a.m. on November 9 to testify at the trial of Neil Cameron Proverbs.

* * *

When Marvin arrived at Toronto's imposing main courthouse as a surprise witness in one of the most sensational trials of the year, he wore a long beige overcoat and a big, impish grin. Reporters instantly loved him, describing him variously as a "pudgy, sometime boxing manager with a rapid manner of speaking," a "self-described political fixer," a "go-between" and "a self-confessed liar." Marvin was uncomfortable with the exposure but, he had to admit, he liked the attention.

Proverbs had been acting on his own behalf at his trial, amicably cross-examining Sergeant Reynolds and others. He was doing a decent job, but when Marvin appeared on the scene, Proverbs handed his defence over to David Humphrey, a prominent Toronto lawyer. On hearing the news that the renowned lawyer would face off against the mysterious witness, courtroom voyeurs started chattering. Everyone wanted to watch the high drama of Humphrey's evisceration of this dodgy shyster. There were murmurs of impatience when court broke for lunch before Marvin was called to the stand.

Marvin walked to a nearby hotel for lunch. There he downed two turkey sandwiches and three martinis. On his way back, he bumped into another leading lawyer in the city. Perhaps as a prank on Humphrey, the lawyer offered a bit of free advice.

"Listen to me, Marvin, everyone is talking about this. They say Humphrey is going to tear you apart. Remember this: don't let him catch you in a lie. If he catches you in a lie, you're finished. If he catches you in a single lie, your credibility is destroyed. Anything he asks you, he is going to have the answer and the proof of it behind his back, so once you say a lie, he'll have the proof right there and you're dead."

Marvin followed that advice almost to the letter, dodging one landmine after another as Humphrey tried to trip him up. His testimony was nothing less than brilliant. Marvin was in his element. He felt surprisingly relaxed, confident. The three martinis had settled him nicely but, with his tolerance for alcohol, had not made him drunk. His comic timing and quick wit had the court in stitches. Spectators sat enraptured from the opening exchange.

"Do you consider yourself a truthful man?" Humphrey asked Marvin.

"Under oath, counsel, I am an honest and truthful person," was Marvin's sharp reply, which allowed him to admit to being an audacious liar, but one who could now be believed because he was under oath. Humphrey then put things to Marvin that anyone would want to deny. Remembering the advice, though, Marvin admitted it all. His previous arrests, charges, past lies, lapses in judgment.

"Oh yeah, I did that," said Marvin. "Yup, that was me."

"Well, if you did all of that, then you must be a very low down, no good person," Humphrey said.

"Well, I never said I was perfect," said Marvin. The courtroom cracked up. Humphrey was getting frustrated. Asked if he was shocked when he was arrested in Calgary, Marvin answered, "I wasn't exactly shocked, due to the fact I read in the *Globe and Mail* a familiar name—mine."

After reading passages of Proverbs's and Marvin's videotaped conversation, in which Marvin suggested he had the cops practically on retainer, Humphrey asked if Marvin had "no pangs of conscience" during the exchange.

Marvin answered, "Due to the fact this conversation took place when I was heavily under the influence of alcohol, I didn't have any pangs of anything."

"When you were having these meetings with Neil Proverbs, then, and saying these things, how did you feel?"

"I felt terrific."

"Why?"

"Because I was drunk."

"So you say the devil made you do it?"

"Well, your client paid for the drinks, if you want to call your client the devil that's up to you." Again the courtroom burst out laughing.

Humphrey, trying to erode Marvin's credibility, noted that in Marvin's conversation with Proverbs, Proverbs had asked him if what he said was accurate, asking if, "Scout's honour," it was true.

"Thank God that's all he said—I was never a Scout," Marvin said, shooting a big grin. "It was this way, Dave," Marvin began in explanation.

"Don't call me Dave," Humphrey interrupted.

"Why, did you change your name?"

Marvin's frank, self-deprecating assessment of his failings won the court over. By admitting his many, many faults, it seemed he had no reason to lie about the other stuff, the stuff relevant to the case at hand. Marvin had a hard time concealing how much he was enjoying it. He couldn't stop smiling, often turning toward the spectators and flashing his apple cheeks.

Did Marvin take money from Proverbs? Absolutely. But, he said, "I know Sergeant Kelly well. I knew there was no way he would take the money and he'd probably kill me first," Marvin said, advancing the police position. Kelly agreed to put him in touch with Reynolds only if it was "one hundred per cent proper," Marvin said. From what he knew of Reynolds, he wouldn't take the money, either, he said. Marvin just squeezed some cash out of Proverbs, he testified.

Marvin admitted he had lied to Proverbs about almost everything.

"It was all a pack of lies," he said.

Marvin then told the court that the only time he had ever met the judge whom he had said was crooked was when, as an usher, he had escorted him to his seat at a public event.

As for Roy McMurtry, the attorney general Marvin claimed was his buddy, he had only met him during his election campaign. Humphrey asked why he would say such things about respected people.

"I didn't realize it was going to turn into a movie. I figured if he ever mentioned any of it, I'd just deny it. Who'd ever think of tapes and video?"

Who could argue with Marvin's assessment? Certainly not Reynolds and Bullied. Even Humphrey told court that the trial was so bizarre it would not be a surprise if the next witness were the Mad Hatter.

For his part, Reynolds stood in the witness box and apologized to those he had run through the mud. The stories, he said, were lies, meant "only as an investigative technique" to get close to Proverbs to learn about a supposed $90-million heroin deal arranged by one of the country's most prominent developers. He and his partner were acting, he said, masquerading as dirty cops to amuse and entertain Proverbs until he told them about the heroin.

With Proverbs lying to get the cops to come to the meetings and the cops saying they lied at the meetings to get Proverbs to talk, the fact that Marvin said he was lying, too, just fitted into the dubious nature of the entire affair. He looked no better or worse than any of them.

In the words of David Humphrey during his closing address: "The only credible testimony from Mr. Elkind was his name, and we can believe that only because they have his mug shot and fingerprints on file at the jail."

That line still makes Marvin laugh.

"Neil Proverbs and I were both con men," Marvin says. "The only difference was he shoots for millions and I nickel and dime."

CHAPTER 22

Stepping from the witness box, Marvin was sad his cross-examination was over. He was having fun. It gave him the adrenalin rush he loved. He walked out of the courtroom with all eyes on him, out the doors and into a private office where the prosecutors and cops were running their case. Inside was Superintendent Fern Savage.

"C'mere," Savage ordered.

Marvin walked over to him, not knowing what to expect. Savage had been so hard on him, Marvin braced for a punch. Instead, Savage gave him a bear hug. The other officers couldn't believe it. Savage wasn't known as an emotional man. Marvin's testimony had thrown the police a lifeline, both in fighting the embarrassment of the corruption allegations and pressing the gun charge.

Savage knew Marvin's testimony on a few key points could have gone one way or another. Savage had impressed upon Marvin the importance of whether Proverbs had known it was cops coming through his door when he reached for the shotgun. During his testimony, Marvin was asked whether Proverbs had ever mentioned that he thought it was crooks coming to get him and, once he realized it was police, was relieved. Marvin said no. In reality, Proverbs had said that very thing. His lie was a favour to the cops, and to himself, so he could avoid the Renfrew charges for which he would have faced five years in prison.

Savage couldn't stop admiring Marvin's job on the witness stand. He loved the way Marvin had stood up under pressure, a rare talent. He was impressed by Marvin's street smarts. He loved that Marvin was a well-known rounder, recognized by all kinds of bad guys stretching back decades. He loved that his connection to Roy Pasquale made him trusted by the Mafia; that his boxing connections made him known to young hoods; that his roots gave him access to the big Jewish gangsters and bookies; and that his connection to Corrigan took him places cops rarely got to see. Most of all, he loved that Marvin wasn't getting respect from the gangsters he worked for.

Marvin was known by all but beholden to none. Savage knew good informant material when he saw it. He loved almost everything about Marvin as a potential fink, although he never used that word. He also recognized the drawbacks. Marvin drank too much. He could be erratic. He was always desperate for money. And he was a bit of a tough guy who had dangerous friends. But Savage was so impressed by his potential that, right after Marvin's testimony, he phoned Detective-Constable Al Robinson in the OPP's Special Services.

* * *

"I want to buy you lunch," Savage said, when Marvin answered his phone the day after his Proverbs testimony.

"Why? You gonna arrest me for something?"

"I wouldn't buy you lunch if I was going to arrest you."

Marvin met Savage at the Village Station restaurant, where a string of old railcars were converted into a dining room. Savage didn't say why he wanted to meet him until after they had ordered drinks.

"Someone is coming for you to meet," Savage said, and Al Robinson, known as Robbie, seemed magically to appear.

"This is Robbie," Savage said. "He handles informants, and you're going to work for him." Robbie sat down. He explained a little about what he wanted.

"We'll have meetings every so often and chat, and anytime we do, anything you have to eat or drink is on me," Robbie said, playing to Marvin's weakness. Robbie had done his homework. Marvin, at that time, was a huge drinker and not a cheap one, with a fondness for Scotch. Marvin listened as he ate and drank. He liked the idea of free drinks and food. He liked having coppers as his friends. But who wanted to be a fink? It seemed crazy. In his mind, Marvin was doing the calculus Robbie knew he would be doing.

"Screw these guys, fuck 'em, I'm not gonna work for them," Marvin said to himself as he ordered another drink. "But I'll con them for a little while, as long as I can, get as much free booze out of them as I can, free food, maybe steal a few bucks off them. I'll milk these coppers for as much as I can and give them nothing. I'm not a fink."

Marvin thought Robbie was a real softie. He didn't realize it was part of Robbie's act, a recruitment technique. Robbie portrayed himself as weak, gullible. Marvin bought it.

"I sized him up all wrong," Marvin says. "I got the impression he would be an easy guy to fool, that he was a really easygoing, nice guy. The kind of guy I could walk all over. Was I ever wrong. It was a trap I fell into. He lured me. Savage was always hard-nosed and tough with me and Robbie was the nice softie when we first met. They played the good cop, bad cop on me.

"I ended up loving Robbie, to the end, for a lot of very good reasons, but he wasn't an easy guy. If things were going his way, he was easy, but if things weren't going his way, he could make life very difficult for people he had an advantage over, like me."

Robbie gave Marvin a number where he could call him. Fortunately for Robbie, he would soon have a chance to prove his value to Marvin, for the Proverbs case still had a few surprises.

* * *

With the threat of going to jail now past, from the Proverbs case and his trouble in Renfrew, Marvin was enjoying the notoriety of being the star witness at the high-profile trial. The newspapers were making him out to be a bad guy who beat the good guys, and in his world that was a good reputation to have. He wanted a memento.

Marvin drove to One Yonge Street, the charmless 25-storey office tower at the foot of what was once the longest street in the world. The tower was home to the *Toronto Star*. At the *Star's* front reception desk Marvin asked for six copies of the newspapers bearing his picture. The woman at the counter must have recognized him and made a discreet phone call, because just as he was getting his wallet out to pay, a young man came up behind him.

"Keep your money, they're on the house." The man introduced himself as John Kessel, the reporter who had revealed the wine-and-dine videos story.

Kessel offered to buy Marvin a drink, an offer Marvin rarely refused, and they sat down in the Print Room, a bar on the main floor. Marvin says Kessel started buying him drinks, telling Marvin he would drive him home afterwards and even pick him up the next morning and take him to get his car. Marvin liked the idea and kept ordering. Marvin understood that the conversation was off the record, meaning the information wouldn't be published.

"I get bombed and I opened my big stupid mouth up a million miles wide," Marvin recalls. "I tell him how the cops scared me, about the plane ride back from Calgary, how I perjured myself, everything. I qualified as the dunce of the century."

Kessel drove him home, and the next thing Marvin remembers is being woken up by the telephone the next morning. It was Kessel saying that Marvin should buy a paper and see that he was true to his word, there was nothing in it about him, Marvin recalls. Kessel said he would come pick him up.

Right afterwards, Marvin's phone rang again. This time it was Robbie.

"You lucky bastard," Robbie roared down the line. "You dumb, stupid lucky bastard."

"What are you talking about?"

"You were interviewed by that reporter Kessel yesterday."

"No, we just had a few drinks," Marvin said.

"Are you crazy? They had a story ready to print with all of the stuff you told him in it, but his editor was madder than all hell that he didn't tape it. The paper called us to confirm it and we said it wasn't right, that Marvin's full of crap. So they're not going to print it. You were telling them all this stuff, how Savage talked you into testifying, you told them everything."

"I guess I did," Marvin said.

Robbie was laughing, almost hysterically, "But it's OK, his editor was yelling at him: 'You had him all that time, he was bombed and you didn't think to tape it?' We saved your ass, Marvin. Now, where's your car?" Robbie knew Kessel had driven Marvin home drunk and was taking charge. This version of Robbie was different from the Robbie Marvin had met in the restaurant. Gone was the meek patsy. Here was a pushy, crafty cop.

"Kessel's coming to get me. It's down at the *Star*."

"You stay a million miles away from Kessel. I'm coming to get you now. Stay there until I come get you."

Kessel didn't get that story into print. He did try to enter the information as new evidence at Proverbs's appeal, swearing that Marvin told him he fabricated his evidence. The Ontario Court of Appeal did not admit Kessel's evidence. In their decision, the judges said it was not a case of whether Kessel could be believed, but whether Marvin could. The transcript of Marvin's court testimony showed he admitted to being a liar who would say anything to keep the free drinks coming. How could the court know that wasn't exactly what Marvin was doing with Kessel?

On November 1, 1983, a full year after the trial, the *Star* gave Proverbs one last front page: even without Kessel's evidence of Marvin's duplicity, Proverbs won his appeal of the gun conviction.

* * *

In his deft, duplicitous rescue of Marvin from the *Star*, Robbie had revealed himself for what he was, a rule-busting, hard-driving, sneaky cop who worked in the OPP's Intelligence Branch of Special Services.

Alan Rook Robinson was born on May 15, 1932, in Hamilton, Ontario, and, as a kid, ran with a group of wannabe mobsters downtown. When he was orphaned at 16—in quick succession, his father died from pneumonia and his mother from cancer—he chose a different path. He enlisted in the

Royal Canadian Air Force a few months after turning 17. In 1965, he retired from the military on a Friday and started with the OPP on the following Monday. Robbie often did his best work outside the formal command structure. As if he were the mould for the renegade cop of countless Hollywood movies, Robbie really was the officer who was being either yelled at by superiors for breaching protocol or rewarded for his creative techniques. He was tolerated by the brass because he got astounding results. The only thing he seemed to fear was the force's promotions exam, and he was never elevated beyond Detective-Constable yet received commendations from all five of the commissioners he worked for in his 28 years of service. When he was on a case, Robbie often gave his title as "investigator," fearing his lowly rank would demean him in the eyes of others, especially given the sensitive cases he worked on.

"Robbie taught me a lot about stress," says Dennis McGillis, one of Robbie's police supervisors, "especially each time he handed in his expense accounts. Official protocol was not his favourite occupation."

Robbie was barrel-chested, with a beer belly. His job demanded an unhealthy lifestyle. He was constantly bouncing around in bars and restaurants. It took him away from his wife and two sons more than they liked, and it was hard on his health. Robbie's hair twisted and hung down too long for him to look like a cop, but was too unstyled to look hip. Just as Marvin collected people who could protect him, Robbie collected—he called it "recruited"—facilitators and sources of all description. His Rolodex was unparalleled. He was a legend within the force, but so much of what he accomplished was secret. Many of his best, and worst, years were still ahead when he was invited to meet another unconventional man, known as The Weasel. When Savage first thought about cultivating Marvin as an informant, he immediately thought of Robbie as his handler, the term for the primary police contact of a street informant.

"Savage figured I was someone who could handle Marvin because he figured Marvin would be someone who would be hard to handle," Robbie said years later. "At the time, I was handling two other regular informants who also needed special handling. But Marvin turned out to be my best."

* * *

Robbie picked Marvin up before Kessel could get there and took him to a hotel bar. He wanted to make sure Marvin wasn't available for a second interview.

"I got bombed out of my head. He was buying and I wanted to get as much as I could out of him because I didn't know if there would be another chance. I slept it off in the hotel lobby. I never picked up a tab the whole time I was with Robbie," Marvin says.

"To me, Robbie became my pillar of strength. I feared him, but I had a great amount of respect for him and I was very fond of him. But most of all, I feared he would be disappointed in me."

Marvin had finally found his father figure.

Marvin learned a lot from the Proverbs ordeal. He learned that sometimes he could get away with lying, but it was sometimes best not to. He learned his mouth could get him into trouble, but also get him out of it. He learned he was a quick thinker under pressure.

But most of all, he learned it was good to have the cops on his side.

PART TWO

PART TWO

CHAPTER 23

TORONTO, 1983

The house looked fine. The trim painted, lawn mowed and siding in good repair. Glancing over it approvingly, Marvin rang the doorbell.

"Good day, ma'am. I couldn't help but see the problems with your siding."

The tin men were back. Marvin was in a crew of four working the neighbourhood. It was the job of three, the door-knockers, to convince homeowners to replace their aluminum siding. The fourth, the closer, would complete the deal whenever a knocker found a sucker. Marvin was a great door-knocker. His friendly nature and apple cheeks helped get him into homes. His specialty was saying his company was just starting in the area and wanted a model home to show off their work. This home—each and every home he knocked at—was the one perfect house for this. Marvin said he'd put up $10,000 worth of siding for $3,000 when, really, he was putting up $1,000 worth or less. This homeowner didn't bite, but others did, which was good for Marvin. It was two weeks after the Proverbs trial and he needed money.

A new sales team from Hamilton had joined them, and their closer, Herbert "Herbie" Asselstine, recognized Marvin's manic grin.

"You're the guy from the Proverbs case," he said, pointing at Marvin. "I read about you in the papers."

"Yeah, that's me," Marvin said.

"Listen, I got a deal going on. We got phoney certified cheques from a bank out in the islands and we're looking for people who can cash them. We're looking to toss these cheques, a couple million worth. You want a piece of it?"

Marvin did. He met with Asselstine and his partner, George Buric, at a pizza joint. With them was the pair's enforcer, sitting disinterestedly beside them. They told Marvin they had access to certified cheques from a flaky bank registered in the Caribbean island of St. Kitts. Certified cheques are treated like cash because, when legitimately issued, a bank has verified the money exists in an account to cover it. The Hamilton men wanted to cash the cheques and flee before anyone realized they were worthless.

"The way you handled yourself in the Proverbs case, Marvin, you'll be the talker, the guy who makes the deal," Asselstine said. Marvin's reward would be 10 per cent. After the meeting, Marvin thought more about it.

"How stupid do these guys think I am?" he asked himself. "I'm doing the most dangerous work and they're giving me the smallest cut. If anyone is going to get pinched, it's me. That article about me and Proverbs must have made me look like an idiot. These guys must think I took one too many hits in the ring. They're playing me for a complete sucker." Marvin grew increasingly insulted. Asselstine and Buric were screwing him.

It was bad timing for them. Marvin was fed up with his treatment in the underworld. He had been hanging around crooks for most of his life, working for Roy, Hoffa, Cotroni, Corrigan, Papalia, Luppino and others. He had gone to jail, kept his mouth shut and worked hard, and still he was dumped on. The disenchantment and frustration, insults and belit-tling jabs came flooding back and Marvin dumped all of his seething anger on the men who had just offered him a lousy share of a con.

"Screw these guys, I'm gonna sell them to the cops," he decided.

Marvin phoned Robbie.

* * *

The harsh scent of industrial-strength cleansers obliterated the warming smell of hand-rolled bagels as Marvin walked past the noisy kitchen and down the 15 steps to the bath-room of the Bagel Plus Bakery at Sheppard Avenue West and Bathurst Street, a much-loved deli in one of Toronto's old Jewish neighbourhoods. It was a place of familiarity and comfort for Marvin as he stepped into a strange world.

Three men followed him. Marvin pushed open the men's room door and made sure no one else was inside. Joining him was Ian Knox and Jack McCombs, officers with the Joint Forces Unit (JFU) in Hamilton, a police task force assigned to fight organized crime. A third officer stayed outside to guard the door. The day before, Robbie had called the JFU about Marvin's cheque tip. They were skeptical that it would lead to much, but were always up for trying something new. In the bathroom Knox and McCombs handed Marvin a large belt made of thick leather and partly covered with Velcro strips. Sewn inside was a series of batteries, a delicate microphone, wires and a radio transmitter. The bulky mess passed as "min-iature" at the time.

"The belt, if anybody saw it, you'd know there was some-thing fishy about it. It was really thick and you could see wires," Marvin says. "You could never pretend it was a normal belt. The only thing you could do was hide it."

Marvin pulled the belt around his waist. It was touch and go whether the two ends would meet, but between the three of them they managed to pull it tight. Marvin tugged the hemline of his baggy sweater and spun like a fashion model as the cops made sure the unnatural bulk was hidden.

It was Marvin's first time being wired for sound. It was March 8, 1983.

Marvin looked at himself for a moment in the single mirror above the sink, standing against the smooth yellow tiles that lined the walls and floor. Despite the dangers of the enterprise he was about to embark on, there was little self-reflection. Marvin was not a man for self-analysis. He was a man of action. He realized he was about to become a police agent, a paid informant. A fink. Snitch. Rat. Stoolie. He knew all the street names for what he was doing, but he was at peace.

The only question he had was, "How much will I get paid?"

Robbie had been enigmatic. "We'll see how the land lies."

Emerging from the washroom wired for sound, walking through the comforting clatter of the deli, Marvin left to meet Asselstine, Buric and their muscle-bound enforcer.

* * *

There was an important stop Marvin's co-conspirators said they had to make before they did anything else. They drove to Hamilton. In the city's north end they stopped at an autobody shop. Marvin loved the place. It looked like a regular low-rent collision-repair garage until the owner pressed a button to release a wall panel that revealed a beautiful office.

Everyone waited inside until an elderly man slowly waddled up the street to join them. He shook everyone's hand and sat and listened silently for a bit as Asselstine and Buric talked up the scam. When the old man stood up, everyone stopped talking and stood up with him. Marvin just followed everyone's lead. The old man then gave his blessing, shook everyone's hand again and left. Marvin had no idea who he was.

Outside, Knox and McCombs couldn't believe their eyes. From their hidden vantage point, they watched the old man shuffle back along the street for a mile until they lost sight of him. They knew him: it was Santo Scibetta, an old revered Mafia don who had come to Hamilton from Buffalo when he faced charges and deportation there. Rather than return to Italy, he had settled across the border in Canada where he continued to represent Buffalo Mafia boss Stefano Magaddino. Mobbed-up crooks in Hamilton were expected to seek Scibetta's blessing before undertaking any significant enterprise.

The Hamilton JFU was no longer skeptical of Marvin's access. Knox and McCombs started making plans for a major operation. To mask Marvin's identity, they gave him a code name that police were to use when referring to him, even in their notebooks. Remembering Marvin's physique in the bagel shop bathroom, they came up with a name easily. For the officers of the JFU, Marvin became "Midge," short for midget. Knox and McCombs then went to the priest of a church next door to the garage for permission to replace one of its windows with one-way glass so they could secretly keep the auto shop under surveillance.

They also tried to bug the secret office but were thwarted by two junkyard dogs that prowled the property at night. A colleague's wife worked at a kennel. She mixed up a bucket of meatballs laced with animal tranquilizer. Knox and McCombs tossed the drugged meatballs over the fence, to the delight of the huge beasts, which gulped them down but remained unaffected. As daylight broke, the tired and frustrated officers gave up, retreating to their church hideout. From there they saw the dogs slowly—finally—start to doze. But it was too late. The sun was up and workers were arriving. The dogs remained immobile all day, one with his legs straight up in the air. Knox and McCombs were afraid they'd killed them and were relieved to hear barking the next night.

Over several days, Marvin met with his co-conspirators, learning the details of their plot. Asselstine and Buric had two supposedly certified cheques totalling $1.7 million from the Bank of Commerce in St. Kitts. Cheque number 1450 was for $965,000 and cheque number 1451 was for $735,000, both payable to "Marsam Innvestments." Marvin took Asselstine and Buric to a bank, ostensibly to gauge the bank's reaction to them, but police had asked the bank ahead of time to discreetly photocopy the cheques for them.

Knox and McCombs then noticed the spelling error in "investments." They told Marvin to tell his co-conspirators that no bank in Canada would accept such large cheques with a typo. The cops wanted to see if Asselstine and Buric could get new ones. Some days later, they had replacements.

Marvin then told them he had found someone who could help. He introduced them to an undercover police officer posing as a black-market jewellery dealer. He arrived with a briefcase jammed full of gold and gems that police had seized on other cases. When he was shown the cheques, the undercover cop said he dealt in rocks, not paper, and introduced him to a second undercover officer, this one posing as a corporate whiz kid. The second cop told Asselstine and Buric that the cheques were too big, and they needed to break them down into smaller amounts. The cops wanted Asselstine and Buric to order new cheques so they could trace where they came from. New cheques eventually arrived by courier from Miami. This time there were four of them, tallying $1.7 million. These weren't forgeries; they were issued by the island bank.

When the new cheques arrived, the cop posing as a business whiz took Asselstine and Buric to a third undercover officer, one who was running what police call a "gaffe company"—a seemingly legitimate business run by cops to further their sting operations. His office in Mississauga, west of Toronto, looked like an import-export company. There was a bank across the street. These multiple layers of undercover introductions were a way of protecting Marvin—putting as much distance as possible between him and the cop that would eventually move to arrest the suspects, and making it less likely that Marvin would be fingered as a fink. Marvin was then largely removed from the conspiracy as the import-export man suggested Asselstine and Buric should cash the cheques across the road at his bank. He'd go with them for a piece of the action, he said.

Buric and two of the undercover cops drove to the bank while Knox and McCombs kept watch. They spotted Asselstine and his enforcer lurking in a car nearby, doing their own surveillance. Even more worryingly, Buric stashed a gun and a knife in his car before going into the bank. He was distressed when the bank manager looked at them as if they were nuts when they showed up demanding that much money.

It was two months since Marvin had put on his first wire, starting the case, and it was obvious to investigators that it was time to close it down. As the men left the bank, one of the undercover officers gave a signal and uniformed police grabbed Buric in the parking lot. Asselstine and the enforcer were nabbed nearby.

* * *

After the arrests in Canada, Ian Knox boarded a plane for Basseterre, the capital of St. Kitts. He was met at the airport by a police superintendent in a black Wolseley 6/80, a 1940s limousine with graceful, bulging fenders and a silver upright grille attached to which a small flag, the green and red triangles of St. Kitts, flapped in the sea breeze. As Knox was squired through town in the state limo, citizens stopped in the street and waved.

The local authorities agreed to co-operate with him. The same cheque scheme had been tried recently in a number of countries and it was embarrassing for the government. Knox met the attorney general and finance minister to discuss the case and was granted a search warrant for the bank's office.

When Knox and local officers raided the bank, above a Hitachi store off a back alley, they found a woman who sat answering every phone call, every fax and every teletype, confirming for each that money was there to cover any cheque she was asked about, even though there wasn't. Knox found 20 cheques identical to the ones that Asselstine and Buric had had, made payable to companies in different countries. It was a global scam that Marvin had tapped into.

"The bank was a strange place," Knox says. "The vault was empty. Here was a bank that didn't actually have any money. The only thing in the boardroom was a pilot waiting to fly back to Miami with a package he was waiting for. There wasn't much in the way of documents to seize. I put all of their records in my back pocket. It was just a place to launder money. Once I executed the search warrant, I got the first flight out of there.

"The banker there was in on it," he says. "We tried to get him to come to testify at the trial and we would have arrested him when he got here. I think he realized that and he wouldn't come."

***

The gang never suspected that Marvin was the mastermind of their downfall. Marvin drove the wife of one of the men to the Hamilton police station to visit her husband. Marvin told her he had connections that could get him out. She gave him $500 for his "intervention." Marvin was still wearing the wired belt at the time and Robbie heard the side deal. Robbie was angry, but he let Marvin keep the money as a bonus.

By June, the gang was working to find out where the heat had come from. They knew there had been a fink, but nobody was sure who it was. Police had interviewed Scibetta, the old Mafia don, and the owner of the auto-body shop. They denied any involvement. One of the gang asked Marvin to find out. He said he would hunt down the damned fink. Not long afterwards, the men questioned why Marvin hadn't been arrested. Then he was given a message from the Hamilton gangsters: they expected him to testify in court on behalf of the accused men, and if he didn't help them, he'd be killed.

"Your guys set me up," Marvin blustered angrily in reply. "You brought me into this thing and I barely got out. You guys better get your act together before I send some guys after you."

The gangsters were taken aback. Marvin didn't sound like a fink.

"Marvin confused a lot of guys," Knox says in wonder.

***

Marvin's first case was a success and now stands as the opening entry in confidential OPP case notes on Marvin's work, notes that would grow beyond anyone's expectations: "Arrest of three subjects and recovery of two million dollars in fraudulent cheques," it says, summarizing the results.

Marvin was officially enrolled as a "coded informant" with the OPP and assigned a four-digit number that would replace his name in virtually all of the force's future documents—protecting his identity, even from other officers. Marvin had obtained yet another name: Informant 0030.

In a memo marked "SECRET" across the top, Robbie summed up 0030 to his boss, the director of the Intelligence Branch: "His criminal past linked him to high-level criminal organizations and recognized organized crime families and groups such as the Papalia, Musitano, Commisso, Cotroni and Volpe families in Toronto, Hamilton, Montreal and areas. He also was linked by Intelligence analysts to recognized crime groups in Detroit, New York City, Buffalo and Atlantic City in the United States." Robbie knew 0030 was a keeper.

Marvin was just as pleased as Robbie. He got tremendous satisfaction watching Asselstine and Buric fall. He hurt them without making a fist.

"It went over big-time," Marvin says. "And I just got so involved with it and was having fun. It was a big adrenalin rush, and all of a sudden I realized—Hey, I'm still in the action, doing my things, but now I've got the cops on my side instead of against me. This is great."

Robbie and the other officers said Marvin was brilliant. He hadn't got many accolades from his criminal cohorts in the past. This was a pleasant change.

"Marvin got the same kick out of working for us as he did when he was by himself. We paid him and I was his buddy and I would protect him—or try to," says Robbie. "Sometimes I couldn't. He was a pain in the ass."

Marvin finally did some soul-searching. He was 49 years

old, and what had his life in the underworld brought him? A little flash money that was gone almost as soon as he had it, some thrills, a pile of war stories and some brushes with the famous and the damned. But also jail time, beatings, abuse, a criminal record, alienation from his family, aggravation with his wife, hassles from the cops. Hardly the riches, power and respect he had hoped for, the way the gangsters lived in the old black-and-white movies he loved. Hollywood had lied to him. Twice before, he had sought promotion in the underworld. He had asked Johnny Papalia and Tommy Corrigan if he could play a bigger role.

"I went to two people to try to get myself bumped up," Marvin says. "Both told me that I'm not capable of it. My problem was that I typecast myself. I wanted to be the guy to hire the muscle and send the guys out, to hire the drivers and give them their assignments. That's what I wanted to do. I never wanted to be a boss. But I wanted to do something more. I wanted it very badly. When they said no, I accepted it too easily. They looked at me as the same muscle I was when I was a kid. It showed the lack of respect the mob had for me."

Even Roy—after 40 years together—was content to have Marvin carry out mere thuggery, driving and errands. The bitterness Marvin felt toward all of them made Robbie's offer irresistible. Still ringing in his ears was the caustic swipe from Corrigan, almost 30 years before when he had hired Marvin, that he was capable of being nothing more than an errand boy.

Looking back, Marvin now knows exactly what Savage and Robbie saw in him. Besides everything else, he wasn't doing well on the streets.

"If you want a fink, you gotta look for a guy who hasn't gone too far, so he's not giving up a lot of money, who's not involved a hundred per cent with just one family so he can move around and nobody will think nothing of it, and he is dissatisfied with the way he is treated. I had a strong bitterness toward a lot of guys," Marvin says.

"I started small in the mob and stayed small."

* * *

Before deciding if his fink caper was a one-off thrill or the start of a new career, Marvin discussed it with his lawyer and childhood friend, Harvey Salem, who had represented him on the fraud charges in the 1960s.

Marvin liked to have two things—a tough, dangerous friend at his side and a wise, straight friend as an adviser. It was like having a wee devil and a tiny angel on his shoulders giving him competing advice, as if Marvin had no confidence in his own conscience. While Baldy Chard was Marvin's dangerous sidekick, Salem was Marvin's wise friend. It was always a coin toss as to whom Marvin would listen to.

"After his bankruptcy, he got into a lot of trouble. He wasn't charged that often, but he was always on the fringe. Always manipulating and getting into all kinds of nonsense," says Salem, who went on to become a judge. "He really needed someone. He would phone me seven, eight times a week. Sometimes it seemed he wouldn't pee without asking me what I think."

When Marvin told Salem about Robbie's offer, his reaction was stern. "You crazy son of a bitch, become a garbageman, do anything else. Don't do that stuff, you're going to get killed."

"But I love the action. I love the action," Marvin replied.

"Don't do it. It's too dangerous. You'll be dealing with some serious, serious criminals."

"Yeah," said Marvin, "I will."

He made his decision and soon discovered he was a much

better fink than he had ever been a crook. Now he was a bad guy, but good.

* * *

There was only one thing that nagged at Marvin about his monumental decision. He was still deeply afraid of Roy. It might have been the lingering childhood attachment or the intimate knowledge of Les Irwin's demise, but of all the dangerous and powerful men Marvin moved with, Roy stood alone in filling Marvin with dread.

Even though Marvin was married with children of his own, he couldn't cut the tie to Roy. The sinister attraction that, as a child, had brought him to worship Roy, remained. As he had in the schoolyard, Marvin still bragged about being "brothers" with the well-known tough guy.

Roy had moved with his wife to Keswick, an hour's drive north of Toronto, and every year Marvin and his family spent the holidays there. Roy loved Christmas. He decorated an enormous tree and had presents for everyone.

"My wife didn't want to go, she hated it, but I was too scared not to," Marvin says. Despite the festive trappings, there was little cheer. "He loved having people over for Christmas, and I would say ninety-nine per cent of them didn't want to be there but were too scared not to go. Most of them owed him money."

Why did Marvin stay hooked up with Roy for so long? "I was afraid to leave him," he says, describing a relationship not unlike that of a crushed woman who can't leave her abusive husband.

Marvin was unsure what to do about Roy. He told Robbie he wanted to avoid finking on him. Even so, he told his handler, if anything important came up he would. Robbie was displacing Roy as the dominant male in Marvin's life. "I had loyalty to Robbie above all else," Marvin admits.

Marvin's concern was short-lived. Around midnight on June 15, 1983, Roy put a revolver to the back of his wife's head, killing Lee Pasquale instantly. He then turned the gun on himself. He was 60 years old.

"It was like karma," Marvin says. "I was worried I would get into trouble from Roy and then—bang—he kills himself." After a pause, he adds: "I had nothing to do with it."

CHAPTER 24

NEW YORK CITY, 1983

Andy Rayne came to the Crossroads of the World to meet Marty Hodas, and the maverick businessman escorted Rayne on a tour of his empire: 42nd Street and Broadway, the key intersection in New York City's Times Square. The dark heart of Manhattan was all about strippers, live sex acts, peepshows, dirty-book stores, grinder houses, body-rub parlours. It was the continental capital of retail smut and most of it belonged to Hodas. Hodas walked Rayne past the racks of dirty movies and books to the back of one of his sex emporiums, where men paid to sit in a booth. A curtain opened revealing a nude woman. Some men reached and groped; others noisily pleasured themselves. As Hodas and Rayne strolled this tawdry streetscape, Hodas put his arm around Rayne's shoulder.

"You can do this in Toronto," he said.

Rayne nodded. "I want to be the Marty Hodas of Canada."

"Son, some day you will be."

Martin J. Hodas wasn't everyone's idea of a role model, but he certainly knew how to make money. His innovation in 1966 revolutionized the sex industry and Times Square. Hodas found young female models through classified ads and paid them $75 to let him film them cavorting nude. He cut the film into two-minute segments and looped them into 13 coin-operated film stands. He placed his coin-ops in a 42nd Street bookstore and, where *Popeye* and *Tarzan* once entertained kids, *Flesh Party* and *Elevator Orgy* now titillated adults. Full-frontal nudity wasn't commercially available until then and, despite the awkward stand-and-look position, Hodas's loops were a hit. He expanded, taking over storefronts around Times Square and becoming a major producer and distributor of pornography. Soon the coin-ops became sit-down booths. Then live models replaced film. The women stripped but the curtains snapped closed just as it got really interesting, forcing viewers to fumble for more coins.

From the late 1960s, Hodas was dubbed "King of the Peeps" and "Porno Prince," and his revenues justified the accolades. His collectors went to the booths emptying quarters from his machines several times a day. The collectors would bring a large set of scales and dump the coins on each end until they were evenly divided, pushing half to the operators and Hodas's half into a steamer trunk. Hodas would then make the collectors take a lie-detector test to ensure they weren't skimming. By 1972, police estimated he was making $13 million a year from porn.

The revolution continued and the new economy brought ancillary vendors and customers: pushers, junkies, hookers and johns. It transformed Times Square into the squalid, crime-riddled sex-carnival strip that would bug every New York mayor until the 1990s, when Rudy Giuliani finally pushed the pornographers out, reclaiming Times Square as a tourist jewel.

Giuliani probably never knew he had help from The Weasel.

Hodas had been charged several times in the past, always mounting a vigorous defence. He shook off charges of arson, bribery, prostitution and a dozen obscenity charges. When Hodas chased off burglars from his bedroom, it was he who ended up being charged. In an undercover operation, New York cops even opened their own porno bookstore, hoping to attract an expected extortion attempt. Hodas poked back at officials, laying lawsuits and fighting freedom of speech cases over government interference with his selling of "First Amendment-protected adult materials." Vice cops believed he was secretly moving really nasty stuff: kiddie porn, violent rapes and "snuff" films—where one of the actors is killed on tape as the climax.

American authorities really wanted Hodas. It was Marvin who gave him to them. Hodas would later learn that Andy Rayne, his new partner in a planned expansion into Canada, was an undercover officer with the RCMP, introduced into a large cross-border porn deal through Marvin in the second case he brought to the cops as a fledgling fink. By the time this case was over, more than 20 officers in two countries would be working on the sting and headlines would be made across the continent.

* * *

It was the bogus-cheque scammers who had started it. Marvin hadn't been sure what his status was or where his deal with Robbie would lead when he'd turned Asselstine and his gang in. Was he just screwing guys who tried to screw him, or was he irreversibly heading down a startling new path? He had decided to take a line out of Robbie's script and see "how the land lies," but the cheque guys had made the decision easier. Before they were arrested, when they still thought they had been lucky to meet an energetic crook with contacts and modest infamy, they had told Marvin about a friend with access to hardcore porno tapes who needed someone with big contacts to help her.

Marvin was surprised to hear it was a woman trying to move the sex tapes, but he said he could help her. He wasn't sexist about whom he sold to the cops.

Marvin met Anna at Kiva's Bagel on Steeles Avenue West in north Toronto. Anna walked in with bleached blonde hair and too much makeup. The two of them, both Jewish, fit in well with the regulars but, unlike the food, their conversation wasn't kosher. The cheque fraudsters had already vouched for Marvin to Anna.

"The Proverbs case gave me a lot of advertising," Marvin quipped when Anna mentioned it. Anna had an unusual business: she collected men's semen to make cosmetic facial creams that were both organic and orgasmic.

"I can get you pornography like you've never seen here," she told Marvin. "I can get you as much as you want—a thousand tapes, two thousand, three thousand. The best. Hard as you want—kiddie porn, S&M, gay, animals, snuff, you name it." What she didn't have was the financing or distribution. Could Marvin bring someone to the deal with money and an organization?

"Absolutely," he said.

Marvin went straight to Robbie's office. Robbie was interested to hear about Anna's nasty tapes. If nothing else, Robbie wanted to test his new fink. Marvin had done well on the cheque scam, but how would he do when he didn't have a score to settle? How good was his information? Could he be trusted?

Bill Gill was an OPP officer in the Special Enforcement Unit, a joint task force in Toronto working to disrupt organized crime. Robbie pushed Gill to go with Marvin that same night, a Friday in February 1983, to meet Anna. A burly man

THE WEASEL | 213

with a thick reddish beard, Gill posed as a crook always on the hunt for a deal. Marvin vouched for him as a man Anna could do business with. She made her porno pitch to the officer.

"Interested?"

Gill played it cool. "Maybe, Hannah, maybe."

"It's Anna."

When Gill next met Anna, she told him the tapes were coming from New York and he would have to smuggle them across the border. Hodas's name never came up, and police wanted to know who was behind the high-volume hardcore. With the New York connection emerging, Gill called a friend at U.S. Customs in Buffalo who passed him along to the Child Exploitation Unit, a joint task force of the FBI, New York City Police Department and Nassau County Police. FBI special agents Steve Skinner and John Thurston joined the probe.

As they planned the sting, the cops gave Marvin another code name. They took one look at his grinning face with a smouldering stick poking from his mouth and knew what it would be: "The Cigar." Marvin liked it better than "Midge."

To play this case through, the cops realized they needed to raise the stakes, more than Gill, who was supposedly a small-time crook, could manage. They needed to introduce a new officer into the mix, someone who could act as a high roller, a boss offering big-money bait to lure the big fish out of the depths. Gill told Anna that he was being pushed out of the deal by his boss, a major cocaine kingpin who could put hundreds of thousands of dollars into it. Anna loved that kind of number.

Enter RCMP corporal Andy Rayne, a brash, easy-talking cop with an olive complexion despite his British background. He resembled Anthony Quinn and, just as the Mexican actor had played an Indian chief, Mafia don, Arab sheik and Greek partisan onscreen, Rayne's ethnically ambiguous look gave him flexibility as an undercover agent. For this role, as a big coke dealer and would-be smut entrepreneur, he dressed to impress: three-piece suit, no tie, shirt open at the neck, a hefty gold chain and a two-and-a-half-carat diamond pinky ring, both borrowed from a jeweller friend of Marvin's. He arrived at the Skyline Hotel on Toronto's airport strip in a rented black Lincoln limo. Rayne became a make-believe Mr. Big. But would Anna—and her New York source—believe it?

Gill introduced Rayne to Anna as Andy Lenew. It was a tongue-in-cheek name, taken from the initials L.N.U., police shorthand for "Last Name Unknown."

Anna repeated the video offer to Rayne. Rayne said he had a distribution network in place for his cocaine and could put the videos all over Canada, but wanted samples first. Over several meetings, each secretly recorded, Anna told Rayne that she couldn't bring the sample tapes to Canada.

"You've got to come to New York, Andy, see them there."

"No way," he said. "I got—what?—maybe a million and a half laid down, do about two or three kilos every two or three months. I don't have time to chase deals to New York. They wanna deal, they come to me."

He called it all off, but Anna phoned the next day.

"OK, maybe they'll consider delivering the tapes to Canada, the ones you order, but you've got to come to New York first," she said. The cops were pleased. They now knew Anna's New York connection was motivated to distribute in Canada. It gave them some leverage.

With the investigation shifting south, FBI agents Skinner and Thurston came to Toronto to plan. It was agreed that Rayne should go to New York and flush out Anna's source. Rayne told Anna he would be in New York on April 11, and he wanted 20 sample tapes.

The police booked two rooms at the LaGuardia Sheraton Hotel in Queens, three miles from the airport. One was for the meeting that Rayne and Gill were hosting; the other, next door, was for FBI surveillance. Rayne and Gill brought a rented videocassette player on which to view samples. Anna arrived with a friend, Sheila Baummel, who had had a relationship with Hodas. That connection explained how Anna had met the porno prince. Anna saw the video player when she arrived.

"There's a mistake. We brought film. I thought you wanted film," she said. "Tomorrow, please wait till tomorrow, we'll bring tapes."

Rayne pretended to be angry but agreed to give them one more day. When they returned the next day, Rayne pretended to fly into a fiercer rage. The tapes the women played were far from the obscene filth the police were after.

"This is softcore," Rayne roared, punching the desk. "The hell you doing? I can get this in Toronto," he yelled, storming out of the room.

Now it was Gill's turn to get back into the act. "What you doing to me?" he said to the women. "I bring you this guy, big guy, you do this? You're going to get me killed."

That same night, the women returned, and this time they showed Rayne and Gill the sort of thing the cops wanted: hardcore, nasty porn filled with violence and animals. Tape after tape of it. After the women left, FBI technicians found the fingerprints of Marty Hodas on the sample tapes. The FBI knew now that they would stick with this case to the end, but they needed to bring Hodas into the open. That opportunity came when Rayne refused to pick the tapes up, insisting they had to be delivered to him.

Anna finally said, "You're dealing with the main man."

"I'm dealing with Marty Hodas?" Rayne asked.

"That's right, you are." Anna told Rayne that he should meet directly with the boss to close the deal, that it was beyond her now. A meeting was arranged in New York.

* * *

It was June 1983. This time, the FBI booked three rooms at the Sheraton New York Hotel & Towers, a complex covering half a city block at 7th Avenue and West 52nd Street. One room was for Rayne to sleep in, one was for the deal to go down in and the third was for the surveillance team.

For the meeting with Hodas, Rayne needed to spruce himself up even more. The FBI fitted him out with a fine-tailored designer suit.

"You don't go play a game like that with a Tip Top Tailors suit on," Rayne says.

He was still outdressed by Hodas. Anna and Sheila arrived at Rayne's hotel room with a stocky man in his early 50s. The man wore casual but expensive clothes and, as if requisite for a porn merchant, a moustache and unbuttoned shirt, revealing greying chest hair and a protruding gut. The man's diamond ring made Rayne's borrowed bauble look like a kid's toy; there must have been 10 carats' worth of stone in it. More than four months after Marvin introduced the cops to Anna, Rayne was finally introduced to Marty Hodas. As the New Yorker sipped vodka in the hotel room and the FBI eagerly recorded the conversation, Hodas chatted amicably.

"I feel very confident about you," he told Rayne. "I invented this business." Then he asked for the money upfront.

"Two months I been negotiating with these ladies," Rayne protested. "There's been lack of communication, there's been screw-ups. I'll show you the money, but no upfront."

"Listen, these broads don't know what they're talking about. These flaky broads don't do my business. I do my business," Hodas said. Rayne and Hodas agreed that Anna and Sheila had outlived their usefulness and Hodas said Rayne should come to his office on Broadway, the centre of his porn empire.

The next day, when Rayne arrived at the office, Hodas greeted him warmly but remained suspicious. He wanted to slow things down.

"I'll tell ya, Andy, I've got a sick wife and this is going to kill her and me if I get caught and go to jail. Let's forget the big [deal] now, do the fifty-to-sixty-thousand-dollar deal first. We'll do two hundred and fifty thousand dollars two weeks later." He told Rayne he never handled kiddie porn himself, but, once a few deals had gone down, he could put him in touch with those who did. Rayne said it all sounded reasonable. Hodas then took Rayne for his tour, showing off the porn mills that had made him rich.

With FBI surveillance agents discreetly taking photographs and recording the audio from vans parked on the crowded streets, Hodas, wearing an open-neck shirt and a gold choker chain, a fashionably wide belt and slacks, steered Rayne, dressed in his trim FBI-issued suit and tie, through his seamy empire. As they walked, Rayne clutched a chocolate-coloured soft-shell leather briefcase under his right arm. In it was $50,000 in $20 bills, courtesy of the FBI.

Afterwards, Rayne pulled $10,000 out and handed it to Hodas, a down payment on his first order.

* * *

When Rayne and Anna flew back to Toronto, Anna had a sample tape of illicit material hidden in her purse to help her own sales efforts back home. Rayne had secretly alerted Canadian border agents to search her and seize it when they arrived at Toronto airport. But on that flight, for some reason—perhaps because she was being cut out of the deal—Anna had doubts about the man she knew as Andy Lenew. As Rayne snoozed on the plane, using the leather briefcase stuffed with cash as a pillow, Anna quietly snapped a photograph of him. Then, unbeknownst to him, she removed the sample tape from her purse and ditched it somewhere on the plane. Her suspicion rose even more when border agents homed in on her purse when she was passing through customs and looked surprised to find nothing.

After having her film developed, Anna wanted to find out if the man in the picture was really who he claimed to be. She went to the one guy who seemed to know everyone. She went straight to The Weasel.

"Do you know who this guy is?" Anna asked Marvin, handing over the snapshot.

"Lemme hang on to this. I'll ask around," he said, folding it in half and stuffing it into his shirt pocket. The only person he showed it to was Robbie. Marvin had introduced Anna to Bill Gill, but not to Andy Rayne, which gave Marvin a little distance. She seemed suspicious of Gill introducing Rayne, not of Marvin introducing Gill. A couple of days later, Marvin got back to her.

"I showed the picture around to some people," he told her. "He's OK. They know him, he checked out."

A few weeks after Rayne returned from New York, he got a phone call at eight o'clock one night. It was Marty Hodas.

"Andy, what are you doing tomorrow?"

"Nothing, why?"

"I'm flying into Toronto on American Airlines arriving nine a.m. Want to pick me up at the airport?"

CHAPTER 25

TORONTO, 1983

It can be harder to pull off an undercover caper in your hometown. Undercover officers and informants risk bumping into people they know, friends or neighbours or people they've arrested or worked with in the past. Even other cops. More than one undercover operation has been ruined by a uniformed officer spotting a colleague in street clothes and, assuming he is off-duty, calling out a friendly greeting. It is even harder to pull it off on short notice.

When Marty Hodas called Andy Rayne to say he was flying into Toronto from New York, he did not give Rayne much time to get organized. That was precisely why Hodas gave so little advance notice: he wanted to check his new friend out. He also wanted to see Toronto's potential as a sex market.

Rayne made some phone calls. He rented the same limousine he had used for his first meeting with Anna, this time getting a fellow cop, a member of the RCMP drug squad, to act as his driver. They picked Hodas up at Toronto airport. Hodas was blown away by the city. He loved the size, the look, the feel. As a resident of midtown Manhattan, he didn't expect to be in awe of a tall building, but the dizzying height of the CN Tower, then the tallest structure in the world, fascinated him.

"I'll take you there for lunch," Rayne said.

Over a $240 meal at the rotating restaurant atop the tower, Hodas admitted to Rayne that he was reluctant to do the cross-border deal.

"Andy, I'll be honest with you. My lawyers say I've already committed an offence coming here conspiring to bring obscene material into Canada. My lawyers told me not to come. I can't do this. I'm going to have to back out of the deal."

Instead, he told Rayne he should open an office in New York and he would help him get started. Rayne said that was out of the question.

After lunch, Hodas wanted to see Toronto's sex offerings. As they walked along Yonge Street, several police agents had been planted along the way to look like crooks who knew Rayne. Some of them engaged him in discreet conversation. One, George Capra, was one of the first Italian members of the RCMP. His expertise on the Mafia had been a godsend years before, when police were struggling to get a grip on the mob. Capra, playing a low-level mobster himself that day, tried to stop Rayne for a talk.

"I haven't got time to talk right now," Rayne said, pushing past him. "I'll call you later." It made Rayne look like a big shot.

In the Zanzibar Tavern, a venerable strip club marked by a gaudy sign that would make Times Square proud, more supposed shady characters greeted Rayne. Hodas, however, had something else on his mind. He couldn't understand Toronto's staid nudity regulations.

Aghast, he pointed at the thong-wearing strippers on stage. "How come they keep their bottoms on?"

Later, at a peepshow, he was further disgusted with the limp offering.

"Soft," he declared of the viewing options. "Old. This is like the stuff I started with twenty years ago."

Hodas told Rayne he was onto something big. Rayne could rent a building and make it look classy to attract the lawyers, doctors, businessmen; charge 50 cents a peep, not a quarter. They would make a killing in Toronto.

"These places aren't making money," Hodas said, dismissing the city's sex emporiums. "If you can't smell cum, you're not making money.

"This place is ready to be raped."

* * *

Andy Rayne had his chauffeur drive them back to the airport. On the way, Hodas revealed the source of his concern. Fuelled by Anna's suspicion, he wondered aloud if Rayne was a police agent.

"You're paranoid," Rayne said. But Hodas didn't know what to believe. He knew the cops wanted to take him down. He didn't want to blow it after winning for so long. But after seeing the potential of turning Yonge Street into Times Square North, he couldn't resist. Before boarding his plane to New York, Hodas put his arm around Rayne again.

"Andy, there is one way this deal might work," he said. "I don't know how to ask you this."

"Am I a cop?"

"No, that's not it. The question is, will you come to New York and take a lie-detector test?"

Rayne quashed his panic and instead smiled serenely, "Sure."

"Thanks, Andy, you're a friend. Come down next week."

The Canadian cops and the FBI agents met to discuss this new wrinkle. Marvin had brought them closer to Hodas than they had ever been before, but how could Andy beat the polygraph test? They threw out ideas in desperation: hypnosis, drugs, refusing the test. None was plausible. The officers knew the importance Hodas placed on polygraphs. He had all of his employees take them. It could be seen as paranoia but, given Hodas's situation, it was more a sign of his intelligence. There seemed no way around it. Rayne would have to take—and pass—Hodas's lie-detector test if the case was to go any further.

***

On June 30, Rayne checked into his New York hotel room overlooking Central Park. Hodas paid him a visit right away, anxious to test him with more than just the polygraph. He knew his relationship with Rayne was tenuous—too many degrees of separation, from Rayne to Gill to Anna to some guy named The Weasel. Hodas had gone back over everything he thought he knew about Rayne and wanted to test it.

Hodas handed Rayne a vial of cocaine.

"Tell me what you think of that."

Rayne was good at handling drugs from his many other cases. He dipped a finger in and rubbed the white powder between his finger and thumb.

"There's a lot of cut in there."

"What do you cut yours with, Andy?"

"D-Mannitol," he said, offering the proper name for the powdered diuretic often used as a cutting agent. Hodas asked how much he paid for his coke in Miami. Rayne said $28,000 a kilo.

"That seems cheap."

"What you gotta remember, Marty, is that's Canadian funds," Rayne said, taking foreign-exchange rates into account. Hodas was satisfied. But the most important question came next.

"Andy, tell me. Are you willing to take this lie-detector test?"

"That's why I'm here."

Rayne had navigated the drug quiz beautifully. In fact, he was thrilled Hodas had started questioning him, since the only plan the officers had concocted to deal with the polygraph test required him to stall Hodas for more than an hour.

"You think I may be an agent. But I also talked to my lawyers, and my lawyer in Miami says I shouldn't take your test. How do I know you're not the one who's an agent, trying to set me up? I answer these questions—do I deal coke, where do I buy it, how much do I pay, how do I deliver it, do I want to buy pornography—and you could be turning me in. I'm in New York, a Canadian confessing to breaking the law. How do I know I won't end up doing time in an American jail? There is no way I'm taking this test with your man. We'll pick somebody we don't know, somebody who's independent. We'll look in the Yellow Pages."

Hodas agreed. Rayne discreetly checked the clock. For this to work, he needed to make the call to a random, privately run lie-detector place as close to the end of the business day as he could. He was shooting for 4 p.m., so the test could not be administered until the next day. It was now 3:30 p.m. Rayne slowly hunted around for the phone book. He pulled out the wrong directory at first, and then slowly flipped through the right book's pages looking for a place. He found several companies offering lie-detection tests and just put his finger on the largest ad on the page, Safeguard Polygraph. They went down to the hotel lobby to use a pay phone. That was a precaution Hodas could appreciate. Rayne phoned the company. To his dismay, the receptionist said to come over now. With the New Yorker standing beside him, he completely ignored what she had just said.

"You mean you're getting ready to close? How about tomorrow at ten? That OK?" He looked at Hodas with an apologetic shrug. The confused receptionist said that would be fine, too.

After Hodas left, it was time for FBI agents Skinner and Thurston to do their part. The agents visited Safeguard Polygraph and flashed their badges. By sheer good fortune, the owner of the company was a retired FBI agent who had worked on the bureau's polygraph team. Skinner and Thurston explained the situation and he agreed to help. That night, Rayne was secretly hooked up to the polygraph unit and took a test, truthfully answering simple questions from the former agent. They were ready to put one over on Hodas. The next morning, though, it was clear that Hodas had considered just this scenario.

"Take the test from my guy. You could have infiltrated that polygraph company," he told Rayne.

"Jeez, Marty, I can't deal with a person that's that paranoid. You want to do this or not?"

When they arrived at the polygraph office, everything looked normal. The former agent ushered the men inside and sat Rayne down in the chair for the test. The bogus polygraph charts from the night before were ready. Hodas handed the operator the three questions he wanted Rayne to answer while hooked up.

"Are you an agent or affiliated with law enforcement?"

"Are you being truthful about your business?"

"Are you ripping Marty Hodas off?"

After Rayne answered each question with a clear, emphatic no, the operator gave the bogus results to Hodas.

"You can take them to any approved operator to be verified," the operator said. "He answered all three questions truthfully."

"Now, Marty, are you satisfied?" Rayne asked.

"It only proves one thing—that Anna is a filthy, lying bitch."

* * *

Hodas and Rayne reclined by a motel pool on the outskirts of Buffalo. It was less than a month since Rayne had taken the polygraph test, and almost immediately afterwards the deal had moved forward. The tapes Rayne had ordered were on their way, arriving in Buffalo courtesy of Hodas's people. The FBI had rented out a small warehouse where they were going to be unloaded and handed to Rayne. The FBI had also given Rayne $60,000 to pay Hodas for the shipment, the first of many deals Rayne and Hodas had arranged. For the drive out to Buffalo, Rayne had tried to rent the same black limo he had used to show Hodas around Toronto, but it was unavailable. He settled for a dark brown one and hoped Hodas wouldn't notice the colour change.

"I've got a truck driver," Hodas explained, "who is a former Buffalo policeman. He's prepared to handle any screwups." To Rayne, that meant the driver would be armed.

"We've got thirty-three boxes of tapes in the truck. There's another fellow in a car, the producer of Corporal tapes. He's on his way to Detroit to make an S&M movie," Hodas said. The producer was in on the deal, using his cut to pay for the new movie, so he needed the cash that day. Corporal Video, as in corporal punishment, specialized in low-budget but high-impact bondage and S&M tapes.

"About the kiddie porn: I don't handle it, never have, but after this, I'll put you in touch with the right people."

From poolside, Rayne and Hodas could watch the highway exit ramp that the truck would come down, and they sipped vodka and chatted as they waited. Hours passed before they saw the truck, following a silver Cadillac, pulling off the highway. Rayne and Hodas headed to Rayne's Lincoln, but if Hodas noticed the different colour, he didn't mention it. The Lincoln joined the convoy, taking the lead. Behind, staying out of sight, was Gill.

At the warehouse, Hodas introduced Rayne to Richard Spadafora, the film producer who had been driving the Cadillac. Spadafora explained that the porn tapes marked with a "G" featured gay content. The truck driver and a couple of FBI agents, posing as Rayne's goons, unloaded the boxes of tapes. Rayne, Hodas and Spadafora were soon on the move again, heading back to the hotel for Rayne to pay for the load. In the car, Hodas seemed visibly relieved.

"I was expecting agents to come out of the wall," he said. Rayne laughed.

If only Hodas had waited around for a little longer. As soon as the cars had left, agents arrested the truck driver, seizing the tapes as well as his gun. At the motel, Rayne asked Spadafora to wait in the bar while he and Hodas finished their business upstairs. The producer was arrested as soon as Hodas and Rayne were out of sight. In Long Island, Sheila was being picked up by other agents.

In the hotel room, Rayne handed over a Montreal Canadiens hockey bag stuffed with cash. Hodas counted it all thoroughly. As he was counting and repacking the money, there was a knock at the door. Hodas was too busy with the cash to notice.

"Marty, I'd like you to meet a couple friends of mine," Rayne said. Hodas paid no attention, intent on getting the stacks of bills back into the bag as soon as he could. Rayne tried again to get his attention.

"Marty. These are two friends of mine. This is Special Agent John Thurston and this is Special Agent Steve Skinner of the FBI."

Hodas was now galvanized. His defence mechanism kicked in.

"I never had that money," he said, pointing to the stacks of bills. "This is the biggest case of entrapment in the history of the United States." Then he turned to Rayne, the man he thought he could trust.

"Andy, how could you do this to me?"

* * *

Marvin was called back in after the arrests to do one more thing on the case that he had started. With police tape record-ers capturing it, Marvin phoned Hodas. The porn merchant knew who he was from Anna. Marvin told him he had heard about the arrests and needed to know what went wrong. Where did it go bad? Was it on the Toronto end or the New York end? Hodas walked through the deal with Marvin as they tried to figure out who the fink was. Hodas warned Marvin to look into this Andy Lenew and find out who he really was.

"I'll do that," Marvin said, "thanks."

Marvin was relieved to hear no overt accusation against him. Police decided to leave Anna out of it to help protect Marvin. She was the one who had first met Marvin directly. Since Marvin had vouched for Bill Gill, not Rayne, they hoped Marvin could avoid being pinned as an informant.

As someone who was not arrested, Anna was also a plausible alternative suspect as to who it was that had finked.

In the end, Marty Hodas, Richard Spadafora and Sheila Baummel pleaded guilty to conspiring to ship pornographic videotapes. Hodas also admitted to shipping obscene material across state lines, since the trucker had taken a short-cut through New Jersey on his way from New York City to Buffalo. The court heard of the 1,200 seized tapes worth more than $50,000, with the prosecutor describing the arrests as the dismantling of "a major distribution ring of really raunchy matter." Further, some $6 million worth of videos and equipment were seized from Corporal Video. The evidence against Hodas was overwhelming. From Marvin's introduction to Anna through to Rayne's recordings, Hodas was undone. In 1985, each of the three was fined $5,000. Spadafora received a four-year suspended sentence, Sheila a year in jail. Hodas was given a year on each count, to be served concurrently.

Part of the plea deal required him to get out of the porn business. The authorities finally got their wish.

After Rayne had testified in court and the plea deal had been struck, Hodas asked to speak with him in the hallway.

"I want to shake your hand," Hodas said. "I've been indicted improperly three, four times and beat every one. You caught me clean and got me good."

The FBI was pleased to have convicted Hodas at long last, even though the kiddie porn and snuff films never materialized. Marvin was disappointed that the FBI shut down the operation before getting to the root of that. He wanted it off the street. As someone who was an abused child, Marvin had an enormous soft spot for children in peril. It was one of the reasons—or excuses—he gave himself when deciding to fink out Anna to Robbie. These were the early days when he was still getting used to the idea of being an informant. His payment from the cops, about $3,000, dispelled any remaining doubt.

Rayne and Gill were given special commendations from William H. Webster, director of the FBI, for their considerable efforts. Marvin was never mentioned. Neither was his role revealed anywhere in the extensive media coverage of the case. The newspaper reports said a "chance encounter" between a Canadian cop and Anna started the case off.

Marvin didn't mind being left out of the publicity, although he kept some of the newspaper clippings hidden in his home as a souvenir. He had pulled down another big case without his secret life as a fink being revealed.

CHAPTER 26

TORONTO, 1983

Marvin arrived at the OPP office in downtown Toronto, at Robbie's request, wondering if he was in trouble. Robbie always told him that just because he worked with the cops didn't mean he wouldn't be charged if he were caught breaking the law. Marvin believed him. In the few months that Marvin had known Robbie, he had seen how ruthless he could be. But when Marvin sat down, he found his handler wasn't looking to chastise. He was looking to sweet-talk him. Robbie had received a call from the FBI in Detroit about a fugitive who had threatened a female judge before jumping bail and fleeing. The threat was seen as serious, particularly given the fugitive's reputation for ruthlessness; reportedly, if anyone crossed her, she had them hurt, Robbie said.

"What a gorilla," Marvin thought.

The FBI thought she was working in Toronto, posing as a Jewish girl named Deborah Goldfarb. She had set up a photo business in shopping malls taking pictures of children and printing them on plastic plaques.

Robbie then said to Marvin words that he would repeat over and over in the years to come: "See what you can do."

* * *

That same week, Marvin attended a meeting of his B'nai Brith lodge. He remained a member, even after his fall from grace when convicted of fraud. His work within the Jewish community was rooted in a genuine sense of altruism, and it had earned him a dozen plaques in gratitude. The lodge was a refuge from his exhausting street life. And despite his reputation, Marvin was a tremendously personable guy called on often to be a master of ceremonies. One day, a fellow member, Freddie Nelson, told Marvin about his new job doing photography for a nice Jewish girl from the United States.

"No kidding," Marvin said. "Tell me about her."

Freddie told Marvin about Deborah Goldfarb. It was another example of the remarkable luck Marvin had while working for the cops. This gave him a way into her life, however flimsy. Marvin didn't need much.

The next day, Marvin went to the photo booth and asked for Deborah. When she appeared, Marvin was flabbergasted. He expected the tough fugitive to be a brutish woman, with the hard look of a con. Deborah was gorgeous; tall and graceful with a beautiful face.

"I heard such nice things about you from my friend Freddie," Marvin told her, shaking her hand, "I wanted to meet you. I'm Marvin Elkind."

Her reply gave him his second surprise. "I know you, Mr. Elkind. You own Elk's menswear," she said, mistaking Marvin for his cousin Manny.

Not missing a beat, Marvin replied, "How did you know?"

"One of my girls used to work for you. She's here now. She'd love to say hi."

Marvin's heart sank. Once exposed as a liar, Deborah would shun him. But the former Elk's worker walked up to Marvin and shook his hand. Even though she had worked at Elk's, she had never actually met Manny Elkind. Then she turned to her boss and said, admiringly: "Mr. Elkind is a very wealthy man."

All of a sudden, Deborah wanted to get to know Marvin as much as Marvin wanted to know her. She suggested they get together for lunch.

Robbie wanted Marvin to dress up for the meal. Marvin was supposed to be the owner of a successful chain of clothing stores, so he should look the part, Robbie said. Marvin had only one good suit, a three-piece in grey, black and white flecks. So he put it on, along with his gold watch, and off he went to meet Deborah. The first thing police wanted was to confirm her identity. The plan was for Marvin to take her out to lunch but to make sure she drove, so police could pull her car over for a make-believe infraction to check her ID and the vehicle identification number of her car.

When Marvin met her for their outing, he took the initiative.

"You drive," he said. "I'll want to have a few drinks."

"Sure," she said. "Toss me your car keys."

It was one of a million tiny unplanned things that can blow an undercover operation. Marvin, though, has an uncanny ability not to show when he is flustered or frightened and is an exceptional extemporaneous thinker. The tools were crucial to his longevity as an informant.

"My brakes have been acting up. I'd hate to risk a pretty thing like you," he said. "Can't we go in your car?" She hunted for her keys and they set off in her black Mercedes-Benz. A block away, city police pulled them over. Deborah apparently had experience with this kind of roadside stop. She hiked up her already short skirt, exposing shapely thighs, as the officer came to her window.

"We're in a big hurry, officer," she said. "Is there a problem?"

The officer was so enamoured of her that he seemed ready to let her go before remembering to ask for her documents. She was exactly who U.S. authorities were looking for, although her real name was not Goldfarb; she was not even Jewish.

Marvin was in awe—a thuggish gentile fugitive passing herself off as a demure Jewish businesswoman. She lived in an apartment building where almost every resident was Jewish. She had the old Jewish ladies mothering her and the old Jewish men ogling her. After the traffic stop, lunch went well. They talked about Marvin putting money into her business. Marvin knew she was looking to con him out of the money, but he didn't care—he didn't have any. All he cared about was that she not find out he was also conning her.

* * *

One of the ways that police gather evidence against a suspect is to have an informant introduce the suspect to an undercover officer posing as a fellow crook. Not only is it better in court to hear evidence from a police officer rather than a reformed criminal, it also helps to protect the informant. The last thing Robbie or Marvin wanted was to put Marvin on the stand at a trial. He would then have to testify under oath to being a fink. It would expose him and, it was assumed, end his career.

For this case, Marvin worked with Danielle McLean.

A slender blond woman with a wide smile, Danielle was one of six children—the only girl—all of whom followed their father into policing. One of her brothers, André Bouchard, made a particular name for himself as the head of the Major Crimes Bureau with Montreal police during the bloody motorcycle gang war in the 1990s that left 160 dead. Raised in such a testosterone-filled home, Danielle was well prepared to be a pioneer for women in the OPP, entering the force in the cadet class of 1974, the first class to allow women. It wasn't always easy, and she endured many a sexist prank, but she showed her dedication. A year into her career she transferred to the intelligence branch, where her fluency in French was appreciated. She was soon partnered with Robbie.

Marvin thought the world of her.

"Gorgeous, gorgeous OPP copper," Marvin says. "But I think she was even tougher than Robbie."

To bring Danielle and Deborah together, Marvin told the fugitive he would like her to meet his friend. Danielle drove to Deborah's apartment in a Buick Wildcat, silver with a black top. The trio plowed through Chinese food and booze. As they talked, Danielle sat twirling her car keys around on one finger. Marvin almost gasped. On the ring, alongside the key to the Buick, was a distinctive key—small and straight, with a single tooth—that Marvin recognized instantly. It was a universal police handcuff key.

"Deborah, honey, could you get me some ice for my drink?" Marvin asked. As soon as Deborah was distracted, Marvin whispered to Danielle to put the keys away. Luckily, Deborah hadn't noticed, and she took to Danielle. Danielle said she lived out of town, which was why she wasn't around much. Deborah offered her a key to her apartment so she would have a place to crash.

As Marvin and Danielle got close to Deborah, the case widened. They learned she was having luxury cars stolen in Canada and shipped to the United States. The cars moved through Windsor to Detroit and from Toronto to New York. When Deborah told them that a guy from New York was coming to town, an Italian guy with major connections, Marvin and Danielle wanted to meet him. Robbie assumed the Italian was Deborah's boss, and arranged to have another officer, a young, attractive male officer, introduced into their plot, someone who might catch Deborah's eye in a different way. Robbie's plan was for Marvin to invite Deborah and her New York boss to dinner at a downtown hotel with Danielle. During dinner, the new undercover officer would walk past. Danielle would recognize him, pretend to be an old friend and greet him with hugs and kisses before making introductions all around. Marvin would then invite him to join them for a drink.

On the day of the dinner, Marvin had been out flogging aluminum siding, and he arrived at the Delta hotel wearing jeans, with his one good suit in a garment bag. Robbie and Danielle were coming straight from work as well. Everyone was to get changed in a single hotel room. When Marvin showed up, only Danielle was in the room. She was taking a shower, and wouldn't open the door. Marvin told her to cover up and unlock the door so he could drop off his suit and shoes. He couldn't risk Deborah seeing him carrying his suit, he said. Danielle, a picture of modesty, reluctantly unlocked the door and Marvin burst in, pretending to take pictures as she recoiled and covered herself with a towel. She was mortified—more so when she later met the other officers and found them all smirking. Marvin had regaled them with the details.

When Marvin and Danielle greeted Deborah and her boss, Deborah was perplexed by something she had noticed. Every time she had seen Marvin, he was wearing the same suit.

"You own all these clothing stores. Why do you always wear the same suit?" she asked. Neither Robbie nor Marvin had thought about that, but Marvin came up with an immediate answer.

"I own twenty of them," he said, looking admiringly at his sleeve. "I liked it so much I bought twenty."

"You bought twenty of the same suit? You're crazy," Deborah said playfully.

Marvin had managed to skirt over the slip, but something still went wrong. No one could have imagined it would come from Robbie.

* * *

Robbie was careful, but also impetuous. Like Marvin, he thrived on the adrenalin rush of undercover operations. In this plot, he was only a bit player as Danielle, Marvin and the new undercover saw all the action. At the dinner, Robbie was only on surveillance duty, sitting anonymously at the bar, keeping watch. At least, that was the plan.

With one drink too many fuelling his bravado, Robbie came along with the young undercover officer when he walked past Marvin and Danielle's table. He was introduced along with everyone else, and when Marvin made the invitation for the undercover to join them, Robbie pulled up a chair, too. To make matters worse, Robbie got into an argument with the New Yorker. Something about him rubbed Robbie the wrong way. It got to the point where Robbie and the fugitive's boss seemed on the verge of a fistfight. Marvin had to be careful because he wasn't supposed to have ever met Robbie.

"Look, this guy has had one too many. Let's just ignore him," Marvin said to his guests. Then, turning to the young undercover officer, he said, "Can't you get your friend to settle down?"

Things did simmer down, but away from the table, Robbie's boss was furious. The next day, Robbie was ordered off the case. He knew he had messed up, apologized and accepted his punishment. But Marvin didn't.

"If Robbie's out, I'm out," he said. They had little choice. Robbie stayed.

Meanwhile, despite Robbie's belligerence, the young officer, Deborah and the New Yorker got along well. Perhaps having to deal with Robbie's aggro brought them closer together. The young officer took Deborah out on a couple of dates, infiltrating her circle even further.

One day soon after, Deborah called Marvin.

"I'm feeling low. How about we all go down to Florida? My treat."

Marvin desperately wanted to go. Free travel and a long weekend in the sun sounded perfect. Marvin called Robbie, begging him to let him go. Robbie said it would be up to Danielle. Marvin called Danielle, saying Robbie wanted them to go. To his surprise, she agreed.

Marvin whistled happily as he packed. Robbie gave Marvin enough time to finish packing before calling him again. He had news. Deborah had been arrested. It turned out that Robbie and Danielle had known all about the pending arrest and that there would be no holiday. For Robbie, it was another of the pranks he and his colleagues played. It proved Marvin was part of his team. For Danielle, it was payback on Marvin for embarrassing her in the hotel room.

***

Back in his office, Robbie summarized the results of Marvin's work in a secret case note: "These individuals were from Detroit and New York City. The subsequent investigation resulted in the arrest of one person from Detroit, the recovery of a stolen Mercedes and Cadillac and the seizure of a large quantity of undervalued goods," he wrote in neat, all-capital letters. He was meticulous, almost obsessive, with his note taking, although his spelling was atrocious. Over years he would fill thick notebook after thick notebook with nothing but his documentation of each of his phone calls and meetings with Marvin. "The [fugitive] from Detroit was returned to the U.S. and received a seven-to-fourteen year sentence on fraud charges relating to activities in the United States. A second individual from New York City became a subject of investigation by the FBI on matters relating to fraud."

Robbie locked his notes away and mused about The Weasel. He was now three for three with his cases, all interesting ones, too. He had displayed a quick mind, fast mouth and even cooler head than him. He told Marvin how proud he was. Marvin loved the praise.

He was paid for his frolics, too, and, once again, the people he betrayed seemed none the wiser. As had happened in the cheque fraud case, when Deborah was arrested, one of her friends called Marvin to ask if he could get the charges dropped through his supposed connections.

"Yeah, I can probably do it, but it'll cost money," Marvin said.

"She has twenty-five hundred dollars in cash hidden in her apartment. You can have that upfront and I will give you another twenty-five hundred later." Marvin agreed. He considered it a tip. He was starting to earn real money through the police, although it was never as much as he had hoped for.

"It would be determined by the nature of the case that we would have him involved in," Robbie says. Marvin generated some of the investigations, but he also was given assignments. "Many of them were started by us and we put him into the subjects, so to speak. And we would direct him then on what we expected and what we were looking for and that type of thing. At the end of that—the completion of that investigation—we would take a look at the time that had been spent, and that's how we determined what we paid him. Another factor was the amount—if it was stolen property—it was determined on the amount of stolen property recovered."

* * *

Along with Robbie, Danielle McLean became a big part of Marvin's life in the years ahead. Marvin grew deeply fond of them both. With Robbie as his father figure, Danielle—despite being 18 years younger than Marvin—became a mother figure.

Marvin was cobbling together a new family.

Despite the danger and irregular hours, he loved this latest contortion in his life. The government work was becoming a full-time endeavour for Marvin, and Marvin was becoming nearly a full-time endeavour for Robbie. Between them, they seemed to come up with no end of tips and leads to chase. Both travelled in unusual circles. As they prowled, each stumbled on intriguing leads. Big or small, they would chase them all; Robbie as a workaholic cop, driven to succeed beyond his rank, and Marvin as an adrenaline junkie, driven to make money and find the sense of belonging that he had never had as a child.

CHAPTER 27

OTTAWA, 1984

Inside the sweltering Ottawa Civic Centre arena, more than 10,000 members of the Liberal Party of Canada frantically waved signs and cheered their new party leader. John Turner had beaten six other challengers—easily, in the end, including his main rival, Jean Chrétien—to become prime minister designate, succeeding the flamboyant Pierre Elliott Trudeau. Chrétien would go on to replace Turner as Liberal leader and hold the prime minister's office for more than a decade. But on this night, June 16, 1984, he stood on the huge stage, dejected, humiliated and hurt. With a grim, tight smile, Chrétien accepted kisses from his teary family and supporters, and a hug of condolence from Trudeau, who, for his farewell, wore an all-white suit with a red rose in his lapel. Chrétien prepared to deliver a speech he was dreading, conceding defeat to a party opponent and bitter personal rival.

At the side of the stage, standing next to Trudeau, was a round man with apple cheeks. Marvin had found his way onto Chrétien's private security detail.

As Marvin continued to work for Robbie, he amazed and delighted his handler with the astonishing places he found himself. Although police had always seen him as an excellent source of information on mob plots, Marvin was showing the true depth of his contacts and his chutzpah. Robbie hadn't contemplated how flexible, complex and versatile Marvin could be. Not only was he in tight with gangsters, union bosses, con men and crooks, he was consorting with hugely wealthy businessmen and powerful political figures—although, as Marvin showed Robbie, it could be difficult to tell a mobster and a political operator apart. Marvin had ferreted out political corruption and, without any trouble, had weaselled his way in. What he caught on tape is astonishing.

* * *

The Liberal Party had been a political dynasty in Canada, dubbed the country's "natural governing party." Being in power for too long can incubate a sense of entitlement and engender extravagance and corruption that become an ugly second nature.

As Marvin circulated in Toronto, known as a representative of the Teamsters union, as an associate in a large construction firm and as someone close to mobsters, he always boasted of his political contacts, even though he really had none. It was only a matter of time before he stumbled upon people who did have some. First, a woman Marvin knew through Tommy Corrigan started discussing a chain of nursing homes she was developing. Marvin offered to help and was introduced to her partners, one of whom was Jamie Astaphan, the doctor who in 1988 would give Ben Johnson the steroids that would cause the sprinter to lose his gold medal in the 100-metre race at the Summer Olympics. Marvin was also introduced to Hector J. Massey, a political-science professor at York University. Massey's role was to "take care" of the politicians and regulators. He was in a good position to do that as a 20-year Liberal Party stalwart, organizer and political adviser. Massey, who had emigrated to Canada from Jamaica in the 1960s, had almost as many degrees as Marvin had fingers. He had served as associate dean of York University's Atkinson College, been elected councillor and named finance chairman of King Township municipal council. He had written books on the Canadian military and was an honorary member of the Canadian Forces Staff School and a recipient of a NATO Fellowship.

Massey, in turn, introduced Marvin to friends in his circle: a young, sharp Liberal Party organizer who always dressed as if he were already in high office; an old party bagman; and others. They fell in love with Marvin, with his hard looks, shady pedigree and joyful banter. It was not his vote Massey was after, but his contacts in the building trade and his association with a major contractor in the city. On April 16, 1984, at Massey's horse farm in Schomberg, an hour's drive north of Toronto, Massey said he was going to Ottawa later in the week to meet with the federal caucus and that he could get Marvin government contracts for renovations. He was, Massey bragged, a close friend of Jean Chrétien, then an influential government minister.

"These guys bought me hook, line and sinker, and sinker, line and hook," Marvin says. "They absolutely loved me and thought they had hooked in with a dirty developer willing to work with them. The deal was, they would find out which government construction jobs, public-works projects—like fixing offices, renovating offices, things like that—were being put out to tender in the area. I would put in a bid for about double what it would cost and they would make sure I got that contract. Then we would split the extra money between us."

It was classic political public-works corruption.

Marvin told Robbie about his new find. Robbie didn't shy away from sensitive investigations, like some of his colleagues did. He wanted to chase these guys down the same way he would a drug dealer or blue-collar crook. He set Marvin up with a wire and sent him to meeting after meeting with his new Liberal pals.

By May, Massey was helping to run the election campaign for a provincial Liberal candidate, and he invited Marvin to a campaign-team meeting. Marvin was asked to supervise the door-to-door canvassing and help land the Jewish vote. In return, Massey told him, Marvin would be given government construction contracts. Marvin was starting to see how politics seemed to work, and it looked a lot like the mob. One organizer, a Hong Kong businessman, was promised a student visa for a relative in return for his help. A young organizer was given a well-paying summer job that he didn't need to show up for to enable him to work on the campaign full-time. Marvin brought a police photographer with him to the candidate's nomination meeting on May 23, 1984. Marvin stood smiling between Hector Massey and Jim Coutts, a former principal secretary to Prime Minister Pierre Trudeau. David Peterson, the provincial premier, and Joe Foti, a famous Liberal Party fundraiser, stood with them. It reminded Marvin of the good old days when he and the mob's card-and-dice cheats were clowning around with the political elite.

Marvin introduced his new friends to his supposed girl-friend, who was secretly an OPP officer. They loved her as much as they loved Marvin and, when she wasn't around, they marvelled to Marvin that he could attract such a hottie.

Marvin was given a special tape recorder hidden in an attaché case. Marvin brought it along to the next meeting with Professor Massey, to see if he could catch the crooked talk on tape. He didn't have to work hard. Unlike seasoned mobsters, these guys used no guarded language or code words. They spelled it all out in painful, embarrassing detail: which public-works jobs they had dibs on, how much they were going to make, what they were going to do with their take and on and on. The evidence was richer than Marvin or Robbie ever imagined.

Afterwards, Robbie called Marvin to his office.

"You got to go back to them and get them to say it again," Robbie said.

"What do you mean, 'again'? I got it all on tape. They laid it all out for me."

"I know," said Robbie. "But a technician screwed up and erased the whole tape. It's gone. You've got to get them to say it again."

Marvin couldn't believe it. It never happened when he was working on thugs, only when he was moving in on politicians.

"How am I gonna get them to say it all again?"

"I don't know, but you have to," was all Robbie offered.

So Marvin and the officer who was posing as his girlfriend were wired up again and went to visit Massey at his university office.

"Hector," Marvin said, genuinely feeling the awkwardness he was trying to project, "I told my girlfriend about our conversation the other night, how it will work and how well we're going to do from it. But she thinks it's all my wishful thinking. She doesn't believe me. Can you tell her about it all yourself?"

Massey happily laid the plans out again. He then asked Marvin and his date to come to another planning meeting he was hosting at a Jamaican restaurant near the home of one of his key allies, Joe Foti, who was a legend in the Liberal Party. Foti was the city of Toronto's supervisor of maintenance, a

Marvin, 3, stands with his mother, Beatrice, and stepfather, Morris, at their wedding in 1937.

Marvin (circled) in school in Toronto. "I had a big, round, fat kisser," he says of his emerging form. He was picked on by classmates, few of whom were Jewish.

Marvin's foster brother, Roy Pasquale.

Tommy Corrigan, Teamsters Canada boss.

On February 16, 1958, Marvin married Hannah "Hennie" Guest.

Marvin sport fishing in Mexico in 1965.

Marvin, cigar in hand, clowns with Baldy Chard (left), his monstrous, long-time partner in the collection business, and Benny "Red" Randell (right), their erratic, short-term partner, at the Beaches Boxing Club in Toronto, circa 1975. Baldy was called "the toughest guy in the world," which meant Marvin wanted him at his side.

Al "Robbie" Robinson in 1981.

The toll of Robbie's job showed by 1991.

Robbie at his desk at the OPP Intelligence Bureau headquarters in 1990.

Marvin's first case for police, in 1983, was a $1.7 million cheque scam.
Above: While wearing a secret wire, Marvin meets Herb Asseltine
(white coat), George Buric (dark jacket), and their muscle, at Toronto's
Royal York Hotel. **Below:** Heading to the bank.

Marvin helped catch New York City's "porno prince" in 1983. **Above:** FBI surveillance cameras watch the undercover agent, Andy Rayne, clutching a bag stuffed with $50,000, as Marty unknowingly gives him a tour of his Times Square sex empire. **Right:** The airplane photo that almost gave Rayne away. **Bottom** (left to right): FBI agent Steve Skinner, Rayne, his partner Bill Gill of the OPP, and FBI agent John Thurston celebrate the successful cross-border sting.

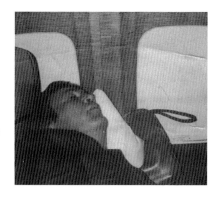

OPP undercover agent John Celentino transformed into a tough mobster and arms merchant known as "Gino" when introduced by Marvin into many of their schemes.

Danielle McLean, Robbie's OPP partner.

Karen Moffatt, Marvin's pretend girlfriend.

Ian Knox

Jack McCombs

Dennis McGillis

Rich Mazzari

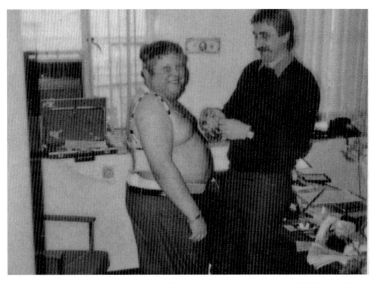

Marvin gets wired up with a hidden microphone in the OPP's intelligence office.

Marvin was among mourners at the funeral for Mafia boss Giacomo Luppino in Hamilton in 1987. He was seated with the family.

In 1984, Aaron "the Hawk" Pryor, junior welterweight champion, boxed Nicky Furlano. Marvin (left), brought along a police surveillance officer posing as a boxing photographer.

Marvin took along a police officer on surveillance to this Liberal Party nomination meeting in 1984. Pictured are Marvin, Jim Coutts, former principal secretary to Prime Minister Trudeau, candidate Joe Ricciuti, David Peterson, then Ontario premier, and bagman Joe Foti (right). At far left is Hector Massey.

Police watch Marvin, sucking on a cigar, carousing with Ernie Kanakis, a Detroit gambler reputed to have killed three Detroit mobsters who came at him with ice picks.

John Celentino hands an AK-47 assault rifle to businessman Nicholas Andreko (middle) as Robbie (left) watches, during a 1987 coup d'état plot against Ghana that was uncovered by Marvin and prevented.

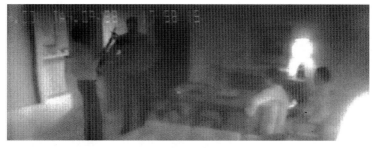

Marvin, in a cap and trench coat, shakes hands as he introduces alleged Chicago coup d'état plotters to his mercenary friends, who are really police agents, as a secret FBI camera records it.

As Marvin reads a newspaper (bottom right), an alleged coup plotter toys with an M60 machine gun. "You look like Rambo," commented Robbie, seated at the table (right).

Despite their awkward first meeting in 1965, three-time Heavyweight Champion Muhammad Ali and Marvin became friends. Whenever the boxing great is in Toronto, often at Marvin's request, he has Marvin drive him around.

Photo by Eimid Ketelaar, FrozenImage.

U.S. Library of Congress

Photo by Adrian Humphreys

(Left) Queen Beatrix of the Netherlands; (middle) Israeli Prime Minister Golda Meir; (right) Canadian Heavyweight Champion George Chuvalo. They all, in turn, have been seated behind Marvin, their driver.

During Marvin's transition back into civilian life, he has been hiding in plain sight, doing modeling jobs that saw his face stretched across buses and subway cars. **Below:** On television where he was in the Mob Stories documentary series.

Photo by Adrian Humphreys

Marvin's enthusiasm for boxing has never waned. He is seen here in 2010 with Neven "No Surrender" Pajkic, Canadian Heavyweight Champ, at a black-tie event in Toronto.

job he had held for 19 years. Robbie set the female officer up with a recorder hidden in her purse to catch the dinner conversation on tape.

Over a deliciously spicy meal, the group discussed with Marvin the next public-works project they were going for, who would be bidding on it, what Marvin's bid should be and how the remainder of the public's money would be divided. Marvin's part in it was to place the winning bid, on behalf of the construction firm they thought he represented. The take would top $200,000.

Marvin was supremely relaxed. It wasn't like his meetings with mobsters—he had no fear of being patted down for wires. These guys didn't even think of it, nor would he have been frightened if they had. If he had been caught, he would have shrugged and walked away. Marvin was also struck by their attitude: it was as if they weren't talking about corruption at all, as if it were their right, their expected reward for working for the political masters of the country.

"All of them thought they were completely legit, that ripping off the government was just the way it was supposed to be. They didn't, in any way, see what they were doing as wrong."

The conversation at the restaurant had been so gloriously incriminating, Marvin looked forward to Robbie's accolades when they got back to the office. When he and the undercover officer got into Marvin's car to leave, however, the cop wasn't as happy.

"We have a problem," she said. "I didn't turn the recorder on."

"What do you mean, you didn't turn it on? They spilled their guts in there."

"I didn't think I could turn it on without them noticing. We were all sitting so close at the table, I didn't want to blow our cover."

Instead of accolades from Robbie, Marvin got a blasting from his handler, who yelled at him for the mistake. Marvin wondered what he could have done about it—he hadn't even known until it was too late. He wondered why the officer didn't just go to the washroom to turn it on, or drop a fork or something. That's when he realized that not everyone had his nerves of steel. The only salvation was that, after dinner, Joe Foti had extended an invitation for the couple to attend his upcoming barbecue, one of the hottest political social events of the summer. This time, Robbie said, no screw-ups.

* * *

Under a canopy of grapevines in the backyard of Joe Foti's home on a pleasant residential stretch of Winona Drive in midtown Toronto, Liberal Party heavyweights and stalwart supporters gathered for an annual summer barbecue that would grow in the years ahead to almost mythical proportions.

Legend had it that Foti had once hosted a small backyard party and a neighbour had complained about the noise, so he'd bought the neighbour's house to end any future squabbles. He then bought two more properties surrounding his, renting out the houses but reserving use of the adjoining backyards for himself. The four yards together allowed his annual barbecue guest list to grow from the dozens who attended the first one, in 1980, to the 700 or so by the time Marvin was there and, eventually, to a horde of five thousand. Foti knew how to throw a party—not the glittery black-tie events the political elites usually went to, but a sprawling garden party set amid the peppers yellowing in Foti's well-tended gardens and fruit ripening on overhanging trees. He would cook hundreds of sausages and steaks and had a pig roasting over a fire pit. He would open case after case of beer and serve his homemade wine. Foti had started throwing the annual barbecue when he worked for the city, and many friends would come from city hall. The mayor, Art Eggleton, was at the first barbecue, and future mayors and wannabe mayors started reserving the date. Provincial and federal members of Parliament, cabinet ministers, even prime ministers came over the years.

For Foti's barbecue, Marvin's undercover date was again wired for sound, but this time she was given a recorder with extra recording time so she could turn it on in Marvin's car before they went into the party. That would prevent any last-minute jitters getting in the way again.

Foti was an affable host.

"Marvin, my house is your house," he told his guest. "Anytime you need a drink, you come here. Anytime you need to eat, you come here. Anytime you need a place to sleep, you come here." Marvin's heart melted with affection.

Foti's folksy and friendly manner, the charm that had won him so many friends, worked on Marvin, too. Marvin felt sick. He didn't like betraying the hospitality of the kindly old man.

* * *

During Marvin's infiltration of the Liberal Party, he was invited by Massey to work at the upcoming Liberal leadership convention in Ottawa. Pierre Trudeau, the long-serving prime minister, had resigned and the party was choosing a new leader, a man who automatically would become the prime minister of Canada, at least until the next election.

Robbie was excited by the idea of having his man there. It would give him a peek into the political machinery, even though there was no hard evidence of corruption beyond the local band of Liberal insiders.

On June 13, 1984, Massey told Marvin the arrangements for his trip to Ottawa. The party would fly him there and put him up in a room at a hotel near the action. Before he caught his flight, Marvin signed the lease to rent premises for the local candidate's campaign headquarters.

When Marvin arrived at the Civic Centre arena to register and be issued a special-access security pass, he was told to fill out a form for a police check. Marvin grimaced. He filled it out with his real name and date of birth and waited for the refusal. To his surprise, despite his criminal record, he was handed photo ID that gave him access to areas of the convention closed to outsiders. He worked hard as one of Chrétien's security guards, accompanying him almost everywhere. He had a great time meeting political bigwigs, even using his ID to let two Liberal senators into an event that their credentials didn't qualify them to enter.

"I found Jean Chrétien to be a great guy. He was real down-to-earth," Marvin says.

Marvin was sad when the convention ended. Before leaving he shared drinks and commiserated with another disappointed man, Eugene Whelan, the minister of agriculture who was famous for always wearing a green Stetson hat. Whelan had come dead last in the leadership vote.

Before leaving town, Liberal Party organizers insisted all staff return their party ID cards. Marvin had no intention of giving it up. In his hotel room, he put the card under the sole of his foot inside his sock, then got dressed. As he left, officials were adamant he return the card, and he swore he had no idea where it had got to. Security bosses searched his luggage and even strip-searched him. As he was undressing in a private room, he was thinking what he would say when the card was discovered. He couldn't convincingly act surprised that the card was in his sock. He decided he would apologize and say he treasured the souvenir of his small role in selecting the next prime minister of Canada too much to turn it in. He had just about concocted the hangdog speech in his head by the time he was nude, but for his socks. He stretched out his arms and spun around to show he wasn't hiding anything. Before he bent down to remove his socks, the security boss just grumbled for him to get dressed. Marvin knew that Robbie would be delighted with the trophy as well.

Marvin used the card only once more.

* * *

Four days after being sworn in as prime minister, John Turner called a snap election. It was a disaster, and after the polls closed on September 4, the Conservatives slaughtered the Liberals, with Brian Mulroney winning the largest majority in Canadian history. As Marvin saw it, his Liberal contacts and the security pass were now irrelevant.

As he watched the election results on television, he saw reporters showing a large victory party for the Conservative faithful at the Royal York Hotel.

"Hennie, we're going out," Marvin called out to his wife. He put on his suit and his gold watch, but when he told Hennie what he had in mind, she refused to go.

"You're crazy," she said. "You'll get thrown out."

Undaunted, Marvin dug out his Liberal ID card and headed downtown. Outside the hotel's Imperial Room, Marvin flashed the card to the Conservatives manning the door.

"I'm here representing Mr. Chrétien. I've come to congrat-ulate you and Mr. Mulroney on your victory," he blustered. The jubilant Tories welcomed him warmly, plying him with consolation drinks and imploring him to go on television to deliver a message from Chrétien. Marvin was tempted, but declined.

"I'm not authorized to do that," he said.

* * *

When Marvin was next called in for a meeting with Robbie, he expected to hear that the Liberal operators had all been arrested. In his office, though, Robbie was blunt with the news.

"The commissioner, in his wisdom, is not going to proceed with criminal charges," Marvin remembers Robbie saying.

Marvin was shocked. He had sat through hours of incriminating conversations, both by himself and with an undercover OPP officer, some of them caught on tape. It seemed an open-and-shut case.

Despite that, Marvin had only one question for Robbie.

"Will this affect the money I'll get paid?"

"Not at all," Robbie said.

"Then big fucking deal."

CHAPTER 28

TORONTO, 1984

The pudgy senior was paying for the sex, so the young woman couldn't complain about the man's lack of stamina. In her line of work, it was a blessing. But with this guy, a married 60-something mayor of a town in southern Ontario, his exhaustion became a routine. He would arrive in Toronto on business, she would come to his room at the Holiday Inn near the airport and strip naked. He would do his business and immediately gasp, roll over and fall asleep.

Despite the small room in an unattractive part of town—she was used to better—she figured this guy must have money. After several trysts, she had an idea. The next time he was in town, she arrived with extra equipment in her bag. When the politician was done and snoozing, she pulled off the sheets, set up a camera and took photographs of them lying naked together. She put her arms around him for one, kissed him for another, all without waking him.

Their next meeting was less satisfying for the mayor. She needed money, she said. Could he give it to her? She was thinking $25,000. Before he had a chance to balk, she added an incentive by handing him the somnolent sex pictures. He was mortified, but retained enough of a grip to say he needed time to get the money. Instead of heading to his bank, he arranged a private meeting with his friend, a senior officer of the OPP. The mayor showed him the pictures and told him of his predicament. Blackmail is a crime, but the mayor's problem with lodging an official complaint was that an arrest would bring his indiscretion to public attention. The officer said he'd see what he could do.

* * *

Robbie was told to discreetly look into the blackmail. The trouble was nobody knew who the hooker was. The phone number the politician used to book her was an answering service that led to a forwarding number no longer in service. And the politician didn't know her real name.

"If anyone'll know her, it'll be Marvin," Robbie's boss said. So Robbie called in The Weasel. Marvin looked at the photos and, after admiring the hooker's professional assets, took a look at her face.

"Yeah," he said. "I know her."

He told Robbie that shortly before this, on June 22, 1984, Toronto fighter Nicky Furlano had fought Cincinnati's Aaron "The Hawk" Pryor, the junior welterweight champ. Marvin and Robbie both remembered the night because Marvin had arranged for a police photographer to attend, posing as a boxing photographer. The officer wasn't subtle enough, though, and the bodyguard of a major loan shark started wondering aloud if the photographer could be a cop because he was more interested in shooting the crowd packed with gangsters than the fight. Before going to the arena that night, Marvin had been with boxing pals in the bar of the Sutton Place Hotel, and someone had introduced him to the hooker, who was working the hotel crowd. He bumped into her again later, a passing encounter between two characters spending too much time in hotel bars.

Robbie loved solving conundrums that others couldn't. He told Marvin to set up a meeting with the woman right away. Marvin asked his friend who knew her to invite her to get together with him for drinks. He said to tell her to meet him where they were first introduced, the Sutton Place bar.

Robbie had a surveillance team outside the hotel, waiting to follow whatever woman Marvin emerged with. The hooker arrived looking the part—leather miniskirt, black tights and a slinky top. She and Marvin had a couple of drinks as Marvin spun a story of big-name boxers coming to town for a match and offered to set her up with some wealthy clients. She thanked him, and they agreed to keep in touch. Marvin walked out with her. Outside the hotel, he heard an unexpected voice.

"Daddy?" It was his youngest daughter, then 22. She worked as a gymnastics instructor and the lessons were sometimes held at the hotel.

"Oh, hi, honey," Marvin said, before saying goodnight to the dolled-up hooker, making sure the surveillance team saw him walking with her. Turning back to his daughter, he asked, "What are you doing here?"

"Never mind what I'm doing here," she said with an icy glare, "what are *you* doing here with *her*?"

Marvin was glad he had told his daughters years ago about his unusual line of work, and that they had met Robbie several times. Robbie had given them his phone number in case they were ever worried.

"Honey, I'm working for the cops. I'm here with Robbie. Please, I want you to go into the bar and you'll see Robbie in there having a drink. I want you to ask him what I'm doing."

She did, and was relieved to hear that her father really was working on a case with the hooker at the hotel.

Meanwhile, as the surveillance team followed the woman, Robbie and Marvin went to celebrate with a drink at the Sheraton, another downtown hotel. As they sipped, Robbie was startled to see the target hooker walking into the bar. She immediately spotted Marvin. He told her he had come to see a boxing buddy at the hotel. She said she was there to meet another client.

An exhausted surveillance team finally followed the busy woman to her home. Soon afterwards, senior OPP officers in dress uniforms confronted her. They came on heavy, with threats of criminal charges. Not realizing it was a bluff, she handed over her copies of the photos and the negatives. Despite the dubious benefit to taxpayers, Marvin was paid by the OPP for his intervention but was also warned never to approach the politician. They were worried that Marvin might try to pull something using his knowledge of the sensitive situation. The OPP closed the case with a summarizing note: Marvin "identified a hooker who was extorting an out-of-town politician. As a result of this identification the authorities were able to recover a number of photographs and the negatives which were being used to extort the politician."

Marvin wasn't surprised when charges weren't laid. He had already seen how politics interfered with policing. This case wasn't over for him, however.

* * *

The day after the police retrieved the photos, the hooker phoned Marvin.

"Did the cops visit you last night?" she asked.

"No, why?"

"There must have been someone watching one of us. They came to my place after I got in."

She called again the next day. This time she wanted to get together to discuss the supposed clients Marvin was bringing in. He agreed to meet her, but when he told Robbie about it, Robbie was suspicious. He said he would have a surveillance team watch from outside, but told Marvin to take Baldy Chard with him, in case the woman had figured things out and brought someone to get revenge. Baldy knew nothing of Marvin's government work. Marvin bamboozled him with the same story of a make-believe boxing event, and Baldy was happy to tag along. When Marvin and Baldy arrived at the bar, the hooker recognized Baldy.

"I know you," she said. "You know my pimp." At the same time that Baldy was trying to remember her pimp—a tall, tough, flamboyant black man who lived up to every stereotype of 1970s blaxploitation movies—that very man was outside the bar watching Marvin. He was disappointed when Marvin arrived with muscle, but then he noticed something else. The police surveillance van was outside, with a blackened one-way window through which pictures could be taken. His street smarts connected the van to Marvin, and he likely figured it all out. He was enraged, but instead of taking it out on Marvin, who sat next to the frightening Baldy, he attacked the van, which seemed an easier target. He started rocking it back and forth. For a moment it looked as if he might tip it. The lone officer inside the van was terrified.

"I had my piece out. I was ready for him if he got in," he told Robbie and Marvin afterwards.

Police were now worried that Marvin's secret life would be revealed, fingered as a fink by the pimp and the hooker.

But if the pair knew of The Weasel's duplicity, Marvin heard nothing more about it.

"They might have been suspicious, but I never had any confrontation or accusation about me being a fink because of it," Marvin says.

Robbie and Marvin both wondered how long that luck could last. Each case, even though he didn't testify in court, seemed to bring him closer to being unmasked. It was one reason that career informants are a rare breed. They usually have a short shelf life. Most quickly disappear into the witness protection program, or they chicken out and quit. Whether he was brave or foolish, Marvin kept going out onto the street and coming back with cases.

Marvin's help in resolving the blackmail brought him one modest favour from the OPP. Marvin again needed money and the OPP owed him some, but Robbie couldn't get it. Everyone was too busy on September 15, 1984, with the first visit to Toronto of Pope John Paul II. As 500,000 people, the largest assembled crowd in Canadian history, descended on the former Downsview air-force base to await the Pope's arrival by heli-copter, Robbie called each of the senior officers with signing authority over the force's "fink fund," and each one told him he couldn't leave the Pope patrol. Marvin was desperate. A bill had to be paid before the end of the day. Then Robbie called the officer whom Marvin had helped on the blackmail case.

"It's for Marvin?" he confirmed with Robbie. "OK, I owe Marvin. I'll come off the detail to get him the cheque."

* * *

The cheque. The money. It always seemed in short supply. Everyone was anxious to get Marvin's information but, he learned, no one liked having to pay for it. The cops were no different from the gangsters that way.

"The biggest problem I had with the coppers was getting my money. They were always holding back money for one reason or another. I was always fighting for my money," Marvin says.

Marvin always needed money. His lifestyle was incompatible with thrift. He made his living hustling and conniving and he was always on the prowl for something he could bring to Robbie. While he waited, he continued to work his collection business with Baldy, and to work for Tommy Corrigan, and sometimes he resorted once again to selling aluminum siding, despite the grief it had caused him, twice getting him into trouble with police. Some good, however, came from the house calls. It was during one of his siding-sales binges in 1984 that Marvin found a clean, quick case.

* * *

Knocking on doors in one of Toronto's less prestigious neighbourhoods, Marvin and a partner spotted two attractive women leaving an apartment wearing beautiful fur coats. Marvin's friend recognized them and went over to chat.

"What's going on?" Marvin asked him.

"These two, I grew up with them. They're living in Toronto now. They're in the hot-fur business," his friend said. Marvin said he knew a guy who would want to buy them. The women asked to be introduced to him, and Marvin called Robbie, who called Andy Rayne. Within a couple of hours, Marvin was in a T.G.I. Friday's restaurant introducing the officer, who was posing as an out-of-town businessman, to the two women.

"What kind of coats you got?" Rayne asked.

"High-end," one of the women replied.

"Where'd you get them?"

"Straight from Creeds."

Creeds was an expensive women's store that specialized in designer fashions. As they talked, Rayne and Marvin coaxed the women into revealing how they had got them. They said they had a tool to cut the security wire from the coats. They would go into the store wearing an old, cheap fur, cut the wire off an exquisite mink, put their old coat on the hanger and walk out wearing the new one.

"I don't buy junk. I want to have a look at them," Rayne said.

"We don't have them with us," the woman said. "And we can't take you to where they are."

"Look, I'm going back up north in two or three hours. I got the cash handy. If you want to bring a couple of coats to show me, I might be interested. So go get some coats and call me on my cellular phone and we'll meet."

Rayne then pulled out his enormous Motorola DynaTAC 8000X, the first cellphone, which had recently gone on the market, and gave them the number. It was a new thing to see portable phones, and they were only in the hands of the wealthy. The women said they would call him in an hour. The moment they left, Rayne used his new portable phone to call the surveillance team waiting outside.

"They're heading for the stash," he said.

Officers followed the women and watched as they walked up a set of stairs to a second-floor apartment. A few minutes later, they emerge carrying two coats each, wrapped in garbage bags. They had just draped them in the trunk of their car when police surrounded them. Upstairs, officers found more furs.

From the OPP case notes on Marvin: "Supplied information on a group of women who were shoplifting fur coats.

Introduced undercover officer to arrange to buy the coats. One female arrested and $150,000 in fur coats recovered." Not bad for an afternoon. The insurance company for Creeds was so pleased with the case—not only with the recovery and arrest, but learning how the coats were being stolen—that they promised Marvin an extra $5,000 reward. After a few weeks of waiting, Robbie called the company to see where the money was. They said they had sent it to Toronto police. When Robbie called the Toronto force, they said they had spent it on their Christmas party. Marvin was furious. No amount of complaining from Robbie could coax the money out of Toronto. Eventually Robbie managed to scrape together $3,000 from his own funds.

"The Toronto cops stole my money," Marvin says. "Who are the bad guys and who are the good guys, again?"

* * *

Money was becoming a regular impediment in Marvin's relationship with the OPP. But with him proving his value on an almost daily basis, Robbie eventually made an impassioned plea to his superiors to ease the strain.

"Placing 0030 on a monthly maintenance salary which would be paid weekly would be far more efficient for the force and would offer an added incentive to the informant," Robbie wrote in a secret three-page memo to Superintendent Steve Ostrowski, director of the OPP's Intelligence Branch. "There is absolutely no doubt that this informant's activities with this force have produced results which would have cost ten times the monies paid out for his information and operational activities."

The unusual plan received strong backing all the way up the chain of command.

"The contacts and ability this informant possesses have made high level projects, investigations and intelligence probes possible where alternative methods would have been prohibitive," said a supporting memo from W.M. Walker, Robbie's supervisor. "0030 as an asset utilizes what should be considered effective techniques that comparatively result in cost efficient operations."

For all the accolades, the funds remained slim. Marvin was given a weekly maintenance salary of $225. "Should 0030 be on holidays for a week or be working for the FBI in the U.S.A., as sometimes occurs, then the OPP maintenance would not be paid," Walker stipulated. Despite the miserly amount, it made Marvin a full-time fink. For successful projects, he was still paid extra.

The cheques from the OPP would be made out to Marvin, who would endorse them and give them back to Robbie, who would cash them at the OPP's bank and give Marvin the cash. Robbie always had Marvin sign a slip of paper acknowledging the money. He kept the receipts tucked in the back of his confidential black notebooks.

Marvin was terrible with money.

"I put it in my pocket and thought I was a rich man until it was gone. I didn't know the meaning of the word saving. And I'm paying the price today."

CHAPTER 29

"We've got a real tough nut we can't crack," Robbie told Marvin, spreading photographs of a tall, handsome, swarthy man across his desk during one of their regular meetings. "He's one of Colonel Gadhafi's boys."

There was a man living in Toronto who was suspected of being a Libyan intelligence agent for the regime of Moammar al-Gadhafi, Robbie told Marvin. The concern was significant. Gadhafi was the Osama bin Laden of the day, but with a large, populous country under his control. At the time, Libya was a renegade state, with a self-styled Islamic socialist revolutionary government that sponsored attacks against the West. Gadhafi was thought to be the principal financier of international terrorism. He had called for the assassination of Libyan dissidents living abroad, and hit squads were sent around the globe, killing at least 25 expats. Gadhafi was blamed as the backer of the Black September Organization, which carried out the massacre of 12 Israeli athletes and a West German policeman at the 1972 Summer Olympics in Munich. Gadhafi was a staunch supporter of the Palestine Liberation Organization, which was waging a guerrilla war against Israel. He was cozying up to the Soviet Union during the Cold War, buying military jets. He was promoting liberation movements in Third World

countries against American interests. And he was national-
izing Libya's vast oil production. Gadhafi was also acquiring
military hardware on the world market, often through sneaky
means, since it faced export bans from the United States and
others. A couple of years after Marvin's meeting with Robbie,
President Ronald Reagan called Gadhafi the "mad dog of the
Middle East."

And here was one of his agents, a former diplomat who was
referred to as a "suspected Libyan terrorist" in Canadian government documents and as a "suspected arms trafficker" by the
U.S. government, living in high style in Toronto. The government was desperate to find out what he was up to, particularly
since he seemed obsessed with asking about military-grade
helicopters. The U.S. government had sent an undercover Arab
agent to Toronto to try to get friendly with him, but he had
failed. The Libyan was canny and careful, engaging in surveillance countermeasures. Through Robbie's contacts in the
intelligence community, the problem had been brought to his
attention. Robbie immediately thought of Marvin, his relatively new but brilliantly resourceful fink.

"We can't get to this guy," Robbie confided in Marvin.
"We want you to get in with him."

"How am I going to get close to him? He's Arab, I'm
Jewish," Marvin said.

"You don't have to tell him that."

Robbie briefed Marvin on the man, named Muftah
El-Abbar. He was six foot two, handsome, something of a
playboy. He lived in a fancy penthouse apartment in Toronto
and drove a Rolls-Royce. He had a gorgeous, six-foot-tall
Canadian girlfriend who was a fashion model and wannabe
actress. He was mad keen on tennis. And his finances were
handled through a Spanish bank in the city.

"See what you can do," Robbie said.

Marvin looked through the material. He saw a familiar name on the list of the bank's board of directors where the Libyan kept his accounts: Stanley Elkind, Marvin's estranged brother. It is another oddity of Marvin's spasmodic life that, while he flitted on the margins, his younger brother, the son born of his mother, Beatrice, and his stepfather, Morris, became a respected lawyer, specializing in mergers, acquisitions and corporate law. In the 1960s, while Marvin was clowning around with gangsters and dice mechanics, his brother Stanley was toiling at Osgoode Hall Law School in Toronto. In 1963, about when Marvin was delivering Roy's land-flip kickback to the Conservative lawyer, Stanley was called to the Ontario bar and started a successful legal career. In 1977, the year Marvin was living in Calgary, hiding from Roy's wrath, Stanley was given the title "QC," for Queen's counsel, by attorney general Roy McMurtry. And in 1983, when Marvin was once again in the news after Neil Proverbs won his appeal of his gun conviction, Stanley was licensed to practise law in New York State. The brothers could hardly be more different. Stanley did not approve of Marvin's lifestyle. Since the death of Morris in 1961, Stanley and Marvin had spoken as little as Stanley could manage. Stanley was not alone within the family in expressing disdain for Marvin. In 1966, Marvin bumped into the cousin whom he used to escort home from school, fighting his schoolyard battles for him. The cousin didn't greet him fondly, saying, "If you were a gentleman, you would change your last name." Marvin humbly said he'd think about it. After Marvin's fraud conviction, Stanley had nothing to say to Marvin. Even so, seeing the connection between his brother and the Libyan's bank prompted Marvin to wonder.

"Leave it with me," Marvin said. "Maybe there's something I can do."

* * *

As America emerged from a recession, the year 1984 started with a burst of economic expansion, bringing rapid growth in consumer spending and business investment. The growth meant many things to many people, but to those in the construction industry it meant a shortage of drywall. The shortage, in turn, provided a way for Marvin to get to the Libyan.

Marvin phoned a builder he knew from Toronto who was involved in a large construction project in Florida, working with one of the biggest developers in Canada.

"If I can get you a million bucks' worth of drywall, would you be interested?" Marvin asked.

"Marvin, if you can get me a million bucks worth of drywall in this market, I'll pay well for the drywall and I'll pay you well for your effort," his friend said.

"I'll be in touch," Marvin promised.

Next, Marvin dressed up nice and went to the Spanish bank. He met the manager, introducing himself by name. Marvin said he needed a letter of credit to cover the purchase of the drywall. He said he already had a buyer, and gave the banker the contact information of the builder and his partners. When the bank contacted the builders, they confirmed their eagerness to buy Marvin's drywall. It looked like a secure million-dollar deal, backed by one of the biggest names in construction. And, the manager learned, it was being handled by the brother of a member of his board of directors, as he didn't know that Marvin and Stanley were estranged. Neither did he know that there was no drywall deal.

"The only trouble is," Marvin told the banker, "my contact in New York, the seller, he's coming to town in a few weeks. I have to entertain him and I don't speak his language."

"What language does he speak?" the banker asked.

"Tennis," cackled Marvin. "He speaks tennis. He's a tennis nut. That's all he ever talks about. Tennis this, tennis that. I don't know anything about tennis. How can I keep him happy when he's here? I hope it doesn't ruin the deal."

The banker smiled.

"I have just the guy for you to meet," the banker said. "I have another client. He loves tennis. Maybe the two of them can get together. Let me call him."

"That would be great."

The banker called his client, Muftah El-Abbar, the Libyan. As a favour, the banker asked, could he get together with these clients? His brother is on the bank's board of directors, they are working on a big deal out of New York and want to talk tennis, the banker explained. Yes, he would love to, the Libyan said.

Now it was Marvin's turn to smile. Leaving the bank, he immediately called Robbie. "We need an agent who knows his tennis," he said.

* * *

While Robbie made arrangements with the Americans to find a tennis-savvy agent, Marvin went ahead and met the Libyan. The two hit it off. El-Abbar was interested in getting in on the business deal with Marvin as well as in talking tennis.

Starting on August 9, 1984, Marvin met for fancy lunches and dinners with the Libyan, whom Marvin found to be charming. Secretly recording most of the chatter, he started to uncover the Libyan's affairs. El-Abbar spoke of how he often flew to Montreal, rented a car and then drove south into the United States, despite not having the required visa. He spoke of his trips to England and Spain. And of his family: his brother Abdul was an officer and pilot with the Libyan air force; his brother Mohamed lived in London, England, and handled much of the family's business interests; and his brother Ahmed was a police officer in Libya.

In October, Abdul came to Canada for a visit and Marvin met him as well. Over dinner at the Four Seasons Hotel in Toronto, he told Marvin he had done his flight training in Miami seven years ago. When his brother left, Muftah El-Abbar was ready to meet Marvin's tennis-loving American business partner.

***

Two United States Treasury Department agents arrived in Toronto to meet Marvin and Robbie to discuss the Libyan. One was young and tall. He was to play the role of Marvin's tennis-loving business contact. The other, older and shorter, was the supervising case agent. Treasury agents work to safeguard the U.S. financial system as well as combating rogue nations, terrorist facilitators, money launderers, drug kingpins and other threats to national security.

The two agents checked into the Four Seasons Hotel in downtown Toronto and Robbie met them in their room as Marvin got ready for a dinner he had arranged with the Libyan. It was one of the things about his new job that Marvin loved, going to some of the best restaurants and not having to pay. Marvin would open a menu, run his finger down the right-hand column, scan the prices and stop at the most expensive entrée.

He would then slide his finger to the left to order it, whatever it was. For this occasion, Marvin had booked a late table at Hy's Steakhouse in Toronto's financial district. Before they headed out, Robbie called Marvin into the hotel room for a briefing with the two agents. The Americans needed two things: an introduction to the Libyan that would translate into ongoing contact, and to get inside his apartment. The younger agent had a miniature camera that could take pictures as he walked.

Then Robbie added, awkwardly, "Here's the thing, Marv. We don't have money for the dinner."

"What do you mean you don't have money?" Marvin said.

"Well, they didn't come in with any money. They thought we were covering it," Robbie said of the two agents, who looked down at the floor. "And we don't have the money because we thought they were bringing it in. We can't use any of our credit cards, so you have to figure a way out of this."

"How am I going to pay? I don't have money or a credit card."

"I've got confidence in you," Robbie said enthusiastically. "If you can't figure this one out, then you're not the fink I think you are."

* * *

Marvin and the young agent went to collect El-Abbar for dinner. A doorman met them in the lobby. Instead of letting them up, he called the Libyan to come down.

"We want to go up," Marvin said.

"Nobody goes up," he replied.

"Gimme that phone," Marvin said, grabbing the receiver from the doorman. "Hey, Muftah, it's Marvin. I haven't seen your apartment but I hear from my banker how fabulous it is."

"Yes, it is," El-Abbar said.

"Well, this guy with me has a fantastic pad in New York. I say yours is probably nicer."

"It probably is. Bring him up."

Marvin gave the agent a quick wink as the doorman let them past. Upstairs, El-Abbar ushered the men inside his wonderful living quarters. As Marvin strolled around admiring the luxury, the agent secretly snapped pictures. Then they set off for Hy's.

Despite the money trouble, Marvin ordered everyone a martini the moment they settled into the plush seats of Hy's dining room, with its soaring ceiling and towering murals. The steaks and wine arrived as they talked and laughed over a drawn-out dinner, with the agent bewildered and anxious about what would happen when the huge bill arrived. Marvin even insisted they order desserts and after-dinner liqueurs, though everyone but Marvin was already stuffed. As the desserts were brought to the table, Marvin whispered to the agent.

"After dessert, get lost. Go to the washroom."

It was the first hint the agent had that Marvin even remembered that neither of them had money. The moment the agent excused himself, Marvin dropped his smile and spoke to the Libyan.

"Muftah, I got a problem. I went to the gym for a workout before coming to dinner and I just realized that, like an asshole, I left my wallet in the gym. I can't pay for dinner. I can't ask him to pay because I'm doing business with him. Can you pick up the tab and I'll make it up to you?"

"No problem, I understand," the Libyan said.

The two secret agents got along well. Marvin kept the conversation rolling with his unparalleled banter. The

U.S. agent and the Libyan agent debated who was the best tennis player, made a date to face each other on the court and talked about going to watch a tournament together in New York. Marvin figured that was an attempt to lure the Libyan across the border so he could be arrested in the United States. El-Abbar liked the agent so much that when Marvin tried to pay him back for the extravagant dinner, the Libyan told him to forget it. He'd had a great time and was happy to pay.

In fact, the Libyan said, he would like to meet him again.

Marvin's role in the spy scheme then largely ended, his mission accomplished: he had got the U.S. agent in close to the Libyan agent. The authorities must have got what they needed. From Robbie's case notes: "This individual was subsequently arrested by U.S. authorities for obtaining a U.S. passport by using counterfeit birth documents." The OPP warned Canadian immigration authorities about their concerns. A few years later, El-Abbar became a suspect in the 1988 bombing of Pan Am Flight 103 over Lockerbie, Scotland, which killed 270 people. He was never charged. According to a published report, El-Abbar later became an informant himself, working for the CIA.

Afterwards, the U.S. Treasury agents called Robbie and asked to meet him and Marvin in Niagara Falls. On the American side of the falls, they had lunch. The agents had something for Marvin. Even though he had already been paid by the OPP for "breaking into" the Libyan, their name for insinuating oneself into someone's life, the agents were so impressed by Marvin and so pleased with the results that they handed him an envelope with another $2,000.

***

On April 5, 1986, about a year after Marvin ended his involvement in the Libyan case, a hidden bomb exploded under a table near the DJ booth of La Belle discotheque in Berlin, West Germany. The nightclub was popular with U.S. soldiers stationed in the city and two American sergeants were killed and more than 50 soldiers injured, along with 178 other casualties in the terrorist attack. Intercepted telexes showed that the attack had been planned by the Libyan secret service and the Libyan Embassy in East Berlin.

Ten days later, bombs started falling on Libya. For 12 minutes, Tripoli airfield, a naval training facility and military barracks were hit by 60 tonnes of munitions fired from U.S. warplanes in Operation El Dorado Canyon, ordered by Ronald Reagan in retaliation for the disco bombing. Among the mayhem that night, six F-111F bombers flying from a base in Britain targeted Gadhafi's home in Tripoli. The colonel escaped but claimed that an adopted daughter had been killed, something he used as a propaganda tool for decades to come.

The OPP was later told that the targeting of Gadhafi's home had come from a trace on a phone number that Robbie had provided to the Americans after Marvin's subterfuge, says retired detective superintendent Dennis McGillis, the OPP's former Director of Intelligence. The Libyan agent in Toronto had had Gadhafi's home phone number with him. It made its way into Robbie's dossier and was passed on to the U.S. government.

* * *

Marvin got enormous pleasure in taking down the Libyan agent. He was able to do what professional undercover agents in Canada and the United States could not. He was helping his country far beyond putting drug dealers, pornographers, con artists and crooks in prison. He had taken down an "enemy of Israel," which pleased him to no end. And he got paid for it twice.

Robbie was later given a plaque commending him for protecting national security. They wanted to give Marvin one, too, but Robbie wouldn't let them.

"He was afraid I'd put it up on my wall and someone would see it," Marvin says.

"I probably would have."

CHAPTER 30

HAMILTON, 1984

The smell of chlorine tickled John "Johnny Pops" Papalia's nose as he walked through the front doors, past the small reception desk and into the wide atrium of the Holiday Inn in Burlington, a city between Papalia's hometown of Hamilton and his hunting grounds in Toronto. Papalia turned at the atrium's swimming pool into Franco's, the hotel restaurant.

For the past three decades, gangsters across the province had bowed to the fearsome Papalia, a Mafia chieftain who held a tenuous grip on the underworld. As the representative of the Buffalo Mafia in Canada, he was used to people grovelling. He loved it. Even as a teenager, back when he had hung around with Roy Pasquale, Papalia enjoyed seeing Roy's brothers and foster brothers quiver when he threatened them, Marvin most of all.

Marvin never liked him.

When Papalia walked into Franco's with his entourage, the manager rushed to greet them. Papalia wanted a table for six and he wanted to be served by *that* waitress, he said, stabbing his finger at a woman in her 40s, heavy-set but not unattractive. She groaned when she saw Papalia. He always insisted she serve him. She was terrified of him, which was why he picked her.

Papalia sat at the head of a table overlooking the pool, joined by his brothers, Frank and Rocco, and his right-hand man, Bruno Monaco, whom police regarded as his consigliere, the traditional adviser to a mob boss. With them were Marvin and a man who had driven Marvin to Hamilton. The waitress was shaking so hard when she brought water that some splashed onto the table, giving Papalia the chance to make his first snide remark. The more he berated, the more she screwed up, bringing more nasty remarks.

"Who's having the roast beef?" the waitress asked, arriving with plates of food.

"Who do you think? The person who ordered it," Papalia snapped. Marvin couldn't stand it. He had been bullied much of his life and knew its sting.

"Why don't you stop picking on that poor lady," Marvin said. Everyone at the table froze. The Mafioso looked at Marvin for a moment and then motioned with his chin toward the edge of the restaurant.

"You see that pool? See that pool over there?" Papalia asked.

"Yeah," Marvin said, warily.

"Want to be in the bottom of that pool? Just keep telling me how to talk to people and you'll be in the bottom of that pool."

Marvin shut up, but Papalia was still irked. Papalia had known Marvin all of his adult life. He trusted him but had no affinity for him.

"I know you're scared of me," Papalia told Marvin. "You act like you aren't, but you are."

Marvin certainly was acting and he was nervous, but not for the reason Papalia thought. Marvin was attending this lunch with the Mafia elite on behalf of police. Underneath his floppy sweater was the enormous secret belt recording their conversation. Could Papalia really sense deception? Or was he just building himself up at someone else's expense? Papalia knew Marvin wouldn't argue, even though, if Marvin was one-on-one, he could beat Papalia into the ground.

"He had the power to have things done to me, bad things," Marvin says. "But I didn't fear him as a man. I was afraid of him finding me wearing a wire. I was afraid of that, but it didn't stop me."

Maybe that was the fear that Papalia smelled on Marvin.

* * *

For years police had been dreaming of arresting Papalia. He had had convictions in the past, doing time for his role in the notorious French Connection heroin-smuggling ring, for instance. When the indictments for that were unsealed in New York in 1961, against Papalia and other mobsters—including Joe Valachi, the Genovese Family soldier who, a few years later, would become famous for breaking omertà, the Mafia's oath of silence—the United States Attorney General Robert Kennedy told his brother, President John F. Kennedy, that it was "the deepest penetration . . . ever made in the illegal international traffic of drugs." Papalia had also been convicted of extortion in a case involving Vic Cotroni and Paolo Violi, the Montreal bosses. But since then, he had become a wily fox.

As Papalia consolidated control over crime in Ontario in the 1980s, undercover officers tried to infiltrate his organization, dressing like hoodlums and hanging out in places Papalia and his associates frequented. It went nowhere. Papalia just didn't trust strangers.

"You couldn't infiltrate Johnny Papalia. It wasn't for lack of trying. He was just too smart. I tell you, this guy was like a fox," says Ron Sandelli, retired staff inspector of the Toronto police intelligence unit. "It would take you forever to infiltrate somebody like that to the extent that you would be a personal trust to him, that he would take you as one of his boys."

They could try forever, or they could look to Marvin, who had already known Papalia for what seemed like forever.

* * *

Marvin started his Papalia caper after connecting with an old friend of Roy's. Howard Halpenny was a scam artist from their old neighbourhood who, after years without contact, called Roy at Romik Carpet. It was actually about carpet. Halpenny had a business partner investing in his idea for a printing business, an early adopter of digital publishing. Halpenny was renovating his corporate offices and remembered that Roy did that kind of work.

"I'm going to put Marvin on it," Roy told him.

Marvin arrived at Halpenny's building on Toronto's Leslie Street with workers who measured for carpet. Marvin and Halpenny knew a lot of the same people. When Papalia's name came up, Halpenny said the gangster was working on huge property deals. Papalia, Halpenny said, was looking at mortgage swindles, with the proceeds being funnelled into building a hotel in downtown Hamilton. The city had just broken ground on Copps Coliseum, a 19,000-seat arena, in the hope of attracting an NHL team, and Papalia figured a hotel nearby would make a fortune. His take on the scheme could reach into the tens of millions. The project, Papalia had said, was his "retirement fund."

Marvin immediately thought of a mortgage broker whom he knew. Marvin thought he could use the broker to insert himself into Papalia's conspiracy and then sell him to the cops.

When Marvin outlined his plan to Robbie, he jumped at it. It was an easy sell to Knox and McCombs as well. Marvin declared he would even wear the secret belt to his meetings with Papalia. The cops were thrilled. Could The Weasel get through the doors that had kept everyone else out?

* * *

Halpenny insisted on driving when Marvin and he made the hour-long trip to Hamilton from Toronto to meet with Papalia. He wanted to show off his success to the gangsters, and few things did that better than his brand-new black Cadillac.

Marvin parked his Buick at Halpenny's office, got into the Cadillac and they headed west. Marvin arranged with Knox and McCombs to meet in a highway truck stop on the outskirts of Hamilton. Marvin told Halpenny he needed to pee and asked him to pull off into the truck stop. Marvin stepped into a stall in the men's room. A cop was waiting for him in the next stall and the electronic belt was passed to him underneath the divider. By now Marvin was familiar with the device and quickly removed his own belt, slung the electronic one around him, then passed his own belt to the cop. He sauntered back to Halpenny's Cadillac, a literal live wire, for the rest of the drive to Papalia's headquarters. Halpenny pulled his Cadillac into the circular front driveway and parked alongside similar cars in the parking lot of 20 Railway Street, a brick warehouse and office building halfway down a mundane dead-end street.

Railway Street was Papalia's fortress. It was where he was born, where his family and close friends had lived for three generations, where most of the properties were owned by his brothers. Railway Street was watched over by a designated enforcer, a man who, Papalia once quipped, "knows nothing but my phone number." Cops who had tried to breach Papalia's inner sanctum for years called his locked and alarm-wired office "Fort Knox."

Marvin walked right in. It was July 20, 1983.

"We were amazed," Knox says. "He was greeted almost like family."

Marvin and Halpenny joined Papalia and his inner circle—his brothers, Frank and Rocco, and his adviser, Bruno—in a lounge, furnished with a couple of couches and several chairs, not flashy but comfortable. There was a well-stocked bar with glasses and a bucket of ice. Papalia told his guests to help themselves.

Robbie had warned Marvin not to drink in Railway Street. He feared if Marvin took one, he would want another and another and not be able to stop. Marvin obeyed and, for once, passed on the booze. Everyone was at ease. In the past, Marvin had hoped for a future with Papalia's organization, but the mobster had dismissed Marvin as a clumsy ex-fighter with only two admirable attributes, one clenched at the end of each arm. But this time, with Papalia's retirement fund at stake, the mob boss had no trouble listening to Marvin when he said he had a friend who could get phoney mortgages.

"Check it out, see that this guy gets mortgages most people can't," Marvin told them. Papalia's men did check before Papalia called and told him. "Go to work. Set it up," he said.

* * *

Robbie wouldn't let Marvin get Papalia a bogus mortgage, so Marvin had to fake it. He swiped some letterhead from the mortgage broker's office. He typed a letter confirming that he was working on the deal, and then had someone sign fake signatures—his own handwriting was deplorable. He gave the letter to Papalia.

"I went in for meeting after meeting and spoke with the Papalias and discussed how they were going to get the money and split it up," Marvin says. The split was 50 per cent for Papalia—recognition that he was the boss—with the others, Frank, Rocco and Bruno, along with Marvin and Halpenny, fighting over the rest. The Papalia brothers' portion was to be invested in constructing a landmark hotel.

Over the next three months, Marvin wore his wired belt to many meetings with Papalia, most of them at the Railway Street bunker, a couple at the home of a lawyer, one at the Holiday Inn restaurant and one at a boxing match in Montreal. With the cops listening in, Papalia, piece by piece, outlined his vision for revitalizing Hamilton's troubled core: an 82,000-square-foot, 100-room hotel with a McDonald's franchise on the ground floor. The cops were amazed to learn of the scheme.

Papalia already had an experienced hotelier, Ray Domenico, involved. Domenico had started as a bellhop at the Royal Connaught Hotel in Hamilton and worked his way up to manager of a Holiday Inn and, later, Toronto's Triumph Hotel. Papalia and Halpenny had an investment firm, Python Investments, and a numbered company ready to help launder the mortgage-scam money when it arrived. They also had a Hamilton lawyer, William Momotiuk, drafting the paperwork and preparing the application to city hall. They even had an architect. In this, Papalia showed good taste. Police records show that he was working with Gene Kinoshita, who typically had more conventional clients, including the Royal Ontario Museum, Art Gallery of Windsor, McMaster University and the University of Guelph. Papalia also said he had a contact at city hall who was helping them steer the proposal through the approvals process. Police wanted to know who.

Papalia's behaviour explained for the cops why it had been so difficult for them to infiltrate him. He was paranoid. One time, the mobster was talking with Marvin inside his Railway Street office when he fell silent. He pulled Marvin to another part of the room.

"We have to go over here, it might be wired there," he said. When they moved across the room and Marvin resumed talking, Papalia stopped him again.

"No, let's move over there, this might be wired," he said, pointing to an office fixture. They walked around the room, stopping and starting the conversation, as he tried to make sure there wasn't a hidden police microphone near him. Then he settled for the spot where they had first started. It never occurred to Papalia that he was moving the microphone with him everywhere he took Marvin. Marvin was killing himself trying not to reveal his amusement.

After each meeting, Marvin would climb back into Halpenny's Cadillac for the ride back to Toronto. He would tell Halpenny he was desperate for a coffee and ask him to pull over at the same restaurant as before. He would go in and swap belts back with the cops under the toilet stall. On his way home from one meeting, however, he went into the washroom and called out for the cop. He got no answer. He waited a couple of minutes and then left, still wearing the police belt. Afterwards, he met with Robbie.

"Everything went great, but I still got the belt. There was no one there to switch belts with," Marvin said. Robbie said the JFU must have been tied up with something, but he then concocted another of his pranks. He told Marvin to call the

JFU office and pretend he'd done the belt exchange. Marvin made the call.

"Tell the cop who I gave the belt to that he never gave me my own belt back," Marvin said to the Hamilton officer. "I want my belt."

The cop taking the call shouted out to the team, "Who took Marvin's belt last night?" Everyone said it wasn't him.

"Marvin, who did you give it to?"

"I dunno," Marvin said, "whatever cop was in the stall. I went in and asked the guy in the next stall if he wants my belt and he says yes, so I gave it to him. But he didn't give my belt back."

The officer started panicking, shouting to his colleagues—"We got a problem!"—until Marvin began cackling with laughter, with Robbie's guffaws in the background.

* * *

There would be no laughter at the next meeting.

The cops were gravely concerned for Marvin's safety throughout the case—more so than Marvin was. Papalia had a dreadful reputation. The last guy to get Papalia into legal trouble had been Stanley Bader, a Toronto stockbroker whom the mobster had swindled out of $300,000. Bader had testified against Papalia in 1976, sending him to prison for four years. Shortly after Papalia got out, Bader, who had fled to Miami, answered a knock at the door of his posh townhouse and was shot in the head and chest. He died on his doorstep.

As Marvin's undercover case went on, concern grew over how much The Weasel could press his luck with the old fox.

As the phoney mortgage and hotel plot coalesced, Papalia told Marvin to join him for a meeting with the lawyer.

Momotiuk was semi-retired, and Papalia, along with his usual cronies, sat with Marvin and Halpenny in the lawyer's Delaware Avenue home in east Hamilton. Papalia really liked this guy. Friendly lawyers were extremely valuable to gangsters. As Papalia looked out the window, surveying the lawyer's backyard, he was surprised by its disarray.

"Your yard needs work," Papalia said.

"Yeah, I got to get somebody in. I'm not up to it anymore," the lawyer said.

Papalia turned to his brother, "Frankie, get some of the boys over here to clear up the yard, make it look nice."

Marvin caught all of these banalities on tape as he sat in the lawyer's living room. Sinking deep into the lawyer's soft, cushioned chairs, Marvin felt the belt bulging upwards, pushing on his gut, a painful reminder of its presence. It made him self-conscious, aware of its bulk, and left him wondering if the others would notice the unnatural bulge.

Marvin was holding the paperwork the lawyer had prepared for the scam when he looked up to see Papalia glaring at him from across the living room with a menacing look on his face. Marvin pretended to read the papers as he watched him. Papalia was looking down, toward his gut. Then he saw Papalia lift himself out of his chair with his arm outstretched, reaching for him, reaching toward his waist. Marvin figured the belt had been spotted.

Marvin's heart pounded heavily, his mind racing and adrenalin surging. He was alone among the wolves. There were no undercover police officers with him, no cop with a gun hidden in his boot. There were officers outside, somewhere, watching the house, he presumed, but they would be of little help at this stage. If Papalia found the wire, Marvin would be dead before anyone outside realized anything was wrong.

Within that tiny moment, Marvin planned his move. As soon as Papalia put his hand on the belt or grabbed at his sweater to lift it, he'd jump up and shout, "You faggot bastard, why are you groping me?" Then he'd throw a left hook at Papalia and run. He would have to hope the cops were watching and could whisk him away.

Papalia kept reaching toward him. Marvin got ready to lash out while he wore the phoniest smile ever.

Then Papalia snatched the paperwork out of Marvin's hand.

"Gimme those," he snapped, before sinking back into his chair, reading them. The mobster hadn't spotted the wire. He was just offended that The Weasel had the important paperwork and not him.

When the meeting was over, Marvin was even more anxious to leave than usual. It had been stressful, but he had never lost his cool. Nobody had seemed to notice his anxiety or, in fact, any change at all in his demeanour. When Marvin pulled off the Velcro straps to return the belt, it seemed to release a huge weight. He was pleased with himself, though. He hadn't acted rashly.

"It showed me I did the right thing—I didn't act until I really knew he had caught me," he says.

When he spoke with the cops at the debriefing that followed each meeting and told them what had happened, they said they'd had him covered.

"Don't worry, Marv," one of the cops said. "If Johnny had touched your belt, we would have had a sniper's bullet in his head before you could stand up."

It made Marvin feel better, until recently, when he was told of a secret police case note on the infiltration: "This operation required the informant to meet with organized crime boss

John Papalia on numerous occasions. The meetings were usually held at Papalia's business on Railway Street in Hamilton. The informant wore a body-pack [microphone] during these meetings. It should also be noted that because of the location of these meetings there was no police support available and the informant was on his own."

* * *

By October, Papalia's mortgages and hotel plans started running into trouble. On Marvin's end, he had to stall the phoney mortgages, and on Papalia's end, the lawyer was questioning why he was arranging an $11.7-million mortgage on properties worth only $2 million. McDonald's had turned down his proposal for a franchise as a ground-floor tenant. The prospect of building and running a hotel was slipping away, and Frank suggested they just sell the idea to someone else and roll the property to people better able to pursue it.

From the police perspective, things were also getting dicey. Marvin had been deeply involved in furthering the conspiracy through the supposed mortgage broker, and they couldn't extricate him from it and replace him with an undercover officer because Papalia wasn't interested in dealing with strangers. To make an arrest without police testimony would mean that Marvin would have to testify in court, destroying his secret identity as a fink. The cops felt that would be a death sentence.

In the end, the JFU didn't get their wish of arresting Papalia. The fox had let The Weasel in, but it didn't lead to criminal charges. Instead, police settled for ruining the deal. They alerted city officials to Papalia's hidden presence in the hotel development, and made sure Papalia's property plans were halted.

"As a result of this project, the authorities were able to scuttle a scheme in which Papalia would have scammed several million dollars," a police case note says. Marvin was delighted: keeping the bully from his money was the next best thing to busting him, and he enjoyed hitting out at Papalia through the cops.

"I had a strong bitterness toward him, right from when I was a kid," Marvin says. "When I did Johnny Papalia, I had a fantastic feeling of pleasure. It was like getting off on a broad almost. I was showing that I was capable of doing more than he thought I could. And Papalia never knew it, as far as I know."

Even after the scheme went awry for Papalia, Marvin successfully did business with the Papalia organization and their mob allies. In 1987, Marvin attended the funeral of Giacomo Luppino, the powerful old Mafia boss of Hamilton, as a police agent.

"At his funeral, they sat me with the family in the church and they put my car in with the family's cars in the procession," Marvin says. He then identified many of the mourners for police and helped them decode the underworld pecking order based on who was seated where, who kissed whom on the cheeks, who was given the cold shoulder and who stayed away altogether. Papalia showed his respect for Luppino by leading a crew of enforcers to—literally—beat the bushes around the cemetery where the old man was being buried to flush out hidden cops or journalists. It didn't occur to him there might be an informant much closer at hand.

Police were worried about one of Papalia's men, though: Carmen Barillaro. The Niagara Falls mob boss was one of Papalia's staunchest defenders, and a hothead. Marvin had finked on him many times, but even after the Papalia caper, Barillaro and Marvin had kept in touch. In 1992, Barillaro arranged to meet Marvin at the Cairn Croft Hotel on Lundy's Lane in Niagara Falls to discuss selling counterfeit passports. The area was the heart of Barillaro's crime empire.

Police worked quickly to wire up Marvin's room to record their conversation, but Barillaro called Marvin down to the pool instead. He said they could go swimming as they talked. It might have been a way of making sure Marvin wasn't wearing a wire, or it might have been part of the buff Barillaro's fitness kick. For backup, one of the surveillance officers called his girlfriend, who was a cop with a neighbouring force, and asked her to whip down with her gun and her bikini. She lay on a lounge chair at the pool, stretched out in her bathing suit with her gun in a makeup bag by her side. Barillaro eyed her up, but not because he was suspicious. Marvin figures Barillaro wouldn't have spent so much time with him if Papalia had told him he was a fink. But Barillaro showed signs of suspicion.

"The one guy who I think suspected me was Carmen Barillaro," Marvin says. "One time, the coppers told me that after I left a meeting with the boys, he followed me for a bit. Police were watching the meeting and they saw him leave after I did and follow me to see where I was going and what I did. He was always very nice with me and always very polite with me, but he might have wondered.

"After it was over and it all went down, the police and myself, we all thought that if they don't bother me, I wouldn't bother them. It never came back to me that they knew. Nobody warned me that they were talking about me."

Most comforting for Marvin, in May of 1988, Papalia asked Marvin to collect a $70,000 debt for him. He also said if he brought loan-shark clients to him he would split the juice with him, 50/50. That didn't sound like someone who thought he was a rat.

"Johnny is the type who wouldn't just let it go. Johnny was the type who would want me to know he knew, just so I would be scared."

* * *

On May 31, 1997, Johnny Papalia, at the age of 73, was shot and killed in the parking lot of his Railway Street fortress. Less than two months later, Carmen Barillaro was shot and killed in his Niagara home by the same hit man. He was 53. Their mob rivals had finally found their nerve.

Police told Marvin to steer clear of the funerals.

CHAPTER 31

NEW YORK AND ATLANTIC CITY, 1984

The Manhattan comedy and music club was famous as a hangout for a long list of celebrities who dropped in to enjoy its cutting-edge performers, so the irony of its name didn't strike Marvin until much later: the Rat Fink Room.

Marvin, of course, was at the Rat Fink Room working as a rat fink, taking in all the talk around him while appearing to be more interested in the double Scotch in his hand than the conversation at his table. With him were Tommy Corrigan, the Teamsters boss, and two friends: one, a Toronto fraudster, and the other, a manager at a famous casino in Las Vegas. They were plotting casino shenanigans while a comedian onstage was picking on people in the audience, pointing them out and skewering them. When the light beamed onto a large, aging man dressed in a suit with a pretty young woman on his arm, Marvin chuckled. The man was in his 70s, the woman in her 20s, and the cut of her clothes suggested she was a call girl.

"Oh, look," the comedian announced, drawing everyone's attention to the mortified man, "another uncle out with his niece. Ain't that sweet." Marvin roared with laughter at the unfortunate schmuck who sat a few tables behind him—until he recognized the man. Sam Shopsowitz was known as Toronto's "Corned Beef King" for the popularity of Shopsy's, his chain of family delicatessens. Marvin coughed on his cigar when the man's heavy features registered through the smoke-filled nightclub. Marvin knew Shopsowitz well. The deli owner didn't like him and had once warned a businessman Marvin was working with in Montreal about his unsavoury connections, calling Marvin a gangster. That was before Marvin had started his government work, when he really was a gangster. The Weasel saw an opportunity to dish the deli owner some aggravation in return.

"Sam, thank you very much," Marvin said, beaming his wide apple grin. "Thank you for giving me some interesting conversation when I get back to Toronto."

Shopsowitz flagged down the waiter and told him that he wanted to pick up Marvin's tab.

"Marvin, before you do anything to embarrass me, come see me at the deli. We'll talk. Please."

Marvin had no intention of telling Shopsowitz's wife about the apparent dalliance in New York. He had just wanted to give Shopsowitz a hard time. But he couldn't let an offer like that pass. Back in Toronto, Marvin went to meet Shopsowitz at his Spadina Avenue deli. The restaurant had a decent humidor, back when smoking was accepted, if not expected. Shopsowitz told Marvin that for the next year he could come in whenever he wanted and pick out a couple of Tuero cigars and eat one meal a day for free—if he just forgot what he had seen in New York.

"Deal," Marvin said, reaching for a menu.

It was a bonus that he had weaselled out of a trip to New York and Atlantic City for which he was already being paid twice. Marvin's expenses and salary were picked up by Corrigan, plus he was getting paid by Robbie for his efforts in uncovering the casino plot. Another day at the office.

* * *

Marvin had flown with Corrigan from Toronto to New York, where they checked into separate rooms at the Waldorf Astoria. Corrigan was on a mission to further his dream of getting a piece of the lucrative casino action in the United States. Marvin was there as Corrigan's assistant and errand boy, rather than a player in the deals being contemplated. Corrigan's brother picked them up at the Waldorf Astoria and drove them two and a half hours down the Garden State Parkway.

Atlantic City is famous for being the inspiration behind the board game Monopoly, where the properties are Atlantic City streets, but to gamblers, nightlife aficionados, hustlers and mobsters, the city on the Atlantic coast is known for its legalized gambling. In 1976, in a bid to reinvigorate a dwindling economy, New Jersey voters passed a referendum to legalize casino gambling, and the first casino, the Resorts International, opened two years later. In 1979, Bally's Atlantic City and Caesars Atlantic City opened and, shortly before Marvin and Corrigan arrived, Trump Plaza brought the Donald Trump brand to the Boardwalk. It triggered a lust among gangsters who longed to make the same kind of killing they had made in Vegas. Mobsters and shady financiers all looked for properties that could be developed into casinos. Corrigan was among them.

While mobsters had little hope of getting approvals for resort casinos, they saw a future in which so-called "sawdust joints" would blossom. These were small dens devoid of any tourist appeal other than raw, hardcore betting. They attracted less scrutiny than the major resort casinos and were easier venues for cheating, sharking and laundering. New Jersey seemed a better place than most for the mob to pull this off, given the state's sad record of corruption. New Jersey was the home of Tony Pro Provenzano, the Teamsters vice-president and Mafia man who had arranged for Marvin to be Hoffa's driver, and about the time Marvin and Tommy were visiting, the city's mayor, Michael Matthews, was sent to prison for extortion after cutting deals with the mob.

In Atlantic City, Marvin was all eyes and ears, noting who was talking to whom and which hotels and casinos were mentioned. He memorized the side deals being discussed, including Corrigan's people trying to secure the contract to supply meat to the restaurants at sister casinos in Atlantic City and Vegas and running junkets there from Toronto and Detroit. At night in his hotel room, Marvin scribbled reminders on Waldorf Astoria stationery to jog his memory. Even when he rolled into the hotel sloshed, he kept enough of his wits to scribble a few notes and tuck them under his pillow. He noted the fraudster's connection with the Vegas casino manager. He noted that Corrigan said financing was coming from his union funds and some was expected from a wealthy Canadian businessman.

Corrigan said he was anxious for the Atlantic City deals to go smoothly, telling Marvin: "If I can get these, then we'll show New York that we know how to do things."

When Marvin returned to Toronto, he met with Robbie, pulled out his small stack of hotel notepaper and gave him a thorough briefing. From the OPP case notes: "[Marvin] supplied information on a group of individuals in the Toronto area who were attempting to do business with casino operators in Atlantic City. One of these subjects had recently been released from prison on fraud charges and another was a representative of an international union. The U.S. authorities were alerted and in turn were able to contact the casinos to protect themselves from possible fraudulent activities."

Corrigan did not suspect his errand boy was the source of this interference. He continued to allow Marvin to stay close to him, day after day, month after month, year after year. In 1986, Marvin tipped Robbie off to Corrigan supplying unregistered guns to friends who needed one. That same year, Marvin and Corrigan returned to New York City, this time meeting several associates of Fat Tony Salerno, of the Genovese Mafia Family, including a hotel manager, a steakhouse owner and a jeweller. The restaurateur's partner was, in turn, a partner in one of Atlantic City's resort casinos. Fat Tony, Marvin's idol from his early days in New York, was not available to meet them personally: he was on trial in the huge "Mafia Commission" case, the racketeering trial prosecuted by United States Attorney Rudy Giuliani against the leadership of the Five Families of New York. Salerno was thought to be the boss of the Genovese Family and was also accused of illegally aiding the election of Roy Lee Williams to the national presidency of the Teamsters. (Fat Tony was eventually sentenced to 100 years in prison.) Marvin's information was given to the FBI and agents launched an investigation.

When Marvin and Corrigan returned to Toronto, Corrigan was given the VIP treatment in the airports at both ends, including going into the customs supervisor's office in Toronto for a private chat.

Not long after their return, Corrigan told Marvin that he needed to have two guests from New York hide out in his home. He would send Marvin's family on a holiday in Mexico to compensate. One of his houseguests was to be Carmine Persico, Jr., the boss of the Colombo Mafia Family of New York, Marvin was told. Persico was in the midst of the same "Mafia Commission" trial as Fat Tony, charged with murder, conspiracy and labour racketeering. It is difficult to see how he could have made such a trip legally. Could he have been planning to flee? Regardless, he never arrived. Robbie alerted the FBI to Persico's purported plans and, a week after Marvin was told to prepare his place, the mob boss was found guilty and given a 100-year sentence. Although Carmine Persico couldn't make the trip to Toronto, Persico's son, Larry, did. Corrigan set him up in a house in Whitby, a Toronto suburb. Marvin told Robbie where to find him.

That, in a way, epitomized Corrigan. Despite the influence and money he tossed around Toronto, he could never become the bigwig he wanted to be. He reached for Carmine but all he got was Larry.

Still, this was not the last or the least of the heartaches Corrigan would suffer at Marvin's hands.

* * *

Paul Volpe, an early crony of Roy Pasquale's who went on to become a substantial Mafia figure in Canada, was something of an underworld visionary. He thought well beyond his city's downtown core, which is the surprisingly insular view of many of his cohorts. In the 1960s, Volpe travelled to the Caribbean and set up a Mafia-funded casino in Port-au-Prince, Haiti, that he ran for a few years. Almost two decades later, Volpe realized the potential in Atlantic City and, through front companies that disguised his involvement, bought properties along the Boardwalk and farther afield. Marvin had known Volpe since his childhood. As Volpe's profile within the underworld grew and Marvin started his police work, Volpe became a regular target of Marvin's tips, including his Boardwalk scheming.

In Atlantic City, Volpe followed Mafia etiquette and sought permission from the Mafia of Philadelphia, an hour's drive away, in whose territory Atlantic City fell. Volpe met with Philadelphia and Gambino mob figures to discuss his plans. Once allowed in, Volpe and his cousin and partner, Angelo Pucci, were able operators, turning over several multimillion-dollar land deals. Marvin knew Pucci, also. Pucci's brother, Frankie, had joined Marvin and Papalia's cheats on their trip to Kentucky when they were caught fiddling with the dice. In 1980, before he started finking, Marvin had also stood up to Pucci and Volpe on behalf of an accountant who had begged Marvin for help getting out from under the mobster's thumb. The accountant had taken on Pucci as a new client. Pucci had then introduced him to his partner, Volpe. The accountant had no idea who Pucci was, but knew Volpe's reputation. The bookkeeper didn't want to be involved and tried to back out.

"You're not getting out," Volpe told him.

Terrified, the accountant went to the only person he knew who spoke the language of the street. He knew Marvin through his synagogue, and Marvin said he would see what he could do. He called his fearsome partner, Baldy Chard, and the pair went to see Volpe.

"Paul, can you do us a favour and leave this guy alone?" Marvin asked.

"What if I don't?" replied Volpe.

Baldy stepped forward and said, "Then you'll have a problem with us."

Marvin would have preferred Baldy said "me" rather than "us," but even a figure as powerful as Volpe was uneasy dealing with the volatile Baldy.

"Aw, fuck it, there are enough accountants around," Volpe said.

Volpe and Pucci's success in Atlantic City had slowed by the early 1980s, after they were caught on film discussing

Atlantic City real estate in an investigative television documentary. The backlash made Volpe a major police target.

The 1980 murder of Angelo Bruno, Philadelphia's Mafia boss, triggered more violence in the area as factions vied for power. It might even have spilled into Canada in 1983, when Volpe's body was found stuffed into the trunk of his wife's BMW, parked at Toronto's Pearson International Airport. The symbolism of the car being dumped at the airport is often seen as a sign that his still-unsolved murder stemmed from problems abroad, perhaps in Atlantic City. Volpe's organization continued without its flamboyant boss and Pucci continued to operate above the fray in Atlantic City, where Nicodemo Scarfo—called "Little Nicky" because of his stature, although rarely to his face—became the new boss.

It was a senior associate of what was left of the Volpe organization who spoke with Corrigan about Atlantic City developments in 1987, rekindling his Atlantic City dreams. Volpe's people wanted to develop some of the dead boss's property and were looking for partners. Corrigan sent Marvin down to examine the properties.

As soon as Corrigan told him to go to Atlantic City, Marvin told Robbie the tantalizing news, and Robbie phoned the FBI. Robbie and Marvin met with FBI agents to discuss the trip, and Marvin agreed to take an undercover agent with him.

***

Rich Mazzari was an Italian-American FBI agent in Detroit who was known for his successful undercover work. He pulled off the mobster look so well that it was impossible not to believe that he was mobbed up. Marvin would work closely with Mazzari over many years. For this caper, the agent pretended to be a Detroit mobster representing Anthony Giacalone, a powerful Detroit figure known as "Tony Jack," notorious for being the gangster Hoffa said he was meeting on the day he disappeared. It would be difficult for Scarfo's men in Atlantic City to discover the lie, since Giacalone was in prison at the time and, as a veteran Motor City cop, Mazzari knew all the Detroit players and places so well he could carry any conversation convincingly.

Marvin flew from Toronto to Philadelphia, accompanied by a man from the Volpe organization. They were met by a driver who was in on the deals. The Volpe man stayed at Caesars Atlantic City and wanted Marvin to check in there, too, but the FBI told him not to. They steered him to Trump's Castle Hotel Casino, the second Donald Trump–owned resort in the city. The head of security at the Castle was a retired FBI agent and the bureau spoke to him about keeping an eye on Marvin and Mazzari, who shared a room.

The driver took Marvin and Volpe's man out, whisking them to various properties around Atlantic City. There was a piece of waterfront property near North Delaware Avenue and Magellan Avenue where there were plans to build a 13-storey apartment building. There were 24.5 acres on Tilton Road, near the entrance to the Atlantic City International Airport, where a 22-floor condominium complex was planned, and others. It was a trip similar to the one Marvin and Corrigan had made a few years earlier. At each of the sites, Marvin got out of the car and was shown around. Marvin asked a lot of questions, making notes as they talked. He wrote down the locations, what amenities were nearby and the estimated value. He even took copies of the blueprints of the planned projects—everything he thought his two masters, Corrigan and Robbie, would want to know.

"I wanted to show it to Tommy. I wanted to show it to Robbie. I was working for everyone," Marvin says.

The next day, Marvin met with another of Volpe's old cronies in Atlantic City. He and Angelo Pucci went to a downtown Atlantic City office building. In a windowless boardroom he met with three Italian-American men who represented Nicky Scarfo's interests. Scarfo had earlier been arrested—along with a city councillor—for extorting a waterfront developer. Marvin was told afterwards by the FBI that the three men were senior players in the Philadelphia Mafia, but the names meant nothing to Marvin. They started discussing various deals in the unlikely hope of getting a casino under their control.

Marvin sweetened the pot of what he said he could do for the Atlantic City group. Not only did he represent Corrigan and the Teamsters' money, he said, he also acted for Irving Kott. Kott was a crooked stock manipulator of legendary proportions. The wealthy Montreal man was fined $500,000 for stock fraud in 1976 (the largest fine at the time), but the sanction did nothing to slow him; in 1979, he was sentenced to four years in prison in another fraud case, but won on appeal. He remained an influential financier and secret mastermind behind dodgy brokerage firms in Canada, Europe, Central America and the United States. One scheme he put together, he bragged, fleeced customers out of $400 million through an Amsterdam boiler room by selling shares in a company that claimed to be able to suck gold out of wastewater. Suckers couldn't get enough of it. Kott did not hide his success, abandoning Montreal winters for a 4,000-square-foot Beverly Hills mansion with a swimming pool and tennis court, once home to Hollywood legend Cary Grant. Marvin really was close to Kott, although the financier had no idea Marvin was tossing his name around Atlantic City. Like Mazzari, Marvin chose his names carefully. Marvin could speak convincingly about Kott and his affairs. Better still, Marvin knew that Kott was in Amsterdam and hard to reach. If anyone contacted Kott's associates, all of them would say that Marvin was a Kott confidant and doing business with them. Even if Kott heard about him using his name, Marvin would tell him he was trying to get him in on a great deal and would likely be thanked, rather than spanked. With Kott's imaginary money in the mix, Marvin dangled $10 million or more.

That grabbed the attention of Scarfo's men, and they insisted Marvin join them for dinner, their treat.

That night, Marvin and Volpe's man met Pucci and two of Scarfo's men for dinner at Caesars. Marvin brought Mazzari along and the agent blended in seamlessly. Marvin was treated like royalty. Being treated like royalty and acting like royalty, however, are quite different things.

One of the marquee restaurants at Caesars Atlantic City, Morton's, had a menu item that caught Marvin's eye: a 40-ounce Porterhouse steak that, if a single diner could consume it within half an hour, was free. Marvin had a magnificent appetite, and Scotch only enhanced it. With a bottle of Scotch at his side, he ordered the enormous steak and dug in, gasping for air between huge bites and chewing noisily while his companions cheered him on.

Bets were soon being placed, with Pucci acting as bookie. Pucci, who had seen Marvin eat before, put his money where Marvin's mouth was. The Philly guys bet he couldn't do it. Marvin cleaned his plate easily, with half the bottle of whisky washing it down. Then he tucked into a plate of mashed potatoes and a basket of bread, but by then he was just showing off. Pucci made $2,000 from Marvin's feat and gave Marvin $500 as his end.

Marvin's antics were not mere buffoonery or gluttony. Long ago, he had learned the value of such bonding experiences. The hijinks brought the diners closer together, creating such a sense of camaraderie and fun—a false intimacy—that it never occurred to any of the gangsters that they were dining with a police informant and an FBI agent. They all got along so brilliantly that Marvin felt relaxed, despite the Scarfo mob's reputation for violence.

Being a fink in Atlantic City was a frightening prospect. Scarfo was notoriously ill-tempered and quick to draw blood. His organization was called "The Mafia's most violent family" because Scarfo purged disloyal soldiers with professional hit men and killed rivals in public to spread fear. If Scarfo and his gang tortured and killed friends over mere slights, what might they do if they caught a real rat among them? Marvin never came close to finding out.

Marvin wasn't frightened of Scarfo's men, but neither was he immune to Atlantic City's rougher edges. One night, when he was returning to his hotel room, reasonably drunk, he was mugged in the hotel elevator.

Before he left Atlantic City, there was one more person Marvin wanted to meet. It was a personal mission. Marvin spoke to the head of security at Trump's Castle and, before he checked out, he was ushered into a lavish office where the security chief introduced Marvin to Ivana Trump, Donald's glamorous wife.

Marvin returned to Toronto and briefed Robbie on the trip. Then he briefed Corrigan. The FBI and Canadian police were now in the loop on the plans in Toronto and in Atlantic City.

***

Volpe's man wanted Marvin to come south with him again in March. This time he asked him to come to Florida to meet a prospective partner in his Atlantic City plans: John Gotti, the notorious boss of the Gambino Family, the most powerful mob family in New York.

When Robbie heard this, he thought Volpe's man was spewing self-aggrandizing lies, but when he called the New York City Police Department's organized-crime section he was startled to learn that Gotti and an unknown man had boarded a train in New York at 6 p.m—destination, Fort Lauderdale, Florida. Gotti had just been acquitted on an assault charge after the victim was frightened into withdrawing his evidence. In a dramatic courtroom moment, the victim said he could not see anyone in court who looked like the man who had attacked him. The case prompted the now famous *New York Post* headline "I FORGOTTI!" and helped build Gotti's reputation as the Teflon Don, a man to whom charges would not stick.

Robbie was anxious for Marvin to go to Florida and see what he could get on the mob boss, but Corrigan said Marvin couldn't go.

"He's the hottest thing in the U.S. right now. Just goin' near him, you get yourself arrested," Corrigan said.

CHAPTER 32

BASSETERRE, ST. KITTS, 1986

Up 20 stairs to the second floor of a scruffy building, amid the lanky palm trees that are the highest points of Basseterre—apart from the mountains that surround it—was an unmarked door. Behind it was a small reception desk, but requests there to speak with someone in charge brought demands to leave or police would be called. It was doubtful the occupants really wanted a visit from police.

This was the head office of the International Bank Ltd.

Not far away, on a poolside deck chair at the condominium apartments of Ocean Terrace Inn, set on a landscaped hilltop just outside Basseterre, lounged Marty Resnick, holding a goblet filled with rye, not his first of the day. Perhaps the rye was what made Resnick chatty when confronted by a newspaper reporter asking about the International Bank and his criminal record.

"Yes, I made some mistakes I wish I hadn't made," Resnick said of his seven convictions for possessing stolen property, six more for fraud and another for counselling to bribe a peace officer, before cracking a joke about his bribery conviction: the cop "wouldn't take the money—so they said I counselled him. Now if he'd taken it, it would have been another matter. I wouldn't have the record, would I?" Resnick said his banking customers were suckers and he was friends with Tommy Corrigan. He would arrange for the reporter, the *Globe and Mail*'s Peter Moon, to meet Corrigan back in Toronto, Resnick said. Resnick soon sobered up and packed up, leaving St. Kitts shortly after Moon started asking questions nobody wanted to answer. Fleeing with Resnick were his seven high-pressure stock salesmen from Canada.

Moon's visit was not an accident. A year before the island bank and its shady proprietors were under investigation, a group of financiers of dubious distinction had gathered in a low-rent coffee shop.

* * *

Laurel Leaf Bakery was a small, almost anonymous tenant of a shopping plaza in north Toronto, but it was jokingly called the "northern office" by Tommy Corrigan, Marvin and a small coterie of colleagues.

Although he maintained real offices for his various unions in a handsome three-storey mansion on Toronto's Madison Avenue in the historic Annex neighbourhood, and another office for his trucking business, Corrigan did most of his dealings in two restaurants. Laurel Leaf Bakery was the "northern office," where the gang would meet each morning, six days a week, at about 8 a.m. They would eat bagels and drink coffee and talk about schemes and scams. They would then adjourn to the "southern office"—the Pickle Barrel, the original 85-seat diner-style restaurant on Leslie Street that started the chain of the same name. There they had their own booth reserved. Corrigan would arrive in his Buick Park Lane, sometimes with Marvin at the wheel. They would eat lunch, drink and continue kibitzing.

Over the years, Marvin would meet at the southern and northern offices with Corrigan and a changing cast of characters as fortunes were made and lost and friendships came and went. William Ginsberg was a regular. A highly strung wheeler-dealer, Ginsberg had made millions in the stock market and with so-called "boiler rooms," the high-pressure telephone sales teams that dupe unsophisticated investors into putting their money into speculative or fraudulent stock. The best of them—and these guys were among the best—set up telephone-laden offices in a number of countries and used a script to woo investors, making off with millions before shutting down and moving on, leaving behind outraged victims and unpaid phone bills. Ginsberg had been charged several times over the sale of securities, but never convicted. He was convicted, however, of peddling obscene photographs. That didn't help his bid for acceptance within the legitimate financial community, although with his full-length wolf-fur coat, heavy gold jewellery and brash personality, he would never have fit in with the banking set.

Arya Dynar was another who met most days at the coffee shop. Often going by the name Al Diner, he had two claims to fame with the Jewish gangsters: one was being a former soldier in Israel, which no one believed until a rabbi confirmed it, and the other was that his wife had been Meyer Lansky's nurse in the 1970s after the organized-crime legend fled to Israel to avoid U.S. prosecutors. Also at the coffee-shop meetings was a guy Marvin remembers only as "Credit Card Jack," named for a huge credit-card fraud he had pulled; Stanley "Bimbo" Grossman, the wisecracking president of a meat-packing company; and a retired bank manager who had also worked for a boiler room in Amsterdam until Dutch police had chased them out of town a few months before.

Billy Ginsberg and Corrigan made a load of money together in the stock market, mainly from insider deals with penny stock. Marvin used to pick up their cheques from the investment company and deliver them.

"When I delivered their cheques to Billy, he would give me a three-hundred-dollar tip. If I had to deliver them to Tommy, he gave me a one-hundred-dollar tip. I hated when Billy wasn't around to take the cheques. Within a year I delivered four hundred thousand dollars to Tommy and eight hundred and fifty thousand dollars to Billy," Marvin says. Ginsberg then reinvested the money with Irving Kott, the crooked Montreal financier.

Much of the talk at the southern and northern offices from 1986 to 1987 was of the island of St. Kitts and the International Bank.

* * *

Basseterre is the capital of the Federation of St. Kitts and Nevis, two Caribbean islands lying 1,300 miles southeast of Miami. With a population of 15,000, Basseterre looks out across a stunning blue harbour on the Caribbean Sea. Its name, French for "low land," speaks to the lush valley it sits in. On the leeward side of the archipelago winds, it is a safe anchorage for ships. In the 1980s, it became a safe anchorage for con men and shysters as well. With secretive and flimsy banking laws, St. Kitts was one of those places where offshore banks could enjoy tax-free status provided they not do business with local residents. One of the first banks was the one that Ian Knox had raided in St. Kitts a few years before, during Marvin's first case with the cops.

In 1986, the government of St. Kitts gave the International

Bank Ltd. official status as an offshore bank. The people behind it were an influential bunch.

One of the bank's local directors was a St. Kitts lawyer who was the prime minister's press and public-relations secretary, as well as the island's ambassador to South Korea and Taiwan. Perhaps the appointment helped the Canadians establish their island foothold: even though a criminal record usually precludes someone from getting a work permit, the Canadians had unfettered access. The island's Ministry of Finance, which controlled the banking sector, and Ministry of Home Affairs, in charge of immigration and policing, were both run from the Prime Minister's Office.

The Canadian end of the bank included a blue-chip portfolio of disgraced financiers.

Leonard Rosenberg's name still brought bile to the mouths of many investors at the time he made seven trips to St. Kitts to help establish the International Bank. In 1982, 10,931 Toronto apartments were bought by Greymac Credit Corp. for $270 million and, on the same day, flipped—twice—for about $500 million. The deal was financed through loans from Greymac Trust Co., Seaway Trust and Crown Trust, which were controlled by Rosenberg and associates. The deal became a public scandal when regulators feared for the solvency of the trust companies and tenants balked at the planned 25 per cent rent hike. The government seized Rosenberg's trust companies and called in the police when it was revealed the sale price had been artificially boosted and investors taken for more than $131 million. Rosenberg faced 36 fraud charges when he was working on the St. Kitts deal. (After 10 years of legal wrangling, he would plead guilty to 13 of them.)

Lyon Wexler was a former Hamilton lawyer who had given up his right to practise law after a criminal conviction. He previously had been fined $4,000 for accepting secret commissions while president of Income Trust Co., and had become a Greymac vice-president. He faced two fraud charges at the time he was running day-to-day operations of the International Bank.

Howard Eaton was a financier from California who joined Rosenberg in St. Kitts for the project. A few years earlier, he had resigned in disgrace as the head of the Edmonton-based Canadian Commercial Bank, after it doled out millions of dollars in loans to Rosenberg, and before it became the largest bank failure in Canadian history. Also involved in the St. Kitts bank, to no one's surprise, was Irving Kott.

And at the centre of it all was Tommy Corrigan. He, too, went to St. Kitts with Rosenberg, Wexler and Eaton to set the scheme in motion.

They established the second-floor office in downtown Basseterre, and issued a prospectus. A prospectus is a legal document that outlines an investment to potential buyers. But those who were talked into buying shares in the International Bank typically did so after a high-pressured sales pitch over the phone. And while a prospectus was mailed to the investor, it was usually too late or ignored by the unsophisticated buyers who preferred to believe the soothing words and assurances they had heard over the phone. Reading it would have alarmed any knowledgeable investor: the bank had virtually no assets and no business record; the controlling shareholders were named as big-sounding institutions, but none of them were fully described or their location given; the favourable business climate in St. Kitts was highlighted, along with an enticing dividend policy—50 per cent payout of all earnings annually.

Marty Resnick and his boiler-room colleagues then went to work, taking advantage of the modern telephone system newly installed on the island.

"When they were holding their meetings, they had me there as their gopher. They had me there to get them cigars, to get cigarettes, to get them coffee. I was at every meeting strictly as an errand boy," Marvin says. "Tommy and the guys, they spent a lot of money setting it up. Every day, Tommy told me how great the place was doing. They were selling phoney stock out of there and they were doing great. I heard it all and I gave all the information to Robbie."

It was a bold move. Corrigan had warned everyone how important it was to keep the deal quiet. "If word gets out," Corrigan had said, "there won't be any threats made, they'll just hit you."

***

Robbie, through Marvin's tips, had been chasing some of these guys and their friends and colleagues from one country to another, exposing their duplicity and shady deals as they hopped from phone bank to phone bank in Europe. Marvin moved with them, feeding information from Holland, Belgium and Britain to Robbie, who passed it on to the local authorities, leaving the con men perplexed about how their deals were discovered so promptly.

In this case, Robbie figured a criminal charge was unlikely. Canadians in St. Kitts were victimizing investors in Britain. It was a clever setup—the international nature of the scam made it difficult to prosecute. But Robbie wouldn't just let it drop. Time and again, sometimes to protect Marvin's identity and sometimes because hard evidence of a criminal act was just beyond reach, police did the next best thing to arresting suspects, which was to strip them of their profits. So Robbie called investigative reporter Peter Moon. Moon and

Robbie had become close over the years. It was one of those occasional relationships where the journalist and the journalist's source were able to work in tandem to meet both of their professional needs—Robbie helped Moon get great stories; Moon raised the profile of police successes and challenges and, in cases like the St. Kitts bank, shone a light on shenanigans that made the subjects scuttle away. Robbie told Moon about what Marvin had dug up in St. Kitts.

"Think there's a story there?"

Moon packed and, given the January cold of Toronto, happily booked his flight for the tropical island to investigate. Soon after he arrived in St. Kitts, he received a threatening message at his hotel. Another caller phoned his newsroom with the same warning to leave. The RCMP contacted the St. Kitts police and Moon finished his investigation under police protection. It was then that he found Resnick basking in the tropical sun with a bottle of rye.

In a moment of rye-induced assessment, Resnick told Moon: "We'll meet again in Hong Kong, maybe Macao, Rio de Janeiro or even Australia, in the same circumstances. And you'll be doing your job and I'll be doing mine. We both have to make a living, don't we? This may close things down here for a week or two, even a month, but it'll go on. The government won't close it down. You haven't stopped anything, you've only stopped it for a while. The people who set this up were careful not to break any laws."

* * *

Broken laws or not, the deal in St. Kitts fell apart under the scrutiny, just as Robbie had predicted. Corrigan and his pals were devastated when Moon's article appeared on the front page of the *Globe* on January 26, 1987. The bold headline read: "Canadian link to St. Kitts bank probed." There was a picture of Rosenberg on the front page, too. Inside were photos of Eaton, Resnick and Wexler and a shot of the bank office in Basseterre. A follow-up story put Corrigan's face, cigar in mouth, on the front page as well.

Because the bank was immediately shuttered, many investors who had agreed to buy stock didn't have to pay the money, saving them all thousands of dollars. The government of St. Kitts asked the RCMP to help investigate and it triggered a national scandal on the island. The Chamber of Commerce sought to cancel the bank's licence, and opposition politicians demanded the prime minister quit because his press secretary had been involved.

"This thing is a scandal. It has brought international notoriety to St. Kitts. Government should resign over this," an opposition leader declared.

Protecting thousands of investors from being fleeced; chasing serial shysters out of a major scam; bringing unwanted publicity to criminal colleagues; and almost bringing down a foreign government: The Weasel was here.

Marvin's information and Moon's article, however, brought consequences that even Robbie couldn't have guessed.

CHAPTER 33

Marvin and Tommy Corrigan were alone at their booth at the Pickle Barrel—their southern office—for a late Sunday brunch and ended their meal with a satisfying puff on their cigars. Two couples at a nearby table took offence to the smoke, however, and one of the men, six foot six and some 300 pounds, lumbered over and growled, loud enough for his date to hear, "Can't you assholes smoke outside?"

"If you'd asked politely, we would," Corrigan said, pausing to draw on his stogie, making its embers glow furiously. "But you didn't," he added, letting the smoke puff out of his mouth with each word. Corrigan then turned away and continued talking to Marvin. The man hesitated, then retreated.

When Marvin and Corrigan had finished moaning about the demise of the St. Kitts operation—dissecting how the nosy reporter might have ended up in St. Kitts and why Marty Resnick had been stupid enough to talk to him—they put on their jackets to leave. As Corrigan passed the couple's table he took a deep suck on his cigar and perfectly timed his puff to blow smoke into the face of the large, belligerent man. The diner jumped up.

"I'll teach you to blow smoke," he shouted as he rushed at Corrigan.

Corrigan, dressed in a suit and tie, as he usually was, held his hands up in mock fear. As the man continued toward him, drawing back his fist, Corrigan calmly took his cigar out of his mouth, placed it on the counter and unleashed a powerful combination—left, right, left; bam, bam, bam. The guy dropped and a woman screamed. The other woman ordered her date to help. He rushed forward and Marvin himself entered the fray, throwing a left hook at the second guy. The restaurant was a chorus of screams as Corrigan picked his cigar back up and he and Marvin left.

* * *

Corrigan's aggression was partly his natural response to insult, but he was also unusually on edge after the St. Kitts debacle. The consortium had invested a lot of time and money into the International Bank and it had promised to generate a record haul. It's premature termination meant lost revenue and inside leaks that needed plugging. This kind of thing always gets fingers pointing as conspirators allay suspicion about themselves by suggesting reasons why it was likely someone else.

One thing was certain, though: Marty Resnick bore some responsibility. His indiscreet talk and acknowledgement of both Corrigan's involvement and the dodgy nature of the deal had sunk any hope of salvaging it. And the scandal it had caused in St. Kitts meant they were now pariahs on what was supposed to be their island paradise. A consensus emerged that it was Resnick who had scuppered the deal and, because Billy Ginsberg had brought Resnick into it, Ginsberg was marked as the responsible partner.

Kott refused to accept his end of the loss and declared that, since Ginsberg had ruined the deal, he was not going to pay back the $850,000 Ginsberg had earlier invested with him. It was, Kott said, compensation for the millions he would have made in St. Kitts. That pronouncement crushed Ginsberg, leaving him a nervous wreck.

Corrigan called a meeting at the northern office to discuss things, telling Marvin and Ginsberg to join him. But Ginsberg didn't show.

"Marv, go to Billy's house and see what's up," Corrigan ordered. It took only a few minutes before Marvin was knocking on his front door.

"Who is it?" Ginsberg called out gruffly.

"It's Marvin, open up."

Inside, Ginsberg, a man known for his ostentatious clothes and glittery jewels, was standing in his pyjamas, his hair a mess, his eyes puffy with dark bags under them. He had sent his two daughters and his wife, a former model, to Florida while he tried to sort things out.

"Billy, what's up? We're supposed to be meeting Tommy."

"I'm too nervous to get dressed. I'm too upset to do anything."

"Tommy said he's going to straighten it all out, so take it easy."

"OK, I'll meet you guys tomorrow," Ginsberg said.

The next day, Ginsberg came to the northern office, as he had promised.

"You're going to Montreal tomorrow, the two of you, to meet with Kott," Corrigan said. "Marvin, you're there to make sure Kott doesn't yell at Billy. If he starts yelling or threatening him, tell him I said to shut up."

Marvin said he would drive, and Ginsberg brightened up. After the meeting with Kott, he said, he'd take Marvin to a Chinese restaurant that would knock his socks off.

Marvin called Robbie as soon as he was alone. Robbie wanted to catch the meeting with Kott on tape. Toronto police could come to Marvin's house to collect his coat and wire it up with a hidden microphone and transmitter for him to wear, but it wouldn't be ready until the next day. They would have to come up with a reason for Marvin to return to his house before leaving for Montreal. Robbie pondered for a moment. He then told Marvin to dress very casually when he went to collect Ginsberg. Robbie knew Ginsberg would be well dressed and would want Marvin looking sharp, too.

"You can then go back home to put on a shirt and tie and pick up the wired coat," Robbie said. A coat would be expected, given the chilly March weather, although it hadn't rained or snowed in two weeks. A police surveillance unit would drive behind their car on the highway, linking up with the hidden transmitter to record the conversation on the way, as well as in Montreal. Marvin would have to drive slowly and steadily to allow the cops to stay close and not lose the transmitter signal, Robbie said.

The next day, Monday, March 16, 1987, Marvin dressed like a slob and went to meet Ginsberg, who looked at him in disgust.

"You can't go to meet Irving Kott looking like that," Ginsberg said. "Go home and change." Robbie was a great judge of character. "When you come back, leave your car in my driveway and we'll take my Mercedes," he said.

As Marvin was about to leave Ginsberg's house, the doorbell rang and Marvin answered it. A short, large woman introduced herself as Ginsberg's neighbour, saying she was checking in on him since his family was away.

"Billy's very busy," Marvin said, anxious to leave for Montreal.

"It's OK," Ginsberg called out, "let her in." Then he told Marvin not to come back for an hour and a half.

"I only need half an hour," Marvin argued.

"I said an hour and a half," Ginsberg snapped.

When Marvin got to his house, the police were ready. He put on a shirt, tie and suit jacket, then pulled on the special coat—it didn't look any different—and slowly drove back to Ginsberg's place. There was a car in the driveway that hadn't been there when he'd left. After an hour and a half on the dot, Marvin rang the doorbell and the woman whom he had left with Ginsberg answered. She was pale and shaking like a leaf.

"Where's Billy?" Marvin asked.

"He's dead," the woman said, bursting into tears.

"What do you mean, he's dead?"

"He said he wasn't feeling good and went upstairs to lie down. I went to check on him and he was dead."

Marvin went to Ginsberg's bedroom. His doctor was there and Ginsberg lay on his bed, dressed, motionless, his eyes open but unblinking. After Marvin got over the shock, he noticed that Ginsberg was no longer wearing his suit and tie, but rather jeans and a golf shirt.

"What the hell?" Marvin said to himself. "He made me get dressed up but he was going to go like that? It doesn't make sense."

Marvin went into another room and quietly called Robbie, who told him to give him five minutes to think, and call back. When Marvin called a second time, Robbie had concocted a plan. He told Marvin the police who were ready to follow them to Montreal would come to the house. Marvin needed to let them in and keep the doctor and neighbour out of the way so the cops could grab papers they wanted for their investigation.

After the cops left, Marvin found himself alone in

Ginsberg's bedroom with the body. Marvin knew Ginsberg had two sets of the exact same jewellery—one in yellow gold, and another in white gold—an expensive Patek Philippe watch, a large diamond ring and a thick bracelet. Ginsberg chose which one to wear based on which best matched his outfit. Marvin noticed he was wearing his white gold. Marvin opened Ginsberg's jewellery box and stuffed the yellow gold set into his pocket.

Robbie, meanwhile, had learned what really happened. When Marvin called to tell him the cops had left, Robbie told him that Ginsberg's telephone had been wiretapped a week before, and while Marvin was changing, police had heard a frantic call made by the visiting neighbour.

"I don't know what to do," the woman had wailed on the phone. "I was giving Billy a blowjob and he died. We're both here nude in his bedroom. What should I do?"

The woman on the other end of the phone had said she should call Ginsberg's doctor. She did, and when the doctor came over, he said he would help her get him dressed so their affair would not be revealed, Robbie told him, chuckling.

"Oh, and Marvin," Robbie added, "be sure you don't take anything."

Marvin hung up the phone, sighed, went back into Ginsberg's room and pulled the jewellery out of his pocket. He looked at it one last time, feeling the heavy weight of the gold, before setting it back in its case.

The cause of Ginsberg's death was a heart attack. He was 61. His family flew home from Florida and the funeral was arranged. Marvin and Corrigan were there, along with Irving Kott and some of the other St. Kitts bank conspirators. Afterwards, friends went back to Ginsberg's house for a wake. Marvin was amused to hear the neighbour telling the crowd, including her own husband and Ginsberg's wife, how she had come to check on Billy to make sure he was eating right while his wife was away, and how he had gone upstairs after saying he wasn't feeling well.

Kott discreetly gave Ginsberg's widow $10,000 in cash, saying it was how much he had owed her husband. Not knowing any better, she thanked him.

* * *

Billy Ginsberg's mischief had kept Marvin and Robbie busy for a year, and his death sharply curtailed Marvin's revenue stream.

In the months before Ginsberg's death, Marvin had tipped Robbie to many of his crimes and conspiracies. He had revealed that a group of Toronto and Montreal swindlers were building a stock-sales "boiler room" in Panama that Robbie put a stop to. Marvin had uncovered a money-skimming operation at a Las Vegas casino by a friend of Ginsberg's. According to OPP case notes: "Information obtained resulted in projects being instituted by FBI in Las Vegas and Metropolitan Toronto Police/ Ontario Provincial Police. Subject identified with skimming and laundering of money from Vegas is now before the courts." The case notes also acknowledge Marvin's help in the dubious grabbing of Ginsberg's documents after his death: "Suspect William Ginsberg died at his home during project involving the stock scam. Mr. Elkind was at residence shortly after the death and assisted intelligence officers in obtaining telephone books etc., from the residence which assisted in the investigation."

Ginsberg knew how to make money out of nothing for himself, but he also helped Marvin make money in ways he never realized.

CHAPTER 34

TORONTO, 1986

Marvin was out of milk. It was well past midnight, but he was used to odd hours. It came with the job—a predator hunts when his prey is out and active. Marvin slipped out of his Toronto townhouse and walked to a 24-hour supermarket. A beautiful blue Rolls-Royce Silver Shadow with personalized licence plates was pulling up in front of the Miracle Mart. Marvin watched a tall, well-dressed black man, dripping with gold jewellery, step out and head into the store. It was June 10, 1986.

"This guy must be something," he said to himself. "I'll have to meet him."

Poking around the aisles, Marvin made sure he bumped into the man and introduced himself. The man replied in kind and gave him his business card, which had been newly printed. His name was Leo James and he had just opened a bar on Vaughan Road called The Three J.J.J.s.

Marvin called Robbie as soon as the sun was up and told him about the man, his Rolls and his expensive gold.

"What do you know about him?" Robbie asked.

"Nothing, yet."

Robbie checked him out on his end, running the Rolls licence plate Marvin had given him. The guy was from Kentucky and seemed well connected. He had criminal convictions and had been flagged by Toronto police's Black Organized Crime Squad, before racial politics led to the unit being dismantled. Robbie told Marvin to become his friend. Marvin started being a regular at The Three J.J.J.s and Leo James started introducing him to his friends and business partners, including Theo Henry, a Trinidadian who was a silent partner in the bar. Everyone called them Theo and Leo.

"This is Marvin 'The Weasel' Elkind. He's a well-connected guy," Leo said.

As the three men talked, over the weeks, Marvin told them several times that he was off to Detroit, and then he would disappear for a few days. It wasn't a lie. Marvin was spending a lot of time in Detroit, where he was working on another case with the FBI. He didn't mention the FBI part.

"I told them I was very well connected to the Detroit mob and they checked it out: I was. Everyone was telling them that I was connected with the bad guys. They called this big fight promoter in Detroit, Emanuel Steward, and he knew me and he said I was always hanging around with the bad guys, that I was well connected with the big mob guys in Detroit," Marvin says.

"They brought me in with open arms. They fed me, gave me money, they treated me fantastic. I became a part of the family."

Marvin started hanging out at The Three J.J.J.s almost every night.

"Everybody got to know me. I became a part of the furniture. We would go downstairs to their office in the bar. They were dealing in all kinds of hot stuff, drugs, prostitution. When they got into trouble with a living-on-the-avails-of-prostitution charge, they needed a good lawyer and I sent them to my lawyer.

"This bar, hardly any white guys ever came in there, ninety-nine point nine per cent of the people were black. They had this Jewish girl working for them there, a hooker. They said, 'Marvin, she's yours because you're Jewish.'"

Marvin couldn't indulge, but the two talked. It turned out she was the daughter of the owner of a major construction firm.

"Does your old man know what you're doing?" Marvin asked her.

"He won't talk to me. I called him on Father's Day and he hung up."

The Three J.J.J.s was a busy place. Men and women drifted in and out. Some never seemed to leave. One night, a car pulled up out front and a man paraded customers and staff over to look at stolen silk suits and fur coats in his trunk. Theo traded some cocaine for a fur he liked. While the deal was going down, a police cruiser pulled up. An officer gave the car driver a ticket for his parking infraction but never asked about the stuff in the trunk.

Within weeks of Marvin bumping into Leo in the super-market, Theo confided to him that they were in a financial bind. The bar's ledgers were already tapped out. They had neglected to account for sales tax in their business plan. They were going to balance their books by moving drugs. They hoped Marvin could help.

On July 11, Marvin and Theo spent the afternoon driving around Toronto. He handed Marvin a packet of money and asked him to count it. Marvin clumsily thumbed through the hundred-dollar bills and said it came to $3,400. Theo then pulled the car to a stop in front of a hair salon, put the money in a briefcase and went inside. He came out a few minutes later looking happy.

"I'm in business," he said.

Later, Theo took Marvin to the Eaton's department store in Yorkdale Shopping Centre in the north end of Toronto.

Theo pointed to a young woman working at the cosmetics counter and told Marvin to watch. A man soon arrived at the counter and discreetly exchanged packages with the woman. After he left, the woman gave Theo the package. Inside was $1,000. Using similar women at similar cosmetics counters, an ingenious distribution network had been built. Ten days later, Theo took Marvin to the Million Dollar Saloon, a strip club in Mississauga, west of Toronto, where Marvin was introduced to the owner. The successful operation was expanding and Theo and Leo were working with him to open Million Dollar Saloons in Niagara Falls and Windsor. Marvin was asked if he would "commit" to their operation. Marvin said he was all about commitment. Immediately Theo asked to borrow Marvin's car keys and then slipped away with them for a few minutes. After they drove back to The Three J.J.J.s together, Theo took six bags from Marvin's trunk and carried them into the bar. Later, Marvin was given $300 for his help moving drugs.

By August, Theo and Leo's money trouble was over and Leo asked Marvin if he could recruit some muscle for them. The new strip clubs were ready and one had competition nearby. They expected a rocky reception. They turned to Marvin because the muscle had to be white and all of their enforcers were black.

For eight months, Marvin hung around with Theo and Leo, working with Robbie to build a case. Robbie usually waited to see if it would lead to bigger, more important suspects before closing a case down. It was not long until Robbie realized just how thoroughly Marvin had penetrated the group.

* * *

Two sisters from Toronto—young twins, absolutely gorgeous—were really freaking out. The pair worked as waitresses at The Three J.J.J.s and, to earn extra cash, made cocaine deliveries in Buffalo for their bosses. Their uncommon looks tempted male border guards to stare places other than their luggage, and the crossings went smoothly. But this time, things had turned nasty in America. The buyers were not as easily distracted as the border agents, and the sisters were ripped off, losing both the drugs and the money they were supposed to collect.

They were now terrified of returning to Toronto empty-handed to face their bosses at the bar. They were afraid they would be accused of stealing and maybe beaten or killed. In their panic, they could see only one solution: reporting the drug theft to the Buffalo police. Crying and begging for mercy, they told the cops everything about the drug run. The detectives had an important question.

"Who sent you? Who are the bosses on the Canadian side?"

The women gave police the names of the top men in the organization: Leo James, Theo Henry and Marvin Elkind.

When Buffalo police checked with the OPP, they were transferred to Robbie. Marvin had been flagged in police databases: when officers ran his name they were instructed to contact Robbie. Robbie took the call on one of the three phones he had at his desk. A manic worker, Robbie was known to juggle calls on all three at once. Robbie told Buffalo police that Marvin was an informant working on a long-term project. Could they do him a favour and keep it under wraps and let the sisters go? They agreed to play along.

The call delighted Robbie. That both sisters had named Marvin as one of the bosses of the gang proved once again how good The Weasel really was.

Robbie wanted to get inside The Three J.J.J.s himself, so he turned to his undercover alter ego: Colonel Al Gibson.

In keeping with the "Mother" tattoo on his arm, his make-believe identity was from his mother's maiden name. Robbie had a set of false IDs to backup the identity, along with business cards for a fake Toronto import-export business. Robbie stepped into the character with confidence, having served in the air force before joining the OPP. Marvin took Robbie to the bar and introduced everyone to "The Colonel."

Because of the cross-border nature of the drug case, focused on strip clubs conveniently located at two major border points, Robbie contacted the FBI and a joint operation began. With the FBI involved, resources expanded considerably.

* * *

Ernie Kanakis was a major gambler from Detroit, a big Greek man who loved to bet and loved to swear. Both would get him into trouble, but he was such a tough bugger he could always handle it. In the summer of 1977, he was hauled into the basement of the Detroit home of mobster Frank Randazzo to receive a pointed message from an angry Nick Ditta, an important member of the Detroit Mafia. When Randazzo, Ditta and a third mobster, Joseph Siragusa, came at Kanakis with ice picks, Kanakis pulled a gun and blasted all three. It had taken police three days to clean up the basement before Randazzo's mourning family could be let back into their house. Kanakis then cut a deal with prosecutors and become a police informant.

Kanakis was brought into this investigation to help enhance Marvin's reputation as a hardened gangster with tight Detroit connections. A couple of times, Marvin took Kanakis around to the strip clubs in Mississauga and Windsor that Theo was involved with. Kanakis was smitten by one of the strippers, buying her roses.

After seeing Marvin hanging around with Kanakis, the strip-club partners were soon asking Marvin about his American connections. This was part of Marvin's plan. He waited for them to come to him with the idea of working on a cross-border deal. Marvin said, yeah, his Detroit friends were, in fact, looking to expand in Ontario.

"But you'll have to talk to them about it. I have the connections, but I don't know much of anything about drugs myself," he said.

He rarely pretended to be an experienced drug dealer. It was too easy to make a mistake if he was asked a drug question for which he didn't know the answer. He stuck to what he knew: ask him about breaking an arm and he could tell you six ways to do it.

The strip-club operators, seeking to impress their American guests, reserved the entire VIP section of their Windsor club. They had their girls dancing, shaking and strutting all around them and the waiters taking free drink orders from the moment Marvin and his three American friends sat down.

Marvin brought FBI Special Agent Rich Mazzari and two other FBI agents to the meeting, posing as his Detroit connection. The operation was bigger than first believed. It was a budding cross-border drug-smuggling enterprise. There were bikers involved in distribution. They were establishing safe houses to protect drug couriers in Los Angeles, Houston, Detroit, Calgary and Toronto. When Marvin and Mazzari had finished arranging a deal to move heroin and cocaine across the border, Mazzari handed one of the club owners a card with his Detroit phone number on it. It was the number to his special hotline, the phone he kept locked in the drawer of his desk on the top floor of the McNamara Federal Building on Michigan Avenue.

***

"They're expecting us. Tell them The Weasel and the Colonel are here," Marvin told the bartender at the long bar at the back of the Million Dollar Saloon.

"I'll pass it on," one of the barmen said, putting down a glass and walking away.

As the bartender headed down to the basement office, Marvin and Robbie waited at the bar. There was a substantial police operation in place at this point. Based on what was said at the meeting in the VIP room, police had been given secret court authorization to wiretap the phones in the Million Dollar Saloon. The list of suspects spinning out from the Three J.J.J.s to the strip clubs continued to grow, encompassing a Los Angeles stock promoter named Kirpal Ahluwalia and members of the Para-Dice Riders Motorcycle Club. Across the border in Detroit, Mazzari was expecting a phone call from the club owner. And while Marvin and Robbie were in the club, waiting for him to come up and meet them, the owner wanted to check one last detail with the American boss. He looked about for the number he had been given, finding it at about the same time that Mazzari was realizing he really needed to pee. Just after Mazzari jogged out of his office to the toilet, he dialled the number from the phone in his basement office. Before Mazzari could finish his business, the phone started ringing and an inexperienced agent walking past Mazzari's office tracked down the curious sound, found the phone in Mazzari's drawer and picked up the receiver.

"FBI Detroit," said the agent.

After a confused pause, the club owner said he must have misdialled.

"What number are you trying to reach?" the agent asked, picking up the base of the phone and looking at the front to see what its number was. The caller read off the numbers on his slip of paper.

"That's the number you dialled. This is an FBI phone. Where did you get this number?"

Click.

Robbie's colleagues in the wire room had heard the call and were in a sweat. Then they heard a second call being made from the club.

"Marvin's been feeding us to the cops. He's upstairs now. We don't know if the guy with him is a cop or not."

Back in the club, Marvin and Robbie had no clue that their cover had been blown, but Robbie decided he should make a phone call of his own.

"I'm going to check in," he said quietly to Marvin, before wandering off to a pay phone in the club. When Robbie called headquarters, he got an earful: "Get the hell out. Your cover's blown."

Robbie went back to the bar, trying to look relaxed.

"They've got us, we're blown," he told Marvin.

"Well, get your piece ready," said Marvin, referring to Robbie's gun.

"I haven't got it."

"What? Why?"

"It's too heavy, it's hard to hide."

"Jesus Christ," muttered Marvin. "There're a million cops in the world and I travel with the one who doesn't like guns."

By then, five large bouncers had appeared and were surrounding Marvin and Robbie. The musclemen were looking at each other. Robbie could tell they were unsure of what to do, and he didn't want to wait for them to figure it out. He told Marvin to start walking toward the front door. The bouncers followed, still looking at each other, waiting for someone to make the first move. When they got near the door, Marvin and Robbie broke into a run, with the bouncers chasing them for a block or so.

It was an embarrassing end to an operation that Marvin and Robbie had been working for almost a year. They were furious when they heard how their cover had been blown, but understood that crazy mistakes sometimes happen. At least they had made it out uninjured. It wasn't long before they were laughing about it.

The bigger concern for Marvin and Robbie was what the revelation would mean for The Weasel. He had been identified as an informant, working with the FBI, no less. Surely that would get around.

"We all thought that would be the end of my career," Marvin says. "But it wasn't. I think these guys were so embarrassed, they didn't want anyone else to know they had been taken in, so they didn't tell anyone." Keeping it to themselves, though, didn't mean they were ready to let it drop.

* * *

Marvin was upstairs in his townhouse watching television on the evening of March 22, 1987, not long after his hasty retreat from the Million Dollar Saloon. The caper had kept him out of the house and away from his family too much in the past few months, and he was enjoying some quiet time. Robbie had made him promise to stay out of sight. Marvin didn't hear the knock at his front door, but Hennie did.

"Marvin, you've got company," she called up to him.

Marvin came down the stairs and saw Theo and another man waiting for him in the hallway.

"What the hell are you doing here?"

"Marv, things haven't been going right for us for a while, and it started when we met you. We're gonna go for a ride and discuss it," Theo said.

"I'm not going anywhere with you."

"You're coming with us. Let's go."

"Go to hell."

As this confrontation began, Hennie walked upstairs, went into the den and sat down to watch television.

Theo and the other guy, meanwhile, grabbed Marvin to pull him out to their car. Through the open door, Marvin saw a third person sitting behind the wheel with the engine running. His fight training would now pay off more than any prize purse. Marvin's left hook shot out in an arc and knocked Theo back. A second struck the other guy. But these two were tough, as well, and a hard, desperate fight started with bodies and furniture bouncing about the small hallway. One of Marvin's daughters heard the commotion and phoned police.

"There are two gangsters in the house trying to drag my dad outside to kill him," she said through tears. She then returned to the hallway and, standing out of the way on the stairs, called out to help her father as best she could.

"Behind you, Dad, watch out! On your left, get him, Dad! You can do it!" The two men grabbed Marvin again and tried to pull him through the door, but Marvin twisted and yanked free, kicking one, punching the other, grabbing the door frame with his right hand.

"You're coming with us," Henry grunted.

"I'm going nowhere. Get the hell out," Marvin grunted back.

The fight went on. Everyone was bleeding and shouting and punching and still police had not arrived. Half an hour passed and there was not even the sound of a siren in the distance. Finally, two officers pulled up in a cruiser and the fighting stopped, leaving everyone exhausted and battered.

Theo, though, was a real smooth talker and calmly met the cops. "Listen, this is just a disagreement between friends that got a little heated. There's no need for police. We're sorry."

The cops turned to Marvin and asked if that was true.

"No, it's not. They're trying to kill me," he said.

The officers took the easy way out, telling Theo and his friends to move along. As Marvin watched through his front window, Theo spotted him. The two men shook their fists at each other like schoolboys.

Marvin phoned Robbie and soon he arrived with Danielle. They noticed the tires on Marvin's car had all been slashed. Robbie called the Toronto police, wanting to know why it had taken so long for officers to respond to the call. A staff inspector looked into it and apologized. The patrol officers admitted that when they were sent on the call they had recognized Marvin's address as the home of a known bad guy—they knew him only as a gangster—and had decided to take their time, thinking it might mean one less troublemaker to worry about.

Police later found the stolen car that Theo and his friends had used. In the back seat was a long bayonet. Police figured they had planned to use the bayonet on Marvin once they had got him into the car. Marvin was glad they hadn't brought the bayonet with them to the door, or they could have stuck him right there.

Robbie was also upset that Marvin's wife had let strangers in.

"You know that nobody in this house opens the door without knowing who it is. What happened?" Robbie asked her. Hennie said she didn't know why she had done it. She was upset and crying, and Danielle took her upstairs. Danielle came down later. She said that at that moment, when the two guys had showed up, Hennie had just had enough and snapped.

Robbie and Danielle both said, "Who can blame her?"

* * *

Although the case ended abruptly, police still considered it a success. In mid-June, a large task force of officers from the OPP, FBI, U.S. Customs, Los Angeles police, Peel police, Windsor police and Calgary police launched the raids that Marvin's former friends had been bracing for, ever since his duplicity had been revealed. Twelve people were arrested, including the landlord, owner and manager of the Million Dollar Saloon in Mississauga; their supplier, Kirpal Ahluwalia; two members of the biker gang; other club employees; and one stripper. Most were charged with conspiracy to import narcotics and conspiracy to distribute narcotics. The dancer was charged with drug possession when she was found with mescaline. After the revelation of the police probe, officers weren't too surprised they didn't find large stashes of dope at the clubs. A little cocaine was found in Mississauga and a kilogram brick seized in L.A., which was found to be 98 per cent pure. Charges against the Three J.J.J.s gang were handled separately.

This time, Marvin was scheduled to testify against the men in court. Theo had earlier sent a message through his lawyer: "Tell Marv's wife we're sorry we came to the house. If we wanted to get him, we shouldn't have done it at his home."

When Marvin arrived for the trial, Robbie walked beside him into the Toronto courthouse carrying a shotgun in an open duffel bag, ready to protect him. Robbie didn't want to be without his piece a second time. To everyone's relief, the defendants pleaded guilty and Marvin didn't have to take the stand.

In court, Marvin saw Theo for the last time.

"I guess everything was a big mistake," Theo said.

"Yeah," said Marvin, "a big mistake."

* * *

It wasn't long afterwards that Marvin bumped into some old friends from Boston at the King Edward Hotel. They started drinking and didn't stop, at least not until they had all passed out. It was an unplanned booze-up and Marvin hadn't called Hennie all day or night.

When morning came and Marvin had not come home, Hennie was worried sick and called Robbie. Robbie hadn't heard from him, either. It was unusual for Marvin to go for so long without contacting one of them. Robbie drove to some of Marvin's usual hangouts. At the King Edward he found no sign of Marvin, but saw his car parked nearby. With a grim face, Robbie went to Marvin's house to get a spare set of car keys from Hennie. He didn't tell her why, but he expected to find Marvin's body stuffed in the trunk of his own car, meeting an end that never seemed far-fetched or too far away.

The trunk was empty, and Marvin soon staggered back to the car, nursing a hangover.

CHAPTER 35

ACCRA, GHANA, 1987

On New Year's Eve, 1981, a young, handsome air-force lieutenant jumped on top of a tank in the centre of Accra, capital of the West African nation of Ghana, clutching a microphone in his left hand, as his right, clenched in a fist, waved aloft, rising and falling dramatically in rhythm with his fiery speech as he exhorted the masses with revolutionary fervour. With his chiselled features, stylish moustache and goatee, athletic movement and glistening dark skin, Jerry J. Rawlings was a striking figure. Wearing aviator sunglasses and a flight suit—sleeves rolled up—he conjured the spirit of Che Guevara for a new generation.

The people cheering Rawlings into the city after his coup d'état knew him well. Rawlings had led a failed coup in 1979, and had been put on trial. The government made a big show of the hearing, which backfired when the articulate Rawlings gave such a rousing justification for his actions in the face of social injustice that a popular uprising swept the country. Rawlings was sprung from jail by fellow military officers, who helped him finish the job of ousting the government. Then, in a surprise move, Rawlings had done what few coup leaders ever do—after a housecleaning that dispatched corrupt government and military leaders, he relinquished power within a few months to an elected leader, just as he had said he would. But emerging democracies can be slow and messy affairs, and an impatient Rawlings had had second thoughts, sparking his return to power this New Year's Eve. This time, he consolidated himself as a dictator, a radical young leader aligned with the hard left, setting up revolutionary committees, eliminating dissidents and spouting socialist slogans.

Few people had more experience in the indelicate art of the coup d'état than Rawlings, who botched one, pulled off two and then foiled at least three against him, all before Marvin found Ghana on a map in 1987.

* * *

The Wheat Sheaf lays claim to being the oldest tavern in Toronto, and its worn brick facade, on King Street West at Bathurst Street, looked it. It was founded in 1849, when Ghana was still a British colony known as the Gold Coast.

It was hotdogs that brought Toronto businessman Nicholas Andreko to a table in a dim corner of the historic tavern on September 14. Andreko had chosen this spot to meet Marvin because of that particular menu item. He raved about their hotdogs and encouraged Marvin to try them. Marvin kept a kosher house, but quietly ate pork outside it, and he enjoyed the Wheat Sheaf's wieners as much as Andreko did. Marvin had known Andreko for years. They had met in Amsterdam when Marvin was investigating crooked stock deals, and they occasionally bumped into each other in Toronto. They would meet at the pub several times in the weeks ahead, with the businessman thinking Marvin was a man with the connections he was looking for. It was another sinister entreaty to The Weasel who, despite his years of finking and occasional exposure, still had a reputation on the street as a wheeler-dealer of the most crooked kind.

The discussions at the Sheaf, secretly caught on tape by Marvin, soon started to sound more like his work against the Libyan agent than more recent cases. Andreko asked about weapons, money, mercenaries and a West African country Marvin wasn't sure he had heard of before.

Marvin knew it would be fun right from the start.

Andreko had spent a lot of time abroad. In fact, he told Marvin, he had been imprisoned in Ghana when he was trying to bring gold out of the country. Though he hadn't much appreciated being in jail, he spoke highly of his captors, noting he was treated "better than at the hotel." It was while in prison in Ghana that he had met some of the men he was working with. When Robbie started listening to Marvin's recordings, he thought Andreko was just a renegade businessman with testosterone-fuelled dreams. But the more information Marvin got, the more concerned Robbie became: there was a large organization of expatriate Ghanaians backing Andreko, including former government ministers, military officers and cultural and political groups around the world. Some of Andreko's colleagues had been locked up for an anti-Rawlings plot before and somehow had managed to escape, fleeing to South America and then travelling north to the United States. Others had moved to Britain. Andreko was arranging weapons and money for them to take another crack at a coup aimed at toppling Rawlings, using an army of hired mercenaries and Ghanaian dissidents.

"The black guys, they're good fighters, but they've got to have some white guys ahead of them. If they don't have white guys ahead of them, they run," Andreko said.

Marvin told him he would arrange for him to meet his favourite arms dealer, Colonel Gibson.

Robbie was fired up at the prospect of delving into another case of international intrigue. It was the type of improbable operation that kept coming his way, setting him apart from most of his peers.

Robbie brought a second undercover officer into the mix, Detective-Constable John Celentino of the Ontario Provincial Police. As a teen, Celentino had flirted with a Niagara Falls street gang, an experience that had given him street smarts and basement tattoos, made with heated pins and India ink. Escaping the bad life, he had joined the cops and been a natural to pose as a mobster in undercover operations. Whenever Marvin introduced the tough-talking Celentino, their targets saw the crude cross on his left hand between his thumb and forefinger, a common prison tattoo. When Celentino rolled up his sleeves, they would see the dark dagger and the heart with a cross and a letter M in the middle, a homage to the Virgin Mary, and he was instantly believable. Celentino often went by the undercover name Gino to emphasize his Italian heritage.

Celentino liked the sound of this case, too. It was a nice change from drugs. The trouble was, for a purported arms dealer, he knew nothing about guns. He was put on a crash course with a police tactical team, learning how to assemble, load and clean assault rifles and combat pistols and about the advantages of certain weapons over others. He stuffed one of the guns into a hockey bag and checked into the Harbour Castle Hotel on the Toronto waterfront where he spent hours in repetitive practice. By the time he was called to meet the coup plotters, Celentino could break down and reassemble an assault rifle with his eyes closed.

When anyone asked about his merchandise, he was ready to show off.

* * *

Celentino and Robbie's room at the luxurious hotel was wired with a hidden camera and microphones when The Weasel arrived with Andreko on November 5, 1987.

"Hey, how are you? Good to see you, good to see you. Everything OK?" Marvin said as he shuffled in, doing brief introductions.

"Take your coat off, relax," Marvin told Andreko.

"You gonna have a drink?" Robbie asked.

"Why not?" said Andreko.

"What's your pleasure? We got Scotch, we got other things."

"Scotch is fine. Scotch is my drink."

"Marv?" Robbie said, expecting him to get the drinks.

"Yeah, Scotch is great," Marvin said, thinking he was being offered a beverage. Robbie shot him a look—"You gonna tend bar there?"—and Marvin started pouring. As Marvin brought drinks, the men settled into plush hotel chairs.

Andreko held up his glass, "Well, cheers, gentlemen." One of the cops chimed in: "To success."

Marvin had told Andreko that Gino and The Colonel could furnish them with an arsenal. To prove the point, the AK-47 assault rifle that Celentino had been practising with was whipped out. Andreko's head snapped up when he heard the distinctive click of the assault rifle.

"How the fuck did you get that across the border?" Andreko asked.

"Don't ask," Celentino replied, as he started taking it apart on the table, showing it to Andreko.

The businessman talked tough to his new partners.

"I have a saying, the only good cop is a dead cop," he told

them. The cops smirked awkwardly. Andreko then outlined the plan.

"These are the three targets you have to take over. The broadcasting house, you can see, it's very small, right. There are only two guys there. The Castle is the heavy one. The airport only has one runway here, so all you have to do is drive a truck with gasoline on it and light it so nothing can land," Andreko said.

The plan called for the weapons to be transported to Florida, where a ship had been arranged to sail to Ghana's western neighbour of Côte d'Ivoire, where dissidents were gathering for their strike on Rawlings. The Ghanaian leader was ensconced in the 17th-century Christiansborg Castle that formed the seat of government in the coastal capital of Accra. The easiest way to get him, the plotters said, was when he was arriving or leaving in his helicopter gunship. That's why they needed a couple of anti-aircraft missiles. Robbie was surprised at the level of preparation and planning that had gone into the mission. With the detailed plans and the American connection to Chicago, Robbie contacted the FBI.

* * *

The plotters' timing was terrible. Throughout the early years of Rawlings's regime, the radical leader had been seen as a threat to Western interests in Africa. He courted Libya's Colonel Gadhafi and praised Cuba's Fidel Castro. Libya had invested heavily in the country after Rawlings's revolution and there was suspected influence by the KGB, the spy service of the Soviet Union. It was more than enough to have made Western governments nervous, perhaps nervous enough to support a pro-capitalist coup. The U.S. government might well have tried. A spy scandal had further damaged relations between Ghana and the United States, when Ghanaian security agents had learned the identity of CIA agents in Ghana and, in the United States, a relative of Rawlings had been arrested for espionage. The agents had all been swapped in a 1985 prisoner exchange. The following year, a ship of mercenaries and weapons had been seized off the coast of Brazil. It was believed to have been destined for Ghana and supported by the CIA. They were not the only challenges Rawlings had faced. A coup attempt in 1981 had failed to dislodge him and at least seven people involved in it had been executed.

With five successful military coups in its short 30-year history, Ghana was not an impossible choice as a coup target. But just as this new coup plot was being hatched, Rawlings was shifting course, imposing financial restraint and pushing for economic recovery and conservative politics. Acknowledging the need for participatory democracy and signing deals with the International Monetary Fund, Rawlings, his domestic record on human rights notwithstanding, was starting to be seen as an emerging model of Third World governance. In another sign of further thawing in Ghana's relationship with the United States, just one year before Marvin met Andreko in the Wheat Sheaf, President Jimmy Carter had visited the country and been warmly greeted by Rawlings. When Robbie took his coup plot to the American authorities, it was greeted with the intention of thwarting, not supporting, the operation.

Robbie and his colleagues mapped out their own mission plan. They wanted to draw all of Andreko's colleagues out into the open and get them into the United States where they could be arrested. Undercover agents with the FBI and U.S. Customs posed as the American arms merchants who were a part of The Colonel and Gino's supposedly nefarious consortium. The FBI's contact was Robbie's friend Rich Mazzari, from Detroit, who had recently worked with Marvin in the close call at the strip club. From U.S. Customs, it was agent Ed Yarkovichs. Marvin spent New Year's Eve arranging a series of meetings between the consortium and the plotters, each one set to draw Robbie further up the ladder of power within the Ghanaian dissident faction.

* * *

On January 9, 1988, Marvin delivered Andreko and Sam O'Dame, the secretary of the Ghana Democratic Movement's U.S. branch, to Room 615 of the Novi Hilton, outside Detroit, and provided introductions.

"Sam, say hello to Gino," Marvin said, motioning to Celentino as the hidden video camera captured the action.

"And this is Colonel Gibson."

"Would you like coffee or a drink or something?" Robbie offered.

"I'll take a drink," O'Dame said. "Scotch."

Marvin knew his role this time.

"Where's your bar, over here?" he said, and then started pulling out glasses. He broke the ice as he offered ice: "A rabbi and a priest went to the fights. Fighter crosses himself. Rabbi says 'Father, what does that mean?' Priest says, 'It don't mean a damn thing if he can't fight.'" As the men laughed, Marvin wandered to the side of the room, picked up a newspaper and sat down to read it, keeping silent and out of the way.

At the board table, Robbie offered a toast: "Here's to business."

What business it was. O'Dame talked openly about "this organization to topple the government" and his dislike of

Rawlings. He laid out the details of their group, their people in Baltimore, New York, Chicago and Detroit. Their leader was in London. He even talked about who would likely take what role in the new government. They had launched a failed coup in 1981, which had led to a "slaughter."

"Any time we planned to do something, somebody leaked things out. As a result, people either get killed for nothing or we're not successful," O'Dame said. "The reason why we failed in the past, we haven't been well prepared and planned according to the way it should be done."

"All right, Sam, then what can we do for you?" Robbie asked.

"We have the people that can do the job, people well trained. We have generals, two of them now in Togo, one in Nigeria," he said. "What we need is money to buy the equipment, the necessary tools to do the job."

O'Dame spoke of Rawlings's helicopter and the need to "knock out that first." Take out Rawlings and his security chief and "the government will fall. There are a few diehards that are going to resist. You'll have some trouble dealing with those, so you have to eliminate those."

"You want money," Robbie said, "and we're certainly prepared to discuss that. But we're also prepared to discuss selling of equipment. That's one of our businesses as well."

"We got some merchandise if you're interested," Robbie added casually, walking toward the kitchenette to get another drink.

"I'll look," O'Dame said.

A belt-fed M60 machine gun with a bipod stand was hauled out.

"Ever see Rambo, Sam?" Robbie asked.

"I saw Rambo, yeah."

"That's what he used."

O'Dame groaned as the heavy gun was dropped into his arms.

"You look like Rambo," Robbie said.

"I'm impressed, believe me."

* * *

On February 28, 1988, Marvin collected Sam O'Dame and Dr. Edward Mahama at the Detroit airport and drove them to meet his consortium at the Omni Hotel downtown. While Robbie was pleased to meet the man O'Dame said was his boss, Robbie was disappointed that the overall leader, a former finance minister in the government Rawlings had overthrown, wasn't with him. The former minister, who was based in London, was the political leader of the dissident faction, the plotters had said. Apologizing for the absence, the doctor said the government official was not allowed into the United States.

By May, however, their leader, based in London, was regularly calling Marvin from London. In a bid to entice him to meet them, the U.S. Customs agents borrowed a missile from the U.S. Marines as bait. It was deadly merchandise. Easy to carry and simple to use, the FIM-92 Stinger was a portable one-man surface-to-air missile-launch system. Hiked up onto the shoulder and weighing less than 35 pounds, it could hit a plane 15,000 feet away and 12,500 feet in the sky with its infrared homing system. They were highly sought after on the black market, with terrorists, mercenaries and foreign governments lusting for them.

Marvin arranged another meeting to close the deal, a show and tell, as cops call it, when they show off the merchandise they were offering to dazzle and ensnare the buyers—all of it to be caught on video. All of the coup conspirators, who were living in Canada, Britain and the United States, were invited to it.

On the day of the meeting, Marvin met with Andreko, Robbie and Celentino and they drove together from Toronto to Detroit. The American agents had arranged with the border guards to let them through without inadvertently sending them for a secondary inspection that might ruin the operation. When Marvin's car pulled up at the U.S. border, the border agent asked them the usual questions—did they have anything to declare, what citizenship were they, where were they headed—and then waved them through.

They were gathering in a boardroom owned by a Detroit automobile-parts manufacturer who had agreed to lend the space to the FBI. A safe, secure and controlled site was a must, as the agents had deadly armaments to show the conspirators. There could be no slip-ups or thefts.

"Whatever you do," the U.S. Customs agent sternly told Marvin, "don't touch the merchandise."

* * *

The Canadian contingent arrived at the Detroit office and were joined by the Ghanaian expats living in the United States. The former minister, however, still could not be coaxed onto American soil. The meeting went ahead regardless, and as the men took their places around the boardroom table, a Stinger missile with its launcher made an engaging centrepiece. After pleasantries and introductions, an agent picked up the weapon and handed it to the plotters.

The Stinger was passed between them, with some of the men hoisting it up onto their shoulder to firing position and peering through the aiming sight, as if they were already on the battlefield in Accra. Marvin kept quiet and pushed himself back against the wall as he looked at the armaments. He placed his arms behind his back and even grabbed one hand in the other to help him resist the urge to get in on the macho posturing.

The visitors were impressed by the show and tell.

"There was two parts to this deal," Robbie explained afterwards. "One was a supply of arms, and the second part was supplying two million dollars in cash, so that they could operate and pay the mercenaries that were going to be involved in the overthrow." The money was seen as an investment. For two million dollars, the investor would gain access to a friendly new ruler of a nation that was one of the world's leading gold producers and the second-largest producer of cacao. Ghana was blessed with other natural resources of interest to a business consortium: oil, timber, diamonds, minerals. The consortium said they certainly wanted casino rights in the country as a minimum.

Robbie and Celentino felt they had what they needed to make a great case. Celentino, in particular, was looking forward to making arrests, especially after the crack about the only good cop being a dead one.

"These people were deadly serious, and if they could have got the weapons, they certainly had the capabilities to do what they were intending to do," Robbie explained afterwards.

Because of the international-intrigue angle of the case, however, police brass needed to inform the federal government. Robbie and his boss, Dennis McGillis, went to Ottawa to brief Joe Clark, the former prime minister who was now Canada's secretary of state for external affairs in the Mulroney government. With a member of the RCMP and a couple of Parliamentary security officials sitting in, Robbie and McGillis gave Clark a briefing and copies of the surveillance tape of the Toronto hotel meeting. There were wider interests and diplomatic sensitivities beyond this investigation, they were cautioned. Canada had a cordial relationship with Rawlings. Of particular interest to Canada was Ghana's off-shore oil reserves: Petro-Canada International, an oil and gas company owned by the Canadian government, was prospecting oil reserves in Ghana's Tano River Basin. That same year, Canada also cancelled the Ghanaian debt of $77.6 million.

Robbie and McGillis left Ottawa with a bad feeling about the future of their operation and were not surprised when it was taken out of their hands. The reports on Marvin's infiltration were sent in the diplomatic pouch to the Canadian Embassy in Ghana, and the information was shared with Rawlings and his security officials. Robbie and McGillis were then told to meet with a delegation arriving in Ottawa from Ghana.

In September 1988, the entourage from Ghana arrived. The OPP booked a large suite with soaring ceilings at the picturesque Château Laurier in the heart of the capital, next door to the Parliament Buildings. Robbie and McGillis watched a long black limousine pull up to the hotel's impressive limestone portico. Dressed in his flashy military uniform, decorated with medals and surrounded by four of the biggest bodyguards the cops had ever seen, the Deputy Director of Internal Security for the government of Ghana emerged and hurried inside.

Once in the suite, Robbie offered drinks. The deputy director loved Canadian beer and, as they talked, he kept asking for another, soon draining the suite's bar fridge and forcing Robbie to order up more. Robbie and McGillis outlined for him what they knew about the coup plans, and then popped a tape into the video player. On the hotel's television they watched the secret surveillance videos of Marvin introducing the plotters to the Canadian and American agents.

"That's them," the deputy director roared, when he saw the faces of the plotters. "I can't believe it, that's them." He recognized some of the men from previous sedition. He fumed that they had managed to get out of Ghana.

His face betrayed his smouldering fury as he listened to the men discuss the assassination of Rawlings and the overthrow of the government. He seethed as he watched them hoisting and fondling the weaponry. For him, it was personal. He wanted Robbie and McGillis to let him grab the plotters off the street and bundle them onto his plane to face justice in Ghana. The cops got the impression the suspects would never see the coast of Ghana under that scenario, but would become fish food somewhere in the Atlantic. That wasn't part of Canada's plans, but neither, as it turned out, were arrests.

"I believe that the steps for conspiracy had been completed. However, there was no prosecution. It didn't go that far, so we had to take other steps to protect the government; at least alert them to what was being planned," Robbie explained.

"Politics played a big part of that," says Celentino, who was disappointed he didn't get to make the surprise revelation that the tough, mobbed-up arms dealer was really a cop. No charges were laid against Andreko or anyone else in Canada. Later, when asked if he was involved in the plot, Andreko claimed to know nothing about it, saying, "Absolutely not, and I don't know what you're talking about."

It was left in the hands of the Americans and the Ghanaians. What happened from there, Marvin doesn't know.

The OPP says Marvin's infiltration and the operation that ensued thwarted a coup, saved a great loss of life and may have saved a teetering independent nation.

"This was an important international incident. It was fascinating the things that came through Marvin," McGillis says.

Hearing that, Marvin smiles. "Somebody owes me something, but I don't know what."

CHAPTER 36

TORONTO, 1988

There were about 700 people watching—sharp-suited businessmen, outlaw bikers in their leathers and everything in between—as George Chuvalo, the former Canadian heavyweight boxing champion, stood at the front of the Canadian Room in the Royal York hotel. Wearing a bow tie and tuxedo, his gut testing the strength of his electric-blue cummerbund, he was oozing contentment after some hard times, basking in the appreciation of boxing fans and fellow-fighters at a $100-a-plate dinner in his honour on November 2, 1988.

"I was known as a body puncher," he said to the crowd. "I was trying to make my opponents' kidneys scream. In the ring, you want to do damage to your opponent. Yet, when the bout is over, you have mutual respect. It's a hell of a way to make friends, but I have some great friends here."

He nodded to those in the audience and those at the head table. It was an illustrious bunch, including Muhammad Ali, Floyd Patterson and Rubin "Hurricane" Carter. Chuvalo joked that he should have used a solid head-butt against the fast-footed Ali during their two punch-ups. Ali rose from his chair and cocked his fists jokingly, as if he were ready for a black-tie rematch. The crowd loved it, chanting, "Ali, Ali, Ali."

The crowd also chanted for Chuvalo's admission into Canada's Sports Hall of Fame, an oversight that was finally corrected two years later. But the rarity of Ali being in their midst made him the star, and he was swarmed before and afterwards for autographs.

It almost hadn't happened. Organizers had been after Ali to attend for weeks, without success. Ali had retired from the ring in 1981 and been diagnosed with Parkinson's disease in 1984, but his fame endured and he was increasingly in demand. The year of the Chuvalo tribute, Ali had led the 1988 Tournament of Roses Parade. Calls had been placed but the requests turned down. Then Marvin called. He spoke to Yolanda, Ali's wife.

"Lonnie, I'd really appreciate him doing this," Marvin said.

She checked with her husband.

"OK," she said, "he'll be there. No charge."

* * *

The first time Marvin met Muhammad Ali was on February 2, 1965, in New York City, when the Canadian champ George Chuvalo was in town to fight Floyd Patterson at Madison Square Garden. Chuvalo arrived with a cheering section from Toronto, including Marvin. Most of the out-of-towners stayed at the Loews Midtown Hotel, across from the stadium. Marvin was able to arrange for special perks because of his time there with Jimmy Hoffa.

At the fight, which Chuvalo lost by decision, Marvin sat next to Sugar Ray Robinson and, afterwards, he ran across to the hotel to collect something from his hotel room. Muhammad Ali must have done the same, because Marvin found himself in the hotel elevator with the charismatic champ, who had recently changed his name from Cassius Clay and beaten Sonny Liston for the world heavyweight title.

"Any time you're in Toronto," Marvin said to him, "you gimme a call and I'll take care of you."

"I have no plans to be in Toronto and, if I did, I wouldn't want to bother with you," the champ said, brushing him off and exiting the elevator.

Marvin told his friends about the slight and, the next morning, as people grabbed some breakfast and milled about the hotel getting ready to leave, Marvin saw Ali in the lobby talking to Joe Louis, the renowned heavyweight great from 20 years earlier. Marvin quipped to his friends that he should insult Ali back, and they all said he was too chicken. He wasn't.

"Champ, you're the greatest," Marvin called out brashly as he approached the pair in the lobby. Ali turned and said, "Thank you."

"Not you, you bum, the *champ*," Marvin said, grabbing Joe Louis's hand to firmly shake it. Ali didn't say a word. Louis laughed.

A year later, Ali was, in fact, in Toronto. He arrived to fight Chuvalo, the first of their two tough clashes, this one at Maple Leaf Gardens in Toronto. Ali was training before the bout at Sully's Gym and Marvin was hired by promoter Irving Ungerman to drive the champ around while he was in town. Ali was staying at the Lord Simcoe Hotel downtown. Everyone working there knew Marvin because Tommy Corrigan represented the employees.

"I walk in there to collect Ali and everybody was saying 'Hi, Marvin' and 'Good to see you, Marvin,' and then I get to Ali," Marvin says. The champ recognized Marvin from New York.

"What happened in the elevator in New York, it was all an act," Ali said.

"What happened the next morning was all an act, too," said Marvin.

They became friends. Many times since, the three-time world heavyweight champion has been with Marvin and, every time, true to his promise in the elevator, Marvin has taken good care of him.

Despite his reluctance to become a driver in the first place, Marvin ended up being a decent one. And a driver of such character deserves, in return, to have real characters as passengers. Muhammad Ali, Jimmy Hoffa, Vic Cotroni and the Mafia bosses of New York are not the only unusual passengers to have sat behind Marvin.

Some have been even more surprising.

* * *

Golda Meir, the fourth prime minister of the State of Israel, wrapped up her hour-long speech to rousing applause and a standing ovation from 5,000 people at Toronto's Beth Tzedec synagogue, one of the largest on the continent. The popular, tough-minded politician who had recently stepped down from high office brought her call for international support for Israel to Canada on December 17, 1974, during difficult times in the Middle East. She left the synagogue under tight security. Meir and her two Israeli bodyguards climbed into the back seat of the black four-door Oldsmobile 98. As the bodyguards bent to get in, one on either side of the VIP, guns poked out of their shoulder holsters. Then an RCMP security officer climbed into the front passenger seat. He, too, was armed. Finally, the driver sat down inside.

"What is your name?" Meir asked the driver.

"Marvin Elkind, Madam Prime Minister."

"How do you feel?"

"I'm nervous and scared."

"Don't be nervous," she said in her grandmotherly tone. "And please don't be scared. Everything will be fine."

Before Marvin set out to drive the prime minister from the synagogue to a private reception at the home of Ray Wolfe, who owned a grocery empire, the officer in charge of the RCMP security detail had come over to Marvin's side window. The street in front of the synagogue had been closed for her protection and a dozen plain-clothes officers were scattered about, but in order not to attract attention, he said, Marvin would be driving without a police escort. There would be no convoy of flashing lights for him to follow, as he had assumed. There would be unmarked police cars along the route, but he was largely on his own. It was about 10 p.m. and pitch-black.

"Please, dear God," Marvin silently prayed as he pulled away from the synagogue, "don't let me make a mistake, don't let me take a wrong turn and don't let me drop her off at the wrong house."

Marvin had come to this unlikely driving assignment through his volunteer work with the Jewish Defence League, providing security for Jewish organizations, and through one of his employers, David Satok, who was the owner of a large building company and involved with the Canadian Jewish Congress. Marvin sometimes drove for Satok when he wasn't busy scurrying around with Corrigan or Baldy Chard. Satok had offered his car and driver to Meir, both as a service and for the distinction of having Meir, a woman he revered, in his car. It would give him something to talk about for years.

Marvin's prayers were answered and he delivered Meir and her guards safely to the mansion's front door on the Bridle Path, where Wolfe greeted them. Wolfe even invited Marvin to join them, but he declined, saying his employer had told him not to. Two weeks later, Satok called Marvin into his office and showed him a letter he had received from Meir. In it, she wrote that she was impressed with the courtesy and competence of her driver.

* * *

Even more arrangements had to be made for another special passenger. Five days before this job, Marvin was taken by government officials to be fitted for a blazer and slacks, then to buy a white dress shirt and navy tie with maroon stripes, black socks and a pair of black dress shoes. It was a similar trip to the one he had undertaken before starting his job with Hoffa, but this time a tie was required. Three days later, he was summoned to the King Edward Hotel in downtown Toronto where a large, older woman gave him protocol lessons, including how to bow, how to address people and when he was allowed to speak.

On the morning of his assignment, in mid-May 1988, Marvin put on his new clothes, practised bowing a couple of times for Hennie and set out to the King Edward Hotel to collect Queen Beatrix of the Netherlands and her husband, Prince Claus.

"I had to take protocol lessons but, for me, it was a piece of cake," Marvin says. "It was pretty much the same rules I followed with the mobsters: you keep your mouth shut."

This particular driving job had come about through Corrigan who, as Teamsters president, had unionized the employees of the King Edward and maintained influence there.

Corrigan, like Satok, liked the snob appeal of saying his driver had chauffeured royalty. In today's world of high security and terrorist threats, it seems absurd that a crook like Corrigan could have any say in the travel plans of a head of state for a major Western nation, and that a man like Marvin, with a criminal record, would be allowed to drive them, but drive them he did.

Marvin bowed as Queen Beatrix and Prince Claus came out of the hotel and climbed into his car. Neither of them said a word to him for the entire trip. He drove from the hotel to the airport, this time with a police escort, where the royals caught a flight to Vancouver.

Two days later, Marvin got a phone call from the government. They wanted all of the clothes back.

"Why would you want them?" he asked, incredulous.

"We might want someone else to use them."

"You think they'll fit?"

"Well, we want it all back, that's the way it is."

Marvin ignored the request. Three days later, he got a second call about the clothes.

"My wife sent it all out to get dry cleaned and they lost it all," Marvin said.

"Give us the name and address of the dry cleaner," the official said.

"She can't remember."

"So you're telling us you're not giving it back?"

"I'm telling you it all went to the dry cleaner and never came back."

* * *

The prime ministers and royalty were a rarity as passengers for Marvin. Usually it was a boxer. It kept Marvin in the loop of the close-knit boxing community even though he himself was no longer in the ring or managing a fighter. Many of the fighters he drove were champs; many never made it. Some became close friends; others, enemies. Among the famous fighters he has chauffeured are Jake LaMotta, Willie Pep, Rocky Marciano, Joe Louis, Evander Holyfield, George Chuvalo, Larry Holmes and Lennox Lewis.

"Joe Louis was a great guy, but he could be difficult," Marvin says of the boxing legend. "One time, somebody wanted to make him a free suit, and I told him to go in there and he said, 'No, I don't want one.' I said, 'You don't understand, it's free, they want to make you one.' He got mad at me. I said, 'OK, Joe,' and I just let it go." Marvin still can't understand why anyone would refuse a free suit.

"Rocky Marciano, nice guy, sociable guy, had a lot of laughs with him, but the cheapest guy you ever met in your life. Cheap to a sickness."

Marvin did find unexpected generosity from some.

When Marvin was hired to chauffeur Ray "Boom Boom" Mancini, the World Boxing Association lightweight champion for two years in the early 1980s, Mancini's promoter told him to buy the champ everything he needed while in town and keep the receipts for reimbursement. Mancini insisted on paying his own way, but he gave Marvin all of the receipts to get reimbursed anyway.

Don King was another whom Marvin enjoyed having in his car. King is a controversial boxing promoter known for his ridiculous hairstyle, his long list of top clients and an only slightly shorter list of clients who claim he cheated them. King's former client Mike Tyson summed him up as "a wretched, slimy, reptilian motherfucker . . . [who] would kill his own mother for a dollar." But when King was in Toronto for an International Boxing Federation conference, Marvin found a gracious and engaging man. Marvin picked up King, his son and daughter and a colleague at the airport and drove them to their hotel. He then gave them a tour of Toronto. The next night, he drove them to North 44, a stylish restaurant, one of the best in the city. As Marvin dropped them at the front door, King told him to park the car and join them. At the end of King's stay, Marvin took him and his entourage back to the airport and King tipped him with a $100 bill. Not everyone kindled such fond memories.

"There have only been two people in my car who I hate, and Evander Holyfield is both of them," Marvin says of the former world heavyweight boxing champion, most famous for his 1997 fight against Mike Tyson, during which Tyson bit Holyfield's ear, tearing off a chunk and spitting it into the ring. Marvin was helping with a charity event where Holyfield was to appear, and he picked up the champ at the Toronto airport. The province's boxing commissioner had given Marvin a pair of boxing gloves for Holyfield to sign, and Marvin asked the boxer to scribble his name on them. Holyfield refused. Later, he recanted and offered to sign them, but Marvin told him not to bother. At the charity event, excited underprivileged boys whom Marvin had invited swarmed Holyfield, seeking autographs from the most famous person they were ever likely to meet. Holyfield again refused, even for the kids. When it came time for him to leave, Marvin refused to drive him back to the airport, telling him to find his own way home.

In 1983, Marvin had started driving George Chuvalo on a regular basis when the former Canadian champ didn't have a driver's licence. Marvin was a driver in need of a passenger and the symmetry seemed obvious. He soon found himself helping Chuvalo in a fight that left him hurting more than any boxing match. Heroin had hijacked the lives of three of Chuvalo's sons. Addled by addiction and depression, the youngest, Jesse, shot himself dead in the family home in 1985. Two other sons, Georgie Lee and Steven, overdosed several times before going to prison for robbing a drugstore to feed their habit. In 1993, just weeks after his release, Georgie was found dead in a Toronto hotel with a syringe still stuck in his arm. The pain was too great for their mother, Lynne, Chuvalo's wife, and two days after Georgie's funeral, she called Marvin to the house. She wanted to apologize for not having treated him well over the years, saying he had only been a friend to the family. Marvin told her to forget about it, but she insisted he accept her apology. She kissed him, and he left. Right after, she killed herself with an overdose of prescription drugs. Finally, in 1996, another Chuvalo son, Steven, also died of an overdose. Chuvalo was left with one son, Mitchell, and a daughter, Vanessa.

The pain of loss, piled one on the other, on the other, on the other, was unfathomable. Marvin helped Chuvalo slowly regain his footing and, as Chuvalo pulled himself up, he did what he always did in the ring: he fought back. He found a new calling, preaching against the perils of drugs. The message from such a tough, powerful figure had an impact on young audiences, earning him accolades beyond sport as well as a prestigious Order of Canada decoration. As Chuvalo took his anti-drug message to schoolchildren across Canada, Marvin accompanied him as an assistant, driver, warm-up act and comic relief. Marvin sweet-talked the female secretaries, principals and teachers from the moment the pair walked into a school.

"Hey, doll, you look absolutely gorgeous," he said in greeting to a female principal. Marvin remains unconvinced by the changing etiquette of the times. To a female teacher he blustered, "Doll, if I had a teacher like you when I was in high school, I would still be there." Chuvalo described Marvin's companionship as "three hundred pounds of levity in a sea of serious business."

There was little levity between them in 1993 when Marvin was hired by the new owner of an apartment building to help evict tenants so he could convert the building. Marvin was promised $1,000 for each tenant he frightened away. Robbie told Marvin not to do it, but Marvin needed the money. In a rare moment of disobedience, Marvin took the job anyway. In order to protect the tenants, Robbie alerted a reporter who went and found Marvin—along with Chuvalo—at the apartment building. The former champ said he was not involved in the ultimatums but was there only because his driver's licence was suspended for unpaid speeding tickets and Marvin was driving him around that day.

That bad publicity was largely forgotten by 1994, when there was another tribute dinner for Chuvalo, held by the Rochester Boxing Hall of Fame. Organizers wanted Ali and Joe Frazier there, two of Chuvalo's toughest and best-known opponents. Once again Marvin made the call and landed the star.

* * *

Of all the champs and contenders, royalty and world leaders, mobsters and businessmen who climbed into his car, Muhammad Ali remains a favourite.

"He's a great human being, great fighter, great person. I really like him," Marvin says. He has many pictures of the two of them together, images he loves to show off. Shamelessly. He had a T-shirt made with one of the colour photos of him with Ali printed on the front, and he wears it often to boxing events.

As Ali's fame skyrocketed, turning him into one of the most recognized people on the planet and a hugely sought-after celebrity speaker, whenever the rich and powerful corporate leaders and fundraising powerhouses in Canada wanted to reach out to the champ to invite him to a charity event, they would go through Marvin. Usually, to the amazement of those courting Ali, who would first try big-named promoters and entertainment moguls to land the special guest, it was usually Marvin who would place a call and come through with the arrangements, just as he had for the Chuvalo tributes.

When Ali started to suffer mightily from Parkinson's, a sad consequence of his punishing bouts in the ring, he still struggled to attend charity events, although his appearances were dramatically reduced. His strong rapid-fire voice and outspoken opinions were silenced. His movements—famously self-described in the phrase "float like a butterfly, sting like a bee"—stiffened and slowed.

In October 2002, Ali was to be honoured as "Athlete of the Century" in Toronto at the halftime show of a Toronto Argonauts football game to raise money for Parkinson's research. A star-studded revue of politicians, sports heroes and business magnates would offer tributes. Again, organizers needed to reach out to Marvin to set it up. In return, Marvin arranged for 50 poor kids from a local boxing club to get free tickets to the game.

At the huge event at Toronto's SkyDome stadium, as the crowds pressed in and security officials surrounded the champ to keep well-wishers and excited sports fans back, there—bouncing around beside Ali, barely visible among the tall phalanx—was a blue peaked driver's cap atop Marvin's head. He ushered Ali out of the limousine and into the stadium. The toll of Parkinson's on Ali was striking: his mouth clenched in a grimace as he tried to smile, his movements a slow shuffle. But on his way out, he still made time to sign autographs for fans before Marvin eventually shouted for everyone to get back so the champ could get into his car for the ride back to his hotel.

CHAPTER 37

QUITO, ECUADOR, 1988

The plane had not been in the air long before Marvin discovered that the price of booze had plummeted to next to nothing, a by-product of the airline having switched to South American prices. By the time the plane reached Aeropuerto Internacional Mariscal Sucre in Quito, the capital of Ecuador, Marvin was coming down from a cruising altitude of 35,000 feet and more than 16 ounces. Neither the landing announcement from the pilot nor the hustle of departing passengers roused him from his drunken slumber. The stewardesses couldn't wake him and airport workers eventually carried him off, dumping him beside the luggage carousel.

Marvin stumbled out of the airport, blinking painfully in the bright sunlight, dazed and disoriented. He had no idea even what time it was. He was just starting to remember that he was on his way to Ecuador when he was greeted by a man named Rafael and his beautiful girlfriend. Through his mental fog, Marvin pulled it together. He was on another secret mission, this one for the RCMP, and Rafael, a suspected South American drug importer and trafficker, was his target.

* * *

Rafael divided his time between Quito and Toronto, which was where he had met Marvin in a boxing gym. He had run into legal trouble in Toronto in 1987, when he had been charged with trafficking and possession of cocaine paste, the first time police had found the precursor to powdered cocaine in Canada. The paste is produced in an early stage of the process of turning coca leaves into snortable cocaine. It was a curiosity for the RCMP after a female undercover officer allegedly made the purchase. Facing charges, Rafael had asked for Marvin's help. Marvin said it would cost $15,000: five upfront, and the remaining 10 if charges were dropped. After collecting his advance fee, Marvin spoke to Robbie. Robbie approached the RCMP about dropping the charges so that Marvin could insinuate himself into his life and see what The Weasel might find, but the RCMP weren't interested.

On the day of Rafael's trial, Marvin cringed. His friend was expecting something, but there was no help coming. Marvin was with Robbie in Detroit on the day of the trial, and he called Rafael to spin a story about having to leave town and not being able to work his magic.

"If you're out of town, how am I going to give you the other ten thousand dollars?" Rafael asked. "Just like you said, they dropped my charges. How did you do it? The judge looked like he didn't know a thing. He acted all surprised."

"Well," blustered a stunned Marvin, "what do you expect him to do? Tell the court I bought him off?"

Marvin cut his trip short and rushed home to collect his money. Robbie called the RCMP, who confirmed the case had been bungled and that Rafael had left court a free man. The force was now interested in taking Marvin up on his offer to stick his nose into Rafael's business. They suspected he was moving cocaine through mules—couriers who carry hidden drugs with them when travelling. The coca plant is native to Ecuador and the country shares its northern border with Colombia, where three-quarters of the world's supply is produced.

Marvin's indomitable charm and the favour he supposedly had done for Rafael built a fast and firm rapport between them. Marvin would drive him around to restaurants and boxing gyms. To catch their conversations on tape, a police technician wired Marvin's car, hiding a microphone in the sunroof. Marvin was told to make sure the sunroof stayed closed. When he picked Rafael up, the first thing he did was to try to open the roof's window. Marvin grabbed his hand.

"Don't touch it, the roof is broken. I had to force it closed," he said. Rafael shrugged and opened the window instead. The two got along so well that Rafael invited Marvin to join him in Ecuador. Robbie arranged for Marvin's flight and paid the airfare. That was when Marvin stumbled out of the Quito airport, on June 7, 1988, trying to decide if he was still drunk or just hungover. Rafael wasn't concerned about Marvin's state. He had spent hours in bars with the round man and already knew of his love for booze.

* * *

Robbie was worried about Marvin being so far away without a handler and without police backup. There wasn't even a Canadian Embassy in Ecuador at the time. Marvin wasn't worried, though, and he spent his time happily palling around with Rafael, meeting his friends and family. The South American was popular with the women, as well. One of the first things Rafael arranged with Marvin was a buzzer code for his apartment. Before either of them came up, Rafael said, they were to buzz three times at the bell in the lobby to warn the other—and any company they might have—of the impending arrival. Marvin liked the idea because he also wanted privacy, but for a different reason.

It didn't take him long to spot where Rafael stored secret records. There was a crack in the drywall in a corner of the living room where he saw his host pull out some papers. When Rafael was out, Marvin stuck his hand in and found that, if he reached up high and then down into a little pocket, he could just get his hands on the documents. Among the papers were the names and contact information of about 100 people. It looked like a map to Rafael's entire network.

Once a day, Marvin would go for a walk about town. When he was certain he wasn't being followed, he would duck into a large hotel, one that seemed popular with tourists and visiting businessmen, and call Robbie collect. When he told Robbie about the long list, he was told to copy it.

The next day, when Rafael was out, Marvin reached into the crevice, pulled out the lists and looked around for something to copy it out onto. He grabbed a large stack of Rafael's business cards and started to methodically copy the information from the list onto the backs of the cards. It was slow going. Marvin's left-handed scribbling was deplorably messy. Handwriting had never been his strength. It is one reason his memory is so good—he always relied on remembering things instead of writing them down. In Quito's tropical warmth, Marvin sat at Rafael's living-room coffee table for more than an hour writing out names until he heard three squawks of the buzzer to warn him that his host was coming up. He put the papers back and hid the business cards in his wallet.

It took him three days of furtive scribbling to get to the end of the list, and throughout his stay he never let his wallet out of his sight, even sleeping with it. When he told Robbie, his handler was delighted, but even Robbie's praise over the telephone line couldn't keep Marvin from feeling bad. As he had felt with Joe Foti, the kindly Liberal barbecue organizer, Marvin hated to betray a gracious host.

"In Ecuador, he made me part of his family. He took me with him to his grandmother's one-hundredth birthday party, a big bash in a restaurant with a hundred and fifty family and friends, catered with local food," Marvin says.

Marvin went with Rafael to Guayaquil, Ecuador's largest city and main port, but despite their close relationship, little was said about drugs. Marvin made a second trip to visit him in Ecuador a few months later, and, when Rafael was in Toronto, they continued to socialize.

* * *

It was back in Toronto that Marvin introduced Rafael to his girlfriend, a beautiful stewardess with Lufthansa. She wasn't really Marvin's girlfriend, naturally, nor was she a stewardess. She was Karen Moffatt, an OPP officer who worked undercover with Robbie. She could pull this lie off flawlessly because, before joining the force, she had been a Lufthansa stewardess for two years. She looked the part, too: five foot ten, curvaceous, with long blond hair and sparkling green eyes.

Marvin introduced her as Karen Wolf, and she had fake ID to prove it. The flight-attendant cover story provided an explanation for why she came and went from Marvin's life. She was with him only when police needed her to be. They would take Rafael to dinner or let him take them out with his friends.

"I was Marv's chick," Moffatt says. "If we were at a function undercover and I was with Marv as his girlfriend, the odd time he'd grab my ass or put his arm around me to play the part, to make it look good. Marv would sometimes massage my neck and shoulders. The rule was he could only go as low as the third vertebra and that was it, no further."

One afternoon, Rafael picked Marvin and Moffatt up in his BMW. While they were stopped at a red light, Rafael turned to Moffatt, locked eyes with her and asked her a question in German. It was meant as a surprise test. If Marvin's girlfriend really was a Lufthansa stewardess, she would know what he was saying and be able to answer. Marvin waited nervously. After all the time Marvin had spent with Rafael, he had no clue he spoke German, and Marvin had no idea what Moffatt was going to do or say. He didn't know if she spoke German, either. After a flicker of surprise, Moffatt smiled at Rafael, batted her eyelashes and answered his question in her own beautiful German. Rafael seemed relieved. They carried on a conversation, *auf Deutsch*, for several minutes, with a befuddled Marvin trying to guess what they were babbling about.

"I could tell by his body language and the look in his eye that it set him at ease, he physically relaxed," Moffatt says. "That day and that moment really seemed to solidify that we were authentic. He believed then that we were who we said, and it really built a trust factor between us, to the point where he even shared with us how they were smuggling drugs using commercial airliners."

The scheme was ingenious. Rafael knew someone who worked at an airline who could track the flights and routes of the airplanes. The worker sought flights from South America to the United States that, after landing, were scheduled to continue on to a second destination within America. A drug courier in Ecuador would bring cocaine, often disguised as a package of coffee, onto an airplane in their carry-on baggage. This was in the day when screening of what came onto an aircraft was not as thorough, the main concern for officials being what was taken off—in other words, an international flight was a taxation issue rather than a security issue. The courier would stuff the package under her seat in place of the life vest and, when she arrived in Atlanta or Miami, would leave the drugs under the seat and walk off, which meant there was no trouble with customs since she no longer carried any contraband. The organization made sure to book a second courier onto the next flight that plane was scheduled to take, booking them into the same seat. This second courier would take the package out from under the seat and carry it off the plane with them when they arrived at the next stop. And since the second arrival was a domestic one, there was no customs check.

"Oh my God, was that ever an amazing way not to get caught," Moffatt says. With her experience as a flight attendant, she could see how it would work.

Marvin and Moffatt met socially many times with Rafael, encouraging him to get comfortable with them both. One unexpected meeting, though, was decidedly uncomfortable for Moffatt. Off-duty, she was visiting a lawyer with her husband, who was also a cop, on a matter involving a private lawsuit. As she sat in the waiting room on the ninth floor of the office tower, she saw Rafael walk in. He was still greeting the receptionist when she spotted him, but he hadn't noticed her. She put her head down, mumbled an apology to her husband and scurried out. She left without seeing whom Rafael was with: Marvin. Marvin didn't know Moffatt's husband, but Moffatt's husband knew who Marvin was—he had worked on surveillance, watching Marvin's back several times, and Marvin was unforgettable. Marvin sat down next to him in the waiting room and tried to engage him in conversation. It was a talent Marvin used to meet new people and get involved in their life, always on the prowl for another case. Marvin asked him what he did for a living and what had brought him to the lawyer and so on, as the husband said as little as possible.

"Toronto is a huge city, but a small world," Moffatt says.

Marvin spent about a year working his way into Rafael's confidence and the South American saw him as an ally. He took Marvin into his confidence and showed him three safety-deposit boxes at three Toronto banks. Inside were passports, mortgage documents, cash and a half-dozen gold bars. He said that if he had an emergency down south, he might have to ask Marvin to access them for him. Marvin passed the information on to Robbie.

* * *

Sugar Ray Leonard, three-time world boxing champ, was in Toronto touting his fall title fight at Caesars Palace in Las Vegas against Donny Lalonde, the World Boxing Council's light-heavyweight champion from Winnipeg, with an amusing line: "Donny is a class act both in and outside the ring. You people in Canada should be proud of him," he said. "He's not known that well in the U.S. and my mission on November seventh is to keep it that way."

Lalonde retorted at the press conference at the Westbury Hotel: "Ray has been super, but he's had his day."

The banter on September 9, 1988, was great for selling tickets. Since the match was being held 2,300 miles away, the press conference was an event in itself for most Toronto boxing fans. Marvin invited Rafael to join him and Moffatt at the event. Moffatt asked Rafael to bring her a little something to buy. She said she was in town for five days with her girlfriends and they wanted to party. He said he would take care of her, she says. At the hotel, amid the hoopla of the press conference, Marvin, Moffatt and Rafael slipped into an unused banquet room down the hall. It was dimly lit and private. There Rafael gave Moffatt two grams of cocaine, and she gave him $200, according to police.

"If you're a cop, I'll die," he said, remembering that his last arrest had come after a purported deal made with a woman who turned out to be an undercover RCMP officer. After the sale, police raided the safety-deposit boxes that Rafael had showed Marvin, seizing the contents and turning it over to the tax agency. The RCMP had a measure of revenge for their failed prosecution, but they still didn't have him in jail. Police wanted to let the case go on further, investigating the names on the list that Marvin had brought back from Ecuador.

After the bank raids, though, there was little doubt in Rafael's mind that Marvin must have double-crossed him. Their friendship ended and, from then on, whenever Marvin saw any of Rafael's friends, they couldn't get away from him fast enough.

CHAPTER 38

TORONTO, 1989

Anger and frustration radiated from Marvin, a menacing tone underlining each of his words with a bold red streak, so that the threat they held was clear and believable to the man sitting nervously across from him in a downtown diner.

"You'll be hurt very bad," Marvin warned, locking eyes on him, his left squinting more than his right. For added emphasis, as if the chilling tone, large fists and frightening stare weren't enough, Marvin had brought a younger, larger and even more frightening boxer with him, who sat silently in the next booth.

Marvin wasn't role-playing. This collection was personal, and he was coming to realize that he wasn't nearly as clever a loan shark as his foster brother Roy had been. Marvin's trouble had started in February, with a phone call from his own nephew, who told him that his friend's uncle, Philip, needed a loan that the banks wouldn't give him. Marvin saw a chance to make easy money and met with Philip to discuss terms. They were deplorable for Philip—$2,000 a month in interest alone, 240 per cent annually—but he agreed; the desperate usually did. To get the money, Marvin went to the Casa Commisso Banquet Hall on Lawrence Avenue West in Toronto, headquarters of the Commisso clan, a notoriously dangerous

Mafia group with global ties. There Marvin told Rocco Remo Commisso that, because the debtor had come through family, there wouldn't be problems getting it back. Commisso loaned Marvin $10,000, handing him an envelope stuffed with $100 bills. Marvin pushed it into the inside breast pocket of his suit jacket and went straight to meet Philip, giving him $9,000 and keeping 10 per cent as his fee. Philip made the first few payments, with Marvin then making his own payments to the Commissos. Then Philip went dry.

After Philip had missed three payments in a row, Marvin was frazzled. That's when he tracked Philip down and confronted him in the diner, issuing his warning. Philip promised him the money, all of it, in two days.

On October 26, 1989, Marvin again met with Philip at the same diner.

"Where is it?" Marvin asked.

"The money's in my business account. I'll have to give you a cheque."

"Give it to me now," Marvin said impatiently.

Philip handed over a cheque for the principal and all of the interest, and left. By the time Marvin had folded and pocketed it, two police officers were at the table.

"Give us the cheque," one of them said.

"What cheque? What are you talking about?"

"The cheque you just took. You're under arrest for extortion."

The fink had been finked on. The restaurant meeting had been staked out by the cops. Marvin told them what he was and said his handler needed to be called.

"He already knows," the officer said.

* * *

Robbie had received a courtesy call from the police about Marvin's loansharking and extortion attempt. He was furious with Marvin for not telling him what he was up to. There were some occasions when Robbie looked the other way as Marvin tried to earn a living beyond what the police paid him. He knew about Marvin's collection work with Baldy and his aluminum siding sales, and Marvin gave Robbie daily briefings on any work for Corrigan.

Robbie had made it clear that Marvin was to tell him about anything he was doing that might cause trouble. But, despite having visited Commisso and borrowing mob money, despite having made a street loan and charging extortionate interest rates, Marvin hadn't said a word about it to Robbie.

Robbie might have been able to convince the officers not to arrest and charge Marvin, but he didn't even try.

When Robbie was called and warned that Marvin was going to be arrested, Robbie wanted to be there. He scurried about his office looking for his gun, which he rarely carried. He pushed files about his desk, opened drawers and eventually found the pistol, but discovered it wasn't loaded.

"Look in that drawer there, see if there are any bullets in it," he said to a visitor who was with him in his office.

"Do you really think this is necessary?" the visitor asked, finding a handful of bullets and passing them over.

"Someone is going to get arrested in a public place. You don't know who's going to be around, you never know who Marvin is going to have with him. I need to be prepared."

Marvin didn't see Robbie at the diner but at the police station, while he was being processed, he heard Robbie's distinctive, gruff voice speaking with the other officers outside the room. When Marvin was formally charged and released, pending a court appearance, he got into his car and the car phone that the OPP had just installed rang.

"Meet me at the safe house," Robbie said, and hung up.

Marvin went to the safe house, an apartment on Bloor Street West that was used by the OPP intelligence officers for meeting sensitive sources in private without the chance of them being seen entering a police station. Robbie was there waiting.

"Whose money was it?" Robbie asked.

"You tell me," Marvin answered.

"Commissos'."

"Yeah. What happened here?"

Robbie recounted how the man whom Marvin had threatened in the diner had told his lawyer about it, and his lawyer had called the police. They had checked with Robbie first, and he had said they could charge him if they wanted to.

"Why'd you say that?" asked Marvin.

"You were involved in a crime without telling me. You didn't tell me about this deal. You never said you were meeting the Commissos."

Marvin understood. He knew he had broken the rules, and the law.

"I didn't hold it against him," Marvin says. "I understood the ball game. I just wanted a quick thousand bucks and thought it would go smoothly." Marvin also knew it wasn't a lost opportunity to run a case on the mobsters because Robbie and Marvin had long ago agreed it was too dangerous for Marvin to fink on the Commissos. The Commissos and Baldy Chard were hands-off for Marvin.

Later, after a court appearance, two police officers came over to Marvin.

"We never in a million years thought Robbie would have us arrest you," one said apologetically. "We don't want you to hold anything against us."

* * *

The arrest was annoying for Marvin, but the bigger concern remained the $10,000. As soon as he was out of police custody, Marvin went to Casa Commisso Banquet Hall to break the news to the Commissos. Marvin was needlessly nervous; the mobsters were gentlemen. Marvin told them about the cops and his arrest. They knew it was true because the charges against Marvin had appeared in a newspaper under the headline "Man accused of charging 240% interest." The article had referred to Marvin as a 55-year-old loan shark and boxing manager.

"They were very good about it, they understood," Marvin says. "I told them I would pay it all back to them and Remo Commisso said I just needed to pay the principal, the ten grand, and to forget about the juice, the interest. They didn't come down hard on me at all."

Despite the forgiving gangsters, Marvin still had a problem. He didn't have the money to pay them back, even without the juice. His arrest notwithstanding, Marvin was still gunning for his money. He called his nephew, who was terribly contrite.

"I want the ten grand from your friend," Marvin said, figuring that if he couldn't go after Philip for it, then Philip's nephew, who had started this thing, should cover the loss. Marvin's nephew refused to reveal his friend's phone number. Desperation is the real mother of invention, and Marvin went over everything he could remember from his conversations with his nephew and with Philip. He knew the family was Jewish and originally from Winnipeg, and that Philip's nephew was a dentist. And he knew their name. In the phone book, Marvin found the number for Philip's mother, but not for the nephew, so he phoned her.

"This is Rabbi Bomberb," Marvin said, when she answered. "We're holding a dinner for Jews in Toronto who came from Winnipeg and we want to invite you."

She was delighted, even more so when "the rabbi" said they were highlighting achievements of young successful Jews and asked if she knew any. Marvin knew she would volunteer her grandson—Philip's nephew—and she did. Marvin then asked for his name, phone number and address.

He hung up and immediately called Philip's nephew.

"Do you know who this is?" he asked gruffly, his voice no longer that of the friendly rabbi.

"No," the man replied.

"It's Marvin Elkind."

After a moment's shocked silence, the flustered nephew stammered, "Sorry about what happened."

"Well, I'm glad you're sorry because you're going to make it right. You're going to pay your uncle's ten grand."

He said he couldn't.

Marvin burst into a rage, bellowing out the nephew's home address. "You give me the money or I'll have the bikers there to take care of you. Don't fuck with me."

Once he realized Marvin knew where he lived, he was a changed man. No more lawyers or cops, just $10,000 in cash the next day. Marvin took it straight to the Commissos before he got tempted to spend it.

***

Marvin was pleading guilty to the extortion charge, but wanted to delay his imprisonment until he settled his affairs. His childhood friend Harvey Salem was again handling the case and, at the Toronto courthouse, Salem tried to find a judge who was available to hear his application for a delay.

"OK, I found one, a judge has come in to do some

paperwork and he is going to go into an empty courtroom for us," Salem said.

"Who is it?"

"David Humphrey," Salem said. Marvin jerked to a stop. Humphrey was the man who, as a lawyer, had cross-examined Marvin at the Neil Proverbs trial. Marvin had been told by several people since that Humphrey remained upset over the embarrassment he had felt over their courtroom tussle, which most felt Marvin had won. One mutual friend had told Marvin that Humphrey had said he would never forgive Marvin. Humphrey had since been made a judge.

"Are you nuts? You can't put me before Humphrey, he hates me."

"This is nothing, it's just a remand, don't worry about it," Salem assured.

"Don't be so sure."

Inside the courtroom, Humphrey sat down at the judge's bench and smiled broadly at Marvin.

"Mr. Elkind, what a surprise. Why is Mr. Elkind here?" Humphrey asked.

Salem explained to the judge that they were seeking a remand for a plea and that the prosecutor had agreed to the postponement.

"And how will you be pleading?" Humphrey asked.

"Guilty, your Honour," said Salem.

"Guilty?" said Humphrey, sounding as if he were surprised. "Well, if he's guilty, he should be in custody."

Salem explained that an arrangement had been made with the prosecutor for a remand.

Humphrey asked Marvin how long a postponement he was seeking.

"Can I have ninety days?" Marvin asked.

"No."

"Can I have sixty days?"

"No."

"Can I have thirty days?"

"No."

"Well, how much time can I have?"

"One week."

Humphrey adjourned the case and left, still smiling. A week later, Marvin appeared before the assigned judge and got his 90-day postponement.

Robbie was rattled by the extortion attempt. Marvin had always been a little unstable, but this was different, more troublesome and consequential. It eroded the trust Robbie had in him, even more so in the case of Robbie's bosses. It looked as if Marvin was on a downward spiral, because the extortion had not been his only crime.

***

It was 2:55 p.m. on May 3, 1988, and the spring sun beamed onto the wide boulevard of pleasant shops and bistros of Avenue Road in Toronto. Marvin was in the curb lane, heading north, near Brookdale Avenue, when he crashed his car into the car in front of him.

The driver, a tall black man, climbed out and headed toward Marvin. He looked upset, and Marvin felt threatened. He put his car in reverse and backed away, into the car behind him, then went forward again, hitting the first car once more. When the driver finally got to Marvin's car, an agitated Marvin hopped out and slugged him. The driver fell backwards, breaking his ankle on the way down. A shopkeeper dashed into his store and called police.

Marvin knew he was in trouble and went to call Robbie. When police arrived, they arrested Marvin for assault causing bodily harm and leaving the scene of an accident. At the police station, Marvin explained who he was and said he had left the scene only to call his handler. The cop said he understood, he had done undercover work himself, and he agreed to drop the leaving-the-scene charge. To ensure it wouldn't happen again, Robbie arranged for Marvin to have a car phone. But with the other driver in hospital, there was no flexibility on the assault charge. The officer said he would talk to the prosecutor and see what could be done.

In court on the assault charge, the cop kept his word, but the prosecutor wasn't sympathetic. He had been involved with the case of Cecil Kirby, a Mafia killer for the Commisso clan who had turned informant, and he felt he had been double-crossed by him. He wasn't interested in doing favours for finks and pressed ahead with the charge. His only concession was that he proceeded in the privacy of the judge's chambers to prevent Marvin's status from being discussed in open court.

In judge's chambers, Marvin pleaded guilty to assault causing bodily harm. Judge John Gilbert said that a man with Marvin's background in boxing couldn't go unpunished after slugging an innocent man without provocation. Marvin was sentenced to 90 days in jail, but was allowed to serve it intermittently on weekends—the court's concession to Salem and Robbie, who were both concerned about Marvin's safety in jail.

Robbie tried to arrange for Marvin to serve his time in the infirmary instead of the general population. If word were to get around that Marvin was a fink, there would be nowhere for him to run. It might be a death sentence. But when Marvin showed up at Mimico jail, for the first of his 90 days, he was tossed in with everyone else. After emerging unscathed from serving his first weekend, he called Robbie first thing.

"Mimico is a garbage dump. It's full of drugs."

By midweek, news of his incarceration had spread and Marvin received a phone call from someone he had finked on in the past: "This will be your last weekend in jail." After Robbie's pleas, instead of the infirmary, Marvin was put in solitary confinement.

"It was miserable in solitary. I would've much preferred to risk being in the population," Marvin says. "There is nothing in solitary, and a day became a year. The only thing they gave you was a Bible to read."

While in Mimico, he was still The Weasel. He played cards with one inmate, Joseph Pilgrim, a 31-year-old maintenance worker, who confided to Marvin that he had sold the gun to the man who had killed a York Regional Police officer. Constable Douglas Tribbling, a father of three, had responded to a burglar alarm at a computer company in Markham in 1984. When backup arrived, he was found lying on the floor. He had been shot three times in the chest and twice in the left arm with a revolver. A massive manhunt turned up nothing for four years, until Ronald Carlton York, a career break-in artist, was arrested and charged with first-degree murder. Marvin told Robbie about the gun, and Robbie passed the tip on to York police. Pilgrim was the brother of York's live-in girlfriend. He was later called to the stand by prosecutors and admitted he had sold the accused a .38-calibre five-shooter, one piece of evidence used to convict York of first-degree murder in 1993.

Helping to put a cop-killer behind bars went a long way toward restoring Marvin's reputation with police, who were starting to worry which side he was on.

CHAPTER 39

TORONTO, 1989

"I'm worried about Marvin," Bill Lidstone, the deputy commissioner of the OPP, said to Robbie one day. "He's under a lot of pressure, seems a bit mixed up as to who he is. I think you'd better get him straightened out."

The concern from on high surprised Robbie, and when he talked about it with Marvin, it surprised him, too. But, so long as Marvin didn't have to pay for it, he was game to see a shrink. The concern seemed justified, not because Marvin was weak—he showed tremendous strength in balancing his double life, adopting and shedding multiple personalities and straying so little into delinquency despite the world he was marinating in. It was mandatory for undercover cops to undergo psychiatric assessment and counselling, to reduce the force's liability, if not out of complete concern for the mental health of its members. It occurred to Lidstone that, if experienced police officers who had the support of colleagues, years of training and the protection of a gun and a badge needed assistance, surely Marvin, who was struggling to set his own moral compass, should see a psychiatrist, too.

Robbie called his friend Morton Shulman. The former provincial coroner, politician and crusading journalist was legendary for his outspoken opinions and drive for public accountability on security issues. He had once smuggled a replica machine gun into a nuclear power plant and then brandished it on the floor of the Ontario legislature, as fellow politicians cowered under their desks, to prove his concerns about lax security. He was Robbie's kind of guy. Robbie told Shulman about Marvin. Shulman, who was Jewish, said Marvin should see his Jewish psychiatrist friend who practised downtown. He arranged an appointment.

Marvin didn't know what the psychiatrist expected, or what Shulman had told him, but apparently not much. The psychiatrist closed his office door and Marvin sat down in the soothingly decorated office and unburdened himself. He told him all about his double life in the mob, about his government work and the gangsters and crooks and foreign agents.

Marvin hadn't even got to the really juicy stuff when he noticed the doctor staring at him. His eyes bugged out and his face was flushed. Marvin paused, and the psychiatrist sprang to his door and threw it open.

"You're crazy," the psychiatrist said.

"Why do you think I'm here?"

The doctor called out to his receptionist, "If this man doesn't leave right away, call the police. This is a dangerous man."

"What do you mean, 'call police'? The police sent me."

"Get out of here."

By the time Marvin got to Robbie's office, Robbie already knew.

"I got a call from Morty Shulman. You scared the shit out of his friend," Robbie told him, sounding sympathetic. "But don't worry, we're going to send you to another guy. I went to see him myself and he understood me right away. He's very good."

Eventually Marvin went to see Dr. Peter Collins, the consultant psychologist for the RCMP's new Violent Crimes

Analysis Section. The two talked and talked. Robbie was right: he was a great guy, and Marvin maintains a deep respect and appreciation for his counsel. Collins understood cops and the oddities and complexities of their job. He has become a global expert on violent crime and is a consultant not only to the OPP and RCMP, but to the FBI, U.S. Department of Homeland Security, INTERPOL and the Australian Federal Police. More recently, he has worked with soldiers, having gone on two deployments in Afghanistan.

Over the years, Marvin would see Collins to deal with a number of matters, including a terrifying recurring daydream that he was suffocating. Sometimes, three or four times a week, he had the same dreadful, panicky feeling that he was being smothered. It felt like he was genuinely dying. Collins and a colleague helped him through it.

Collins saw the delicate and intimate relationship between Marvin and Robbie, the fink and his handler. It was a strange bond. They faced danger together many times. Trust was crucial. They were companions more than they were friends, but they also had outside loyalties and directives. They were often at odds with each other, but each depended on the other for his success. They became an enormous part of each other's life. They would speak on the phone many times a day, almost every day and often into the night, for a decade. Robbie's wife, Gladys, would often come down to her kitchen in the middle of the night and order Robbie to hang up on Marvin and come to bed. Marvin and Robbie travelled together, shared hotel rooms, drank together, got into mischief together, played pranks on each other, but Robbie always retained the upper hand. Whenever there was a dispute, Robbie's word was the law.

"To me, Robbie became my pillar of strength," Marvin says. "I feared him, but I had a great amount of respect for him and I was very fond of him. But most of all, I feared he would be disappointed in me."

Marvin was only two years younger than Robbie, but admits he saw Robbie as a father figure.

"He gave me the feeling—very strongly—that he was always on my side. He was there to look after me, as well as use me."

After talking to Marvin, Collins met with Robbie.

"I've got myself a third son," Robbie said. "His name is Marvin Elkind."

* * *

Being a handler isn't a job every cop can do well. It takes more commitment and dedication than most people realize at first. While cops have scheduled working hours, union security and a blue brotherhood to back them up, finks operate without a schedule or support.

"This guy ruled my life," Robbie later explained. "Day and night, he ruled my life, but we got results, crazy results. You're not going to get results if you only work to union rules."

"You have to have patience with an informant," Marvin says. "Robbie had patience with me. When he saw I was going through a hard time, he didn't come on strong with me. But he would come on strong when he really needed something done or when I needed pushing."

Just as few cops were as patient as Robbie, few finks were as reliable as Marvin. This combination was what made their team—this pair—so successful. No matter what force Marvin worked for, or what country he was working in, everything involving Marvin and law enforcement went through Robbie. Officers treated Marvin in different ways. A few looked at him as if he were something stuck to the bottom of their shoe; others hugged him and invited him out for drinks. Most were somewhere in between.

"Marvin wasn't a hardened criminal. He was just associated with hardened criminals," says Andy Rayne, the RCMP officer who often worked undercover with Marvin. "He wasn't one of the bad guys. We could trust him. He wasn't like other informants we worked with. We trusted him and he was part of the team. The golden rule, they always tell us, is don't befriend an informant. Well, I'm sorry, we kind of all became friends with Marvin. Most of us, anyway."

"Marvin just kept popping up all the time. He was always on the outskirts of everything," says Roy Teeft, a retired inspector with the Toronto police intelligence unit. "His information was like a big onion: you peel the first layer off and there is another one underneath. You kept going and going and you always found something. Like an onion, he might make you cry, but he was very successful."

"The big concern with Marvin was that he was going to be found dead," says Jack McCombs. "You try to keep a distance, but Marvin had such a personality that, deep down, you just couldn't dislike him."

Cops sometimes helped Marvin in unofficial ways, such as one time when he needed to pay a fine that he couldn't afford. And Marvin helped officers in return, such as when he got free tickets through his fight contacts for Rayne and Bill Gill and their kids to see Hulk Hogan and other wrestling stars when 64,000 fans filled Toronto's Exhibition Stadium on August 28, 1986, for the World Wrestling Federation's Big Event.

* * *

Marvin was uncomfortable, breathing heavily under a white cloth hood. It was tall and conical, gathering into a point more than a foot above his head and swooping down below his chin at the bottom. He peered out through two perfectly round eye-holes. The mask was unmistakable—the white hood of the Ku Klux Klan—and the sight of the short, increasingly round Jewish man wearing it as he stood next to Robbie was a strange sight.

Robbie and Marvin were at the front of a classroom at the Ontario Police College, a government-run training cen-tre for cops on an abandoned air-force base near Aylmer, 120 miles west of Toronto. In front of them sat 30 police officers from different services who were enrolled in the Informant Development course.

The KKK hood was partly Robbie's showmanship on dis-play, but it was also to protect Marvin's identity, even from the cops. The hood was one of Robbie's souvenirs, a war trophy. Robbie had investigated the KKK in Ontario and helped to infiltrate the group and other white supremacist organiza-tions. In 1989, when a delegation of neo-Nazis from Canada was invited to Libya to celebrate the 20th anniversary of the Libyan revolution, police were trying to find out details of the trip. Robbie had raced over to the hangout of one of the leaders of the Nationalist Party of Canada, a white supremacist group, and made sure he bumped into him.

"Have a nice day," the man said.

"The whole world would be having a hell of a nicer one without one fucking country in the Middle East," said Robbie.

"You're talking about Israel?"

"That's right," Robbie said, instantly making friends. Within minutes the man had told Robbie about the pending trip to Libya. A few minutes later and Robbie knew their air-line, flight time and travel route.

Using another of his finks, Robbie had identified the KKK leadership and seized a set of the white robes and hood of a Klansman during the investigation. He brought them to his office, where he modelled them, to much laughter.

Marvin and Robbie worked so well together that they were often asked to lecture at police academies. At first, Marvin wore a burlap sack with eyeholes cut into it to protect his identity, until Robbie replaced the sack with the seized KKK hood. It made more of an impact. The two regaled academy members with stories of their successes and failures. Robbie would give them tips on cultivating and nurturing good informants, and Marvin would give the fink's perspective, answering question after question.

In 1987, they took their show to Washington, D.C., to train U.S. Customs agents on how to handle informants and in undercover techniques, and to the FBI Academy on a United States Marine Corps base in Quantico, Virginia, where they trained agents in informant recruitment. They gave such a bravura performance that they were invited back three more times, and were introduced as "the ultimate example of a handler-informant relationship." Everywhere they went, people were amazed by the relationship, the friendly banter and jests, their mutual devotion and fondness. They fed off each other.

That didn't mean they didn't fight.

* * *

Marvin and Robbie were sharing a hotel room during an undercover mission in 1984, when Marvin was left alone for an evening while Robbie met with U.S. agents about their case. Bored, Marvin drained the room's expansive mini-bar. When Robbie returned to the room, he was furious over what the hotel bill would be. He was already under pressure about the money Marvin was being paid and the expenses of intelligence officers when they were on the road. This was going to cause trouble. How could Marvin be so stupid? Robbie exploded in a tirade that, if Marvin could remember it through the boozy fog, would have reminded him of his foster brother Roy. But Marvin didn't remember much of anything from that night. He woke up the next morning with a dire headache. Booze didn't usually hit him like that. He staggered into the bathroom to splash water on his face.

In the bathroom he stood, dumbfounded, in front of the mirror. The face staring back at him had a swollen, bruised eye with a cut underneath and a huge fat lip with a gash that was flaked with dried blood.

"What happened?" Marvin asked Robbie, who stood at the bathroom door.

"I slugged you. We got in a fight and I slugged you. I'm sorry. Don't tell anyone, I'll get in trouble."

At breakfast, Marvin and Robbie joined the U.S. agents who had been staying in the room next door.

"What the hell happened last night? What was all the commotion? We didn't know if we should come over," one said. Marvin and Robbie told them it was nothing. Marvin dutifully didn't report the fight, saying he deserved it.

Robbie was more mortified about it than Marvin knew. He anguished over it, bewildered by his own lack of control and the realization that he had cut his prized informant so close to the eye.

"I could have taken his eye out," he moaned to a friend afterwards. "I could have damaged him for life."

On another case, in 1988, Marvin was asked to work with Toronto city police to investigate a large break-and-enter gang. The nimble crooks were getting into stores through the roof, dropping down to pilfer the most expensive merchandise they could find. They had an affinity for furs and jewellery. Marvin had no trouble working his way into the tight-knit group wearing a police wire.

Two officers with the Toronto force arranged through Robbie to meet with Marvin on a Thursday at Town and Country Square. Marvin sat and waited, and waited. More than an hour after the scheduled meeting, Marvin stormed off and phoned Robbie.

"Where the hell are they?" Marvin said.

"They had to cancel."

"No one told me. For Christ's sake, I put the day aside for this. I've come out here and I've waited more than an hour."

"I guess they thought I was going to tell you and I thought they did. That's the way it is. We'll do the meeting tomorrow."

Marvin was angry. He sometimes jokes that it is impossible to insult a fink, but the truth was he felt insulted.

"No," Marvin snapped. "I'm not coming to work tomorrow. I'm taking the day off."

Robbie hung up on him. A couple of hours later, Marvin called Robbie back to try to clear the air. The intelligence bureau's secretary answered the phone. She said she would get Robbie, but soon was back on the line.

"He said you can stay on the line till hell freezes over. He's not going to pick up the phone."

"Fuck him."

Marvin didn't call Robbie the next day, Friday. He didn't call him on Saturday. He didn't call him Sunday. Nor Monday. It was the longest Marvin and Robbie had gone without talking since they had started working together. Even when Marvin was overseas without Robbie, Marvin had checked in frequently. On Tuesday, there was a message on Marvin's answering machine. It was Robbie.

"Are you all right or just mad at me? I want to make sure nothing's wrong."

Marvin called back and they talked as if nothing had happened. Neither mentioned the argument or the days without contact. It was Thursday morning all over again.

"I just got hot at him. I made up my mind not to call him," Marvin says. "I think he thought I would crumble and call him. He wanted to remind me who was boss. But I refused to call him. I told myself I was retiring."

Marvin was relieved when Robbie called. It was hard for him to quit Robbie cold turkey. It was hard for Robbie to quit Marvin as well.

"I guess we both needed each other."

CHAPTER 40

TORONTO, 1989

Marvin and Hennie's eldest daughter finally brought her boyfriend home to meet her parents, after weeks of avoiding it. She was 25, and keen on this lad. He arrived at their home hoping to make a good impression, but Marvin opened the door to greet him and almost had a heart attack. The boyfriend looked at Marvin and almost ran. Neither had realized it beforehand, but the two knew each other. The boy hung out in a tough lounge where Marvin would go to meet his gangster pals. He knew the boy was a hood.

Marvin was firm in forbidding his daughter from dating him, and the boy's mother called Marvin the next day.

"Mr. Elkind, are you any better than my son?" she asked.

"Nope, maybe even worse," he said.

"Then why won't you let your daughter go out with him?"

"Because I don't want my daughter associating with somebody like me. I know what all the mistakes are because I made most of them. Don't take any disrespect or anything, but I know what your son is, because not only was I there, I'm still there, and I don't want your son putting my daughter through what I put my wife through."

His daughter was bitterly upset about her father's intractable stance until she realized how right he had been: one day,

386

someone threw a Molotov cocktail into the boy's house, to settle an ongoing feud. The boy wasn't home, but his roommate was. He escaped the flames by jumping from the balcony, but smashed his head on the way down, causing permanent brain damage. She couldn't help but realize that it could have been her in the house, had their relationship continued.

Throughout the years, Marvin worked feverishly to keep his unusual occupation and pugnacious associates separate from his family life. It wasn't always possible. He was juggling his real life as a husband, father and dutiful son with his double life in the mob. He was honest with his family about what he did, but he also tried to shield them from it.

Marvin's youngest daughter offered him a different problem. She was living with her boyfriend and it drove Marvin mad. This wasn't a boy he was looking to keep his daughter from, but rather a boy he wanted to embrace as his son-in-law. Everyone who knew Marvin knew how much it bothered him that they weren't married. One night, Marvin brought the boyfriend to a boxing match. There Marvin introduced him to George Chuvalo, the retired heavyweight champ. Chuvalo put the startled boy in a tight headlock.

"We are going to the synagogue, either for a funeral or a wedding. Your choice," Chuvalo said. Not long after, the boy proposed.

It solved one headache for Marvin, but created another. Now he had a wedding to pay for.

***

With the marriage on the horizon, Marvin wondered how he would pay for it. He had no savings and no payday on the horizon. His daughter asked him how he would feel if her fiancé's father paid for it. Marvin, the traditionalist, was dead set against it, and she dutifully started planning a small, simple wedding.

Then Marvin got a call from Irving Kott. He was sending Marvin $1,000 to buy plane tickets to go see him in Montreal. He had a job for him.

In Montreal, Kott told Marvin that he and Tommy Corrigan were bidding against each other to take over a waste-disposal company. Kott wanted Marvin to find out what Corrigan's offer was going to be, so that he could beat it—but not by more than was necessary. If Marvin could deliver him a copy of Corrigan's planned bid, thereby assuring that Kott would beat it, Kott would pay Marvin $20,000.

"I probably wouldn't have done it if I hadn't had the wedding coming up, because I was scared of Tommy," Marvin says. "In the biggest way, I wanted to pay for that wedding and make it nice."

Marvin started poking around Corrigan's affairs more than usual and did stumble across the offer. He managed to get it to Kott who, in turn, delivered the $20,000 to Marvin, in cash. Marvin hurried home with it, handing it to Hennie the moment he strode through the door, almost in a panic.

"Take this money and keep it away from me. This is for the wedding," he said.

When Marvin phoned his future son-in-law's father to tell him he had $20,000 for the wedding, the father offered to match it, so their kids could have an amazing event. Marvin agreed to that, and it was an affair to remember, not unlike Marvin and Hennie's own wedding. The guests arrived at the reception at the Sutton Place Hotel and wined and dined in fine style. Marvin had invited a couple of guests whom he was in the midst of finking on, to build a stronger bond.

Marvin hired a couple of boxing friends as security, to make sure there wasn't any trouble, and then he displayed his extemporaneous speaking skills by delivering an impromptu speech that had everyone laughing and crying. Dozens of guests came up to him afterwards and told him it was the funniest speech they had ever heard, but Marvin can't remember a word of it—and not because he was drunk. He was just completely living in the moment. He was perhaps the only person at the reception who hadn't touched a drop of booze. In the days leading up to the event, his mother, wife and both daughters had come to him on their own and made him promise he wouldn't drink at the wedding.

He kept his word. But when it was over and everyone had left happy, Marvin settled into a limousine with Hennie for the ride home, opened up a bottle of Usher's Green Stripe Scotch Whisky and downed it.

* * *

Even the most unusual lives are punctuated by the trivialities, tragedies and frailties of living. Marvin's has been no different. As he danced from disrepute to danger, adventure to adversity, feast to famine, he muddled through health scares and heartaches.

Not long after the high of his daughter's wedding, his mother, Beatrice, was diagnosed with stomach cancer. The doctors told her that, without surgery, she wouldn't live for more than a couple of years. Despite that, she was worried more about the operation than the cancer. She didn't want to go through with it.

"Look, I'm not going to sit on pins and needles for two years," Marvin told her. "You've got to get this fixed."

"My mother, your grandmother, had the same operation and she never got out of bed again," she complained.

"Ma, that was a thousand years ago. Believe me, there's new technology. They've figured this stuff out by now."

"Marvin, it's not the quantity of life that matters, it's the quality."

Marvin and his siblings, Stanley and Marilyn, convinced their mother to have the surgery, although she wasn't happy about it. The night before the operation, the three children visited Beatrice in hospital. They were discreetly pulled aside by the surgeon.

"Listen, I'm a little concerned about something. She seems to not have the fight in her that I need her to have. It's like she's given up before we go in, and I'm not happy about that. See if you can talk something into her," the doctor said.

When the children went into her room, their mother's maudlin fatalism was on full display as she sank her head deep in the hospital pillows.

"I'm glad my three children are here, so we can say good-bye," she said.

"What are you trying to say, Ma?" asked Marvin.

"This is the last time we're going to see each other."

"Are you trying to say that, after tonight, it's curtains?"

"Yes. I'm not going to make it."

"Ma, in that case, can I have the TV?"

A fire returned to Beatrice's eyes. She lifted her head.

"You rotten, no-good—no, no, you can't! Because, just you see, I'm going to survive this. So you can't have it. That's just what I expect of you. You can't have it because I'm going to need it. I'll need it for a long time to come," she berated.

The children left her for the night, feeling better.

Stanley looked at Marvin. "Very good," he said.

Although he was worried for his mother, Marvin had to smile. He beamed even more the next day, when Beatrice pulled through the surgery and, indeed, needed her television.

Some years later, the family was moving Beatrice into Toronto's Jewish Home for the Aged. They had scheduled an eight o'clock meeting with the staff, to discuss the arrangements. Marvin left early for the meeting because of the dreadful weather, rain pouring down, and ended up arriving 20 minutes early. As he waited, he recognized the caretaker as a man he had known from the boxing gym, and they stood in the hallway chatting. Which is where he was when his mother arrived with his sister. They went into the administrative office and Beatrice was seated with her back to Marvin. Marilyn gave Marvin a wave, and they waited for Stanley. About 10 minutes after the meeting was supposed to have begun, the administrator announced that they would have to start without one of her sons, who hadn't arrived yet.

"That's him, all right," Beatrice complained. "Anything to upset me. He's probably at a boxing gym talking to his friends. Or maybe one of his friends got arrested and he's down at the jail talking to him. Or maybe he got arrested."

Marilyn interrupted her. "Ma, Marvin is here, he was here before us. It's Stanley who's not here."

"Well," said Beatrice, "what do you expect, look at the weather."

Beatrice Elkind died on November 11, 2005. She was 94 years old.

CHAPTER 41

DETROIT, 1990

To Marvin it was just noise, a loud, repetitive thumping that bothered his ears; a throbbing bass he felt in his bowels, with computerized melodies and mechanical beeps fading in and out. It reminded him a bit of the disco music he had heard in Toronto's nightclubs a decade before, but this seemed to be fused with the industrial clamour of the nearby car-assembly plants. It was the distinctive sound of Detroit's burgeoning techno-music scene, and it was blasting out of immense speakers inside a warehouse in a real gutter district of downtown Detroit.

Marvin tried to block out the noise and concentrate.

With him was Andy Rayne, the RCMP undercover officer whom Marvin liked to work with. Marvin had confidence in Rayne. Rayne and Marvin, along with Rayne's partner, Bill Gill, were in the after-hours club undercover, on a cross-border drugs and guns investigation. Marvin was trying to introduce his supposed mob contacts to a gang in Detroit. Their enticement to the gangsters was that they would swap drugs from Canada for American guns.

Marvin introduced Rayne to everyone he met as Andy DiNardo. It had become Rayne's regular undercover name. Rayne had borrowed the last name from Joe DiNardo, a Toronto speed fighter, who had himself adopted the name after emigrating to Canada from Hungary. Joe DiNardo was notorious for having been in and out of jail more than anyone else. Marvin had finked on him in 1990, tipping Robbie to his drug-dealing. By using the same undercover name on cases, Rayne was able to establish a profile that he could exploit later. Over the years, Marvin would casually introduce "Andy DiNardo" to his underworld friends, not to build cases against them, but just so they could get to know him. Later, if anyone were to check up on Andy DiNardo, there would be plenty of thugs who could vouch for him. But in this Detroit warehouse, amid the throbbing music and crowd of young people wiggling on the dance floor, nobody knew any of the Canadians.

Marvin took care of that. With his gregarious nature, Marvin easily worked his way into conversations, meeting and greeting some of the guys who looked like high rollers or bad guys. To each of them, Marvin introduced Rayne as a real big hitter from Toronto who was in town looking for guns.

Rayne struck up one conversation with a towering, well-spoken black man, athletic-looking, almost seven feet tall.

"You from Toronto?" the man asked.

"Yeah," said Rayne.

"Let me buy you a drink."

"Of course."

They talked amicably about nothing criminal. The man was quite charming. After a bit, Gill came over and, while the tall man was ordering another round of drinks, whispered to Rayne.

"Do you know who you're talking to?"

"Nope," said Rayne.

It was John "Spider" Salley, a power forward with the Detroit Pistons. The fact that he was an NBA star explained his extraordinary height. Rayne was amused at his brush with a sporting celebrity and moved on, as night turned to day, to those who might prove more fruitful for investigation. The trio eventually returned to their hotel to get some needed sleep. The next morning, they were woken earlier than they would have wished by a telephone call. Gill answered.

"We got a problem," an FBI agent told him. "After you left last night, the disco was bombed. Someone blew the front doors right off the place."

When Detroit police had interviewed everyone they could find who had been at the club, many of them described two shady Toronto mobsters carousing and looking for weapons, who had left shortly before the explosion. The Detroit police had their suspects. Marvin and Rayne had been too convincing.

"The local police are looking for your undercover operators for the bombing. Get your guys out of here," the agent said.

It was a dangerous time for drug dealers in Detroit. The bombing came in the middle of a cocaine war between rival crews jostling for domination with bullets and bombs.

***

As Marvin's reputation grew among law-enforcement agencies, the FBI rented him from Robbie many times to help in their investigations. Marvin enjoyed working with the Americans, mainly because they paid better than Canadian cops.

After hearing Robbie brag about his seemingly unbeatable operative, Special Agent Rich Mazzari at the FBI's Detroit office asked if he could borrow Marvin. There was an Italian bakery shop owner suspected of selling heroin. Marvin walked into the bakery cold and introduced himself to the owner. The baker asked him to come back after giving him a day's notice and he could show Marvin around town. In return, the baker asked, would Marvin take him around Toronto and introduce him to some of his contacts? Every businessman likes to network. When Marvin went back to the bakery, he arranged a $10,000 heroin deal. The baker claimed shocking suppliers: three Detroit city cops and a real estate agent from Windsor. A day later, Marvin and the baker opened a joint safe-deposit box at the National Bank of Detroit in Harper Woods, northeast of Detroit, and the day after that Marvin was introduced to his distributors, the owner of a motel on East 9 Mile Road and the owner of a restaurant across the border in Windsor.

Mazzari had to admit it: Marvin was good.

While the FBI looked into the allegations of dope-dealing cops, Marvin and Robbie turned their attention to the Windsor realtor. Marvin had meeting after meeting with him, trying to get him to engage. The FBI lent him and Karen Moffatt, his undercover "girlfriend," a silver-fox fur coat and limousine they had seized from traffickers, so that they would look the part of high rollers when they took the realtor out for nights on the town. Detroit police provided an officer who posed as their chauffeur. No matter what Marvin and Moffatt did or said, the realtor never discussed drugs. Marvin considers him the one who got away.

The cops almost lost Marvin on that case: at a dinner at Carl's Chop House, a steakhouse marked by a life-size black cow on top of its sign on Detroit's Grand River Avenue, Marvin ordered the prime rib. Desperately hungry, as soon as his meal arrived he cut the giant slab of beef in half, shoved it in his mouth and promptly started choking. Marvin jumped up and ran to the washroom where no one could see him. One of the police officers eventually found him, his eyes bulging, face purple. After a Heimlich push, the meat was dislodged and, after a few minutes of recuperating, Marvin returned to the table for the other half of the beef.

It was also at Carl's that Robbie, Marvin, Andy Rayne and Bill Gill were treated to dinner by FBI agents after working on a case. It was hospitality, not an undercover operation. Marvin was already drunk when they arrived and some officers questioned the wisdom of bringing him, but Robbie assured everyone he would be fine, once he had gotten some food in him. Marvin deserved a nice dinner more than anyone, he said. Marvin ordered the beef ribs and was served enormous racks of drippy, greasy sauce-soaked meat. Boozy and loud, he rolled up his sleeves and gnawed into them, gripping the slippery bones with his equally meaty fingers. But in his inebriated state they proved too much: sauce was soon smeared around his face and running off his hands and down his wrists. He used the tablecloth to wipe his fingers, when he couldn't easily find his napkin. It was a spectacle, and the agents were mortified and amused in equal measure, until the owner came over and hissed at them to get Marvin out of his restaurant. Bill Gill took him to the hotel to lie down. The next day, Marvin didn't remember much of the evening but everyone was making jokes to him about ribs. It took him a while to figure it out.

"I didn't realize I was making such an ass of myself until the next morning. After that, I would not eat ribs in public again," he says. For years, cops would make jokes to Marvin about ribs. When they were out to dinner and looking over the menu, someone would invariably say, "I hear the ribs are good."

The messy manners didn't spoil the FBI's appetite for exploiting Marvin. In 1986, he was sent to Houston to infiltrate a group of suspicious men who owned a large oil and intra-state gas pipeline company. When Marvin arrived, he was greeted by men who thought he represented Irving Kott's millions and they showered him with Texan hospitality.

Marvin uncovered a plot to buy orange groves in Costa Rica with drug money and the agents launched an investigation. In 1990, he uncovered a skimming and money-laundering operation at a casino in Las Vegas that led to arrests.

With the FBI and U.S. Customs, Marvin tackled street gangs, drug traffickers, gun smugglers, money launderers, mobsters and other criminal organizations. But it was another one of Robbie's finks who brought Marvin back to Detroit in October 1990.

* * *

Robbie had been told that Kirpal Ahluwalia, the Los Angeles stock promoter who was arrested as one of the suppliers of the Million Dollar Saloon network that Marvin had infiltrated in 1987, had already served his time and was up to his old tricks. It was to Kirpal's great fortune that, although he spent most of his time in L.A., he was arrested at a ranch near Calgary, meaning he was sentenced under Canada's more lenient provisions. Although the tip came from another fink, it was Marvin whom Robbie called in to get close to Kirpal. Although Marvin had been discovered as a fink during the Million Dollar Saloon probe, he had never had anything to do with Kirpal's end of the business and the two had never met. Robbie gave Kirpal's phone number to Marvin, and Marvin called him up out of the blue.

"I understand you're into some business that I might get involved in and make some money, and make you some money," Marvin said.

"Where did you get my name and number?" Kirpal asked. Marvin said he was recommended by a mutual friend, and gave him a name. Kirpal checked Marvin out. The mutual friend confirmed Marvin's shady past and their association, but was perplexed by the call and confronted Marvin about it.

"What do you think you're doing, using my name?" the man said. Marvin convinced him that he really had given him Kirpal's name and number.

"You've got a lot going on, you must have forgot. Don't worry about it," Marvin consoled him.

Marvin was soon meeting with Kirpal and being introduced to his friends. They talked a lot, but not about drugs. After three months, Kirpal introduced Marvin to the owner of a chain of dry cleaners. Marvin worked his way into his life, as well. In turn, he introduced Marvin to a man he referred to as their boss, Balbir Ahluwalia. Balbir, Marvin was told, worked out of a Toronto lawyer's office. Robbie took it to mean that he was the go-to guy for the drugs Marvin kept hinting about. But all Balbir wanted to talk about was an oil and gas venture. Marvin began to believe the tip about drugs was bogus.

"I think this one's a dead end," Marvin said to Robbie one day, after months of meeting with Balbir and Kirpal and getting nary a sniff of dope.

"Keep trying," Robbie insisted.

Robbie had Marvin calling Balbir and visiting Balbir and bumping into Balbir over and over again. Balbir must have been getting sick of him, but he showed grace and patience, even when Robbie woke Marvin one day at 2 a.m. and told him to go and visit Balbir right then, and try again. Marvin dutifully got out of bed, apologized to Hennie and crept out of the house. Marvin buzzed Balbir at his penthouse apartment in Toronto.

"Hey, I can't sleep," Marvin told him. "Let's talk business."

They sat in Balbir's living room where, with a sleepy sigh, Marvin listened to Balbir explain his gas company. Balbir was trying to buy up 300 independent gas stations in Ontario to form a new chain. Marvin was convinced Balbir was interested only in petroleum products, and he even considered trying to find some money to invest with him.

Then it hit him: investors.

Marvin said he had wealthy friends from the Middle East living in Detroit who might want to invest in his gas company—and other deals. In January 1991, Marvin convinced Balbir to take a phone call from one of his supposedly wealthy investors. By then, Robbie had called the FBI about the case, and the FBI had brought one of their informants into the operation, Frank Makdesion, who knew the drug trade and was co-operating with the government, Marvin was told, to avoid deportation back to the Middle East. The team of U.S. agents and Canadian police formed a joint operation, code-named Project Motown, in homage to Detroit.

Marvin put Makdesion together with Balbir. Over the next month, the three of them met and talked several times. Balbir's resistance seemed to be waning. When Marvin chatted up Balbir's apartment manager, he learned Balbir was having money trouble.

"When he first moved to this building he was driving a Mercedes, then it was a Nissan. Now he's walking," the manager said.

On February 21, Balbir met with Makdesion in Windsor. According to an agreed statement of facts signed by Balbir, he gave Makdesion a sample of cocaine, something he later denied. In early March, Balbir and Makdesion met again in Detroit. Makdesion drove him around the city and then suddenly told him to drop the charade of the gas company and sell him some drugs. Makdesion put a gun to Balbir's head and said he would shoot him if he didn't supply him with drugs,

Balbir later said, an allegation Makdesion denied. If true, it is strange that Balbir met with Makdesion again to spend most of the next day with him. A deal was struck at $26,000 per kilo, $1,000 less if it was collected in Los Angeles.

Marvin also made headway. Balbir's partner said he checked Marvin out in Detroit. All the hoods there said he was "a great guy." He invited Marvin to come to Kenya with him to appraise some young boxers he was working with.

In his notebook, Robbie underlined his thoughts on this: "'M' told, under no circumstances is he to go to Kenya." He knew Marvin would be tempted.

After six months of meetings, on March 25, Marvin sat with Balbir in the King Edward Hotel in downtown Toronto when a drug deal finally was struck. Although Marvin had been talking about it for months, he had always made it clear that he didn't personally have much knowledge of drugs. He had friends and associates who were the experts, he would say; he just wanted to make money. He said he would need to take a sample to his buddy for testing.

Marvin met Balbir in a grocery-store parking lot. Marvin pulled his car up close beside his. Balbir popped open his trunk, took out a knife and cut off the corner of a block of cocaine that was wrapped in white paper and gave it to Marvin. Marvin took the sample to a coffee shop and slipped it to an undercover drug cop, who went into the washroom to test it. When he came out, he told Marvin that it was good, go buy it. Marvin returned to the parking lot and acquired a kilo brick of cocaine. Finally, there was a drug transaction. Robbie was relieved his instinct hadn't been wrong.

There is nothing like selling a brick of cocaine and not being arrested to give a dealer confidence in a buyer. The parking-lot transaction broke the logjam. By May, Makdesion was discussing a five-kilo deal with Balbir, but settled on a one-kilo sale, followed by other sales over the next three months, while police wiretapped his telephone. In August, Balbir offered to add heroin to the merchandise.

On August 14, Makdesion introduced Balbir to an under-cover officer. They cut a deal for two ounces of heroin and, soon after, Balbir and some co-conspirators were arrested and charged with trafficking in cocaine and heroin, possession of cocaine and heroin and laundering the proceeds of crime. Balbir pleaded not guilty.

Marvin was disappointed when told he would be called to testify. His role in the case as the initial drug buyer made his evidence indispensible to prosecutors. Robbie accompanied him to court. When Marvin was reunited with Makdesion, the two finks embraced. Marvin's testimony was typically insightful. Makdesion testified, as well, but with less suc-cess. Balbir also took the stand, testifying on his own behalf. He said he had sold the drugs under duress after Makdesion threatened him. The case ended in a mistrial. Before a new trial was scheduled, Balbir and his co-accused changed their plea to guilty on some of the charges. They signed an agreed state-ment of facts, but, after three adjournments of the sentenc-ing hearing, Balbir claimed that police had entrapped him. After a lengthy hearing, at which Marvin and Makdesion were called to testify again, the claim was dismissed and, in January 1997, Balbir was sentenced to seven and a half years in prison. After his conviction, he was ordered deported back to India. He appealed the rejection of his entrapment claim, which put the deportation on hold, because Balbir had some-thing new to work with.

Balbir's lawyer learned that Makdesion had lied in his testimony. The American informant had said he had a single charge of drug possession dating from more than a decade ago. In fact, he had also been convicted of assault with a dangerous weapon and drug possession less than a year before—while he was employed by the FBI. It cast a bad light on the prosecutors.

"The fresh evidence compels the conclusion that Makdesion committed perjury at the trial when he testified about his criminal record," Judge David Doherty wrote in the appeal ruling in 2000. "Makdesion was an important witness and his credibility was very much in issue, especially as it related to his testimony that he did not threaten [Balbir]." It might have been enough to "destroy his credibility entirely." The convictions were tossed and a new hearing was ordered on the entrapment issue. The appeal was even worse for Marvin than the trial, which had been ignored by the press. The appeal judgment was a searing indictment of a government witness who had perjured himself, with the possible co-operation of the prosecutors or police, and it was widely reported. In paragraph nine of the appeal decision, Marvin's secret identity was revealed, much to his discomfort, in black and white: "Constable Robinson arranged for Marvin Elkind, a long-time paid police agent for the OPP, to make contact with Kirpal." Luckily for Marvin, reporters focused on Makdesion, the lying fink, and left him out of it.

* * *

Even after arrests were made in Canada, the case still bore fruit in the United States. Marvin kept tabs on Kirpal Ahluwalia, his original target, as hunter and prey moved back and forth between Canada and the United States.

Marvin then introduced Makdesion to Kirpal and his friends, and things progressed more quickly in California. On

July 29, 1992, Makdesion met Kirpal at the Embassy Suites Hotel in Irvine, less than a mile from the John Wayne Airport and a 45-minute drive from Los Angeles, to discuss the purchase of 65 kilos of cocaine. They met there again the next day, and then drove together to the coast, at Newport Beach, to meet Kirpal's two colleagues. One, a woman, made a series of phone calls from a nearby pay phone to arrange the deal. They said that the first 14 kilos were on their way, and they set off to get it, dodging in and out of traffic to shake off anyone who might be following. In a parking lot 30 minutes away, in Anaheim, they met three others before returning to the Embassy Suites. Kirpal drove Makdesion back to the hotel, where they were all reunited. As the exchange was made, Kirpal and his two friends were arrested. The United States portion of the investigation was codenamed Motown II.

Authorities seized 21 kilos of cocaine and three kilos of heroin as a result of Marvin's introductions. In 1993, Kirpal pleaded guilty and was sentenced to 10 years in prison. In 1996, he cut a deal for a reduced sentence of five years, but prosecutors made sure he wasn't eligible for transfer to Canada under the countries' prisoner transfer treaty. He was released a year later, anyway.

* * *

The courtroom slips of Makdesion and his handlers showed the vulnerability of police evidence when paid informants were called to testify. Paid informants were usually dodgy people with a questionable moral compass. The Balbir Ahluwalia case—and the stiff dressing-down from the appeal court—highlighted why many prosecutors dislike using informant evidence and why some officers give finks a cool reception.

They give the better defence lawyers something to pick at, and many informants can't stand up to such scrutiny. But Marvin always could.

Project Motown I and II, in Canada and the United States, reinforced the faith Robbie and the other officers had in Marvin. Not one word of criticism came Marvin's way from the court. The appeal judges noted that, when Marvin was asked something that he didn't know, he seemed forthcoming in saying he didn't know or didn't recall. His evidence was believed, accepted, and his actions on the case were deemed persistent but appropriate.

After the last of Marvin's Detroit cases, Robbie's summary case notes were enthusiastic: "This informant was successful in infiltrating this criminal group and was also successful in introducing an FBI informant into the same group. As a result of our informant's actions, a major drug trafficking organization has been broken. The FBI in Detroit have seized twenty-one kilos of cocaine, three kilos of heroin and made ten arrests. Three individuals have already been convicted and are awaiting sentence. Their investigation is continuing. The street value of the drugs seized is $7 Million . . . It took six months of persistence by this informant before he was able to penetrate their operation. In addition, he purchased the first kilo of cocaine."

PART THREE

CHAPTER 42

TORONTO, 1992

Joe Natale solemnly greeted visitors as they arrived at the funeral home to pay respects to his dead brother, Gene, and most of the mourners thought the same thing: Gene, in the casket, looked better than Joe standing beside it. It was not a good time for the Natale family, and Joe, a Toronto loan shark and bookie, was suffering mightily from cancer. From a young age, Joe Natale had had his heart set on being a mobster, which was unfortunate because he was a natural-born salesman and could have forged a fine honest living. He was so good at selling cars at a Ford dealership that, even when he started getting arrested, he wasn't fired. Among those who shook Natale's hand in sympathy was Marvin.

The two had known each other for years, first working together under Roy Pasquale. Natale once sold broadloom to a woman in Fort Erie through Roy's carpet store, but after installation she refused to pay, and Roy sent a thug nicknamed Snow White—because of his dark complexion—to scare her. The next day, two large Italian men visited Roy's office and opened their jackets to show they were carrying guns. They told Roy the woman was a relative of Stefano Magaddino, the dead, but once-powerful, Mafia boss of Buffalo.

"Roy almost had a fucking heart attack. So did we all. We

didn't know who she was," Marvin says. "We found out later that Natale, the asshole, knew who she was but didn't say nothing."

Soon after, in 1986, Marvin got Natale back, tipping Robbie to his crooked business arrangements with Johnny Papalia, the Hamilton Mafia boss. Marvin introduced Natale to two undercover OPP officers: Karen Moffatt, who pretended to flirt with the gangster to get his attention, and Bill Gill, who had done the first undercover work with Marvin on the New York porn case. Later, Marvin helped Natale obtain a strip-club licence through a friend who was a licensing official with the City of Toronto. Natale paid Marvin—the licensing official refused payment—and then Marvin finked about the new strip club to Robbie. Natale dodged the investigation, but not in the way he would have wanted; he died of cancer soon after it began. Marvin didn't shed a tear at Natale's funeral, in 1988, but if he had, it would not have been so much for the loss of a friend but for the loss of a job. Natale's premature death robbed Marvin of the chance of pressing that case, and he figured it gave him less finking work to do. He couldn't know that, in death, Natale would bring him more work than he would ever have in his life.

* * *

Lorraine Latter was Natale's girlfriend who, after his funeral, called Marvin about her money trouble. Chicago boxing promoter Donny Elbaum had owed Natale $100,000 from a big fight they had worked on together, she said. She wanted Marvin to ask Elbaum to pay. Marvin knew Elbaum and called him.

"Marvin, I've got the promissory note here, it's bullshit. It's for ten thousand dollars, not a hundred," Elbaum told him. "Are you calling to collect it?"

"Lorraine needs the money," Marvin said. Elbaum and Latter cut a deal for $7,500. Latter called Marvin again, the next time she had trouble. This time it was with Morris Monte Friesner, who appeared to be a financial guru who could land enormous loans from exotic sources. Marvin already knew Friesner. He had finked on him twice.

"Friesner had a lot of confidence in me," Marvin says. "He looked at me as an ally. He was telling me all kinds of things he was involved in."

Back in 1985, Marvin had learned Friesner was fraudulently taking over a Thunder Bay hotel, claiming to be a lawyer. Robbie alerted the owners and the scheme withered. Friesner never learned how police had uncovered his plot, and the following year he told Marvin that he had just convinced Steve Fonyo to let him be his business manager. Fonyo was the young Canadian who had lost a leg to cancer and then set out to emulate Terry Fox's marathon across Canada to raise money for cancer research. Unlike Fox, who had had to abandon his run when his cancer returned, Fonyo had completed the journey and done the same across Britain. His gruelling runs had brought in $14 million, and the idea of someone like Friesner getting near that money worried Robbie. Seeing nothing criminal in the relationship, yet, Robbie intervened in another way. He again leaked information to Peter Moon: it had worked so well on the St. Kitts bank. The front-page newspaper story, about a man with convictions for arson, assault, fraud, possession of stolen goods and (denied) links to organized crime managing the then-national hero, had the same effect on donors and sponsors as it had on Robbie. Fonyo soon fired him.

At the time that Lorraine Latter was complaining to Marvin about Friesner, the con man had moved on to running a company with the respectable-sounding name First

Federal Bancorp (Canada) Inc. He told clients he could get multimillion-dollar loans from Kuwaiti lenders in return for an advance fee of $500,000. One of the suckers was Latter, who had borrowed most of the advanced fee from friends so she could buy a hotel. Latter told Marvin of other victims who had also paid at least $2 million in fees for loans that never materialized. Marvin passed the tips on to Robbie.

After Robbie started investigating him, Friesner declared bankruptcy in Toronto—listing liabilities of $11.4 million and assets of just $200—and relocated to Oklahoma, where he sped around in a Porsche 911 and raised Arabian horses. Robbie gave his evidence to the FBI in Tulsa, and in November 1992, Friesner was arrested. At his trial, the prosecutor summed up Friesner's life, saying: "So many lies, so little time." He was found guilty on 21 counts of fraud and money laundering and sentenced to seven years. Judge Thomas Brett spoke of the Canadian's silver tongue: "Frankly, I think you could sell iceboxes to quite a few Eskimos. You have an unusual talent and ability at salesmanship."

It was another good case courtesy of Marvin, but Lorraine Latter's inadvertent tips would yield bigger fish. She didn't know how Marvin was able to solve her problems, but she appreciated it and wanted to give him something in return.

* * *

"I've got a guy to introduce you to," Latter told Marvin, soon after Friesner's arrest. They were words Marvin still loved to hear, almost a decade after he had first started working for Robbie.

Marvin and Latter met on June 22, 1992, at the Sutton Place Hotel, where she said she could get him quality fake

Canadian citizenship cards, all he wanted, for $3,000 each. Marvin said he would talk to his people and get back to her.

When Robbie heard about the offer, he was excited. In the years before the terrorist attacks on the World Trade Center on September 11, 2001, a card like this would be accepted as proof of Canadian citizenship both in Canada and abroad. At that time, Canadians didn't need a passport to enter the United States; anyone with one of these cards could slip easily back and forth across the border. Terrorists, foreign agents and criminals had already been passing themselves off as Canadians to do covert work around the globe.

"Let's go for it," Robbie said.

Marvin met Latter's card man, saying he'd be buying in bulk.

"But I need to take one to show my people," Marvin said.

"No way. I'll show you one, you can look at it all you want, but I can't let you take it with you," the man said.

Robbie told Marvin that it was essential to get a sample. Was it a legitimate card pilfered from the government, or was it counterfeit? If it was a real card, who was stealing them? And if it was a counterfeit, how good was it, and who was making them? These were questions Robbie needed answered.

So Marvin phoned his contact back.

"Listen, I'm coming over to look at one of those things," he said, in mimicry of the way crooks talk obscurely about their activities over the phone in case it is wired. "But I'm in a big hurry. Can you meet me outside your apartment, so I don't have to come up? I'll check it out, place an order and push off to an appointment."

"I'll be waiting out front," the man replied.

Marvin then did something he almost never did. He involved Hennie, his wife. Not telling her much about what he was doing or why, he asked her to drive him to the man's apartment. About a block away, Marvin told her to pull their Buick to the side of the road.

"I'll meet you right back here, wait for me," Marvin said as he got out, and then he walked around the corner. The man handed Marvin one of the cards. Marvin took it in his hand, looked at it for a second, as if he were going to examine it, and then he stuffed it in his pocket and walked away.

"Hey, you can't take that," the man squawked.

"Yeah, I gotta. I gotta show my people," said Marvin, still walking toward the corner where he had told Hennie to wait.

"Give it back. You can't take it."

"Don't worry. They need to see one before they buy."

"Give it."

"Can't."

Marvin walked faster, with the man hounding him. He broke into a jog as he turned the corner, with the man now grabbing at him. Marvin stopped dead. Neither Hennie nor the car was there. The street was empty. He was flabbergasted.

By then, the man was in front of Marvin, blocking him, demanding, threatening and grabbing at Marvin's pocket, where Marvin kept his meaty fist clamped around the small card jammed deep inside. Marvin continued to push him away with his free hand, while trying to calm him down.

"Listen, you'll get it back. I'm borrowing it. I gotta show my people."

The man was a big guy, but not especially tough. The Weasel could handle him, if push came to shove, which it did. Marvin looked up and down the street, wondering where Hennie could be. He considered his options as the confrontation verged on an all-out brawl. Just when it looked like Marvin would have to clobber the guy to shut him up, the

Buick drove up. Marvin gave a last shove and jumped into the car, telling Hennie to floor it.

"What happened? Where the hell were you?"

"I didn't know how long you'd be," she said, "so I did a little shopping."

Marvin, recalling it, lets out a sigh.

"I tell you, this finking has not been an easy business."

* * *

Marvin took the borrowed card to Robbie, who called Andy Rayne. The veteran officer had by then left undercover work and was with the RCMP's Passport and Immigration section.

"Andy, Marv's got a connection to fake citizenship cards, a lot of them. They look good. You interested?"

Rayne had long ago stopped being surprised by what was dredged up by The Cigar, as he still calls Marvin. Rayne knew this was not the first case that Marvin had uncovered that protected international border integrity. In 1986, Marvin had identified a large, Mafia-backed fraud involving the sale of land and a casino investment project in the Caribbean island of St. Maarten, a Dutch protectorate. Investment packages of $100,000 or more included a Dutch passport in return. Marvin even obtained one of the passports as a sample for Robbie. One of the conspirators was a former Cabinet minister on the island at a delicate time: the government was falling under the influence of the Sicilian Mafia. Robbie alerted Dutch authorities, who shut down the operation. Marvin's evidence helped prompt a government investigation into alleged ties between the mob and the island administration. Two years later, Marvin uncovered a similar plot involving organized crime figures from Taiwan who were offering investment packages that included a passport for a Commonwealth country. After Marvin's tip, that was also shut down.

Rayne was pleased to work with Robbie and Marvin again, although this time he wouldn't be undercover. Rayne examined the blank citizenship card. It was a superb fake, barely distinguishable from the real thing. In fact, Rayne knew that these same fake cards were already in use, having encountered several dozen of them over the past year in the hands of bogus immigrants, in fraudulent applications for Canadian passports, in thwarted incidents of smuggling foreign nationals into the United States, used to obtain other pieces of personal identification and in welfare and Medicare frauds. The RCMP were anxious to find out where they were coming from, and the force was on board, Rayne said. Robbie gave the card back to Marvin, who took it back to his source.

"Look, I'm sorry about that. I don't understand what the hell your problem was," Marvin said, tossing the card back to him. "To order as many cards as we want, I needed to show it to my people, and they sure aren't coming out here to see it," he said. It was an old standby that Marvin often fell back on to explain some of the unusual things he had to do undercover—passing the blame off on rich, powerful and dangerous bosses. It reminded the target that Marvin was representing much bigger interests, and it also appealed to their greed. Big bosses usually meant bigger sales.

"You did what you had to do," the card man said.

Marvin next needed to wangle an introduction to the card maker. He achieved this by ordering such a large number of cards that it was beyond the middleman's authority to handle the deal. Marvin said he would be ordering cards by the hundreds and wanted a bulk-rate discount. He was told that would have to be discussed with his partner, who was in Israel and not returning for a few days. The man who was doing the work, Yehuda Segel, was an Israeli who ran a Toronto print shop. Marvin haggled the price down to $500 a card from the original $3,000.

With Marvin introduced up the food chain, he in turn introduced Segel to a Trinidadian RCMP officer who was posing as a Tamil smuggler with links to foreign militants. The officer ordered 300 cards. People were so impressed by Marvin's connections that, while the cards were being worked on, an offer came to meet colleagues who were into guns, cargo heists and other swindles.

"Would you be interested?" someone asked. It's a wonder people bothered asking; Marvin was always interested.

Marvin was introduced to Edward Bradshaw. Bradshaw had recently been released from prison and was making up for lost time. An energetic hood, Bradshaw and his pals were hijacking tractor-trailer loads of consumer goods and, in no time, he was advertising his wares to Marvin.

He had $300,000 in counterfeit U.S. currency: $100,000 was spoken for, but the rest was for sale at 25 cents on the dollar. He had 20 skids of hijacked Neilson Iced Tea: 50 cases per skid for 90 cents a case. He had 1,100 cases of vodka and rum, that was en route to Virginia when it was nicked. He had flashlights, 4,600 of them, that sold for $20.99 apiece retail. He would sell them for $3.30 each if Marvin bought the whole load. And more.

Marvin was also introduced to a guy running a stolen-car ring that was moving hot vehicles back on the street to unsuspecting customers through a leasing company. And there were other prospects. There was "Yogi," "Frenchie," "Al the Driver," "Kanada" and "Fitz" all involved. The operation went from being designated a "case" to a "project," in police lingo. The joint-forces project included OPP officers, RCMP and police in Toronto and Peel, west of Toronto, home to the international airport. Marvin's role as a successful underworld broker gave officers a code name for their investigation: Project Broker.

"They kept introducing me to other guys and we were doing more and more and more stuff," Marvin says. He had tapped into a particularly rich vein and was busy meeting all of the enterprising crooks trying to sell him their wares. With the cargo thefts, truckers were being bribed to let the crooks know when they would be carrying a load of particularly desirable merchandise. Drivers would take a coffee break at a certain restaurant, and when they returned to their rig, it would be gone. Feigning surprise, they would call police. The crooks made off with transport trucks loaded with all kinds of stuff, some of it easier to sell afterwards than others.

While the RCMP worked with the citizenship card supplier, Marvin put Bradshaw in touch with John Celentino, who again went undercover as a mobster. On July 17, Marvin introduced Bradshaw to Celentino at the Prince Hotel in north Toronto. They settled on $13,000 for the first truckload. Bradshaw's instability, however, was starting to show. Marvin heard that he was working on another deal and when he grew suspicious, Bradshaw put a gun to the man's head and demanded credentials. He checked with his references before releasing him, Marvin was told. Even with the added prospect of gunplay, Marvin, Robbie and Celentino wanted to see just what the various crooks in the widening probe could offer. They wanted to put on a show for them, to reveal their extensive resources—to establish credibility as major operators. The problem was the cops didn't have much in the way of resources. The OPP didn't have the money for the kind of imaginative operations some of its members dreamed up.

Robbie needed to recruit some private assistance.

* * *

Robbie loved a good party. It was at a Christmas levee at a Toronto hotel, packed with ranking police officers, spies and former cops from most of the law-enforcement and security agencies around Toronto, that he had met Jack Taylor. Taylor had retired as the deputy chief of York Regional Police, an affluent area north of Toronto, and become director of security at Magna International, a multibillion-dollar automotive-supply company founded by Frank Stronach.

Taylor noticed Robbie in the room long before they met: he seemed to know everyone there. When Taylor was finally introduced to Robbie, he mentioned a problem that he was having at work, which Robbie immediately sorted out. Afterwards, Robbie took Taylor to a bar where they met one of Robbie's other long-time informants, one who had been out of the country for two years. Taylor was astounded at the way the pair carried on. He was used to seeing cops view informants as a necessary, but unseemly, part of their business, a resource to be drained and then discarded, rather than valued and nurtured.

"The rapport I witnessed between Robbie and the informant was an education," Taylor says. "He was as comfortable dealing with the informant as he was clowning around with his fellow officers."

It was after this that Taylor had got a call from Robbie. Robbie asked if Magna, with all of its resources and facilities, could help him and his team boost their credibility with the crooks. Robbie was looking to steal a page from the gangster's playbook and build his own front company. It took a five-minute meeting between Taylor and Stronach for the boss to agree. Stronach gave Taylor a free hand to act as a good corporate citizen. Dozens of times over the next few years, Taylor would give Robbie access to warehouses, offices and other corporate resources from the sprawling Magna empire for police-sting operations. Taylor sometimes got in on the action, like the time he arranged for Robbie to borrow Magna's private unmarked Gulfstream jet so that he could make a grand arrival at Detroit airport for one of his undercover operations. Being the only two guys to get off a private jet is certainly an attention grabber when you are trying to pass yourself off as an accomplished, but shady, businessman coming to arrange a lucrative deal. Robbie and Taylor walked off the jet together and the targets of the operation were there waiting to pick Robbie up, taking it all in with greedy eyes.

But for Project Broker, Robbie's needs were simpler. All he wanted was a warehouse where tractor-trailers could be unloaded and stored. Taylor said that wouldn't be a problem, and he made a few phone calls.

* * *

Jack Taylor groggily answered his phone at 3 a.m. to be greeted by Robbie, sounding as fresh as if he had just started his day. It was July 21, 1992. Robbie told him that he needed the warehouse in an hour. Taylor headed down to an unmarked building on Wildcat Road in a north Toronto industrial park, walking around in the gloom, turning off the alarms and making sure all of the employees were gone. He checked the interior loading dock and staging area, storage rooms and the freight elevator. There was a forklift and room enough to store a couple of full-sized transport trailers, a bonus since the trailers they were expecting had been stolen recently along with the goods they carried. The warehouse was a minor concern in the context of Magna's sprawling empire, but to an enterprising, independent crook fresh out of prison, like Bradshaw, it looked mighty appealing.

Taylor called Robbie and said he was inside, the front door was unlocked and the alarms were off. Robbie and his partner, Danielle McLean, parked a dozen buildings away and walked over to make sure their cars weren't seen. At about 4:30 a.m., Marvin and Celentino arrived at the warehouse, followed by Bradshaw, two partners and a stolen transport truck. The truck was backed into the loading bay and the doors were quickly shut. The trailer was packed full of dishwashers and washing machines. Bradshaw was impressed by the warehouse setup. It seemed as if he had hooked up with some well-connected, organized hoods. When the truck was opened and the contents inspected, Celentino gave Bradshaw $13,000. As they finished the transaction, Bradshaw offered other services as well.

"You need guns? I can get you guns."

Marvin shrugged, "Sure, what kind?"

He had a dozen or more 9mm Browning semi-automatic pistols, the same side arms Canadian soldiers carried, for $600 each. A larger shipment was arriving in 10 days that included Uzi submachine guns. He also had a load of 12 million cigarettes that he would sell for $1.2 million. And he had refilled his counterfeit currency supply and now had $5 million in bills for sale. That might work nicely, Celentino said.

As Marvin escorted Bradshaw outside and said goodbye, Bradshaw looked happy. He was very pleased with Celentino, Bradshaw told Marvin.

When Marvin returned to the warehouse, he was surprised to see that the seemingly deserted space was now throbbing with activity. A couple of well-armed cops were standing against a wall. Robbie was already driving the forklift into the trailer and hauling out huge pallets of appliances onto the floor, where they would be photographed as evidence. Marvin was even more shocked to see that Robbie had a rifle with him, resting against the side of the truck. Danielle came out of the shadows, wearing a pistol in a shoulder holster. Marvin had thought that he and Celentino were alone with Bradshaw; he didn't know that police had considered him to be so dangerous that they had hidden snipers around the balcony to watch him.

Then the door of the warehouse rattled, and opened.

In walked Bradshaw.

The unexpected reappearance of the target of the sting could have ruined it all, but, luckily, Danielle, Taylor and the other cops were far enough away from the door in the dimly lit warehouse that they silently sank down behind fixtures and boxes. Robbie, dressed in a lumberjack jacket and work-boots, just kept working away with the forklift. He must have looked like another member of the gang. If Bradshaw noticed Robbie's rifle, he never mentioned it.

Marvin asked what was up. Bradshaw said he had forgotten to take the licence plates off the tractor trailer. After the trucks were stolen, their plates had been changed to prevent their being discovered by police after the thefts were reported. He wanted his dummy plates back, he said. He collected his plates and left, none the wiser.

Project Broker would offer Marvin even more surprises.

CHAPTER 43

NIAGARA FALLS, 1991

The rumble of cars and SUVs couldn't drown out the dreamier thunder of five million cubic feet of water crashing over Niagara Falls at the Rainbow Bridge, one of the passageways across the Niagara Gorge from Canada to the United States. With commercial trucks diverted to other crossings, the Rainbow Bridge is popular with tourists exploring the geological wonder.

On October 3, 1991, after the summer hordes had thinned, a Chevrolet Suburban and a Buick were stopped at the border while trying to cross into New York State. Inside, U.S. Customs agents found four men with incriminating documents. There were aerial photographs, floor plans and interior videos of the huge Vishnu Hindu temple, north of Toronto, and the India Centre Theatre on Toronto's Gerrard Street East. There were instructions for how to enter one of the buildings through the window of a men's washroom; bomb-making recipes and diagrams showing how to place explosives at natural-gas lines to inflict maximum causalties; paperwork on personnel assignments for a "hit team," a "guard team" and a "recon team"; a receipt from Radio Shack for three alarm clocks of the type that can be used as bomb timers; and Federal Express documents showing $6,000 in cash being shipped to Toronto. There was also a letter that contained the words, "dying as a soldier of Allah."

Retrieved from the disturbing haul was a cellphone from which someone had recently called an apartment in Brooklyn, New York, at least 30 times. When the Joint Terrorism Task Force raided the Brooklyn apartment, they found nine loaded automatic and semi- automatic rifles and pistols, as well as a large cache of ammunition. Police in Canada searched the two buildings that were the apparent targets of a bomb plot and found no explosives. But they remained gravely concerned about the potential. The plot called for the attacks to have been carried out during Diwali, the Hindu festival of light, which was to be celebrated that same month, when both venues would have been packed to capacity, meaning a loss of life of as many as 4,500 people. Two men from Toronto and three men from Texas were arrested, while another wanted man fled to Pakistan. They were charged with conspiracy to commit murder and conspiracy to commit mischief. The men were linked to the Jamaat ul-Fuqra, an Islamic criminal extremist group consisting mainly of black Muslims. Authorities said the spiritual leader of the nebulous organization was Sheikh Mubarak Ali Gilani. It was Gilani whom *Wall Street Journal* reporter Daniel Pearl was on his way to interview, in 2002, when he was abducted and beheaded.

In among the terrorist cell's administrative papers, police found a handwritten list of things left to do. One item on the list was to obtain false identification.

It seems that last part of the plan involved the citizenship-card counterfeiting ring that Marvin had infiltrated. During undercover meetings that Marvin arranged, the counterfeiter, Yehuda Segel—despite being Jewish—admitted that he was associated with a Muslim extremist group that was involved in a "bombing experience" on Gerrard Street in Toronto, the location of the India Centre Theatre. He also said he wouldn't deal in Israeli documents because the Mossad, Israel's security service, would kill him. It made the cops wonder if "spook activity"—a police term for spies, or foreign secret agents—was involved. Was the counterfeiter just a greedy crook willing to sell to anyone, or was he trying to divert attention from his true loyalties? Had he secretly engineered the border stop of the terrorists as a foreign spy, or had he been paid to help facilitate it? Police weren't sure.

"We thought he might be Mossad," Andy Rayne says bluntly. Another person involved in the probe came to the same conclusion.

* * *

The intrigue brought a renewed sense of urgency to Project Broker, just as the probe was looking like it could spin on to encompass breaches of the entire criminal code. The RCMP were getting nervous. The number-one priority for the federal government was the counterfeit citizenship cards, and the printer at the centre of that was looking fishier and fishier by the day. Officers were told Segel had employee travel credentials, forged or otherwise, for El Al, the national airline of Israel. With this documentation, and whatever else he could conjure up in his state-of-the-art print shop, he could board an El Al airliner without buying a ticket, which meant that police would have no warning of his travel plans and he could flee their jurisdiction at a moment's notice.

When Marvin's order for the cards was ready for delivery, he arranged for the RCMP officer who was posing as a Tamil militant to complete the purchase. The RCMP planned a "flash-and-grab," an operation during which an officer shows money to a suspect and gets merchandise in return before springing the trap with an immediate arrest.

Marvin took the officer to the Howard Johnson hotel on Warden Avenue in east Toronto where they met the printer in the coffee shop. After short pleasantries, Marvin was thanked and asked to excuse them while they went to a room to wrap up the deal. Upstairs, the officer showed the printer $75,000, and the printer handed over 247 forged citizenship cards. The hotel room was wired for sound, and as soon as the exchange was made, the undercover officer spoke a codeword and uniformed officers used a passkey to rush inside. While other officers seized the cards and secured the cash, Rayne arrested the surprised printer.

Police then raided the apartment where Marvin had been introduced to the citizenship-card middleman by Lorraine Latter. They seized his computer, using Marvin's description of it for their affidavit, and arrested him. Latter, along with Bradshaw and others, were arrested as well.

"I had introduced the cops and vouched for them, and they knew they were really cops when they were arrested, so it exposed me," Marvin says. "Robbie and I felt the case should have been allowed to go on a lot further, but the bust blew my cover. Once one arrest was made by the Mounties, we had to wrap it all up because it wasn't safe."

* * *

Project Broker hit the front pages of the newspapers. It was a tantalizing story, criminals dealing in counterfeit citizenship cards and explosives, although after 9/11 it would have rung far louder alarm bells. And even though the high-security trial of the men involved in the foiled Jamaat ul-Fuqra bomb plot was going on at that very moment in St. Catharines, Ontario, the connection between the cards and the terror plot was never revealed.

"Hundreds of top-quality phony citizenship cards are circulating in the Metro Toronto area, police said yesterday after a joint-forces operation cracked an alleged crime ring specializing in theft, counterfeiting and forgery," read the *Globe and Mail* on September 16, 1992. "More than $400,000 worth of liquor was seized, along with several thousand dollars worth of phony U.S. currency and three kilograms of explosives. . . . As part of the investigation, dubbed Project Broker, undercover officers infiltrated the group, and found the citizenship cards." The *Toronto Sun* started their story with police officers seizing explosives, while the *Toronto Star* led with the prospect of an in-depth undercover operation, offering: "Nine people have been arrested in a two-month joint forces police operation in which undercover officers infiltrated a fraud, forgery and stolen property ring. . . . Police said undercover officers were introduced to members of the group and managed to recover three trailer-loads of stolen property, as well as explosives and 247 forged citizenship cards."

Marvin kept a couple of the articles as mementoes, even though they made him uncomfortable. The prominent mention of undercover cops having been introduced into the conspiracy would have left little doubt for those arrested as to who the fink was.

It was a decent news story, although a bit thin, and it might have ended there, if not for nagging suspicions about the card forger, Yehuda Segel, also spelled Jehuda Segel. Crime reporter Lee Lamothe was at work at the *Toronto Sun* when he got a phone call from a well-placed government source who told him to meet him within the hour at a downtown Toronto pub. After Lamothe arrived, he was joined at the bar by the man, who told him not to look at him while they talked to make it appear that they were there through happenstance, and not for a secret meeting. The man seemed nervous, careful, concerned that someone might be watching. It was real cloak-and-dagger stuff that would have been dismissed as silly paranoia had it not been for the unimpeachable pedigree of the source. The source drew the reporter's attention to the Project Broker arrests. There were connections to the Mossad, he said, with El Al used as cover.

"This'll be the story of your career," the man said, before getting up to leave. Lamothe went to the bail hearing for Segel, who was facing conspiracy and forgery charges for the phoney citizenship cards. In court, RCMP officer Fred Bowen said of Segel, "He appeared to be a very well-trained individual . . . very surveillance-conscious." The cards he was selling were "of extremely high quality." He also said Segel had implied that he was involved in the 1991 bomb plot, and had said he feared the Mossad.

Special Crown Attorney Hugh Campbell asked Segel directly if he had ever been "an agent of a foreign government."

"No, sir," he replied.

Marvin was oblivious to such intrigue. What he focused on was his exposure as an informant. During the endgame of Project Broker, Marvin's secret world started to split apart. The warning signs appeared everywhere.

* * *

Because Project Broker had started with Lorraine Latter, it was only appropriate that the first evidence of Marvin's exposure should come from her. Latter confided to Marvin one day, over coffee—before the arrests—that she had recently bumped into Sam Shirose at a local restaurant. A contemporary of Marvin's, Shirose was a gambling specialist of the old school, from back when Jewish gangsters had run the rackets in the city before the Mafia had taken over. Shirose had organized high-stakes poker games with Paul Volpe, and a home- improvement scam with Johnny Papalia. He was as well placed to pick up on underworld tittle-tattle as anyone. Latter told Marvin that when she mentioned his name to Shirose, he had recoiled, saying, "Be very careful. We think he works for the cops."

Latter was rattled at first, but dismissed the notion.

"I know he's lying, but he's bad-talking you," she told Marvin a few days later. "It's vicious stuff he's saying about you, but I thought you should know."

"That dirty bastard," Marvin replied. But it sent him deep into thought. Marvin had finked on Shirose several times in the past. Which one had gone wrong?

A year earlier, Marvin had introduced Shirose to an undercover cop when Shirose was trying to sell a truckload of counterfeit designer jeans. More recently, Shirose had told Marvin that he was looking to buy large amounts of U.S. currency and asked if he had contacts with U.S. border guards. Robbie suspected cross-border money laundering was being planned, and Robbie and Marvin went to Buffalo to meet with U.S. Customs agents about Shirose's interest. They arranged for an agent to go to Toronto, where Marvin would introduce him to Shirose. They were to meet in a Toronto restaurant, but Marvin never got there. Another case that Marvin was working on at the same time took an ugly turn: Marvin was arrested. Marvin still gets angry remembering the screw-up.

He was targeting Jonathan Sagadin, a dealer in fine art and prints, some of which police suspected were stolen. Marvin went to Sagadin's house seven or eight times, banging on his door, asking his neighbours about him and leaving his phone number. Sagadin called Marvin to ask him what on earth he wanted.

"I'm interested in art," Marvin said.

"Why didn't you just call me, instead of lurking around my home?"

"That's my way," Marvin said. He told Sagadin that he was referred by a mutual friend who had fled to Brazil after Marvin finked on his attempt to sell $500,000 in gems smuggled from South America. Marvin said he wanted to buy Sampson-Matthews silkscreens, signed prints made by the famed printing firm that released works by the Group of Seven artists.

"All you can get," Marvin said.

Sagadin wanted a signed offer of purchase and a $250,000 deposit, but Marvin needed to slow things down. The case involved the OPP and Toronto police, and the two forces were at odds as to how to proceed. The Toronto cop on the case didn't want an informant involved, thinking it muddied the waters. So Marvin was withdrawn, and he stalled and stalled. Sagadin grew annoyed.

"Stop wasting my time," he told Marvin one day. "Either give a written offer or stop calling me."

"I know exactly where you live and where to find you," Marvin shouted.

"Are you threatening me?" the dealer asked.

"Don't fuck with me. Just don't fuck with me."

A little while later, investigators found a new avenue of investigation, and again they asked Marvin to try to insinuate himself into Sagadin's life. The trouble was Danielle McLean had forgotten to inform her Toronto police counterpart. When the city cop learned that Marvin was contacting Sagadin again, he was furious, and when he heard Sagadin complain that Marvin had threatened him, he snapped.

"When he spoke of himself as a boxer, I got the feeling that he was representing himself as the rough, tough enforcer type," Sagadin told police. "I am concerned that he may do something of a violent nature. I don't know what his capabilities are."

The Toronto officer issued a warrant for Marvin's arrest, noting on the warrant that Marvin was a "dangerous ex-fighter with uncontrollable temper." Which meant that, at 10:30 a.m. on February 5, 1992, no fewer than four police cruisers swarmed his townhouse. He was charged with threatening bodily harm. Marvin tried to explain that he was working for the cops. In the interview room at Toronto's 52 Division, he was asked where he had got Sagadin's home address.

"It was given to me by the OPP," Marvin said.

"For what purpose?" he was asked.

"Apparently he had a lot of art prints that he had illegally . . . I was trying to get some samples to give to the OPP." Marvin didn't help matters after the interview by telling the Toronto officer: "Make sure I don't do any time for it and I'll owe you a couple." By the time the cop had calmed down, it was too late. The charge had been laid. When the case finally wound its way into court, the charge was ordered dropped if, in exchange, Marvin agreed to stay away from Sagadin. But by then, the planned meeting with Shirose and the undercover U.S. Customs agents had long since passed and the case evaporated. His case against Sagadin was destroyed by the arrest, too, although less than a year later the dealer was arrested for theft after Sagadin took an oil painting of Halifax Harbour, painted in the 1760s, to Sotheby's auction house for an appraisal. It had been stolen from the walls of the Toronto law firm Blake Cassels and Graydon. Marvin's arrest left a paper trail in court of his work and further jeopardized his secret-informant status, which infuriated Robbie.

Marvin had taken one last crack at Shirose. The old gambler had introduced Marvin to a man who had been ripped off in a drug deal and was looking for revenge. The man wanted his money back and the perpetrator "busted up." Marvin tried to introduce an undercover cop into the conspiracy as the leg-breaker, but the infiltration failed. The first meeting was cancelled when the Peel cop couldn't make it in time. For the second meeting, a perfect-looking officer came—a hulking guy who looked like he belonged in a biker gang. But by then, the target of the investigation was so high on cocaine and paranoid during sleepless binges that he wouldn't leave his house or meet anyone.

Marvin wondered what had caused Shirose to suspect that he was a fink. Something about one of those scuttled cases, or perhaps the accumulation of them, had caused Shirose alarm.

Marvin didn't have long to contemplate, however. After the RCMP arrested Segel, the citizenship-card printer, the other officers moved in to arrest the remaining Project Broker suspects before word got out that they had been caught in a splendid sting.

The officers who made the arrests were jubilant. A wrap-up party was organized to celebrate. Everyone who had been involved—except Marvin—was invited. Although he was left off the invitation list, he wasn't forgotten.

The senior Toronto police representative on the project task force was there, a man whom Marvin had tried to avoid because he always spoke gruffly to him. At the party, he stood up, raised his drink and, in his booming voice, made a toast.

"Let's drink to Robbie and his informant. They put this whole thing together."

Project Broker was a success and the value the government placed on catching the citizenship counterfeiter was clear when the RCMP arranged for one of Marvin's biggest paydays: $10,000.

It was an appreciated sum but the job cost Marvin much in terms of his secret identity and personal safety. What with Shirose's vocal suspicions, the long list of dangerous crooks who had just learned Marvin had double-crossed them and the art-theft arrest—all of it happening in such short order— he was feeling more exposed than ever.

Threatening phone calls started coming to his house in the dead of night. When Hennie answered the phone one night she heard a male voice say, "We're going to crucify Marvin." Marvin answered a call at four in the morning and was told to look in his back yard. When Marvin went outside, glistening under the moonlight were two gutted pigeons, prominently displayed. Then a close friend from boxing said he had been told that Marvin "would be dead by the end of the month." After a fearsome thug—a former heavyweight boxer who had sold his soul to the mob—marched up to Marvin as he sat in a café in Toronto's Little Italy and started calling him a fink, Marvin decided he needed more reassurance than Robbie could provide.

* * *

Marvin just came out and asked Tommy Corrigan the question.

"Tommy, can you get me a piece, sooner, rather than later?"

"What do you need a gun for?" Corrigan asked.

Marvin was ready with an answer, spinning a lie about having been caught fooling around with a rich guy's wife, and the guy was now looking to get him. Marvin even told Corrigan the rich guy's name, choosing a man whom he knew Corrigan detested. It meant there was little chance the two would start chatting and, as it turned out, Corrigan was so tickled by the possibility that Marvin might shoot the guy that he gave Marvin a Röhm Model 66 .22 Magnum, a preposterously long-barrelled cowboy-style revolver with a polished wooden handle, for free.

Marvin, the dutiful fink, mentioned it to Robbie in one of their rare off-the-record conversations. Robbie didn't like it, but he understood it. As a personal favour to Marvin, he pretended not to know and let him keep it, but made him promise to use it only in a life-or-death confrontation.

Marvin hid it away under his bedroom mattress, hoping that he wouldn't need it.

CHAPTER 44

TORONTO, 1992

Marvin leaned in as close as his belly would allow, pushing his head and shoulders across a table at the Laurel Leaf Bakery, the "northern office" of Corrigan and his crew. He was trying to look like he wanted to listen carefully, but was really making sure his hidden police microphone was as close as possible to his friend Arya Dynar.

"There's ten thousand dollars in it for you if you break both of his legs and both of his arms. Not just hurt, but broken," Dynar said, revealing his animosity toward Irving Kott, the Montreal financier. An alternative would be to place a bomb in Kott's Montreal office. Marvin saw Dynar at breakfast almost every day at the deli, but that didn't stop him from letting Dynar fall into his and Robbie's trap. A battery-powered recorder and transmitter were pushed into the small of Marvin's back, held in place by an elasticized halter and strips of tape. The microphone wires were taped to his skin as they ran up and over his right shoulder and left to rest on his right breast, not too close to his own mouth but facing forward, where his target sat. When Dynar had finished incriminating himself, Marvin got up to leave.

"Then I did the dumbest thing a fink could do," Marvin says. "When I walked outside, there were two gangsters there

I knew, and instead of getting into my car and going to see Robbie like I was supposed to do, I went over and talked to them, still wearing the wire."

As they chatted, Dynar came out to join them. The hustlers started joking about rats and stoolies and how hard it was to know who to trust.

"Anyone could be a fink these days," one said, "any one of us."

As they laughed, another said to Marvin, "Are you wearing a wire?" and, in jest, made a move for Marvin's shirt, grabbing a fistful of wires along with the cotton-poly blend.

Marvin called him a "fag" for trying to undress him, and roughly pushed him away before storming off, feigning insult. Robbie had been listening over the transmitter from a nearby van and was ready to rush over and "arrest" Marvin to pull him to safety, but didn't need to. A minute after Marvin huffed off, as the gangsters stood bewildered, Corrigan arrived at the deli and went inside, where the gangsters joined him.

Marvin and Robbie discussed what to do. Had the gangsters realized Marvin really was wearing a wire? Had the crook got a look at what he had obviously felt under Marvin's shirt? Had they told Corrigan about it? Corrigan was a little smarter and a little more paranoid than the others, and was the one most likely to put it all together if anyone were to mention the wires under Marvin's billowy shirt. Corrigan was also the most dangerous of the bunch by a wide margin.

Robbie took Marvin to a medical-supply store and bought him an occupational back-support brace, a system of wraps around the lower abdomen and suspender straps that went up and over the shoulders; the thing was meant to protect workers who do heavy lifting. Marvin put it on the next morning and headed down to the deli, as he always did.

"I knew they were going to bring it up the next morning and if I wasn't there it would be seen as confirmation of what they thought they found," Marvin recalls. "Robbie and I figured I had to go there and not look afraid."

When Marvin arrived and sat at the table, he was immediately confronted.

"What the hell was that all about yesterday," one of them asked.

Marvin stood up at the table.

"I'm sick of this bullshit," he announced loudly, with other customers starting to stare. "Everyone knows I have a bad back from one of my fights."

He then pulled down his trousers and lifted his shirt to reveal the back brace.

"Everyone knows I have to wear this damn thing," he said, turning this way and that to show everyone the brace.

"Ohhh, Jesus, put that away," they bellowed, wincing and recoiling from the sight of Marvin's exposed flesh.

"Jeez, Marvin, we were only joking. We know you have a bad back. You're too sensitive," said the man who had grabbed the wires. Marvin did up his pants, sat down and ordered his coffee and bagel. Nothing more was said about it.

Marvin laughs about it now.

"The last thing these guys wanted to believe was that one of their friends was a fink," he says. It dispelled any concern they had about Marvin. So much so that even after Dynar was arrested by police, as he boarded a plane to Miami, Marvin smoothly moved on to target another man sitting at the table, another member of Corrigan's northern-office crew.

* * *

Throughout his entire turbulent life, Stanley Grossman had suffered with the nickname "Bimbo" since he was a kid. To relieve the burden, his buddy Tommy Corrigan had started calling him "The Butcher" instead, because Grossman owned a meat company. It wasn't the only favour Corrigan tried to do for him.

Grossman, who was 59, hung around with Corrigan and the clique of crooks and rogues who gathered most mornings at the Laurel Leaf Bakery. Grossman fit in well with the conniving crowd, having been convicted of conspiracy to commit theft and conspiracy to intercept private communications. Grossman's business partner in the Mississauga meat packing company, Sydney Rosen, had himself been convicted of perjury and fraud. Grossman and Rosen made a good team, with Rosen a financial genius and Grossman knowing meat. Both had two sons working for the company. When Grossman began to have marital difficulties, Rosen warned him that he could lose his share of the firm if his wife went after his assets. Rosen convinced Grossman to give him his shares for protection. Sometime later, when a dispute broke out between Grossman and one of Rosen's sons, Rosen played his hand and fired Grossman, asserting his ownership, despite the circumstances of how he had come by it.

Outraged, Grossman went to Corrigan with a plan. There was a third man involved in the company, Bernie Jessel, who was friends with everyone: Grossman, Rosen, Corrigan and Marvin. Grossman figured Jessel knew about Rosen's duplicity, and he wanted Corrigan to get Jessel to reveal what he knew, while Corrigan was carrying a hidden tape recorder, so that Grossman could sue Rosen. Corrigan said he wouldn't wear a wire, but he volunteered Marvin for the job. Corrigan didn't know that Marvin was a fink, but he knew he was The Weasel.

For a fee, no problem, Marvin said.

For the meeting, Marvin stuffed a tape recorder in his shirt pocket and pulled a suit jacket over it. Once things got underway, Marvin chuckled to hear Jessel say that Rosen wanted Marvin to spy on Grossman for him.

For a fee, no problem, Marvin said.

After each meeting, Marvin would take the tapes to Robbie before sending them to Grossman or to Rosen. He was being paid by Grossman to spy on Rosen, by Rosen to spy on Grossman and by Robbie to spy on both of them. The Weasel was in his natural habitat.

* * *

During this intrigue, Grossman also hired Marvin to do some collecting work for him. One job was to go after a guy in Tampa. Robbie said that Marvin should go to Florida, call the debtor and come on really strong and threatening, to scare him into calling the police. That way, Marvin wouldn't have to turn Grossman down; nor would he be breaking the law by strong-arming the guy for the money. Robbie then talked to the Tampa police to make sure they didn't arrest Marvin. It worked perfectly. Marvin returned to Toronto and told Grossman the cops had come after him and he had had to flee. Grossman checked it out and found that the guy really had called police. The second collection was to go after a young woman. Marvin caught Grossman on tape saying that he had loaned her $5,000 because he couldn't say no at the time, because she was giving him a blowjob. That is never a good conversation to have on tape at any time, let alone while preparing to commit a felony.

On November 22, 1991, Grossman met Marvin in the Laurel Leaf Bakery in north Toronto and announced a new plan for his former meat partner: he wanted Rosen beaten and ordered to pay $500,000 into a Hong Kong bank. If he refused, he was to be told that his children would be killed, one by one, starting with his eldest son. Grossman told Marvin to bring in a couple of his mob associates from Detroit for the job, and he would pay them $50,000. Marvin said he knew just the guys.

By January, it was finally time for Marvin to bring his friends in to discuss the job. On January 17, 1992, a bitterly cold day, Grossman was scheduled to meet Marvin and his heavies at the Chimo Hotel north of Toronto. Rather than a pair of thugs from across the border, Marvin's friends were really John Celentino, the undercover cop who had helped to foil the Ghanaian coup, and Claude Chapados, a York Regional Police officer. Before Grossman arrived, Marvin asked Celentino if he had remembered to change the licence plates on his car to the Michigan plates he had in his trunk. Celentino said it was too cold and miserable out; Grossman wouldn't look.

When Grossman got there, Marvin introduced everyone and The Butcher laid out yet another plan: instead of a beating, he wanted Rosen's 32-year-old son kidnapped and held until Rosen gave him back his shares. The four men then left the hotel in Marvin's car. With Marvin driving through the snow-covered streets, Grossman showed them where Rosen's son lived, and where he worked, and he gave Celentino $300 to cover expenses.

As Marvin drove them back to the hotel, Grossman asked how the drive from Detroit had been in this crummy weather. The cops said it had gone fine. When Marvin pulled into the hotel parking lot, Grossman told him to take him to the visitors' car, so he could check the car's plates. Celentino stayed cool and told him they had come with a third buddy, who was out in their car. Grossman looked rattled.

After Grossman left, Marvin said to Celentino, "Your first mistake, Johnny."

The slip still bothers Celentino.

"I buggered up," he says. "Marvin was a little sharper than us because it was his life on the line, not mine. They're not going to kill a cop, but they'd kill Marvin. I felt terrible."

* * *

Marvin was sure the deal was dead after that, but Grossman called him a day or so later and asked him to bring his friends back to town. It was time to do the job.

The cops were particularly careful for the next meeting. Celentino and Chapados packed luggage for a week's stay in Toronto, even though they would be staying for only a few hours. After checking into the Sheraton Parkway, they hung suit jackets and winter coats in the closet, unpacked underwear, socks and jeans into drawers and put toothbrushes and shaving tackle in the bathroom. Celentino made certain his car had the Michigan plates. The room was wired with hidden microphones, and armed officers were waiting in the room next door. The plan was to capture Grossman plotting the kidnapping on tape, and then to arrest him and Marvin as they left the hotel. Marvin's arrest would hide his role as an informant.

When Grossman arrived, on January 21, he still had his suspicions. He walked around the men's hotel room, opening the closet and looking in drawers, all the time muttering, "clippety clop, clippety clop." The cops knew what he was saying. The sound of a horse's hooves was a reference to the Royal Canadian Mounted Police, often referred to in the underworld as the "Horsemen."

"Yeah, I'm Sergeant Preston of the Yukon," Celentino said sarcastically, referring to the old television show about a hero Mountie and his sled dog. Grossman looked relieved to see the luggage and toiletries.

"OK, walio," said Grossman, a derogatory nod to Celentino being Italian, "let's do business."

Grossman clarified the plot—and a second job. He also wanted them to go to New Jersey to beat up and pry $80,000 out of a former client.

Marvin and Grossman then left together. Police were waiting in the lobby to arrest them when they stepped out of the elevator. But Grossman hit the wrong button by mistake, and instead of stopping on the main floor, the elevator went down to the basement. When the doors opened, Marvin and Grossman realized their error, but saw a door to the parking lot and went out that way instead of going back up. The cops were confused when the empty elevator opened on the main floor until an officer spotted them trudging through the snow toward Grossman's car.

"Mr. Grossman? Mr. Elkind? You're under arrest."

Both were handcuffed and placed in separate cruisers. When the back door was shut on Marvin, the officer turned to him. "The handcuffs aren't too tight, are they, Marv? I can loosen them."

"Don't worry about it," Marvin said. "Just get me to some-place warm."

Grossman was charged with two counts of counselling to commit extortion and one count of counselling to commit kidnapping.

* * *

Grossman was outraged at having been charged, and instead of taking a plea bargain and going away quietly, as Marvin and Robbie had hoped, he hired a skilled lawyer named Joseph Bloomenfeld.

Although Marvin had worked on hundreds of cases, he had been needed to testify in only a few of them. Prosecutors usually found a way to avoid calling Marvin to the stand in court. The cops would instead call the undercover police officers Marvin had introduced into the schemes. They would say that they had received information from a confidential source whom, in the public interest and for the safety of the person involved, they would decline to identify. The rules of evidence allowed that back then.

One of the worst days for the finks of Canada, however, was November 7, 1991—the day William Stinchcombe, a Calgary lawyer charged with breach of trust, theft and fraud, won his case at the Supreme Court of Canada. Stinchcombe wanted access to a witness statement taken by authorities before deciding whether to call the witness. Prosecutors refused. After years of challenges to that decision in the lower courts, the highest court made a landmark declaration: "The Crown has a legal duty to disclose all relevant information to the defence. The fruits of the investigation which are in its possession are not the property of the Crown for use in securing a conviction but the property of the public to be used to ensure that justice is done."

Part of the fallout of *R. v. Stinchcombe* was that prosecutors could not always hide their informants; defence lawyers, the court said, needed to know about them and were entitled to call finks to the stand and grill them in open court. *R. v. Stinchcombe* had come down two weeks before Marvin's meeting with Stanley Grossman in the Laurel Leaf Bakery, so when Bloomenfeld was preparing Grossman's case for trial, prosecutors were obliged to tell him about Marvin.

* * *

"Now, Mr. Elkind, I understand that in years past you've had an association with the Ontario Provincial Police, is that right?" Lynne Saunders-Gartner, the prosecutor at Grossman's trial, asked Marvin, who had been called to the stand and had sworn on a Bible to tell the truth.

"That's correct," Marvin answered.

"And throughout a number of years, I understand that you've provided the police with information through that association?" he was asked.

"Yes, ma'am."

"You are, or were at one time, what is typically referred to as a police informer?"

"Yes, ma'am."

"How long have you had that relationship with the OPP?"

"I had it for approximately twelve years, ma'am."

When it came time for Bloomenfeld to cross-examine Marvin, he clawed at Marvin's arrangements with police.

"Mr. Elkind, are you presently employed?" Bloomenfeld asked.

"No," Marvin replied.

"When was the last time that you had an ordinary job?" he asked.

"Do you call being an informer with the OPP an ordinary job?"

"No," Bloomenfeld said.

"About twelve years ago," Marvin answered, and then told him about his aluminum siding sales.

After Bloomenfeld interrupted him during an answer, Marvin objected, "You asked me a question, you never let me answer." When the lawyer appealed to the judge to rein Marvin in, the judge sided with Marvin.

"If you're going to ask questions, you're going to take the answers as you can get them," Judge J.R. MacKinnon said.

Bloomenfeld asked Marvin how he had found people to fink on. Marvin said they came to him because of his street persona.

"One reputation was that I worked for the Detroit mob. One reputation was that I had loan-shark connections. One reputation was that I had government connections," Marvin said. He was known as a "put-togetherer," he said.

"As a matter of fact, my reputation on the street was always of being a pretty dumb guy."

About Grossman, Marvin said, "I'll bring it to the crunch of it—his timing was just wrong. Of all the people he knew, he came to get that job done, to meet those heavies, to an Ontario Provincial Police informant."

But Marvin's timing was also wrong, pulling this sting after the Stinchcombe decision.

The only thing that backfired for Grossman in the cross-examination was when Bloomenfeld asked about Marvin's collection work on Grossman's behalf. The question prompted prosecutors to play the recording in which Grossman spoke of receiving a blowjob from the young woman. When the tape was played in court, Grossman's wife was in the gallery. She stood up and left.

Grossman was found guilty on all counts. He then pressed an argument of entrapment, accusing Marvin of setting the whole thing up. Entrapment occurs when police or a police agent provide a person an opportunity to commit a crime, without having reasonable prior suspicion that the person is already engaged in criminal activity, or when the authorities go beyond merely providing an opportunity and act to induce the person to commit a crime.

Grossman testified that Marvin had initiated the kidnapping idea. Marvin and Robbie also testified. Credibility was a key factor for the judge.

"I found Mr. Elkind to be a thoroughly unsavoury witness," Judge MacKinnon began his assessment. "He admitted being a thief, a liar, a drinker and a bully. He admitted to memory problems. . . . I keep in mind that since he is a paid informant, I should be extremely cautious in accepting his testimony."

Judge MacKinnon then appraised Grossman.

"I found the accused to be evasive and shifty in his demeanour while on the witness stand, both on this application and at trial. . . . I find the accused's testimony as to who hatched the plan and as to the supposed inducement to be untrustworthy, unreliable as not capable of belief."

In the end, Judge MacKinnon sided with Marvin and Robbie, referring to the former as "a reliable, successful informant over a twelve-year period," and to Robbie as "a sensitive and credible witness."

"Robinson was at all material times the handler of Marvin Elkind, a paid police informer," the judge wrote in his reasons for judgment on January 26, 1995. "Mr. Robinson's duties as Mr. Elkind's handler continued from 1983 through 1994 and involved investigations with approximately 160 major occurrences resulting in a forty percent to fifty percent arrest rate and on which there were no court dismissals. Mr. Robinson believed Marvin Elkind to be truthful and reliable in his dealings with him."

That stands as an official assessment of Marvin's judicial success to that point. Combine that with the endless tips, cases and undercover work that didn't go to court in Canada—such as his work for law-enforcement agencies in the United States, England, Amsterdam, Mexico and other jurisdictions; his many cases that went to the stock securities regulators for intervention rather than conviction; his cases involving the Libyan agent, the Ghanaian coup attempt and other spies and intrigue; his daily calls, tips, ideas, assessments, underworld news—and it makes Marvin Canada's most prolific known police informant.

There have been more explosive rats, such as hitman Réal Simard, who killed five men for Montreal Mafia boss Frank Cotroni during the 1980s and struck a deal to testify against his boss. There have been finks with a higher body count, such as Yves "Apache" Trudeau, who pleaded guilty to 43 murders and was sentenced to seven years in return for testifying against fellow members of Quebec's Hells Angels Motorcycle Club. But most informants are forged in a single act of self-preservation, co-operating with police to save themselves, offering testimony against co-conspirators in exchange for reduced punishment. These guys burst into the headlines, provide their testimony and then disappear into witness protection. Marvin is different. He kept going back into the street and reeling in case after case, year after year. He didn't disappear. He doesn't hide his face. He hasn't changed his name.

Informant 0030 was "a unique find and a coup to intelligence gathering," says a secret OPP report from 1991. "His initial assignments were very much controlled with cautious optimism due to his criminal history and association to criminal targets. It was relatively a short time before 0030 proved himself to be a valuable source of reliable information. . . . There are very few informants of this person's calibre who have operated successfully for so many years . . . his knowledge is tapped on a daily basis." Another secret police report declares, "Informant 0030 is an extremely valuable asset." A 1993 memo calls him "invaluable" as the longest known informant. "During his tenure in this capacity he consistently proved himself to be loyal and reliable," it says.

Despite his record of success, the Grossman case—on the record and in open court—widely demolished Marvin's secret identity within his milieu. There was no ambiguity. No room for cuteness or excuses or Marvin's great talent for obviation and obfuscation, his special ability to confuse and befuddle and misdirect. No fake back brace could erase this evidence; no lie or threat could change these optics. This was in black and white, available to anyone who looked or to anyone who spoke to Grossman or Bloomenfeld. And neither of them felt they had any need to keep Marvin's secret.

* * *

Eddie "Hurricane" Melo was a brilliant boxer who had dropped out of high school and beat the reigning Canadian middleweight champ, taking the title as soon as he was old enough. The in-ring fury that earned him his nickname was appreciated by Frank Cotroni, the Montreal mobster, and Melo started working his way up the ranks of mob muscle in Montreal and Toronto.

Marvin and Melo were close friends. Through his union contacts, Marvin had got Melo a dummy job at a construction site. Melo would go to the job site each morning and clock in, but would immediately leave to train in the gym before coming back at the end of the shift to clock out, ensuring he got paid. None of the real labourers had the guts to squeal on him. Marvin and Melo's friendship never got in the way of business. When Marvin owed money to Melo's trainer, Melo had given Marvin a punch in the head to help collect it. Likewise, Marvin had passed on several tips about Melo to Robbie over the years, including in 1991, when Carmen Barillaro had told Marvin that Melo was working for him as a collector. Later that same summer, when police were trying to find Melo, Marvin had told them he would be at the wedding of Frank Cotroni's son, Frank, Jr.

Melo had many brushes with the law, and his lawyer for many of those cases was Joseph Bloomenfeld.

Shortly after Marvin testified at Grossman's hearing, he was at a boxing match at Toronto's St. Lawrence Market when Melo confronted him. Melo started hurling invective; the three-letter word "rat" stung more than all of the four-letter words that accompanied it. Melo ordered Marvin outside to fight. Marvin knew he didn't stand a chance against the younger Hurricane, so he planned to jump on Melo's back the moment they were at the door and gouge his eyes with his thumbs. He figured that was his only chance to avoid leaving in an ambulance, or worse. But before the fight got started, George Chuvalo's son, Mitchell, stepped in and told Melo that if he wanted to fight someone, to fight him. That would have been a fairer duel, but it also could have brought the wrath of George Chuvalo onto Melo. He refused, and Marvin slipped away.

Marvin quickly realized that life after his Grossman testimony was going to be a lot more difficult.

CHAPTER 45

TORONTO, 1993

Marvin pondered what to do after his testimony that had damned both Stanley Grossman and himself. Should he hide? Would Grossman tell everyone? Would the gang who met each day with Tommy Corrigan find out that he had finked on one of their own and wonder if Marvin was a party to their own downfalls? Most important, would Corrigan know, and what might he do?

Despite the temptation to flee, Marvin knew that, if he had any hope of preserving his reputation as a bona fide bad guy, he needed to act as if he had nothing to hide. If there was gossip, staying away would only feed it. He also wanted to see, first-hand, how the gang treated him. Over the years, he had become extremely perceptive in reading people's reception of, and reaction to him: living a double life as a fink and a mobster had made him almost psychic that way.

The morning after his courtroom grilling at the preliminary inquiry in the Grossman case, he left his home at the same time as usual and drove to Laurel Leaf Bakery for the morning ritual of bagels and coffee. He made sure to act as if nothing had happened, and he was greeted by the guys as if nothing had. They sat and kibitzed. No one asked him how he had had the audacity to show his face, or even what was going on: two reactions he had braced himself for. If any of them knew, no one gave a hint. Marvin was relieved, but remained wary of one important fact: Corrigan wasn't there yet.

When the crew adjourned to the southern office, Marvin drove to the Pickle Barrel and joined them at their customary booth. Then Corrigan arrived. Halfway between the door and the booth, he stopped and pointed at Marvin.

"C'mere," he growled, "I want to talk to you."

Marvin, hiding his fear, which grew with each step, shuffled out of the low seat of the booth and walked toward Corrigan, who was standing between Marvin and the exit. Corrigan had been told of Marvin's startling admissions, and it had all suddenly made sense to the union boss, how the cops had spoiled his St. Kitts bank scheme, his Atlantic City casino plans, how they knew about so many of his private moments and indiscretions. Marvin had even been to Buffalo, not long before, to brief U.S. Department of Labor officials on Teamsters activities and Corrigan's crimes. Corrigan now understood where all of the inconvenient leaks had come from that had cost him millions and afflicted and perplexed him. Corrigan was a powder keg of barely controlled rage as he walked with Marvin to the door, before stopping and grabbing his arm. Corrigan pushed his ruddy face close enough for Marvin to smell his smoky breath as he spoke.

"One day soon, you'll feel a cold piece at the back of your head, and when it goes off, I want you to think of me."

* * *

Marvin decided not to wait to feel a gun at his skull. He went on the offensive with a ploy that only The Weasel might concoct. He phoned Corrigan's wife.

She had been at Marvin's wedding and they had chatted at many social events over the years. She had been a concert singer, and at Corrigan's Christmas parties she would sometimes sing. Marvin always told her how beautiful she was and what a great voice she had.

"There is something I have to tell you, but it is very important you don't tell Tommy you're meeting me. Don't tell anyone, but I have to meet you to tell you something," Marvin said to her. "My conscience is bothering me."

They met at a coffee shop where they were certain Corrigan had never been and Marvin told her that Corrigan was cheating on her. She said she didn't believe it.

"Believe me, I'll tell you where and when and who."

She asked how he knew.

"I've driven the girl there, he's had me drive her there, he's had me drive her home," he said. He even told her about a bizarre phone call that Marvin had received from Corrigan in the middle of the night.

* * *

Marvin was woken by the telephone at 2 a.m. to hear Corrigan barking an order.

"Get over here," he said curtly, giving Marvin a room number at a downtown hotel. Like many of Corrigan's haunts, Marvin knew the place well because its employees were with one of Corrigan's unions.

When Marvin stepped out of the elevator, he found a young woman sitting naked on the floor outside a room, her legs pulled up tight to her breasts and her arms wrapped around her knees. She was sobbing heavily, tears streaking mascara down her high cheeks. Despite the messy makeup, the woman was a real looker. Marvin knocked on the hotel-room door.

"Who's there?" Corrigan called out.

"Tommy, it's Marvin. What's going on?"

Corrigan opened the door and tossed the woman's clothes out.

"Take this bitch's clothes and take her home," he said. She slipped on her short dress and high heels. She stuffed the rest—bra, panties, nylons and small purse—into a hotel laundry bag. Marvin saw that Corrigan was with another woman, his regular mistress. He escorted the sobbing woman home.

Marvin reported the bizarre incident to Robbie. Robbie was curious. He wanted to investigate a possible assault and told Marvin to set up an undercover meeting with the woman.

A couple of days after the strange night, Marvin invited the woman to lunch. When he arrived at the restaurant with her, he introduced her to Robbie and Karen Moffatt, both passing themselves off as close friends of Marvin's. After they all had a few drinks, Marvin brought up the incident.

"I was telling these guys about the other night at the hotel. What the hell happened with Tommy?" Marvin asked.

She told them how Corrigan had hired her to have a ménage à trois—a threesome—with him and his mistress. The mistress seemed OK with the idea, and the three of them had started fooling around in the hotel room. When they were naked in bed, though, the mistress had got jealous and attacked the younger woman. Corrigan realized it was a bad idea and had carried her into the hallway and dropped her like a cat being put out at night. She knocked and cried and begged to be let back in to get her clothes, but Corrigan wouldn't open the door. It was a strange tale, but nothing in it suggested that Corrigan should be charged.

Marvin told Corrigan's wife about that encounter—leaving out the bit about the undercover cops—and other details of Corrigan's marital failings. She listened grimly.

Marvin recalled the rumours that Corrigan's in-laws were heavily involved with the Mafia in the United States. He hoped that word of Corrigan dishonouring the family would spread among them.

* * *

Tommy Corrigan died on May 6, 2001.

Marvin heard he was poisoned under the same mysterious circumstances as two of Corrigan's old business partners: Sam Salla, the mild Arab who had partnered in Corrigan's waste company; and Jack Brock, a scrap-metal dealer who had driven off with a load of recycled copper after Corrigan had bought it from him. Corrigan had hinted to Marvin that he had had them both killed by poisoning.

In an official release, Teamsters president James P. Hoffa, son of Jimmy Hoffa, Marvin's old boss, offered this tribute: "Members like Corrigan are what made the Teamsters the great union that we are."

Marvin was likely the happiest person at the funeral.

CHAPTER 46

LOS ANGELES, 1993

It was a heavy burden of infamy to have to carry, killing three made members of the Detroit Mafia and living to tell the tale. Ernie Kanakis had had good reason to think he had little choice but to draw a gun and not stop shooting until he was the only one still breathing, after the mobsters had come at him with ice picks. He might have been able to convince a jury of that, but there was no way the mob was going to see his point of view. His solution, in 1977, had been to become a police informant. As it did with Marvin, being a fink allowed him to lead a semblance of his old life while being offered some protection. Still, Kanakis would have some close calls over the years. In 1985, a veteran Detroit mobster was convicted of soliciting his murder. For some, the fear of mob reprisal might give a sense of the fragility of living life as a fink. For Kanakis, it seemed to turn his heart to stone.

His Detroit handlers had rented Kanakis to Canadian police to help Marvin make an impression when he was infiltrating the Million Dollar Saloon crew. It was a successful venture. He then was given a second job in Canada to help press some investigations into organized gambling in Toronto and Windsor.

For more than a month, Kanakis lived at the OPP safe house. Robbie stayed there with him and, each day and each night, Kanakis and Marvin would roam the gambling dens and cafés, Marvin in his trench coat, cap and cigar, and Kanakis in a sports jacket and collared shirt. Marvin introduced him to everyone as the professional gambler that he was. Few people knew more about gambling than the tough Greek; he knew every game, every trick, every angle in the racket. Everyone Marvin introduced him to was impressed by Kanakis, and he started getting invitations to their underground card games and black-market casinos. Marvin reported everything to Robbie, and various probes and investigations were set in motion.

One place Marvin made sure to take Kanakis was to the Casa Commisso Banquet Hall. It was the headquarters of the Commisso clan, a Mafia group with global ties and a reputation for intense violence. Marvin and Kanakis were greeted that afternoon by Cosimo Commisso and his brother, Rocco Remo Commisso. Marvin knew them from his years of toiling in the underworld and, after one of the Commisso brothers had married a Jewish woman, they had found they had more friends in common. Marvin introduced Kanakis to the Commissos, telling them he was a pro who was going to be operating in Toronto for a bit. Cosimo invited them to sit down. As they chatted, he had the banquet-hall staff bring them pasta, meatballs and drinks. Kanakis had been told by Robbie not to let Marvin drink too much, and after Marvin had downed a few double Scotches and ordered another, Kanakis grabbed the waiter gruffly, saying, "Don't bring him another." The Commissos seemed to like his firm approach. Kanakis offered them some advice on operations and the gangsters seemed impressed, enough so that they sat and chatted for hours.

"It made me look good," Marvin says.

Kanakis was still a crook at heart, though, and he took a wad of the expense money he was given and bought a fancy pair of eyeglasses in downtown Toronto. He then told Robbie that he had taken a suspect to the racetrack and lost the money while gambling to impress the target. Another day, he wanted a break from the non-stop round of introductions. He pressed Marvin into taking a day off with him, and they goofed around. They went to a movie and strolled through Little Italy, drinking and eating. Kanakis then made up a list of places he said Marvin had taken him, to pretend that they had done a serious day's work.

Marvin felt uncomfortable duping Robbie. Afterwards, he confessed to Robbie that they had goofed off all day and been to none of the places Kanakis said. He also told him about the glasses and the expense money. Robbie spontaneously hugged Marvin.

"I'm so happy you told me that," Robbie said. He then pulled out a small stack of black-and-white photographs that showed Marvin and Kanakis cavorting about. Marvin hadn't known it, but Robbie had had a police surveillance team following them the whole time.

Robbie and the team were disappointed with Kanakis and the operation was stopped. He was sent back to Detroit, with Robbie noting in his report to the Americans that his own informant had been straight with him, while theirs had stolen from him and lied to him. The Detroit cops were embarrassed, and they decided to punish Kanakis. They knew he was running a gambling game in the city. They had turned a blind eye to it because of the assistance he had given them on their gambling files. But after his breach of etiquette in Canada, they raided his game one night and arrested him.

After that was dealt with and Kanakis found himself back on the street, an officer, for some bizarre reason, told him why he had been arrested and how they had known about his shafting of the Canadian cops, letting him know that it was Marvin who had finked on him. A furious Kanakis phoned the cop in Windsor who had arranged the operation and blasted him.

"I'm just going to let you know now," Kanakis told him angrily, "that I'm calling the Commissos in Toronto and I'm telling them exactly what I am and what Marvin is and why he brought me to them."

*　*　*

The moment he heard of the threat from Kanakis, Robbie sent an OPP squad car to collect Marvin. The Commissos were feared in Toronto, perhaps more than anyone else. More than a decade before, they had sent their trusted family hit man, Cecil Kirby, on something of a rampage, and had conspired—unsuccessfully—to kill rival mob figures Paul Volpe and Peter Scarcella. It was too risky to ignore the possibility that Kanakis might be serious, and that the Commissos would try to punish Marvin. Marvin and Robbie knew that Kanakis could be impetuous and petulant, and the Commissos could be deadly.

Marvin was whisked away into witness protection.

Robbie and Marvin both had many friends in the FBI, who were happy to help. Marvin was flown to Los Angeles and put up in a room at a Marriott near the airport. He was told he could eat and drink as much as he wanted; to just sign for it on the room tab. Everything was being paid for by the authorities—except, he soon learned, the overly generous tips he was adding to the bills for the hotel staff. The excitement of the warm sun, palm trees, pleasant outdoor pool and unlimited food and drink soon waned, however.

"They told me I had to stay in the hotel. I had to eat at the hotel. They didn't want me going out. They told me I couldn't go to nightclubs or to a boxing gym or to a boxing match. I couldn't call my wife, I couldn't call my friends. The only person I could speak to was Robbie, and that was once a day. They basically wanted me to drink myself into a stupor, so I wouldn't go anywhere. They figured the drunker I was, the less trouble I'd get into," Marvin says. He asked if Hennie could join him—he'd even pay for her flight—but they said no. He spent most of his time sitting by the pool, drinking.

"I found it a very lonely existence. The only thing I had going for me was the food and the booze, but even the booze wasn't doing much for me. I prefer to drink when I'm happy, not when I'm down. I was drinking alone."

He slipped out to a phone booth one day and called a boxing buddy to catch up on the street gossip. The next day, his FBI handlers came to his hotel room and yelled at him for it. They had the pay phone wired, they told him.

After a month of this strange existence, soaking in Scotch and sunlight, bored to tears and slowly pickling as he tanned, a young rock band checked into the hotel. Marvin met the four young men at the pool and ordered them drinks from the bar, signing for it all on the FBI's tab. He was delighted finally to have company. The band stayed at the hotel for two weeks while they played gigs in Los Angeles, and Marvin kept buying them poolside drinks whenever they met. He never showed any interest in their music and never knew the band's name, nor did they ever invite him to one of their gigs, although he would have been prohibited from going because of his agreement with police.

On Monday, June 7, 1993, Marvin took a seat beside the pool, ordered a double Scotch on the rocks and opened the newspaper. In the sports pages was an article that caught his eye: George Foreman and Tommy "The Duke" Morrison were set for a 12-round heavyweight punchout that night at the Thomas & Mack Center in Las Vegas. He longed to go, and by the time he had finished reading about the showdown, Marvin was joined at the pool by the young rockers. He ordered them drinks and told them about the boxing match. By coincidence, the band was playing a gig that night in Vegas, just a few blocks from the arena where the fight was scheduled. They were going to Vegas aboard the airplane owned by their record label, a five-seater Piper Malibu. Being a quartet, the band had an extra seat, and they offered it to Marvin for a free trip to Vegas.

"Hold on," Marvin said, heading into the hotel.

He called the Vegas arena and asked to speak with George Foreman. The guy who answered said he would try to get one of Foreman's people to come to the phone. After a few minutes, Archie Moore, a former light-heavyweight world champion who was working with Foreman, picked up the phone. Marvin knew Moore from the times he had driven him, including in 1956, when the champ had beat James J. Parker in Toronto.

"Marvin," Moore asked, "what do you want? Wanna come to the fight?"

"Yeah, I do," Marvin said. "I'm in L.A., but I'll be in Vegas in a few hours."

"There will be a ticket at the door for you, my friend."

Marvin told the band he would join them. He yearned to get out of the hotel and out of the sun and back into the sweaty boxing milieu. At the match, he bumped into Lennox Lewis and stuck with his entourage. The TV cameras tailed Lewis, as well, since he had been named World Boxing Council heavyweight champion earlier that year. Afterwards, Marvin met up with the band at the airport for the return flight to Los Angeles.

* * *

The next morning, there was a knock at Marvin's door at the Marriott. Bleary-eyed, he answered, trying to focus on the men in the hallway, recognizing the FBI agents standing there impatiently. Inside, one of them laid into him.

"One of the specifics of you being here is you don't leave the state," he said. "One of the specifics is you don't go to boxing matches."

"What are you talking about?" Marvin protested.

The agent screamed, "We saw you on television in Vegas."

They asked Marvin if he wanted to go home, and he said yes.

"It's funny, of all the things I did, fear never got to me. I'm not saying I wasn't ever afraid, but it never got to me. Fear, I can handle it. If I'm scared, you'll never know it. But I can't stand loneliness. Loneliness—it got to me. The loneliness."

The FBI weren't the only ones to have recognized the round, cigar-chomping guy lurking near Lennox Lewis on television at the Vegas fight. Several of Marvin's friends in Toronto had spotted him, too. During the weeks that Marvin had been out of town, Robbie had checked every source he could and found no evidence that the Commissos were gunning for Marvin, or that Ernie Kanakis had acted on his threat. When Marvin returned, he checked in with sources of his own. He called up some of the people he knew who were friends with the Commissos, including Domenic Russo and George Bagnato, and no one seemed to pay him much bother. He then gathered up the nerve to return to the Casa Commisso Banquet Hall.

He was greeted with the usual warmth. He ordered a meal, and when he tried to pay, was told not to worry.

"For the first fifteen minutes it was nerve-racking, but after that I could see that everything was cool, there wasn't a problem here."

Word of Marvin's secret life was getting around, but much slower than Robbie imagined. As Project Broker and the Stanley Grossman case slowly wound through the courts, life started to get more treacherous.

An intermediary met with Marvin and warned him not to testify against Bradshaw. If he did, he was told, he would be killed. The intermediary said that Grossman was spreading the word about all of the cases Marvin had done. Then Marvin got a call from a biker friend who said he heard that a contract for Marvin's life was being offered around prison.

Robbie was worried. There was another wrinkle he knew was coming, but he had not yet told Marvin about it.

CHAPTER 47

There was a meeting that Robbie needed to arrange, but he kept putting it off. He expected it to be awkward when the legendary OPP intelligence officer sat down with Cosimo Commisso, the legendary Mafia boss, to ask a favour, of sorts.

Robbie was retiring.

With almost 28 years of service behind him and still a detective-constable, he was making plans to jump into private security. He had tried it once before, quitting the force in 1975, in favour of a larger paycheque working for the American investigative firm Intertel, Inc. But he had missed the action of the street, and had quit Intertel less than a year after starting and re-enlisted with the OPP, picking up his old job where he had left off. His colleagues wondered why he had come back.

"I missed the action," Robbie had told them.

This time, however, he was ready. His family had put up with his erratic schedule, late nights, business trips and the constant calls to his home from Marvin and his other finks for too long. Robbie didn't make a sudden leap, though. Instead he spent a year wrapping up his work, closing files, protecting sensitive documents, passing along information and suggestions to his colleagues who would carry on without him; and disengaging from Marvin. That was the hardest part. Robbie

461

felt great fondness for his best fink. He also felt a deep sense of responsibility for him. For all of his toughness and swagger, his indomitable confidence and unassailable bravado, Marvin was also fragile. He was his own worst enemy, in many ways. Robbie wanted to protect him as best he could.

Robbie assessed the damage from their hundreds of escapades and investigations over the past decade, laboriously going through the cast of characters of who might cause trouble for Marvin. There were many possibilities, but Marvin seemed to have mitigated the situations or confused most of the crooks. However, Robbie remained deeply concerned about two: Carmen Barillaro in Niagara and the Commisso clan in Toronto, even though Marvin had never really finked on the Commissos. The clan had carved out a harsh reputation and, as emigrants from Calabria, they retained an Old World outlook on matters of honour. Robbie was worried that any association between them and a career informant might bring a death sentence for Marvin. The last time Robbie had worried about the Commissos, it was enough for police to whisk Marvin into witness relocation in Los Angeles.

Robbie knew both Barillaro and the Commissos knew about Marvin by now: their network of contacts was staggering, and Marvin's testimony in the last flurry of cases had been profoundly incriminating. Robbie felt he should visit the mobsters personally to discuss it before he retired. He asked John Celentino to come with him. Even Robbie didn't want to go alone.

On April 5, 1993, Robbie and Celentino met first with Barillaro in Niagara Falls. The mobster said he had no use for Marvin and wouldn't waste the money to put a contract on him. Robbie told him to make sure it stayed that way.

The next day, they visited the Commissos' new restaurant north of Toronto and were greeted by Cosimo. By the time the cops had got there, Barillaro had already been. Cosimo had been upset at Barillaro's visit because he was still on parole and was not to associate with criminals. If he objected to the policemen stopping by, he never showed it. Over 45 minutes, Cosimo was polite, cordial, but wary. So were Robbie and Celentino.

"Yes, he's been a fink," Robbie told him, "but he never did anything against you. He was always loyal to you and your family. I want you to know that."

Robbie asked for their assurance, as gentlemen and men of honour, that they would not go after Marvin. He left an implied threat: if anything did happen, he and Celentino and the rest of the intelligence officers were ready to retaliate.

"There is nothing Marvin can do to me that would cause me to retaliate," Cosimo said, according to Robbie. "Others have done worse."

Robbie thanked him. And he believed him.

***

What to do with The Weasel without Robbie there to handle him had become an important and difficult question within the senior ranks of the OPP.

There had been worries about The Weasel in the past; in fact, there had been worries from the start—concern over his drinking and sometimes erratic behaviour, fears for his safety and security. There had been audits by the OPP management of the money being paid to Marvin, and of the expenses for Robbie, Marvin and their colleagues when working on their cases. Marvin's two recent arrests for the extortion and assault had caused significant anxiety for police. If anything were to happen to Marvin while he was doing his government work or, worse, if anything significant were to happen to a civilian because of Marvin, there could be financial liability and issues of public accountability.

Right from Marvin's first case—the bogus island cheque scheme—he had faced danger when pressured by Hamilton gangsters over questions of his loyalty. His second case, the New York porn caper, had left Anna knowing that he had brought undercover police into the conspiracy. Marvin's blackmailing hooker case had left an angry pimp gunning for Marvin and, later, Barillaro had suspected something was fishy. There was also the time his crooked buddies at the café had accidentally grabbed the wire he was wearing. The gangsters from The Three J.J.J.s, who had tried to drag Marvin out of his house, had brought the threat to a new level, but still Marvin had carried on. But in the last year, his secrets had been revealed as never before. There was his testimony at Stanley Grossman's trial that had reached the ears of Eddie Melo and many others in his milieu, the gossip from Sam Shirose and the exposure from the Project Broker arrests. Even Celentino had felt the heat after that last one. Afterwards, he had had to retire his long-time undercover name and shred his false ID; "Gino" was now too tainted on the street.

Marvin's health was also deteriorating. His absurd lifestyle was catching up to him.

"Elkind is 58 years old and in extremely poor health," warned a secret OPP memo from Detective-Sergeant Peter Lollar to the director of the Intelligence Branch. "He is five feet six inches in height and weighs over two hundred and seventy pounds. He is diagnosed with an inoperable brain tumour in his inner ear and because of his obesity is developing diabetes. Following a medical examination one week ago, his doctor stated that he is a 'walking heart attack.'" (In the years since, his tumour has continued to be benign.) The cumulative apprehension was too much for OPP brass, even though Marvin was OK with it. The OPP could come up with only one solution. With Robbie leaving, an order came down: The Weasel was being forced into retirement.

"Marvin needed an eye kept on him because he was hell on wheels sometimes," says Dennis McGillis, Robbie's former boss.

After a little negotiation, a severance package was arranged.

Lollar made the case for the payment to senior management: "For over one-quarter of his adult life, Elkind has been an agent for police, betraying friends and criminal associates, resulting in successful prosecutions and gathering of valuable strategic intelligence," he wrote in a memo on January 18, 1993. "Elkind does not have a pension plan and in his present state of health does not appear to have a long life expectancy. He does, however, have deep concern for his wife and would like to be in a position of providing for her. He has had to completely sever all ties with his underworld associates for fear of being set up and killed."

Another memo says: "An extremely high threat assessment places 0030 at great risk."

Marvin had to agree.

"I didn't want to retire, but it was hard to argue," Marvin says. "I had been exposed. Too many people were talking about me and Robbie was getting ready to retire. They thought it was time. They told me: 'You can't work for us anymore because if you do, you'll get yourself killed.'"

* * *

"This agreement made as of the 13th day of May, 1993, between the Ontario Provincial Police and Marvin Elkind," began the contract, typed onto four pages of plain white paper. It consigned Marvin to retirement.

"Whereas Marvin Elkind has acted as an informant in various Ontario Provincial Police investigations since approximately 1983; and whereas with the assistance of Marvin Elkind prosecutions were commenced against various individuals on charges of a serious nature; and whereas the police are satisfied that the information and evidence of Marvin Elkind was an important part of the investigations and subsequent prosecutions; and whereas Marvin Elkind was and may continue to be required to make court appearance in Ontario to give evidence as part of the case against such individuals; and whereas as a result of providing assistance it is recognized that some disruption has been and will be caused to the ability of Marvin Elkind to earn an income; and whereas Marvin Elkind has declined to enter the Witness Protection Program and will be making arrangements for his own security and that of his family, and as a result will require assistance to relocate and/or maintain a more secure place of residence; now therefore the parties agree as follows."

On Marvin's part, the contract stipulated: "He acknowledges that he was offered entry into a program or relocation and security but has declined to enter into such a program, and has freely chosen to make his own arrangements for the relocation and security of himself and his family, notwithstanding being repeatedly advised by the Ontario Provincial Police of the high safety risk in doing so."

But the line that attracted Marvin's attention was not the fears for his safety, but the lump-sum payment of $60,000.

Signing the severance contract on behalf of the OPP was Detective-Sergeant Jack McCombs. It was fitting that he should sign, since McCombs had worked on the Hamilton

JFU with Marvin on his first case, the phoney-cheque scheme, on March 8, 1983. As McCombs scribbled the date, May 13, 1993, he and Marvin could hardly believe that more than 10 years had passed since that first meeting.

Marvin awkwardly picked up the pen in his left hand to sign. There was no hesitation or pause for introspection—just as when McCombs had helped Marvin to put on the electronic belt in the bathroom of the bagel bakery, before heading out on his first mission. Marvin was not one to be overwhelmed by sentimentality, or by a sense of occasion.

He scribbled his messy signature at the bottom.

"My retirement was bittersweet. It had become a way of life for me. I was sorry my career was over, but I was anxious to get the money."

Marvin took $10,000 in cash to put toward his immediate relocation, and McCombs wired the rest to the bank account of Marvin's younger daughter, who was living on the West Coast of Canada, where Marvin was going to join her and her husband. Hennie remained in Toronto. This was a temporary move, for a year, the OPP said, while things settled down.

* * *

McCombs bought Marvin a one-way plane ticket to Vancouver and drove him to the airport, where they said goodbye.

But Marvin was no more able to settle on Canada's West Coast than he was in Los Angeles. He had the company of his daughter and son-in-law, but it wasn't home. Toronto was home; the boxing club, with his dog-eared friends, was home; Hennie was home. Marvin wanted to be there.

"I got bored, I got homesick and all this crap," Marvin says.

Just weeks after he arrived on the coast, he abandoned the relocation. He was back in Toronto for two weeks before he even told Robbie. McCombs was sitting in his office at OPP Intelligence when he heard a cackling laugh that he recognized instantly.

"No, it can't be," McCombs said aloud, as he went to investigate.

There was Marvin, wearing the same big grin he had flashed when McCombs was waving goodbye at the airport.

"Marvin, you crazy son of a bitch, what are you doing here?"

"I missed the action," Marvin said.

Everyone but Robbie thought he was nuts. Robbie understood completely.

Still, Robbie couldn't stop worrying. The pressure on Marvin had hardly abated. With Robbie heading into retirement, their interaction dwindled and on December 1, 1993, Robbie made his last entry in his special notebooks dedicated to Informant 0030.

Marvin had called Robbie at 7 a.m., the earliest he dared bother him, he wrote. Three hours earlier, Marvin had been phoned at home by an anonymous male who said: "Your death warrant was signed when you testified."

CHAPTER 48

TORONTO, 1994

Marvin first knew something was wrong after a car carrying two tough-looking thugs drove slowly up and down the street in front of his townhouse complex, peering at the homes. When they saw a neighbour, they stopped.

"Which house does Marvin Elkind live in?" the driver asked.

"He doesn't live here anymore," the neighbour said.

After making a couple more passes of the street, the car left, but not before the neighbour wrote down its licence-plate number. He gave it to Marvin, who did still live there. The neighbour didn't know that Marvin was a career fink, but he knew Marvin was a friend who had reason to hide. Marvin called the police, although he soon knew what the visit was about. Shortly after the thugs had given up the search of his street, Marvin had received a phone call from a hooker he had befriended, on Robbie's orders, years ago.

"We know who you are and we know what you did," she said.

"What are you talking about?" Marvin answered, this time truly confused.

"They used your name at the door to get in. We know you set us up."

Marvin thought back to one of his early cases, the operation to find the mystery hooker who had blackmailed the small-town mayor with the sex photos. Marvin recalled how he had met a second hooker when he was celebrating with Robbie in a hotel bar after cracking the case. How Robbie had sent him over to find out what was going on after he'd seen a well-dressed man— obviously a guest at the hotel—saying goodbye to an apparent hooker in the lobby. Marvin had introduced himself to her, got her phone number and then done what he did so well: insinuated himself into her life. Using various excuses and pretences, he'd worn a wire and met with her several times, becoming her friend, quizzing her on her business and, most important, finding out about her boss. Marvin remembers being nervous about one cop who was watching over him during the meetings. He was a gun nut who had tried to put Marvin at ease by saying he didn't need to worry, he was ready for anything. He had then flashed his four pistols—one on each hip, one in his waistband at the back and the fourth tucked into an ankle holster. It was a contrast to Robbie, who rarely had his weapon handy.

"If anybody shoots me," Marvin thought, "it'll be him."

Over time, Marvin had uncovered a prostitution ring the woman was involved with in two neighbouring apartments on Don Mills Road in east-end Toronto. One apartment was used as an office where a husband and wife ran the business, advertised as an escort service; the other was where the young women waited, sitting around in shorts and T-shirts playing video games and reading magazines, until they were called on. They would then quickly put on their working clothes and head out. Marvin can't remember why, but the investigation had been put on hold, and he hadn't thought anything more of it until the disturbing visit from the thugs and the accusing phone call from the hooker.

What Marvin didn't know was that police had launched a joint-force anti-prostitution initiative in the Toronto area and officers were looking to mop up whatever cases they could muster. One of the case files brought forward was the prostitution ring on Don Mills that Marvin had infiltrated. On the night of the police raid, officers staked out the building's exits, while other officers gathered in the doorway. One officer buzzed the apartment from the lobby and asked to be let in. When the pimp asked who it was, the cop said the only name he knew that might get them through the door.

"Marvin Elkind." The cops were buzzed in.

When the officers got upstairs, they burst into the two apartments, arresting the couple and the bevy of young women next door. Because of the officer's indiscretion over the intercom, those arrested knew whom to blame and they immediately started looking for Marvin.

When police ran a check on the licence plate of the car seen outside Marvin's home, they found it was registered to an associate of the prostitution-ring operators. Marvin and the OPP knew they had a problem.

* * *

For Marvin, this wasn't too close to home, this was home. He was incensed—the cops hadn't even paid him for the use of his name.

For the OPP, it put them in an awkward spot. It had been one of their officers working on the prostitution task force who had brought Marvin's name to the table in the new operation, even though the OPP had previously closed their books on Marvin. He was not supposed to be used as an informant any longer because of the concern for his safety and the force's potential liability. The fact that a member of the force had inadvertently reactivated him, putting him back in harm's way as a known informant, made the contract Marvin had signed with the OPP null and void.

Despite having already paid Marvin his $60,000 severance in lieu of witness protection, the force was responsible for The Weasel once again. The only option this time seemed to be the witness protection program: to give Marvin a formal change of identity and permanent relocation far from Toronto.

* * *

Marvin and Hennie resigned themselves to a move that neither of them wanted. Sitting in the office of the OPP's witness-relocation program officer, they listened as the plan for them was outlined.

Marvin and Hennie were told to pack up what they wanted to keep. Everything had to fit in Marvin's car; nothing could be shipped later. The contents were to be transferred from his car to police custody. Marvin and Hennie would be taken to a rural location—a cabin, basically—for safekeeping while they awaited new identities and documentation. Then they would be taken to their new home.

The first difficulty they had was that the officer wouldn't tell them where they were going. "East coast," they were told. They would find out when they got there, for security reasons. The only thing they knew was that the place had a synagogue.

Their daughters couldn't go with them, and there were severe restrictions on how and when they could get in touch with them. They were to have no contact with friends. Like his other relocations, in Los Angeles and Vancouver, Marvin was never to go to a boxing club or boxing match. When he asked about his car, he was told it would have to be sold or abandoned. He said he would have to buy a new one as soon as he got to wherever he was going. He was told he wouldn't be able to, since he wouldn't have any credit history or collateral.

"How're we supposed to get around?" he asked, bewildered. He was, after all, a driver. By public transit, he was told, but the synagogue would be within walking distance. The government would pay for rent and groceries.

"What if I want to make extra money?"

"That's OK, as long as we approve it first and it won't put you in the public eye," he was told. Nothing public, nothing dangerous and nothing criminal? Marvin was at a loss over what he could do.

"They were telling us, 'You can't do this, can't do that.' They made it sound like getting bumped off would be better," Marvin says.

After hearing it all, as she sat with the officer, Hennie turned to Marvin.

"I'm not going," she said. "If you want to go, I will be waiting for you when you come back, but I don't want that kind of life."

Marvin was thrown into turmoil. This was a Friday. He was scheduled to leave on Monday morning. He was supposed to say goodbye to his family and his mother that Sunday. Marvin spoke to Robbie, who was now retired. Robbie was angry at the way Marvin was being treated, especially since he was in danger because of a screw-up by the cops, but there was nothing he could do.

Marvin pictured himself alone out east, a nobody who knew nobody, without a car, stripped of his family, barred from enjoying his hobby.

"I started thinking about doing this by myself, but loneliness is not my ball game. I figure that if I go, I'll end up sitting in a room on my own, drinking myself to death."

On Sunday night, hours before he was to depart, he decided not to go.

The decision came as a relief to police. In hindsight, Marvin thinks they may have been laying on the grim existence to nudge him toward declining the relocation, saving the government a ton of money and bother.

Marvin did, however, agree to testify at the prostitution trial of the people running the hooker ring in Don Mills. For his court appearance, the OPP relocation officer headed Marvin's security detail. Marvin was escorted into the University Avenue courthouse in Toronto by four armed officers and whisked into a private elevator. His testimony was pristine, yet again.

He and Hennie then moved to another house, far enough away to cover their tracks but close enough to feel like home.

CHAPTER 49

Many repo men had tried, but all had failed to bring home the Chrysler Intrepid. A crafty professional gambler had long ago stopped making his lease payments on the four-door sedan, but whenever any of the leasing company's hired repossession agents showed up at the gambler's condo to grab it, the Intrepid was either not there or locked in a garage. This job was going to need a little extra something.

They called for The Weasel.

Marvin was struggling to acclimatize to his new life, a life without his umbilical cord to Robbie, always walking carefully in case he ran into any of the myriad who wished him dead, and without the income stream of being a fink on retainer. In his portfolio of piecemeal work was the rough-and-tumble world of car repossession. It wasn't easy work for a man of his size and in his 60s. What Marvin lacked in pace, though, he made up for with ingenuity. His career as a police agent had given him skills that few others had. He was cunning, tricky, bold. An audacious liar.

If the gambler carefully secured his car when it was parked at home, Marvin reasoned, then he would have to get it while the gambler was out. He asked around in Toronto's gambling community and learned that the man was a regular at an Italian restaurant on Toronto's St. Clair Avenue West. Marvin asked a leasing-company driver to take him there. He went inside, looked around and asked the owners if they had seen the gambler.

"He's not here, they left," the owner said.

"What do you mean, 'they'? Who's he with?" Marvin asked.

"His bodyguard. What do you want him for?"

"I got fight tickets for him," Marvin said, showing him a business card that identified him as an official with a boxing federation. "A pair of ringsides."

"Oh, he'll like that," the restaurateur said. "You can leave them with me."

"Naw, I gotta put them right into his hand."

"Maybe try his cousin's place."

Following the man's directions, Marvin's driver cruised north and along Eglinton Avenue West, with Marvin looking from side to side.

"There," Marvin called out, pointing his thick finger. Parked in front of Sabatino's Ristorante was the elusive Intrepid.

Marvin walked over and quickly opened the door with the key that the leasing company had given him, and he started it up. He gave his driver the thumbs-up sign and his partner drove off.

Marvin was carefully backing the car up, to give him room to turn out into the traffic, when the gambler and his enormous bodyguard charged out of Sabatino's.

"Stop! Thief! Stop!" they both screamed.

The gambler ran in front of the car to block him, while the bodyguard ran out into the street to go around to the driver's side, hoping to open the door and yank Marvin out of the car. Marvin cranked the steering wheel as far to the left as it went and jammed the accelerator, hoping he had enough clearance to spin out of the parking spot without hitting the gambler. With the bodyguard in the street ahead of him, blocking him, he kept going in a tight U-turn and sped away in the other direction.

About six blocks away, he was starting to relax when he heard a siren. In his rear-view mirror he saw the throbbing red lights of a police car trying to pull him over. The gambler had flagged down a passing cruiser and sent the officer after the supposed car thief. It took ages for Marvin to clear it all up and be on his way. The job hardly seemed worth it, but for Marvin, money was always worth more than his time.

Marvin knew his retirement wasn't going to be easy.

* * *

Robbie's retirement party, in 1994, had attracted many of the officers and agents who had worked with him on so many capers. It was a vintage cop send-off, a boozy affair with representatives of several forces presenting him with baseball caps, golf shirts, plaques and certificates bearing their logos and words of appreciation for Detective-Constable #5442, some wrapped in risqué wrapping paper and most expressing inside jokes.

As the festivities went on, a mystery guest was announced. Over the loudspeaker came a recording of a raspy voice as Celentino sat on the stage, in the white KKK hood, and pretended to be doing the talking.

"Hello, Robbie," it began. There was a roar of instant recognition; almost everyone in the room knew Marvin's voice.

Robbie left the police to work as a security director at the Windsor Raceway, a harness-horse track. He kept in touch with Marvin, but the weaning process had begun. Old habits were hard to break.

Robbie was in Windsor for most of the week in mid-March 1998. On Thursday, Robbie and his friend Jack Taylor drove back to Toronto together. On Friday, Robbie and Marvin reprised their dog-and-pony show at the police academy, leading another informant-development class. It was something they both enjoyed, and it allowed them to revel in past glories and soak in the adulation of the young cops. It was the perfect way to ease into retirement. Afterwards, Robbie headed to his pleasant home north of Toronto. That night, he drove his son, Mark, and daughter-in-law, Diane, to a local bar.

Robbie woke early on Saturday with a brutal headache. He looked at the clock: 5 a.m. Not wanting to wake his family, he crept to the bathroom, grabbed a handful of aspirin and headed to the kitchen to brew a big pot of coffee. He went back to bed but realized something was wrong. He reached out toward his nightstand for his glasses but his body wouldn't co-operate. He slipped helplessly off the side of the bed, becoming wedged between it and the wall. Unable to speak and barely able to move, Robbie lay there in undiluted despair, struggling to bang the wall with the one leg that he could rouse until his family woke and found him.

"As soon as you looked at him you knew he'd had a stroke. One side of his face was all droopy, he couldn't move," says his eldest son, Mark.

Fresh snow lay thick and heavy over their country lane and firemen frantically dug a 400-foot-long path to the front door from the spot where the ambulance was forced to a stop. They then helped carry Robbie to it on a chair.

In hospital, Robbie's problem seemed to be easing, some movement returning. A doctor put his finger in Robbie's palm and asked him to squeeze. The doctor started screaming in pain, ordering him to let go. Robbie couldn't. He'd been hit by another stroke at that moment, and his muscles were frozen in an iron grip.

Robbie became paralyzed down the left side of his body, his arm and leg now immobile, his left eye blind, his ability to speak badly affected. It was a grim diagnosis for the energetic man of constant action. An incapacitated Robbie was a dispiriting sight for the parade of colleagues and friends who came to visit him at first, and it was even more alarming for his wife, Gladys, and two sons, Mark and Michael, who had just started to get used to the pleasant notion of not having to share Robbie so widely.

When Danielle told Marvin that Robbie had had a stroke, he couldn't believe it. He had always viewed Robbie as invincible; learning of his sudden frailty hit him like a child realizing for the first time that his parents weren't going to live forever. Marvin visited Robbie a few times, but he perceived tension with Robbie's wife. For so long she had seen Marvin as the one who had taken Robbie away from the family. She seemed to be out of patience with Robbie's "third son."

Marvin saw Robbie again when Taylor took over Magna's corporate box at the SkyDome stadium for a Toronto Blue Jays game. Many of Robbie's friends were there. Marvin and Robbie's sons were also invited to watch the baseball. Robbie was carried in.

Robbie didn't respond well to rehabilitation. The stroke was severe, and the impact on him psychologically was almost as debilitating. He and everyone around him were distraught. Confined to a wheelchair and needing frequent attention, Robbie was moved into a nursing home in Newmarket, north of Toronto. During Robbie's visits with some of his pals, his thoughts turned dark and he sometimes asked for his old service revolver to be smuggled in so that he could end it all. After seeing him like that, some were tempted.

Robbie knew that Marvin had agreed to recount his undercover life for a book, and he supported the decision.

He was helping as best he could, telling his half of the stories, confirming the bits that seemed improbable and fighting through his impediments to tell of their exploits. He had some of his notebooks retrieved from storage and, ensconced in his elaborate wheelchair, worked to awkwardly flip through the pages to slowly read passages aloud. It seemed to soothe him.

For a man with no joy in the present and no hope for the future, the past is a delicious thing.

On Wednesday, January 8, 2003, at 5:15 p.m., Alan R. Robinson, legendary cop, undercover specialist, extraordinary handler, father, husband and friend, died at the Newmarket nursing home. He was 70 years old.

Robbie's death touched many, Marvin among them. It made him feel impotent, lost and vulnerable. He had thought that he and Robbie would move into retirement together. He had always figured Robbie would be there to watch his back. Robbie's dreadful demise, however, also made him realize that, however lean his retirement was going to be, circumstances could be worse.

* * *

There was a sudden hiss and squeak from the air brakes as a city bus pulled over at a crowded stop. Students lined up to get in, knapsacks on their backs and earphone cords dangling. As they reached for their fares, few seemed to notice the larger-than-life colour photograph on the side of the bus. There, dressed in a T-shirt, with large arms stretched up behind his head, was a man with a pair of rosy apple cheeks, his left eye twitching into an ironic wink.

Underneath Marvin's distinctive face was a slogan offering three guesses as to who he might be: Biker, Trucker or Your Secret Internet Chat Girl. Beside the photo of Marvin's face was a picture of a bag of Crispers with another list of options: A Chip, A Cracker, Totally Different.

The large bus and subway-car advertisement campaign was one of the fruits of Marvin's modelling career, another way he tried to make a living after retiring from the OPP. He had long looked as if he had been sent straight from Central Casting to fill the role of a mob thug, and since the look rarely got him work from the cops these days, he was looking for a new means of making money from that face.

He appeared in a fashion spread for *Cream World* magazine, posing as a boxing-club denizen. That was hardly a stretch for him; the other models were given clothes to change into, but the photographer asked Marvin to wear what he already had on. His face was on the front cover of *Toronto Life* magazine, touting the "Summer Fiction" issue, a picture of him dressed up as a butcher to suggest that everyone can enjoy literature. He also did a dramatic turn as an abrasive umpire ruling a baseball player out at home plate in an ad for the Chapters bookstore chain that appeared in magazines, newspapers and on billboards.

"But I never got asked to do underwear ads," he says.

It was an odd way to make money for a fink who was supposed to be in witness protection, plastering his face around the country as a character model. More than one person who knew Marvin's secret was startled when they recognized the unusual face staring out at them. But it paid well.

The modelling started when he was in a boxing gym and a woman from a casting agency asked if she could take his picture for possible modelling work. He heard the word "work" and said yes. He went to several auditions for television commercials and movies, but only the print-advertising roles came his way.

Marvin couldn't stay away from boxing and continued to

drive visiting fighters around whenever they were in town for a match. By now, he was an institution in the industry and many boxers followed Muhammad Ali's lead and asked promoters to hire Marvin to look after them. He also did a little boxing management, getting enthusiastic over new, young fighters and offering to help their careers. He has been working lately with a woman boxer with indomitable determination. In 2003, the Rochester Boxing Hall of Fame honoured him with the Outstanding Canadian Award, declaring him "Canada's boxing goodwill ambassador." But there was never much cash for him in boxing, even when he was in the ring.

The Weasel still snagged the occasional police informant's fee. Although the OPP wouldn't use him anymore, other forces did, if he had something to offer. It led to a couple of freelance jobs with forces in and around Toronto, one of them against a husband and wife loansharking team. He also went back to the police academy to lecture on informant development. It wasn't the same without Robbie, but the cops were just as engaged and entertained by his stories and always bombarded him with questions.

One of his most dangerous assignments came well into his retirement. In 2009, at the age of 75, Marvin was contacted by the FBI. The agents, along with the Policía Federal, Mexico's national force known as the Federales, were investigating a drug cartel in Mexico City. Among the men working with the cartel was the nephew from Italy of Mama Pasquale, Marvin's former foster mother. As a child, Marvin had played with him when he was visiting Sicily. They had gotten along wonderfully and periodically kept in touch. They called each other "cousin" and Marvin knew he had moved to Mexico in the 1960s. The agents were looking to exploit that coincidence to get Marvin—and them—inside the cartel.

Despite his age, Marvin was anxious to do it. He needed the money and, frankly, the action. Marvin called his cousin and said he was coming down on business, letting him know without saying—in that way gangsters do—that he was talking about drugs. Because the investigation was in December, he arranged for the government to put his wife and daughters up in a Puerto Vallarta resort and he would fly from Mexico City to the resort during breaks in the month-long operation. The cousin met him at Benito Juárez International Airport. The cartel was already larding dope into the United States, but every seller likes new buyers and it wasn't long before Marvin was invited to meet cartel bosses inside an office tower. The FBI wanted Marvin to wear a wire to the meeting. The Federales said that was suicide; if it were discovered, the Mexican police boss said, there would be no escape. Informants in his jurisdiction were killed without quibble in acts of grotesque cruelty: In the months before Marvin arrived, 24 bound-and-gagged bodies, victims of a mass execution, were found not far from where he was to meet his cousin's amigos; and the body of a suspected informant was dumped in a public square, his hands had been tied behind his back and a plastic bag taped over his head before bullets ended his misery. With the corpse was a blood-stained note: "This is what happens to informants." The Americans said they would swoop in and save him. The Mexicans laughed.

"They're nine stories up in a tower," the Mexican cop said. Marvin said he was willing to take the risk but the local officer wouldn't allow it. A dead Canadian informant was not what he needed. Marvin went to the meeting unencumbered and was glad he did it that way; he was told to strip and step into a sauna with the cartel chiefs.

"OK, where are the broads?" Marvin joked as he unbuttoned

his shirt. They all laughed and got down to business. For the next four hours, Marvin worked to remember details on upcoming shipments of cocaine to the United States that were discussed. He and his family left Mexico before the arrests, escorted by an RCMP officer. As he was saying goodbye, the Mexican officer passed him a phone. On the other end of the line was Mexico's President Felipe Calderón. He thanked Marvin for his bravery.

"You'll always have a friend in this country," he remembers President Calderón saying.

"This simple peasant is both honoured and humbled," Marvin replied. He was paid when he got back to Canada. Just $2,000.

He had always had trouble making ends meet while on retainer with the cops, and life after Robbie became even harder.

"Some people live day-to-day," he says. "I live minute-to-minute."

* * *

When Robbie retired, he had passed his responsibility for Marvin over to his former partner, Danielle McLean. Even though Marvin wasn't doing undercover work for the OPP anymore, he still needed a contact person. There remained a level of responsibility for the man whom they had helped to create.

After Robbie had his stroke, he had one piece of unfinished business involving Marvin that he needed to pass on to her. When Danielle dropped by for a visit, Robbie told her about Marvin's gun. He explained to her how Marvin had got it from Tommy Corrigan to protect himself, and Robbie had quietly let him keep it. He felt she needed to know. Despite their affinity, Danielle was a different cop from Robbie and she couldn't even begin to understand how her mentor could tolerate leaving Marvin with a gun. Maybe it was "a guy thing," she later mused.

Danielle left Robbie and called John Celentino, the undercover operator whom she knew Marvin deeply respected. She told him about the gun and asked if he would go to Marvin's house and get it from him. Celentino refused. He understood why Marvin wanted it and why Robbie had let him keep it. Danielle played by the rules, though, and she called Marvin and ordered him to bring her the gun.

"What are you talking about? What gun?"

"Marvin," she said coolly, "if you don't have that gun on my desk by ten a.m. tomorrow, I will be executing a search warrant at your house."

Marvin knew she wasn't bluffing. He unloaded the gun, put it in a briefcase and drove it to her office. She greeted him fondly, like a different person from the authoritarian on the phone. She bought him a coffee and they chatted warmly, mostly about Robbie.

Danielle retired in 2004. After her retirement, she called Marvin and asked to borrow a pair of boxing gloves. A landmark birthday for one of her five brothers was coming, she told him, and she wanted to make a special card for him. When they were children, she had once beaten this brother up, a story often told among the family, and she wanted a card with a photo of her wearing boxing gloves as a light-hearted reminder. The day she returned them was the last time Marvin saw her.

On September 13, 2008, after taking ill with a rare form of cancer, Danielle died in Toronto General Hospital. She was 56.

Marvin was devastated. It had never occurred to him that he might outlive Robbie, let alone the young, vivacious Danielle.

CHAPTER 50

TORONTO, 1998

Marvin cut a distinctive figure as he stood outside a distinctive building. Beth David B'nai Israel Beth Am synagogue stands like a giant, intricately carved shoebox in a residential neighbourhood of north Toronto, its concrete facade and curved windows a swirl of enormous Talmudic symbols and designs. Marvin stood like a pumpkin on the front doorstep, scanning the masses arriving for the Sabbath service, grinning at those whom he knew and squinting suspiciously at those whom he didn't.

Marvin was on duty, but not for the cops or any of his gangster friends. He was providing security, volunteering amid heightened fears of terrorism and anti-Semitism. Already that month, Islamic militants had bombed the U.S. embassies in Tanzania and Kenya and, in retaliation, the United States had sent cruise missiles slamming into Afghanistan and Sudan. And with hysteria over feared weapons of mass destruction in Iraq, a second Gulf War loomed. Security was heightened in both the Jewish and Muslim communities around Toronto. As Marvin greeted people outside the synagogue entrance, a familiar, but unhappy-looking man started up the short set of steps. Jack Tully was 70 years old and a regular attendee, along with his wife and daughter, son-in-law and two young grandchildren. As the jowly and bespectacled Tully drew closer to Marvin at the doors, he paused.

"I'm told that you know how to straighten people out," the old man said.

"Yup," Marvin answered. They arranged to meet the following week.

It was similar circumstances—swirling rumours of war—seven years before, that had seen Marvin sprung from jail, where he was spending his weekends while serving his sentence on the assault conviction after his car crash. And it was local community tensions, during the first Gulf War, that had brought Marvin to his post at Beth David's glass doors.

* * *

An aerial bombardment of Iraqi targets by a U.S.-led coalition announced the start of the first Gulf War on January 17, 1991, with a thunderous roar and the chattering of all-news television networks. "The mother of all battles has begun," Saddam Hussein declared. The ensuing war wasn't much of a military challenge for the coalition, but its impact on ethnic and social tension in Canada was nonetheless pronounced.

As the coalition drove the Iraqi army from Kuwait, Saddam fired Scud missiles into Israel hoping to provoke a counterattack, which, he hoped, would drive Arab nations out of the U.S.-led coalition. That never happened, but the old distrust and tension that Saddam was counting on was felt within Canada's Jewish and Muslim populations, with each seeing a sharp rise in vandalism of religious institutions, bomb threats and harassing and threatening hate mail.

What with the coalition's bombs, Saddam's Scuds and the percolating local anti-Semitism, Marvin felt he was needed.

He was not the only one who felt it was a waste to have a man of his talent idling in jail in times like these. An application was made for Marvin to serve his sentence doing community service instead. It was supported by the rabbi at Beth David, who requested that Marvin provide security at the synagogue, whose dramatic and distinctly Jewish architecture made it a natural target. Arrangements were made and Marvin started his patrols. In terms of hours spent, jail would have been easier. Each day and at night, whenever he wasn't meeting his crooked pals, or working on a case for the cops, or doing one of his short-term jobs, Marvin kept an eye on the synagogue. It was fulfilling work. Finally, his rough upbringing and tough demeanour had found a useful place within his faith.

Each Sabbath, Marvin was suddenly front and centre at the synagogue doors or in the parking lot at the start and end of Saturday services, watching, checking people out, even asking an occasional stranger to open a bag and let him look inside.

He took the job seriously. It was a difficult time in the community and Marvin got misty-eyed when mothers told him they sent their children to Hebrew school or to choir practice in the evenings only because they knew he was there. He met leaders in the local Palestinian community to discuss their mutual issues and found them to be good people. One night, he caught some kids attacking the building. They turned out to be not Palestinian, but Vietnamese, young troublemakers taking advantage of the times.

Among the congregants, Marvin, the serious-minded security chief, became a figure of gossip and speculation. It didn't take long for people to learn about his conviction. But cynicism over his motivation—to get out of jail—dissipated when, long after his sentence was finished and the war in the Persian Gulf had ended, he kept his volunteer vigil.

It was while he was still working that Sabbath sentry duty, amid rising new tensions, that Jack Tully asked him about his rumoured special abilities.

* * *

"That's my problem. People only come to me when they want somebody killed or hurt," Marvin says. "Nobody comes to me and says, 'Give me a scientific answer to this,' or 'What do you think of this mathematical problem.' They never ask me that." Certainly for Tully, it wasn't trouble with science or math that brought him to Marvin. It was gossip among the congregation about the dark background of the security chief.

At a meeting in a Tim Hortons coffee shop on Steeles Avenue, Tully told Marvin about his problems with his son-in-law, Martin Fisher. Fisher and Tully's daughter were in a tumultuous relationship and Tully didn't like him or the way he treated her. Then Fisher started to interfere with the joy and delight of Tully's life: his grandchildren, aged 10 and five. Tully grew desperate when his daughter, Lynda, faxed him a letter telling him that he couldn't see his grandchildren without Fisher's permission. He wanted Fisher out of the way, Tully told Marvin.

Marvin knew Fisher, from the synagogue and from boxing. Fisher was a fight fan. Tully suggested that Marvin invite Fisher to a bar to watch a boxing match and ply him with drinks, get him bombed; that would be easy, Tully said. Then, when Fisher left the bar to drive home, Marvin could call the cops and have him arrested for impaired driving. A stint in jail for Fisher would give Tully the time he needed alone with his daughter to break Fisher's spell over her, he said.

Marvin hated the idea.

"Jack, there's a couple of problems with that. Before the cops pick him up, what if he gets killed driving drunk?"

"Then that will really end my problems," Tully said coldly.

"There's another problem, Jack. He could kill someone else. He could wipe out someone else's family. I couldn't do that. We'll have to think of something else."

To show he was serious, Tully gave Marvin $1,000 as a down payment. Marvin took the money but did nothing about Fisher until Tully contacted him again. Tully was excited when they met for a second time at the same Tim Hortons.

"I've got the perfect way for you to kill him without getting in trouble," Tully announced. He told Marvin that Fisher had a severe allergy to peanuts. Any amount of peanut could send him into anaphylactic shock and kill him. He would give Marvin another $1,500—in instalments, so his wife wouldn't notice the missing money—if Marvin took Fisher to a bar and put peanut butter onto his sandwich or his chicken wings and put a drop of peanut oil in his drink, Tully told him. It was shortly after Robbie had his stroke and Marvin had thought his finking days were over, but this put him in an awkward spot. He didn't want to put the old man in jail, and he certainly wasn't interested in killing Fisher. But if he just left it, Tully might kill the guy himself or hire someone else to do it. Marvin went to the local police, York Regional Police Service, and spoke to an investigator he knew. The policeman understood his dilemma.

"We'll do it this way, Marvin," the policeman said. "Meet with him again and we're going to get you wired and we'll video you two, and if we think it's just loose talk, that he's just angry and blowing off steam, then we'll just warn him. But if it looks like he's serious, we'll have to arrest him."

Marvin liked the plan. Better still, he would get paid as a police agent once again. He was registered with York Regional

Police as a confidential informant, signed waivers absolving the force of responsibility for his safety and relocation and The Weasel was back in business.

Shortly before 3 p.m. on September 2, Marvin arrived back at the Tim Hortons for another meeting with Tully. York police had placed a hidden video camera aimed at a specific table in front of the shop window and, just like old times, Marvin was wired up. He was impressed by the advance in miniaturization since his finking heyday. There was no bulky belt that could be spotted at the wrong moment, not that he was afraid of Tully, if he were to find out. Marvin arrived early, bought a coffee and sat down. He was waiting, reading a newspaper and watching for Tully, when he suddenly realized he was sitting at the wrong table. He was a little rusty.

He moved to the right table just as Tully arrived.

It didn't take long for Tully to show how serious he was about the murder plot. Tully placed a grocery bag on the table and slid it across toward Marvin. Inside were the murder weapons—a jar of Kraft peanut butter and a bottle of peanut oil he had bought two hours before. Tully pointed to the peanut butter and said he just needed to jam a little bit of that into a sandwich. Then he showed him the oil and told him to put a splash of that in his drink, that'd finish him.

"Jack, are you really certain?" Marvin asked. Tully was adamant; it was the only way he would find peace.

"Well, I'll need some money to buy the drinks," Marvin said. Tully gave him another $200. Police were listening to the conversation. There was no doubt of the old man's intention. After Marvin and Tully said goodbye, Tully went to his car in the parking lot and police stopped and arrested him, charging him with counselling to commit murder. He still had the receipt for the peanut products in his pocket.

* * *

Jack Tully hobbled into court in January 2001, leaning on a cane on one side and his wife's arm on the other, looking as frail and bewildered as he could. Representing him was a lawyer who knew all about Marvin: Joseph Bloomenfeld, who had defended Stanley Grossman in the case that had forced Robbie and Marvin to testify to their long-standing relationship. Shaking his mane of white hair in disgusted wonder, Bloomenfeld could hardly believe that Marvin was still reeling in cases after all these years.

Marvin calls Bloomenfeld "my arch enemy."

Bloomenfeld calls Marvin "an abscess on the ass of humanity."

But before Bloomenfeld had been hired for Tully's case, Tully had had a lawyer who didn't know much about Marvin or his storied past. When Marvin had testified at the preliminary hearing, the young lawyer had asked him if he had been a police agent before.

"Yeah," answered Marvin.

"How many times?"

"I'm not sure."

"Was it two, three?"

"More," said Marvin.

"Five, six?"

"More."

"Well, how many, fifty?"

"More than that."

"A hundred?"

"More."

"Two hundred? More? Two hundred and fifty?"

"Yeah, about that," Marvin said, smiling. By now,

admitting to such a thing in court didn't cause the same stress for him. Like finking itself, Marvin could get used to almost anything if he were being paid.

The prosecutor and judge were laughing. The defence lawyer stood silent for a moment, floored.

"Where?" he finally asked.

"Canada, United States, Europe, South America. . ."

In the end, with Marvin's testimony, the seized weapons, the incriminating grocery receipt, the police video and even the store's own surveillance videos, all pointing to his guilt, Tully pleaded guilty to counselling to commit murder. Shortly afterwards, Marvin was phoned by a local newspaper reporter asking about the case. The reporter had been tipped to it by Fisher, but Marvin denied knowing anything about it.

"Look," Marvin lied, "you got the wrong guy."

Tully's sentencing made for a strange hearing, even by Marvin's standards. It featured an acrimonious Bloomenfeld; Marvin, trying to avoid any publicity; Tully, trying to look as frail and infirm as he could; and Fisher, the target, asking that the man who had tried to kill him not be sent to jail.

Bloomenfeld described Marvin in court as a "despicable con artist."

Judge Edward Minden wasn't as harsh but, while accepting Marvin's testimony as truthful and accurate, he had no glowing praise for The Weasel.

Marvin "recognized an opportunity when he saw one," and "unquestionably assisted in creating an atmosphere" that gave life to the murder plot, he said in his decision. Judge Minden—taking his cue from Fisher's plea for leniency—sentenced Tully to a year of house arrest.

The only one who seemed happy about Marvin's intervention, besides the cops, was Martin Fisher.

"I know that Marvin probably travels with a different crowd than the average accountant does in the [Jewish] brotherhood," Fisher says, "but I owe him a huge debt. He may have saved my life. The intended hit man may have saved my life, and the twisted irony of this thing is that I may have helped save my father-in-law's life because jail is not the place for him. He would have been dead before he finished his sentence."

After all of that, Tully got what he wanted. Fisher and Tully's daughter split before the case was over.

* * *

Marvin, although feeling bad about Tully, enjoyed being back in the action, rekindling the rush of being a police agent and getting paid. But a story like this one couldn't go without the press catching wind of it. No self-respecting newspaper editor could resist the bizarre murder weapons and the opportunity to use peanut-butter puns in headlines.

In one story, Marvin was disappointed to read this line: "Marvin Elkind had once been on the wrong side of the law and was now a police informant." In the age of the Internet, it wasn't like the old days, when a newspaper story disappeared by the next day. The stories linger on-line. Marvin started getting phone calls about the story from friends and acquaintances. Some people at the boxing gym or at the fights confronted him about it. Marvin told them they didn't understand, it just meant that he had gone to the cops to save Fisher's life, that he was too old to bust guys up anymore. Most seemed to accept that.

He even turned the notoriety into a bit of profit—and another adventure. After a story appeared in the *National Post* revealing the intimate details of the peanut plot, a screenwriter was tickled by the tale and invited Marvin to dinner. As he tucked into a massive steak smothered by onion rings at a Toronto steakhouse, Marvin, licking his fingers between sentences, recounted the story to screenwriter Michael Amo—without mentioning his long career as a fink.

"If this works out," Marvin said, as they finished, "I want Robert Redford to play me." The movie did work out, but instead of Redford, The Weasel was played by the more appropriate Danny Aiello, a Hollywood veteran who had appeared in *The Godfather: Part II*, *Once Upon a Time in America*, *Moonstruck*, *The Purple Rose of Cairo* and *Do the Right Thing*, for which he had been nominated for an Academy Award. Cast as the Tully figure was Judd Hirsch, who had appeared in *Independence Day* and *A Beautiful Mind* and had been nominated for an Academy Award for *Ordinary People*. Mercedes Ruehl, who had won an Academy Award for *The Fisher King*, also starred. Called *Running with the Hitman* in the United States and *Zeyda and the Hitman* in Canada, it was released in 2004.

"It's *The Sopranos* meets *All in the Family* in this pitch-black comedic drama," said the promotional material. Marvin got a kick out of it.

After the Tully case, Marvin remained a controversial figure at the synagogue. Some felt he had damaged the reputation of the Jewish community by turning Tully in. Tully's family and friends were angry with him. But many others understood; after all, it was Tully, so sure-fired hot to kill Fisher, who had started the trouble. Some felt Marvin had saved a life: Fisher's. And then there was Marvin's demonstrated good work on the security beat. That was something no one could deny. He volunteered for years, winning many supporters by helping them, week after week.

"Because of my security work at the synagogue I was given this certificate and allowed to write a letter in the holy book. Some objected to it, but the rabbi said I deserved it. I earned it. The Torah is the holiest book and they let me write a letter in it and gave me this certificate. I was greatly honoured."

EPILOGUE

TORONTO, 2010

Marvin didn't want to screw up this meeting. It was too important to him. He took a long shower that morning and gave himself a close shave, not an easy task with his drooping chins. He splashed on Hugo Boss aftershave, but not too much, because it's expensive and he would have to wait until next Father's Day for another bottle from his kids. He put on his good suit, but before doing up his shirt buttons, he took off all of his jewellery.

He undid the gold choker given him when he was driving Jimmy Hoffa. He pulled a long, thin gold chain with a charm dangling from it, a pair of gold boxing gloves—given him by the World Boxing Federation—off his chest and over his head. He undid another chain on which hung two ornate letters of the Hebrew alphabet, spelling *Chai*, a word for "living," worn as a good-luck charm; it had been brought back from Israel for him by his wife's family after a young relative had got into trouble in Florida and Marvin had managed to extricate him. There was a heavy gold chain received in payment after he and Baldy Chard had scared a man into giving his former wife joint custody of their children. From his bulging pinky he pulled a gold ring, a gift from a jeweller who had been selling fake gold bars. Marvin had been given it when

497

he was getting to be his buddy, before Robbie arrested the jeweller for fraud.

It was a glimmering pictorial of his past. His life in chains.

The jewellery had long been a part of his image. The bling made him look tough—like a gangster—but there was a time and a place for that look. Today, he didn't want to look like a hood.

Marvin had a job interview.

It was for a straight job and it wasn't glamorous. It was simple, menial work, part-time. It wouldn't give him the war stories of mixing with gangsters or provide the familiar company of boxers or the adrenalin rush of his government work, but it would be honest labour with a steady paycheque. He had applied to work at the movie theatre that he and Hennie had been going to for years. Marvin had always loved the cinema: from when he was a kid sneaking into old movie houses to his first date with Hennie to just the previous weekend when, after watching a new release, he had asked at the theatre if there was work available—any kind, he wasn't fussy—and he had arranged this interview with the theatre manager.

Marvin had done other work in recent years of the type that books aren't written about. He had been an attendant in the parking lot of a large medical clinic, where he prevented drivers who were not patients from pulling into the reserved parking spaces. Later, after a story on him was published in the *National Post* and he appeared in the *Mob Stories* television series, Lee Nefsky, the colourful CEO of TCH International, had recognized his beaming apple cheeks. He took a liking to Marvin and offered him a job driving documents around the city, going to banks and making deposits. When Nefsky called in his financial officer to arrange it, the man had asked if Marvin was bonded, and Nefsky and Marvin both just laughed. Marvin loved that job. He loved being trusted and he loved flirting with the bank tellers. He always liked to be noticed when he went somewhere, and it was comforting for him to walk into a bank and be greeted by a chorus of "Hi, Marvin." It didn't last, though. The company was sold to a larger American firm, and as soon as they found out about Marvin, he was fired. He also worked alone in a warehouse for a company that sold mannequins. It was a cavernous, gloomy place with fake body parts spilling everywhere, and he hated it and had to quit. It was a funny thing to spook a man who doesn't show fear.

More recently, Marvin picked up some work from Mitchell Worsoff, a Toronto lawyer who was a boxing fan. They became friends. The young lawyer called him "Uncle Marv," and Marvin introduced Worsoff to a parade of boxing greats, including Jake LaMotta and George Chuvalo. Worsoff was pleased to become friends with the former champ who had twice faced Ali without being knocked off his feet. Chuvalo joined Marvin at the *bris*, the Jewish circumcision ceremony, for Worsoff's son, with Marvin saving him a seat beside him in the front row. As the mohel went about the messy business, Chuvalo watched in horror. A non-Jew, he had never witnessed such a thing at such close range.

"Look what they're doing to the poor little guy," he said to Marvin.

The next thing Marvin heard was a bang. He whirled around to find Chuvalo unsteady and stumbling. Several people turned to see what was wrong when Marvin jumped to his feet.

"If Muhammad Ali had known this, he would have held a *bris* in the ring," he called out. By the time the chuckles faded, Chuvalo had recovered and the ceremony continued.

Worsoff had Marvin working part-time, delivering legal documents to courthouses and prisons and even, sometimes, representing clients in court to arrange remand dates. But it wasn't enough to sustain Marvin.

He needed another steady paycheque, no matter how modest.

"I was two months behind on the rent and Hennie didn't know," he says. "Every time I tried to tell her, I chickened out. She deserved much better. I didn't want to admit I was having trouble."

Marvin drove out to the cinema, with his hopes pinned on landing a job. He was perfectly punctual, as always, and went inside ready to make a good impression.

The manager wasn't there. He didn't even show up for the interview.

* * *

Shortly before his aborted interview, Marvin had been driving downtown and a man behind him was leaning on his horn, making gestures to Marvin, wanting him to go faster. Marvin turned down a side street and pulled over. The other guy pulled in behind him. Marvin got out of his car and stormed over.

"You want to start a beef, we can do it right now," he said.

The man looked at Marvin and said, chuckling, "You think I'm going to hit an old man?"

It struck Marvin—again—how much his life had changed. There was a time when the driver might have soiled himself as Marvin approached. Marvin realized the absurdity of his challenge. He started back to his own car, stopped, and returned to the other driver.

"Thank you for being a gentleman. I'm sorry for being a

jerk," Marvin said. The man laughed and waved it off. Marvin wasn't laughing.

"I'm growing old ungracefully," Marvin says. "I don't want to grow old, damn it all."

His government work had given him the adrenalin rush he craved, a surrogate family in Robbie and Danielle and unlimited memories. He had earned enough money to live on at the time, but there had been no corporate pension, retirement plan or medical and dental benefits.

"People say to me, 'You're still working, eh? I guess you love it.' I wish I was doing it because I loved it. I hate it. I'm doing it because I have to pay the bills. I gotta do the same shit at seventy-six as I did at forty-six, except that it's much harder now. I'm seventy-fucking-six years old and I still have to hustle and connive and this and that and so forth. And it gets a lot harder as you get older. I got to remember what I said to this guy yesterday and what I'm supposed to say to this guy tomorrow."

Being a weasel is a young man's game.

"I regret today that I didn't field myself larger ambitions. Had I have, I might have done better in life than I did."

It was getting Marvin down, beyond feeling blue and into black. It's likely that he suffers from some form of stress disorder. Medical professionals say direct personal exposure to extreme events involving real or threatened death or serious injury can create all sorts of psychological damage. That would describe Marvin's hard life over and over again. He's about as happy talking about depression as he is recounting his childhood abuse, but about eight years ago he suffered something of a mental breakdown. A lot of things were going wrong. He felt as if he were drowning. He went to see a shrink, and the doctor was so concerned, he wanted to hospitalize him.

Marvin knew the loneliness would push him over the edge. The doctor made him hand over his car keys instead. Marvin recovered and put it behind him.

But after the aborted job interview at the movie theatre, he started to have some of those same dark feelings.

He was having difficulty facing the oddity, for the first time, of living an ordinary life; the life of a senior citizen unable to keep up the frenetic pace of his former lives. He has kicked the booze and cigars and he eats sensibly now. Gone are the hours and days lost in the foggy swirl of an emptying bottle of Chivas, the sloppy gorging on bloody steaks, messy ribs and the two-turkey-sandwiches-and-three-martini lunches. Now it's a glass of milk and a slice of cheese on a buttered kaiser roll, and a snack in the afternoon to keep his blood sugar up because of his diabetes. The former adrenalin junkie who sauntered into the fortress of a dangerous Mafia boss wearing a police wire, because he "loved the rush," now dozes off in his black overstuffed La-Z-Boy before getting to the end of *Law & Order* on TV. The man who travelled the world ensnaring drug traffickers, gangsters, pimps, pornographers, con men, money launderers, mercenaries and spies has difficulty pulling himself out of the back seat of a van.

He has outlived so many. The untimely death of Robbie was a stunner for him. Danielle's sad premature death knocked him badly. Fern Savage, the cop who first spotted his potential, died of Parkinson's recently. So many of those he finked on have also died. No one ever imagined that Marvin might be the last man standing.

Marvin had friends who committed suicide, including his foster brother Roy. He never understood it. He thought it crazy, pathetic. But once he felt the grip of depression himself, he had a glimmer of understanding.

"I have been through so much in my life," Marvin says. "I was scared, but never depressed. They are very different things. When you are scared, you think about running for your life. When you're depressed, you're thinking of a way to end your life."

* * *

Then his phone rang.

Muhammad Ali was coming to Toronto for two intimate charity fundraisers, and he wanted Marvin to drive him. The visit in late November of 2010 was to be low-key. The media were never told. The champ had two stops: one, with Lionel Richie and 15-time Grammy winner David Foster, in aid of life-saving organ transplants for children; and the other, a private soiree with Warren Buffett, the famed financial whiz and philanthropist who is one of the world's wealthiest people, at a mansion on the Bridle Path.

"That Friday, I had a case of depression that was awful. Hennie was going to take me to the hospital. Then I got the call about Ali, it picked me right up. It was like a cure. Ali is mentally fine, but physically not good. I picked him up at the airport again and it was great, great to see him again and be with him again. At the estate, Warren Buffett was holding court, too," Marvin says.

The party was a microcosm of Marvin's bizarre life—going from anguish to elation at a moment's turn; from feeling like a complete nobody to being with one of the most famous men on the planet and one of the world's richest.

This time, as far as Marvin knew, there were neither gangsters nor cops standing beside him. And The Weasel was nowhere in sight.

ACKNOWLEDGEMENTS

My first words of appreciation go to Marvin Elkind and his family for indulging and enduring my relentless invasion of their privacy. There is both joy and pain in these pages and they bravely dealt with it all in an incredibly forthcoming manner—and with good humour. I hope this book stands as an adequate testament to a unique life.

Al "Robbie" Robinson was gracious in fighting through his impediments to assist in this project. Robbie did outstanding work, most of which has remained unknown and unheralded by a public that owes him a debt of gratitude. After his devastating stroke, as he spoke with me about his exploits from his wheelchair or nursing-home bed, it was clear he remained a man of action whose mind was locked in an uncooperative body. To Robbie's family, who lost a tremendous man far too soon, thank you for sharing him, and your thoughts, with me. I owe particular appreciation to Mark and Diane Robinson.

Similarly, Danielle McLean was a great friend to Marvin who also helped with this book before she was taken in a frightfully untimely manner.

Many former colleagues of Marvin's and Robbie's helped me put the pieces of this puzzle together. The enormous amount of material that came my way—memories, notebooks, photos, videos, audio tapes and stray documents—was terrifically important. Among those whose efforts aided me greatly are Jack McCombs, Ian Knox, Jack Taylor, Andy Rayne, Dennis McGillis, John Celentino, Karen Moffatt, Rich Mazzari, Dr. Peter Collins, Les Young, Roy Teeft, Larry Tronstad, Ron Sandelli, and Barry Berscht.

I am indebted to Peter Moon for first introducing me to The Weasel 13 years ago, for commenting on drafts of the manuscript and for his endless enthusiasm; and to Phil Mathias for taking me to meet Robbie, 11 years ago. I also appreciated the memories and thoughtful considerations of Harvey Salem, a former judge who is Marvin's oldest friend. Several other participants in this slice of gritty history— including a few whom Marvin finked on, several boxers and some lawyers—spoke to me over the years, on and off the record, and their contributions were also helpful.

I enjoyed the labour of others in assembling this story. Thanks to Lynn Philip Hodgson, author of *Camp 30*, for answering questions about Bowmanville and the Nazi PoWs and telling me of the Red Cross visit. *Sweethearts* by Catherine Wismer offered background on the Atlantic Acceptance scandal. *The Devil's Playground* by James Traub, *The Forbidden Apple* by Kat Long and Michael Hanlon's stories in the *Toronto Star* helped with the "prince of porn" caper. *The Hoffa Wars* by Dan E. Moldea and *Hoffa* by Arthur A. Sloane were useful primers on Jimmy Hoffa and his era. *Eclipse: The Last Days of the CIA* by Mark Perry helped me trace El-Abbar, the Libyan. Moon's coverage of Corrigan in the *Globe* and John Kessel's coverage of Proverbs in the *Star* were terrific. Mafia historian Andy Petepiece kindly helped chase down various mob ephemera and *Mob Rule* by James Dubro helped me understand the Mafia's shenanigans in Atlantic City. Eric Mayne and *Motor City Mafia* by Scott Burnstein provided some details on Detroit-Windsor mobsters. A report by CTV News on the Ghanaian coup and an episode of the CBC's *On the Road* were useful. Various contemporary newspaper accounts of the people, places and things dealt with here were invaluable as they always are.

In terms of this book's manifestation, I benefited greatly from the talents and efforts of Terry Miosi, Hearn Audio, Don Loney, Elizabeth Schaal, Mathew McCarthy, Mitchell Worsoff, Melissa Deslières, Elizabeth McCurdy and Brian Rogers. The constant encouragement and advice from Lee Lamothe and Stewart Bell was appreciated. Thank you, also, to my agent, Michael Levine.

Last in this list but first in my heart are Paula and the kids. You sacrificed much to make room for *The Weasel* and I will always cherish your love, consideration and kindness, which you show in a million different ways.

INDEX